When Romeo Was a Woman

TRIANGULATIONS
Lesbian/Gay/Queer ▲ Theater/Drama/Performance

Titles in the series:
Tony Kushner in Conversation
   edited by Robert Vorlicky

*Passing Performances: Queer Readings of Leading Players
in American Theater History*
   edited by Robert A. Schanke and Kim Marra

*When Romeo Was a Woman: Charlotte Cushman and Her Circle
of Female Spectators*
   by Lisa Merrill

When Romeo Was a Woman

Charlotte Cushman and Her Circle of Female Spectators

Lisa Merrill

Ann Arbor

THE UNIVERSITY OF MICHIGAN PRESS

Copyright © Lisa Merrill 1999
All rights reserved
Published in the United States of America by
The University of Michigan Press
Manufactured in the United States of America
♾ Printed on acid-free paper

2002   2001   2000   1999   4   3   2   1

A CIP catalog record for this book is available from the British Library.

Library of Congress Cataloging-in-Publication Data

Merrill, Lisa.
    When Romeo was a woman : Charlotte Cushman and her circle of
female spectators / Lisa Merrill.
        p.   cm. — (Triangulations)
    Includes bibliographical references and index.
    ISBN 0-472-10799-2 (cloth : alk. paper)
    1. Cushman, Charlotte, 1816–1876. 2. Actors—United States—
Biography.   I. Title.   II. Series.
    PN2287.C8M47   1999
    792'.028'092—dc21
    [B]   98-41314
                                                                   CIP

For Denise

Contents

Illustrations

Foreword
Jill Dolan

One could argue that the formative years of gay and lesbian studies in the American academy were marked by an attention to history and to the ways in which world events and narratives of an American past were framed by a heterosexist perspective that failed to consider sexuality as an influential factor in human social, cultural, and political affairs. Historians, such as Martha Vicinus, Martin Duberman, George Chauncey, and Eric Garber, among many others, have collected for the first time records of contributions made by gays and lesbians to the unfolding of a collective cultural past. These historical excavations contextualized much of the scholarship that has followed over the last twenty years, providing an intellectual foundation for subsequent work in theory and interdisciplinary forays into the broad spectrum of influence that gays, lesbians, and queers have had on world culture.

This early work in gay and lesbian theater and performance studies appeared at a time when the academy was very much influenced by post-structuralism and deconstruction. As a result, scholarship in gay and lesbian performance concentrated mainly (although not exclusively) on theoretical issues around gender and sexuality, spectatorship and reception, and didn't see the flourishing of work in history and biography that marked gay and lesbian research in other fields. The Triangulations series' inaugural titles focus on redressing these historical and biographical omissions in theater and performance studies.

When Romeo Was a Woman, Lisa Merrill's authoritative account of the life of Charlotte Cushman, investigates from a historical perspective many of the questions posed by contemporary queer theory. How can we define "lesbian" in a historical moment in which this terminology was unknown and perhaps even unthought? Without parsing or ignoring more recently formulated identity categories, Merrill manages to respect the conventions of nineteenth-century sexual and gender practices while simultaneously re-reading Cushman's relationships through a queer lens. While she admits to the complications and contradictions of writing a biography that accounts for sexual practice, Merrill's work is invigorated, rather than enervated, by these challenges. She considers Cushman a liminal figure, one whose life tread "the borderland of nineteenth-century notions of masculinity and femininity" and "complicated the various ways her most intimate relationships were understood by those around her." Merrill's research considers the ways in which Cushman understood and performed her passions for other women, lacking even a language that would help her name her longings, desires, and sexual practices.

Merrill looks across the trajectory of Cushman's career, setting aside categories of naming that finally might somehow trivialize the import of her theatrical and her life performances. Working at the interstices of gender, sexuality, and nationalism, Merrill interrogates Cushman's status as an American icon, a performer whose productions in Europe stood for something much more than themselves. Her biography offers a nineteenth-century case study of performativity, testing a current theoretical notion against a life in which the edges of the theatrical and the social often blurred, in ways not unlike those twentieth-century lesbian performers Peggy Shaw and Lois Weaver have demonstrated for contemporary theorists. Such comparisons across U.S. history, readily and richly available in the Triangulations series, allow readers, scholars, and teachers to connect historical moments without collapsing their important differences and distinctions. The poignant performativity of sexuality and gender had different meanings in the nineteenth century than it did in the twentieth, but the fact of its exercise means a great deal to gay/lesbian/queer thinkers researching and writing across moments in time.

Merrill's work is imbued with respect toward the materiality of history. She carefully marks the difference of her own historical moment as she reads back through her subject's archives. Merrill questions her own ability to see, and the methods of her own reading, as she sorts through the artifacts of Cushman's life, wondering at how they've survived to be perused by a new generation of differently situated lesbian writers. Handling the diary Cushman kept on her first journey across the Atlantic Ocean over 150 years ago, Merrill acknowledges the rich passage of time and marvels at the preservation of words that now resonate with renewed passion and perhaps more specific implications of sexual practice and longing, desires that Merrill argues fuel Cushman's theatrical and social performances. At the same time, she acknowledges the missing words, the gaps and aporia that confront a late-twentieth-century scholar of the nineteenth century writing about an unconventional woman. Merrill knows that the preserved letters are no doubt a fraction of the hundreds that were discarded out of fear, perhaps, of what they might come to mean to posterity.

Merrill's biography is not meant to solidify the once and for all "real" story of Cushman's life but to explore the ways in which it was variously represented, by herself and others, and to account for what these representations meant to her contemporaries and what they might mean to later historians and scholars and spectators of American theater and culture. As Merrill's eyes and hands pass over each artifact from which she reconstructs Cushman's life, Merrill's own pleasure in these texts and the elegance with which she makes their many meanings resonate highlight the ways in which objects and subjects change over time. Merrill's writing evokes the many human hands and minds that pass over and through a subject's life and her thoughts and her things while everything they mean continues to change across time. The meaning of "lesbian" is no more secure today than the meanings of "actor" or "American"; the writing of biography and history is a material reminder of the fluidity (and perhaps fragility) of present definitions and understandings, to which we cling sometimes too readily.

Merrill relates that "Charlotte bragged that, rather than play with dolls as a young child, she had cracked open their heads so that she could see how they think." Writing a biography requires something of Cushman's aggressive curiosity, built as it is on a desire to know that can finally never be sated but must always be pursued. When the head breaks open, even if nothing is there but the imaginings and reconstructings of the child (or the biographer herself), much has been gained by the labor of prying open and investigating such a life and such a mind. American theater practice and scholarship is all the richer for what such reopenings contribute to our understandings of how Cushman (and her performances, in plays and in her relationships) worked.

Preface

The life of an actress is to the world at large a terra incognita,
peopled by forbidding phantoms of evil, or seductive visions of
pleasure and success.
  —"S" [Sarah Anderton], "A Few Words about Actresses
  and the Profession of the Stage"

American actress Charlotte Cushman (1816–76) lived in a tumultuous age
when thinking about gender was in flux and the social status of women on
the stage was being debated in the popular press and fiction as well as in
private drawing rooms and personal correspondence. The particular phantoms and seductive possibilities that many of Cushman's contemporaries
recognized or resisted in actresses had much to do with their understandings of and concerns about women's passion. And Charlotte Cushman—a
woman who loved other women—was a lightning rod for many of these
cultural shifts and changes. In a period when most middle-class women
were admonished to be passive, submissive, domestic, and, above all,
chaste, she endeavored to support herself, her family, and, later, the women
with whom she shared her life through her labor in the sexually charged
arena of the stage.

Despite the impediments she faced, Cushman was extraordinarily
successful. At the height of her career she was considered America's greatest actress and one of the best-known women in the English-speaking
world. According to theater historian Charles H. Shattuck, for many of the
millions of fans who had seen her in her four decades upon the stage,
"admiration of her art passed almost into personal worship." When she
retired from the New York stage, she was accorded "the most spectacular
farewell ceremony in the history of the American theatre, surrounded by
civic, literary and theatrical notables."[1] Thousands came to witness the
fireworks and the candlelight procession through the streets of New York
in her honor.

Why was she so successful? Charlotte Cushman represented different
things to different people. To those who believed in the "inherent" moralizing power of women, she was lauded as a model of virtue whose disinter-

est in men helped to purge from the theater associations with impropriety. To advocates for women's rights, Charlotte Cushman was a staunchly independent woman who could play male roles and claim male privilege to manage her own career and support her loved ones. To some observers, such as Henry James, Cushman was "markedly destitute of beauty or of the feminine-attractive,"[2] while female fans, such as novelist Geraldine Jewsbury, maintained that "although Miss Cushman was not handsome . . . [s]he conveyed the impression of protection and strength; . . . to me she always looked beautiful."[3] Cushman was the first American actress to be received favorably by the British, who were both impressed with her precise, "proper" articulation and fascinated with her "masculine" vigor, which they found "distinctly American." To her countrypeople, Cushman's fame was a source of national pride, but her gender transgressions onstage puzzled as well as pleased them.

How was Cushman able to bridge so many dichotomies? It is my contention that *both* Charlotte Cushman's extraordinary celebrity *and* the posthumous eclipse of her fame are attributable to shifting definitions of female sexuality, particularly with regard to women who loved other women.

In November 1874 Henry Alden, editor of *Harper's Magazine,* wrote asking the almost fifty-nine-year-old actress "to offer to the public . . . such reminiscences of your career as you may consider most appropriate and interesting to our readers." Alden was particularly eager for such an article because he thought she represented "the development of the loftiest features of the histrionic art in this country" and "the grandest possibilities in Art by Woman without derogation of her womanliness."[4] Charlotte Cushman refused, as she had refused numerous such requests before.

But Cushman had already taken an active hand in her own representation. Like her carefully crafted onstage performances, her voluminous correspondence—still largely unpublished—served as a series of autobiographical "performances" in which she played multiple parts. As with her theatrical presentations, Cushman's private letters, diaries, and even the photographs or paintings she sat for were attempts (albeit not always conscious ones) to position herself both within and against dominant cultural narratives of gender and sexuality and to frame others' responses to her. It is these artifacts that serve as the basis of my study of Charlotte Cushman and her circle.

During her lifetime, as Cushman became an object of extraordinary renown, an object of public consumption, she came to be seen as an icon, or "sign," in whom the threads of gender, nationality, and sexuality were interwoven for spectators. As a performance historian, I come to Cushman's artifacts—the theater reviews and published memoirs of her contemporaries as well as her own correspondence—as an interpreter, attempting to decipher and narrate conversations in print that existed without me, to locate them in their historical moment as well as to consider them *as* performances. This book is both a biographical treatment of an individual woman and an exploration of the various circles of spectators, fans, friends, lovers, and critics for whom Charlotte Cushman metonymically evoked their multiple and often paradoxical responses to female performers, to independent professional women, and to the possibilities of lesbian desire.

While I have been researching and writing about Charlotte Cushman, as well as engaging with her artifactual performances for more than a decade, my thinking has changed and grown as it has been informed by several theoretical approaches that offer particular sets of lenses through which to view Cushman. The word *theory,* like *theater,* has its roots in the visual, providing a way of seeing. What I have come to observe in Charlotte Cushman is influenced by several predominant bodies of theoretical speculation. Current work in gender studies and performativity suggests that what is experienced as gender is composed of a series of socially constructed, repetitive "acts";[5] examined through this lens, Charlotte Cushman's contemporaries' general willingness and occasional resistance to accept her as a "masculine" woman, both in theatrical roles and in everyday life, take on new valences. In an era that largely accepted the "realism" of female Romeos but decried the "unsexed" performances of women who engaged in professional careers, Cushman's fluidity in traversing gender roles was particularly compelling. Furthermore, a recognition of everyday life experiences *as* performance allows for an interrogation of Cushman's strategies for presenting herself and signaling her desire offstage as well as on.[6] Scholarship in gay and lesbian history suggests ways to historicize Charlotte Cushman's relationships and how they were seen by her contemporaries.[7] Viewed through this lens, her private correspondence offers an opportunity to witness the active negotiation of lesbian desire in a period during which the very possibility of such desire was not generally recognized, and women who spent their lives in long-term passionate relationships with other women were assumed by many of their contemporaries to be chaste "romantic friends." Charlotte Cushman's simultaneous position as a cultural icon as well as a liminal figure on the borderland of nineteenth-century notions of masculinity and femininity complicated the various ways her most intimate relationships were understood by those around her. Finally, my reading of Cushman is informed by a concern with the process of spectatorship and the available meanings a performer evokes for those who witness her.[8] Theoretical work in women's and lesbian spectatorial positions and points of view has led me to consider the range of "meanings" Cushman made available to female viewers and to call into question notions of objectification and dominance that do not account for the possible readings of lesbian spectators.

I have envisioned this book in several sections. This study of Charlotte Cushman opens with both actual and metaphorical boundaries that she traversed. The first chapter starts at a particular moment in time, October 1844, when Cushman was crossing the Atlantic Ocean prior to her first British appearances. During these few weeks aboard ship Cushman kept a diary in which she reflected on her accomplishments on the American stage and expressed her concerns about the future and about what she was risking by choosing to perform for British audiences. Chapter 1 is drawn largely from that unpublished diary, which, fortunately, still exists in its original form.

After setting the stage for Cushman's international acclaim, chapters 2 and 3 establish both the formative personal experiences that led up to her 1844 voyage and the cultural milieu she encountered in the early-nine-teenth-century Boston, New York, and Philadelphia theater. In these chapters I map some of the social and cultural cross-currents that shaped both the particular environment of Charlotte Cushman's early life and the general climate for women in the nineteenth-century theater. Drawing upon letters, theater reviews, and contemporary biographical sketches of Cushman, I examine the various narratives that were constructed by her or by sympathetic friends about her childhood and her reasons for embarking on a theatrical career as I explore questions of performance and respectability in the United States at a time when the very act of putting oneself onstage, subject to the public gaze, was suspect for women.

The middle section of this book, chapters 4 and 5, features the most ephemeral and iconic of Cushman's representations: the characters she portrayed onstage. Here I explore Charlotte Cushman's public persona from the time of her arrival in England: her major roles, her use of her body, her effect on spectators.

Focusing first on reactions to Cushman's major female roles, in chapter 4 I note how some reviewers and fans praised her performances as validation for new, powerful social roles for women, while those who equated Cushman's onstage depiction of dominant women with social movements they did not support were decidedly critical. Drawing upon descriptions of "epicene," "strong-minded," and "mannish" women by her contemporaries, I contend that reactions to Charlotte Cushman's gender performances were largely conceptualized in terms of her national identity as an American.

In chapter 5 I focus on Cushman's remarkably successful stage depictions of male characters and her on- and offstage flirtations with female lovers/friends/spectators in the guise of these male characters. Although women's "breeches" performances were common on the nineteenth-century stage, some spectators evidently read Cushman's cross-gender performance as transgressive; again turning to contemporary accounts, I explore how a woman's onstage depiction of desire for another woman resonated with Cushman's female/lesbian spectators.

In chapters 6, 7, and 8 I return to the tensions and slippage between public and private accounts by and about Cushman as I explore the relationships with women that formed the emotional center of Charlotte Cushman's life. In these chapters I investigate how she integrated her female lovers and friends into social and familial networks that allowed for a redefinition of family in which she could apply the expectations of commitment, partnership, and responsibility to the women she loved.

In chapter 6 I explore Cushman's reception in England by a loosely knit community of women, some of whom provided invaluable support that helped sustain her as a professional artist in her first years in England, while others shared with her more intimate bonds.

Against the backdrop of Charlotte Cushman's personal relationships with other women, I discuss the letters written to and about her by female friends, lovers, and fans who saw her onstage. I contend that Cushman's performances paradigmatically constructed a virtual community of female spectators, many of whom were empowered by her example.

In chapter 7 I discuss the intimate circle Charlotte Cushman created with those women with whom she lived in Rome. From her first venture to Italy in 1852 with writer Matilda Hays, her volatile partner of ten years, through the next twenty years, which she lived with sculptor Emma Stebbins, Cushman reveled in playing host to women artists and performing at home for their Roman expatriate community. Chapter 8 focuses on Charlotte Cushman's relationship with Emma Crow, her "little lover." Some of Cushman's most passionate correspondence and her clearest efforts to control how that passion was perceived are evidenced in the unpublished letters between them. Cushman's correspondence demonstrates that in all of her relationships she managed the representation of her personal and professional roles with an eye to how her behavior, associations, and bearing would be read by others. I also explore Cushman's ability to master and deploy dominant social codes with reference to family, romantic love, and homoerotic love *so as to undo those codes.*

In chapter 9 the book concludes with my explication of how Charlotte Cushman and her sexuality were read immediately after her death and after "the love that has no name" *had* a name. It is my contention that the posthumous trivialization of Charlotte Cushman's life and achievements

Charlotte Cushman's Eye. *(From the Art Collection of the Folger Shakespeare Library.)*

coincided with and resulted from a growing climate of discomfort and homophobia in the wake of the increasing general acceptance of the theories of the late-nineteenth- and early-twentieth-century sexologists. In a historiographical synopsis in which I examine specific depictions of Cushman in theater history texts as well as later biographical sketches and posthumous newspaper accounts, I theorize the relationship between the erasure or diminution of Cushman's acclaim and the homophobia directed toward "mannish" lesbians as they became increasingly visible.

Throughout the text, as I speculate on how Cushman's contemporaries saw her, I invite readers to engage with particular visual images of Cushman. My favorite picture of Charlotte Cushman is not one of the stage illustrations that heralded her performances, attempting to capture the image of a fleeting moment, nor one of her carefully posed paintings or photographs, many of which, she felt, "libeled" her, making her appear "more ugly than my looking glass and even the critics tell me I am."[9] No, my favorite is the miniature of her eye. Not much is known about it. Like most miniatures, it is painted on an oval piece of ivory, designed to be worn as well as displayed. Synecdotal of the assertive, direct woman it represents, this eye gazes, as if through a peephole, just past the viewer. There are hints of sadness in the arched brow, a "knowing" look, a possibly wry smile teasing at the corners of a mouth we cannot observe. Seen in person (in the collection of the Folger Shakespeare Library), this miniature is eerie. In its gold frame, resting in a velvet box, it almost might be her *actual* eye, reduced now to a talisman. It is shocking in its directness, singular and specific; a sole piece that stands for a larger picture.

All representations are partial, and this book, like the miniature of Charlotte Cushman's eye, is no exception. There is no complete narrative of a life, and I do not attempt one here. By focusing on a particular aspect of Charlotte Cushman—her performance of gender and sexuality and the ways that performance was received—I have necessarily left other, equally compelling aspects of Cushman for another exploration. What I have looked for and seen in Cushman is inevitably guided, as it has been for all her spectators, by my desire.

A final note on the text: In quoting Cushman's manuscript letters I have modernized her punctuation and abbreviations where to do so would not affect the meaning or alter the tone of her text. All biographers are faced with the task of deciding how to refer to their subjects. Because this book incorporates so many private accounts and discusses other members of Charlotte Cushman's family, I have tended to use "Charlotte" throughout. This choice does not so much signal my relationship with Charlotte Cushman as situate her within private as well as public contexts.

Acknowledgments

After Charlotte Cushman's death, her friend Geraldine Jewsbury wrote that Cushman "had to fight every inch of her way with her own hand—and one can only hope that few of the women who are now seeking careers and employment will have so hard a life." Fortunately for this writer, thanks to the help of several colleagues and friends, the research and writing of this book was not a lone, hard fight but an exciting and rewarding adventure.

In the years during which I have hunted through repositories transcribing letters, identifying references, following clues, I have been ably assisted by a number of particularly helpful archivists and librarians pleased to share my excitement about discovering the treasure troves lying in their midst.

I am grateful to the staff at numerous institutions, including the Library of Congress, Washington, DC; the Rare Book and Manuscript Library at Columbia University; the Library Company of Philadelphia; the Folger Shakespeare Library; the Harvard Theatre Collection in the Houghton Library, Harvard University; the Schlesinger Library, Radcliffe College; the Huntington Library, San Marino, California; the New York Public Library; the Players Club, New York; the New-York Historical Society; the Museum of the City of New York; the Charlotte Cushman Club, Philadelphia; the Pierpont Morgan Library, New York; Bibliothèque Marguerite Durand, Paris; the Keats-Shelley Memorial Museum, Rome; the National Library of Scotland, Edinburgh; the Fawcett Library, London; Girton College, Cambridge; and the British Library.

Some efforts deserve special acknowledgment and thanks. At the Fawcett Library, David Doughan's enthusiasm, help, and interest were a beacon, pointing me toward previously unknown sources and illuminating unanticipated connections. Kate Perry, the archivist at Girton College, Cambridge, generously shared her knowledge of the *English Woman's Journal* circle with me. At the Library of Congress, Michael Klein's thoughtful mention of Jenny Lorenz's collection of Cushman memorabilia enhanced this study immeasurably. Mary Ison's and Jan Grenchi's willingness to pore over uncataloged photographs from Cushman's own albums allowed for the inclusion of much of a visual record of her life. At the Harvard Theatre

Collection, Michael Dumas was similarly helpful with illustrative as well as manuscript material. At the Players Club, illuminating conversations with Ray Wemmlinger of the Hampden-Booth Theatre Library about our mutual nineteenth-century friends added to the pleasure of this research. Jean Ashton and Bernard R. Crystal of the Butler Library, Columbia University, graciously facilitated my examination of Cushman's diary and letters. In addition, I am most grateful to Alec Cushman for sharing with me Cushman family stories and photographs.

My thinking about Cushman and her circle has been enriched by the generosity of many colleagues and friends willing to share their own fields of expertise with me. I am grateful to Jane Rendall for sharing her notes on Matilda Hays and the *English Woman's Journal* as well as for her hospitality in York, England, and to Nancy Anderson for our conversations about Cushman and Eliza Lynn Linton. Joy Dixon's insights about the history of Victorian notions of sexuality and the sexologists were invaluable, as were her thoughtful editorial suggestions and her willingness to look over this manuscript at various stages. Emma Donoghue's scholarship and sense of humor enlivened our talks and my thinking about lesbian history. John Wynne encouraged this project from the beginning. Long conversations and comradeship with Craig Gingrich-Philbrook informed my theorizing about Cushman and performance studies, and Laura Cohen's constant support and interest has helped keep me grounded. As always, Kalman and Eleanor Cohen's belief in me was a continuing source of encouragement. I appreciate as well the support of Hofstra University, whose awarding of Presidential Research Awards and a scholarly sabbatical afforded me the time to travel to archives and conceptualize this book.

Numerous friends and family members, far too many to mention, have sat through readings of different versions, chapters, and ideas for this text. I appreciate their interest and helpful responses, as I do the reactions of audiences to my conference presentations of early versions of various chapters at the American Theatre in Higher Education, National Communication Association, Performance Studies, and Women's Theatre Program Conferences over the past several years. I offer particular thanks to John Anderson, Judith Hamera, and Stacy Wolf. Jill Dolan's early work on spectatorship excited glimmerings of my own. With this Triangulations Series I am once again pleased to be in her company.

I owe special gratitude to LeAnn Fields of the University of Michigan Press. LeAnn's insight, encouragement, and talent as editor have helped shape this manuscript. So much of the scholarship that has shaped the various disciplines that inform this work has come to print under her thoughtful stewardship. The pleasure of our lively discussions has been an added and delightful benefit, sustaining me through the long process of writing this book. I appreciate as well the suggestions of the anonymous readers and the members of the University of Michigan Press's editorial board. While I gratefully acknowledge all the help I have received, any errors in the book are, of course, mine.

I have been working on some version of Charlotte Cushman, her career, and her circle for the past fifteen years, from the time I first sat down in the manuscript room of the Library of Congress and attempted to decode her correspondence for my doctoral dissertation. But this book would not have been possible in its present form without the insight, intellectual companionship, and thoughtful assistance of my partner, Denise Quirk. For the past five years together we have prowled through archives, transcribing letters and checking obscure references. Her faith in this project has been unfailing. Her training and talent as a historian and an editor have been enormously valuable in all phases of this project, and her good humor and patience while living with Charlotte Cushman as well as me for these past several years is deeply appreciated. This book would not exist without her. It is with heartfelt gratitude and much love that I dedicate this book to her.

Crossings

Passion Embodied and Remembered

A dead calm . . . the water as smooth as a gentle lake. Not a rip-
ple upon it. The gulls sitting upon the water as calm as possible
and not a breath of wind. The captn [sic] promises however
that we shall pay up well for this indulgence. If I only had Rosalie here, I would not care how long we were situated thus.
— Charlotte Cushman, 5 November 1844

I am impatient and fear that I shall not be successful abroad—
if not—I am worse off at home than if I had not gone. However, time will show all, at all events, it cannot deprive me of
her love & I should care for nothing else.
— Charlotte Cushman, 10 November 1844

It is a small diary, approximately four inches by six inches, with a hard,
marbleized cover, like a composition notebook. Imprinted on the cover is
"Diary 1844." This notebook—now carefully filed away in the rare book
room of Butler Library, Columbia University—is filled with tiny notations
of expenses paid, parts played, and money earned. The notebook belonged
to Charlotte Cushman, who took it with her when she set out for England
on 26 October 1844. With it she crossed the ocean, passing physically and
metaphorically from the experiences of a promising twenty-eight-year-old
American actress to the world of acclaim she was to achieve on the English
stage. Charlotte Cushman was to succeed beyond her wildest imaginings,
but at this moment, during this passage, she recorded, along with the
minutiae of daily life, her fears and her desires.

Every time I request the diary, I wait a few impatient minutes while the
librarians retrieve it. The diary is fragile, guarded, filed away. During the
voyage Charlotte scrawled in pencil in tiny script as the ship lurched toward
a future she felt was uncertain at best. She was leaving the family she supported: her mother, sister, brother, and nephew. She was leaving friends,
and she was leaving her lover, Rosalie Sully. The pencil marks are faded and
smudged. I hold the diary carefully in my hand and note how Charlotte

Cushman, a lesbian in an era before some claim the word—or the self-identification—existed, wrote about the woman she was leaving behind. Others have seen this diary—certainly the partner who survived Charlotte and the few twentieth-century researchers who wrote or attempted to write biographies. What do I see that they have not? How has the shared referentiality of lesbian experience and recent work in gay and lesbian history allowed me to see and understand the apprehensions and the longing Charlotte felt as she sat on shipboard, more than a century and a half ago, summoning up the memory of her lover?[1]

> Mon., Oct 28, 1844 . . . my sole thought was Rosalie, dear Rosalie. . . . Oh how miserable I am. My thoughts of home instead of bringing me comfort in the recollection of the love borne to me, render me only more wretched that I had left, as it were, comfort, a home, for uncertainty. Oct 29, 1844 . . . Felt tolerably well and with courage to go on deck, dressed myself but not able to get further than the Ladies Saloon . . . so tired and homesick that I cried myself to sleep. Read a little and thought of Rosalie.[2]

Eyes blurred by tears, Charlotte Cushman wrote: "Wed., Oct 30, 1844 . . . I see Rosalie in her painting room, in the front room and in the parlor. . . . I feel almost her arms about me and then weep again—till I almost wish I could sleep away six months."[3]

Charlotte's original plan was to be gone only six months. Rosalie Sully knew the importance of Charlotte's career. Rosalie, herself an artist (although one traditionally dependent upon her family for support), had encouraged Charlotte. While she envisioned "dear Rose [Rosalie] in her painting room, working away as for her life,"[4] Charlotte remembered Rosalie's words to her, charging Charlotte not to give way to despondency: "Think how soon six months will pass and how happy you will then be that you are coming back to those who love you and how short your absence will then appear."[5]

But this diary is not just a love story; it is also the account of an extraordinarily ambitious, successful, and independent woman who embodied, onstage and off, new roles for women. Carolyn Heilbrun, in *Writing a Woman's Life*, speaks of "the conventional marriage or erotic plot" as the only narrative available to most women.[6] As a woman who loved other women, Charlotte's erotic relationships were certainly not conventional, but neither were they the sum total of her existence. And so I cannot read Charlotte Cushman as a lesbian merely in terms of her lovers but, rather, in relation to her sense of self, of possibility, of ambition. Her story is as irreducibly tied up in her autonomy as it is in her attraction to and identification with other women. Without a personal narrative that allowed for a male supporter, rescuer, or champion, she created herself, inscribed her own story, represented herself, first in these tentative pencil scratches and later in playbills on two continents and in the life she had the audacity to live.

The twelve months prior to Charlotte Cushman's sailing to England had been an especially important time for her professionally. Just a year before this voyage she had performed with the great British tragedian William Charles Macready during his American tour. Although in the years since her official stage debut, in 1835, Charlotte had become successful enough locally to serve as manager as well as leading actress at Philadelphia's Walnut Street Theatre, Macready's positive reaction to her Lady Macbeth had signaled a new high point in her performing career and brought with it new opportunities. Throughout 1844 Charlotte Cushman acted opposite Macready during his New York appearances, making the strenuous commute between Philadelphia and New York every other day to perform in both cities. The American press, critics, and fans had already constructed Charlotte Cushman as a serious, professional performer and had applauded her portrayals of some of the greatest roles in the English-speaking world. But it became increasingly clear to her that, if she were ever to achieve success equal to Macready's, she would have to go to England and try her luck with British audiences—and she was not willing to settle for less.

Once on board, however, she began to have second thoughts, and occasionally her doubts overtook her. Whether crying herself to sleep in her stifling, small stateroom or walking the deck to ward off seasickness, her one constant, her anchor, was the thought of Rosalie: "The one bright spot of my existence, the one hope that bids me toil on, the one care to live if only to enjoy her affection which is to me all the world. . . . I reproach myself that I was not content with moderate competency . . . but must in the hope of gain thrust myself from the delights that I was permitted to enjoy, for this miserable, frightful uncertainty, this lingering doubt which at last may end in disappointment."[7]

The acclaim that Charlotte Cushman sought, that she was on the precipice of realizing, would grant her fame and a fortune virtually unparalleled for women of her era. But it would only be achieved at the price of risking whatever security she had already attained. Charlotte was seeking independence and enough money to buy her more than "the delights" she had been "permitted"; she yearned for the freedom to live as she chose, with another woman. As she sat on the deck writing in her diary, she paused to repair her gloves, remembering that Rosalie had mended them for her on the last night they spent together. Every memory, observation, and dream seemed to Charlotte to be charged with meaning, signifying a possible future event.

"Shall I ever make sufficient money to have her with me always?" Charlotte mused, wondering what it would take to be wealthy enough to live beyond the limits that constrained would-be-respectable nineteenth-century women who loved each other from spending their lives together. "Oh dear . . . how I hope it, how I sigh for it—if she was only differently situated it might be *now*. I could work with much more cheerfulness if she waited my coming to comfort me with her dear voice and sweet endearing smiles."[8] In many ways the relationship Charlotte envisioned resembled the bourgeois heterosexual marriages she saw around her, with Charlotte as the provider toiling at her art in public while her partner waited at home for her. But in her world the only way that two women could make a home together would be for them both to be financially independent, not "situated" as Rosalie was, within a nuclear family to whom she was close and dependent upon for support; or else one of them would need to be so successful that no social censure or financial obstacle could constrain them.

One of Charlotte Cushman's biggest fears, as she pondered her chances of success abroad, was her sense of "otherness" as an American in Europe. Would she be accepted on the British stage? The cultural competition between British and American performers, particularly serious Shakespearean actors, was intense. British performers, like Macready and her friend Fanny Kemble Butler, had achieved much acclaim in the United States, but no American woman had been as successful performing the work of British playwrights on British soil. Strolling on deck, Charlotte overheard "many very disgusting arguments going on around me between the English and Americans on board as to their respective merits." As she listened, Charlotte began to experience "that feeling of pride in home, which Mr. Sully told me I should never know until in a foreign land."[9]

Rosalie Sully and her father, acclaimed portrait painter Thomas Sully, had accompanied Charlotte, her mother, and her brother to New York to see her off. Charlotte appreciated Sully's almost familial concern. In addition to a copy of Charles Dickens's *Martin Chuzzlewit* that Thomas Sully had brought along as a going-away gift, he left Charlotte with advice gleaned both from his own lengthy trips to England and from his childhood experience in a family of actors who, in 1792, had emigrated to the United States from England, when Sully was nine years old. Charlotte confided in her diary that she didn't much care for the novel, which she vowed to get through for "father's" sake, as she often referred to Sully, but his observations about the perception of her national identity as an American she weighed seriously.

Charlotte pondered the social implications of her geographical crossing, since in crossing the ocean to seek her livelihood she was hoping to attain a certain cultural prestige afforded to all things English by the rising American middle class. In the mind of many of her contemporaries, the British were associated with high culture, dignity, refinement; the Americans with impetuosity, physicality, directness. Macready had noted these distinctions in his own diary and, in a fit of pique, claimed, "I am sick of American audiences; they are not fit to have the language in which Shakespeare wrote."[10] Yet, as Charlotte Cushman was soon to see, the very attributes associated with nationality were also markers of social class and of gender, for the expression or absence of "refinement" was generally considered an indication of whether or not women were "ladies." She was not "feminine" or conventionally attractive. Although the determination and directness she embodied had been labeled "masculine" by some of her critics at home—as were other vague, unidentifiable aspects of her bearing and demeanor—these qualities had served her well as an independent professional woman. While Charlotte contemplated how the English might react to her, she was not above fostering prejudices of her own, and she confided in her diary how many of her fellow passengers, even the English, seemed "decidedly vulgar."

On board ship Charlotte, lonesome and homesick, was confronting more than hostile anti-American feelings; she was faced as well with the stereotypes about and biases against actresses common on both sides of the Atlantic. Charlotte had been warned that the British audiences had even more delicate, or more conservative, sensibilities with regard to acceptable roles for women—perhaps because notions of respectability were both so gendered and so class bound. Since, for many people, any woman who placed herself onstage, to be gazed at by spectators for a fee, was morally suspect, Charlotte Cushman's colleague Junius Booth had suggested that when in England she studiously avoid any characterizations, like her startling and moving portrayal of the prostitute Nancy Sykes in *Oliver Twist,* which, while dramatically successful in the United States, might lead British spectators to equate her with the persona she enacted. "It will give you a vulgar dash you will never get over," Booth had advised.[11] Charlotte, for whom respectability was the driving force behind many of her choices, listened. Several days into her journey Charlotte made friends with a Mrs. Bliss, whom she described as "a very amiable little woman": "whether she meant it as a compliment or not I do not know," Charlotte went on to relate, "but she says that she thought that people in my profession were very different from what she finds me."[12]

But, regardless of the widespread biases against the theater, Charlotte Cushman was committed to her profession and determined to succeed. As she examined large maps of England and London and arranged the voluminous letters of introduction she had brought along in her portfolio, she occasionally gave voice to her concerns. With Macready's reputed encouragement and with letters from friends and managers of American theaters, she was reasonably assured of some employment. Yet on shipboard Charlotte contemplated the possibility that "I may not have an opportunity of acting or I may fail—either of which would make me unhappy and perhaps prevent my getting home as soon as I expected for if I act, I will not go home until I succeed as they would have me, and a week longer than I promised myself away will seem a year. However, I must hope for the best."[13] With formidable determination Charlotte followed every mention of her apprehensions, even in her own diary, with a stoic rejoinder, reminding herself not to give up now that she had come this far. Even at her loneliest, when Charlotte moaned that she would "give worlds" to be at home with Rosalie, she conceded, "I have cast the dice otherwise and now must abide it."[14]

I read these passages with a mixture of irony and admiration, for I know what Charlotte Cushman, writing them, did not: that within two years of this voyage she was to be considered by many as the finest performer on both sides of the Atlantic. And, even more paradoxically, that much of her acclaim would come from spectators' perceptions of the *male* roles she played onstage coupled with their notion of her unassailable moral character. How much of her fame, I wonder, is attributable to her courageousness and innovation and how much to a curious mix of naïveté and dismissal that rendered invisible to many people the passions that impelled her as a woman who loved other women?

Other than the companionship of Mr. and Mrs. Bliss, the ship's captain, and the ministrations of Sallie Mercer, the fourteen-year-old African American young woman Charlotte had brought along as her maid, Charlotte spent most of her time fighting off seasickness and thinking of Rosalie. In addition to rereading Rosalie's last letter to her numerous times, Charlotte tried to capture in her diary her memories of Rosalie, as though by repeating them in words, on paper, to herself she might hold onto the image and the feelings they represented. The faint scrawl covers pages filled throughout the long transatlantic voyage. Continuing onto the endpapers in the back of the diary, Charlotte wrote:

Fri., Nov. 1, 1844. The clouds have just broken away and through the window of the Ladies Saloon I observed a pure bright star. I called it "Rosalie" and with such[,] sound my prayers to it. God bless her—if she ever knew how constantly she possessed my thoughts—how often I traced her features, how frequently I was dreaming her occupations through the day. Where she was in her family rooms, where in the third story, where in the parlor and oh how I shall long to be in the front room at the family gatherings.[15]

The next day Charlotte was too seasick to move, but she noted, "on Sunday took my book and pencil and tried to trace my thoughts of the last two days," since the weather had been too rough to write. Several months earlier, in July, Rosalie, a painter, had given her lover a miniature of herself on a bracelet. Thinking of Rosalie, Charlotte wrote of "her sweet eyes as they gaze up to me now from her picture on my wrist. . . . I love them for their dear art and gentle influence upon me, which serves to remind me in my unhappy wretched moments that there is one heart at least in which I am faithfully remembered. I only wish I could hear her voice and see her dear lips move to kiss me. I verily believe if I had her by me at this moment I could press the breath out of her body."[16] *Press the breath out of her body.*

Lillian Faderman, in *Surpassing the Love of Men*, describes Charlotte Cushman's relationships with other women as "passionate romantic friendships" and "Boston marriages" that were generally considered acceptable by nineteenth-century mores because women were assumed to be incapable of carnal desire. Faderman has claimed that "romantic friendships were love relationships in every sense except perhaps the genital, since women in centuries other than ours often internalized the view of females as having little sexual passion." According to Faderman, romantic friends "might kiss, fondle each other, sleep together, utter expressions of overwhelming love and promises of eternal faithfulness, and yet see their passions as nothing more than effusions of the spirit. . . . If they were sexually aroused; they might deny it even to themselves if they wished."[17] They might. Yet the longing that Charlotte Cushman felt for Rosalie Sully was clearly embodied. It is evident that the desire women in earlier periods felt for each other meant different things to them than those feelings might today. But to suggest that the feelings expressed between women can be captured in a single definition of "romantic friendship" is perhaps to overlook their complexity. The meanings of same-sex desire were not simple or constant—but, rather, were multiple and contradictory. Tensions and ambiguities existed within and alongside romantic friendships, despite a wide acceptance of women's sentimental expressions of affection and the absence of a categorizing or pathologizing term with which to label those feelings.

Without a label, like *lesbian,* to contain her, to identify and demark

Charlotte's love for women from the sentimental attachments so popularly accepted in her era, how did Charlotte and those around her understand her desire? Some theorists and historians have suggested that before the term *lesbian* or *homosexual* existed in common parlance—that is, before medical authorities and sexologists defined "homosexuals" as identifiable kinds of persons—women who felt emotional attachments and even erotic desire for other women did not perceive of themselves as "being" different, having a specific identity, but merely as having feelings for each other and perhaps even engaging in erotic acts as a result of those feelings. While erotic acts or feelings might be directed toward the same or opposite sex, this argument runs, there was no notion that sexual behavior defined what an individual "was," merely which specific sexual "acts" that individual might engage in.[18]

The absence of the labels such as *lesbian* and *homosexual* may have afforded women like Charlotte Cushman greater freedom to express their closeness to other women, but what became clear to me during my first study of her private correspondence fifteen years ago[19] is that, contrary to those theorists who claim that women who loved each other in earlier time periods experienced their attachments to each other as innocent, socially acceptable romantic friendships, Charlotte's diary, letters, and those of women in her intimate circle are filled with their own active negotiation of how much of their intense, passionate feelings for other women they could safely display. My study of Charlotte Cushman reveals the concerns that underlie her negotiations, revealing that women's erotic desire for each other was legible—to anyone who could read the "code." Like Martha Vicinus, Emma Donoghue, and Terry Castle, all of whom intentionally employ the term *lesbian* to signal this awareness, even when located in women who lived before the term was commonly used, I am interested in how women in earlier periods struggled to understand themselves and their passions.[20]

Throughout the summer before her voyage Charlotte had spent more and more time with Rosalie, riding alone with her in the early mornings, "passing hours of sweet companionship" on what Rosalie referred to as "our sofa" on the third floor, opposite the backroom door in the Sully's South Fifth Street Philadelphia home, a location that they each associated with their most intimate moments.[21] On shipboard Charlotte recounted how she would try to will herself to dream of Rosalie and then described the dreams she remembered: "I was in the upstairs . . . sitting on the sofa—Rose by my side with her arm around my neck—her cheek resting against mine and my lips pressed upon her hand." It felt so real to Charlotte—she could even hear her lover's voice.[22]

During her voyage Charlotte repeatedly attempted to summon up specific images and memories of Rosalie, for, as apprehensive as the actress was about the professional success she was seeking, she was secure in the commitment the two women shared. On 1 June, while performing with Macready in New York, Charlotte had sent Rosalie a ring for her birthday two days later.[23] The ring was more than a birthday present, however. It portended even greater intimacy between the two women, for on 5 July 1844, Charlotte noted for the first time that she "Slept with Rose."[24] Although *slept with* may not have had a sexual connotation in an era when it was not uncommon for same-sex friends to share a bed, clearly the closeness between the two women was heightened and marked by this experience, because on the very next day Charlotte's diary entry reads: " 'R.' Saturday, July 6th 'married.' "[25]

At first I wondered what this cryptic entry meant to her. Clearly, if Charlotte referred to another literal, heterosexual marriage, there would be no need to cite it, to set it off with quotation marks. Instead, this was "like" a marriage. This commitment, forged by the two women after whatever intimacies were shared when they slept together, was noteworthy to Charlotte but had to remain coded, indicated by initial and quotation mark even within the privacy of her own diary. But what did *married* mean to nineteenth-century women who loved other women?[26] Certainly, it implied a passionate commitment, one Charlotte reiterated in her journal. Even as she crossed the ocean, Charlotte affirmed that "now that I have known the luxury and dear happiness of her love I would not care or wish to live an hour deprived of her love and affection. . . . While she cares for me, as I know she does, I promise most solemnly never to love anything else. I could not if I would."[27] Similarly, Rosalie was to assure Charlotte in a letter the following May: "I am as fondly yours as I was the 6th of July last—that pledge I still wear. Were my feelings towards you the least changed I should remove it from off my finger for I never deceive either in word or in action."[28] And Charlotte, for her part, knew that Rosalie's covenant with her was sincere, passionate, and long-lasting: "She is not hasty in making promises, as I can prove, hard to convince, but once satisfied—no matter what comes after, the dearest consolation of my heart . . . is 'She loves me'—not the love of a day, but forever. She is mine in every thought. I know it, I feel it, everything else sinks into insignificance."[29]

On 16 July 1844, four months before this voyage, to seal further the closeness between them, Rosalie had given Charlotte the bracelet on which she had painted her own likeness, a representation of herself to accompany her lover. On board ship, after they parted, Charlotte invoked the memory of the woman she loved to gird her through the fears: "I laid thinking of dear Rose for more than an hour, speaking to her—calling on her by the most endearing names and begging for an answer—I only saw her lips move to kiss me! and almost springing from my berth at the bare thought of my usual reply to that sweet expression from her, I sunk back again and almost imagining I had her head upon my shoulder, I dropped asleep."[30]

Whatever Charlotte's "usual reply" to Rosalie's kisses, there are no other letters between them to offer clues. On Wednesday, 24 July 1844, after having slept together on Charlotte's birthday the night before, the two women had gone to Charlotte's Clover Hill home in Philadelphia and "burned letters." What had Charlotte felt the need to edit? Throughout her life she managed her representation of herself masterfully, carefully noting when she received letters and when she responded. She didn't want any letters lost, found by others, their contents revealed to unintended spectators. None of Rosalie's letters to Charlotte from this period have been found. But Charlotte's diary and the scores of other letters that remain from other relationships with women make it apparent that women were the romantic and passionate center of her life.

By the end of this voyage, Charlotte despaired that Rosalie's image was fading from her mind; she was no longer able to will herself to dream of Rosalie. And, when Rosalie *did* appear in Charlotte's dreams, she looked sad or ill. With a prophetic sense of foreboding, Charlotte noted that she would have to remind Rosalie to take care of herself for Charlotte's sake, if not for her own. Although Charlotte was primarily narrating her feelings for herself, to understand her fears and desires by expressing them, in some sense she imagined herself to be chronicling her experiences *for* Rosalie— her reactions and introspection a gift for her partner— a way they might at some point in the future share this adventure. But as she "sat and ruminated, thinking of home till [her] heart ached," Charlotte wrote, "What a monstrous existence to attempt to make a journal of [,] yet she for whom it is written will make it worthy by reading it."[31]

But Rosalie would never get to read the small diary I hold in my hands more than a century and a half later. Just as Charlotte could not anticipate the future acclaim that awaited her, she could not imagine that she would never see Rosalie again; for in little more than two years, while Charlotte was enjoying the fruits of her first British success, Rosalie Sully, the aspiring and energetic young artist Charlotte had loved so much, would be dead.[32]

As the British travelers on board ship eagerly anticipated their arrival home, Charlotte calculated how soon she would be able to write to Rosalie and what vessel returning to the United States would convey her letters home. She had glued the transatlantic steamer schedule to her diary. On Friday, 15 November, when the ship was only a few hundred miles from the English shore, Charlotte noted that, "if we are fortunate, we shall be in

Charlotte Cushman, by Rosalie Sully. Behind this 1844 ivory minature in its gold frame are intertwined locks of Charlotte Cushman's and Rosalie Sully's hair. *(From the Art Collection of the Folger Shakespeare Library.)*

Liverpool . . . about 9 o'clock Monday." Charlotte hoped to be there in time to have a letter to Rosalie delivered early, by the returning steamer leaving that day. "Oh what will dear Rose say when the letter is put in her hands? She cannot expect to hear from me until the middle of Dec. and getting one by the 1st she will hardly believe her eyes."[33]

On the next day, the weather was damp and uncomfortable; the deck, covered in a thick drizzling mist, was so wet that Charlotte felt "compelled to remain in the wheelhouse," and so she "happened to be standing by the man at the wheel when he spied *land;* he pointed it out to me and then called to the mate, who instantly shouted 'Land Ho.'" With all of the excitement that ensued Charlotte could not help noting:

> with what different feelings I looked upon the land to what the other passengers do. . . . [I]nstead of joy, a feeling of sadness pervades my heart and I find myself unconsciously shedding tears at my lonely situation—I am indeed a stranger and I feel it—my only hope can be that I may not long feel so; if I do it will break my heart. The morning is thick and miserable as we get nearer. The fog is more dense and the English on board are smacking their lips as if they could recognize the taste of their own air. . . . I can well understand the desire to do so, for if I was within 1000 miles of Phila[delphia] I am sure I should imagine I could scent Phila[delphia] air."[34]

Filled with loneliness and anticipation, Charlotte's thoughts drew her back to the long road that had brought her to this moment. At this time Charlotte looked to the past, and so do I, trying to make sense of the events that had brought her this far. Along with her diary, thousands of her letters have been saved, offering clues, and there are hundreds of reviews and articles about her and her performances. Many of the letters are to and from women who formed the various circles of her most intimate life: groups of friends and lovers from these early years in the United States and, later, the circles of women who filled her life in London and in Rome. As I struggle to provide coherence, to understand Charlotte Cushman, I am painfully conscious of all the artifacts that are missing. No other diary of hers exists. For every letter saved, how many others have been destroyed? What is left is fragmentary, partially the result of what lovers and family members who outlived her wanted to preserve, partially the result of her own intentional editing. Both the saving and discarding were influenced, no doubt, by what Charlotte and her nineteenth-century contemporaries deemed important, significant, remarkable—or embarrassing, painful, or merely unnecessary.

What would Charlotte Cushman come to signify for the women who knew her? Whether in memoirs, fiction, poetry, journalism, or fan letters, women who felt close to Charlotte Cushman articulated in print the feelings and reactions she evoked in them, and their texts, too, are part of her story. Charlotte was many different things to the different women who knew her, but the independent, autonomous woman who loved other women was first and foremost an *actress*. In the mid-nineteenth century the predominant image of the actress was as a woman cut off from polite, middle-class society by her "unwomanly" behavior, offstage as well as on. For many readers of texts that featured performers as characters and for spectators at actual theatrical events, actresses were seen as the representative embodiment of artifice, self-promotion, sexual availability, and public display at a time when middle-class women were enjoined to be selfless, chaste, domestic, and "true." Theatrical reviews, fiction, and articles in the popular periodical press were therefore sites in which images of the actress were constructed and debated, but Charlotte had a hand in representing images of her various "selves" in other, more personal contexts as well.

Inevitably, what I find as I sift through her letters and diary is as much a result of my fashioning of the fragments she and others have left—imposing an order, a structure, a meaning—as it was for her contemporaries. At first, I envisioned this as a study of Charlotte Cushman's concentric circles; like the broadening ripples encircling the boat that bore her to England, I pictured Charlotte's close, intimate circles of lovers, family, and friends surrounded by her more public circles of fans and spectators, her actual communities ebbing out into virtual communities. At the center of all, as in a whirlpool, were her signature roles. In these celebrated characterizations those who personally knew her recognized aspects of the woman she was, while for others who only knew *of* her Charlotte Cushman's portrayals made available in the cultural imaginary new and potentially transformative images of female ambition and desire.

But now, instead of concentric circles, I have come to see Charlotte Cushman's circles overlap, like ripples encircling several stones, each extending into the next. Women who started out as fans or friends in one period of her life became lovers. Some lovers became "family." Writer friends created and publicized images of her, framing what she would come to mean to the larger community of their readers, and Charlotte Cushman herself constructed narratives about her life that were in dialogue with these images.

What do I see, emphasize, ignore? Unlike her other biographers, I am not interested in creating a laudatory tribute to a now-forgotten theatrical "star" or in telling the story of her life as I understand it—as if there *were* one *true* story. Instead, this study of Charlotte Cushman is an exploration of representations. As I sit here, decoding her diary, I am drawn to consider other ways she represented herself—in interviews, in her personal letters, and in the characters she portrayed onstage. What hints, whispers, clues lie just under the surface in her accounts and in others' accounts of her? Her enormous popularity, was, to some extent, due to the range of possible readings others brought to these representations. Along with historian Jennifer Terry, I aim to be "a reader-against-the-grain who recognizes traces of deviant subjects revealed through the conflict within dominant accounts."[35] Charlotte Cushman is, on many registers, a "deviant subject." As I read her diary, I feel part voyeur and part archaeologist, questioning my entitlement while I dig deeper. The secrets and feelings Charlotte expressed here and strove to keep hidden elsewhere were her most personal and intimate passions, encoded in language shaped by her era—language that framed the way she saw herself, fraught with meanings and connotations I can only try to imagine.

Yet, in recognizing Charlotte Cushman as a lesbian, the particular history I struggle to transcribe, decode, uncover, and contextualize is my history as well. Her words are slippery and fading. It takes a long time to read the cramped, nineteenth-century handwriting, to differentiate between the letters—double *s*'s written like *f*'s. Inevitably, some of the words elude me, announcing the paradox of their connotations so long ago. This document, this artifact, is a marvel to me. For more than a century and a half it has existed, passing from Cushman's hands on that first squally voyage and through many others till it resides safely here, in this archive, protected. Still imbued with the poignancy of its historical moment, it is a window into the hopes and fears and longings of America's greatest nineteenth-century actress at the very moment when, unbeknownst to her, she was on the verge of achieving unprecedented celebrity. But in order to read this artifact, to comprehend how Charlotte Cushman came to be seen not just as a remarkable performer but as an icon, I need to understand what came before. As I attempt to uncover the details of her early life, to understand the conditions that created her and allowed for her success, I turn first to her genealogy: to the stories she told and those that were told about her.

The Hero in the Family
and on the Stage

> I bless my mother, or rather my grandmother, for one element
> in my nature—ambition!
>
> —Charlotte Cushman

"I was born a tomboy."[1] So begin the recollections of her childhood that Charlotte Cushman dictated just months before she died. As Emma Stebbins, Charlotte's companion for the last twenty years of her life, explained:

> In those days this epithet, "tomboy," was applied to all little girls who showed the least tendency toward thinking and acting for themselves. It was the advance-guard of that army of opprobrious epithets which has since been lavished so freely upon the pioneers of woman's advancement and for a long time the ugly little phrase had power to keep the dangerous feminine element within what was considered to be the due bounds of propriety and decorum.[2]

Emma Stebbins, writing in 1878, after Charlotte Cushman's death, was conscious of how language was then being used to categorize and label young girls and women who attempted to transgress gender stereotypes. *Tomboy* was a label that had the power to constrain women, "to keep the dangerous feminine element" within socially acceptable bounds. Yet Charlotte, looking back at her early life, was not only *not* limited by the impropriety of the label; she *claimed* it as an identity category into which she was born, one she embraced despite its "danger."

How else did she see herself? And how did she want others to see her? Her letters and memoirs, the interviews she gave, the texts she wrote, and those written about her were all efforts to make sense, in different ways, of her life, identity, desire, and career. Whether consciously or not, a person fashions a sense of self in the stories she chooses to tell and retell, or authorizes to be told, about her. All narratives are constructed in a context and are, therefore, shaped by and in dialogue with the values and beliefs prevalent in the storyteller's life; in this case the context included the Cushman family, the milieu of the nineteenth-century stage, the experiences of women who loved other women, and the dominant social expectations of appropriate "masculine" and "feminine" behavior.

As Charlotte Cushman selectively fashioned the "facts" of her life into stories, letters, and published accounts, she represented multiple and sometimes contradictory selves, in part to account for her life choices. Sometimes the details in the stories she told or authorized are changed, stretched, rearranged—not necessarily to mislead (although occasionally with that effect) but to emphasize or to illustrate a point, to have a hand in the aesthetic construction of her life narrative. Literary scholar Stephen Greenblatt has used the term *self-fashioning* to describe the "manipulable and artful process" by which a person forms and expresses her identity through the "representation of one's nature or intention in speech or actions." The selves we fashion in the accounts we tell others are multifaceted and reveal, in Stephen Orgel's terms, not only the ways we want others to see us but also the ways we want to see ourselves.[3] As we fashion our narratives, we impose a structure on the events we recount, implying causality, for example, by saying, "these are the events that led me to pursue this career, or that partner." Our stories are also "performances" constructed with and addressed to specific or imagined listeners or readers for whom we wish to suggest a particular shared meaning or set of values to be gleaned from our circumstances or actions. Whether to specific correspondents in her letters or to particular interviewers and critics in the press, Charlotte told stories about the events and people in her life, shaping for and with her readers the ways she would be known and remembered. And so, as I attempt in this chapter to examine the various narratives that were constructed by Charlotte Cushman or by sympathetic friends about her parentage and her reasons for embarking on a theatrical career, I recognize that I, too, am constructing a narrative, one in which I am less concerned with the absolute veracity of the facts she told than I am with the meanings she, and her supporters or detractors, attempted to wrest from her circumstances to account for her extraordinary success.

Charlotte was an unlikely candidate for such public celebrity. Standing five feet six inches tall, with a large forehead and square jaw, even in her youth she looked powerful and substantial, not at all the diminutive, feminine part most women played in the cultural imaginary of the period. The stories she told or authorized about herself were all shaped in some relationship to the dominant images of middle-class, nineteenth-century women. Even in her private correspondence Charlotte Cushman's self-fashionings were bound up in what Felicity A. Nussbaum refers to as "cultural definitions of gender—those assumed, prescribed and embedded in their consciousness, as well as their subversive thoughts and acts in contradiction to those definitions."[4] And, so, in this chapter I explore the narra-

Charlotte Cushman. This portrait of Charlotte Cushman was probably completed in 1845, shortly after Cushman's arrival in England. *(Harvard Theatre Collection. Houghton Library.)*

tive construction of Charlotte Cushman, reading the often repeated stories of her early life against the backdrop of her era, an era that made possible and necessary some of the meanings Charlotte attributed to her own behavior and allowed for some of the resistant readings that help constitute possibilities outside of mainstream norms.

Charlotte grew up with a mother and a grandmother who had each in her own way overstepped the bounds of propriety. Although some of the facts of Charlotte's genealogy are sketchy, a basic outline can be determined. In 1810 Mary Saunders Babbit packed up her three children—seventeen-year-old twins, Mary Eliza and Winthrop, and seven-year-old Augustus—and set off with them for Boston, leaving her husband, lawyer Erasmus Babbit Jr., in Sturbridge, Massachusetts. The exact reason for Mary Babbit's move remains difficult to ascertain; Erasmus Babbit was known to be more frivolous than his strong-willed and ambitious wife, and the low fees he earned may have exacerbated whatever was wrong between them.[5] Once settled in Boston, Mary Babbit's daughter Mary Eliza managed a school, until, at the age of twenty-two, she married forty-six-year-old widower Elkanah Cushman. Elkanah Cushman, whose own parents had died when he was thirteen, was a sixth-generation descendant of Thomas Cushman and Mary Allerton, both of whom were connected with the earliest Puritan settlements on the American continent. Thomas Cushman's father had petitioned the English Crown to allow the Puritans to settle in Plymouth; Mary Allerton was a passenger on the *Mayflower*. When Elkanah Cushman and Mary Eliza Babbit met, Elkanah was only three years younger than Mary Eliza's father and was an established Boston shipping merchant. On 23 July 1816, Charlotte Cushman, the first of their four children, was born.

This tale of Elkanah Cushman's Puritan ancestry is part of the standard narrative of Charlotte Cushman's heritage, repeated in articles and reviews time and again and featured prominently in a lengthy, early article about Charlotte by her good friend Mary Howitt.[6] Howitt, who undoubtably received her information from Charlotte herself, befriended Charlotte shortly after she arrived in England and was unquestionably sympathetic. And yet this genealogical narrative of Pilgrim forebears may be partly apocryphal, deployed by Charlotte because she felt her fame called for a story of respectable origins. Shortly after Cushman's death, Manning Leonard, a distant relative, claimed that "the friends and acquaintances here of the Babbit family, always maintained that the husband of Mary Eliza was a foreigner, an Englishman, and I was surprised when the newspapers stated that he was connected directly with the Plymouth families, but the work of Hon. H. W. Cushman explains it." Leonard was referring to an 1855 published genealogy of the Cushman family that identified Elkanah's father as an American loyalist who "embarked with the British Army in 1776."[7]

Charlotte Cushman's Pilgrim heritage, however, was considered an important component of her success. Tracing her family to the *Mayflower* meant claiming a Puritan pedigree, an inherited prestige that provided the highest qualifications as an American, both at home and abroad, and Charlotte capitalized on the effect such claims could have on her career. Such a pedigree established her as a source of pride for other Americans and helped defuse the antitheatrical prejudices so vehemently articulated by the "moralizers" who believed, as had the Puritans, that the theater was an immoral endeavor. Leonard ultimately claimed that Charlotte's father's background was immaterial in the story of her life; what mattered were the *women* in Charlotte's family, the female relatives she had known: "It seems to me that the personal appearance, and all prominent characteristics of

Charlotte Saunders Cushman were transmitted through her maternal ancestry," Leonard suggested.[8]

Whatever the specific facts of her heritage, Leonard at least corroborated Cushman's contention that she was born into a family with two earlier generations of strong, unconventional women. Her mother had been a self-supporting teacher, and her grandmother, in a move extremely uncharacteristic for the early nineteenth century, had left her husband and raised her three children alone. As the eldest child in the third generation of such a family, Charlotte was not deterred by the "ugly little phrase 'tomboy.'" Instead, she elaborated upon it. Charlotte bragged that, rather than play with dolls as a young child, she had cracked open their heads so that she could see how they think. She preferred building toy furniture to sewing doll clothes. Climbing trees was "an absolute passion."[9] Like her grandmother, Mary Saunders Babbit, who lived with the Cushman family, Charlotte was a gifted mimic. Charlotte claimed that her grandmother was "remarkably clever, bright and witty, and so dominated her household and children, that although qualities descended, her immediate family had little opportunity to exercise them in her presence."[10] Charlotte was accustomed to powerful, captivating, dominant women whose sphere of influence may have only extended to an individual small family yet was absolute. And Charlotte learned early that with her own precocious talents, she too could entertain others and hold sway over their attention. The private, everyday performances she witnessed at the dinner table, and engaged in herself from time to time, were assertions of personal and social power.

Contrary to the expectation that girls be shy and retiring, from the time she was very young Charlotte enjoyed being the center of attention and was loathe to share the spotlight. In 1818, when she was two years old, her brother Charles was born, and four years later, on 17 March 1822, her sister, Susan. By her own admission, and with some bravado, Charlotte claimed that she was "tyrannical to brothers and sister," although she clearly favored and was quite protective of her youngest brother, Augustus, born in 1825.[11]

Charlotte's father, by contrast, appears in most stories of her early life as a shadowy figure whose "age and fiscal worries prevented his being the strong, responsible head he might have been."[12] The year Augustus was born, Elkanah Cushman suffered severe business losses that dramatically changed the family's financial circumstances. Then fifty-six years old, with grown children from his previous marriage, Elkanah Cushman drifted from his second family as his business worsened. Thus, although Charlotte lived in an age marked by the expectation of strong, patriarchal authority figures, the only consistent male influence at this point in her life was her uncle Augustus Babbit. Babbit was only thirteen years older than his niece and took a special interest in Charlotte. Despite the commonly held notion, supported by medical belief, that "the female brain and nervous system . . . [were] inadequate to sustained intellectual effort,"[13] Babbit offered his niece prizes to encourage Charlotte in her studies, and one of his special interests was the theater. In 1826 he took Charlotte to the theater for the first time to see Shakespeare's *Coriolanus,* starring British tragedian William Charles Macready on his first American tour. Since Augustus Babbit was a stockholder at the Tremont Theatre, Charlotte was able to attend performances often, and her mother also became acquainted with Augustus's theatrical friends. "Thus," as Charlotte remembered, "we had many opportunities of seeing and knowing something of the fraternity."[14] Although she had no idea that she was to become one of the most celebrated members of this "fraternity," Charlotte's familial association with members of the theatrical profession left a strong early impression upon her.

In school Charlotte enjoyed reciting and reading aloud, just as she had enjoyed participating in the rollicking mimicry at her dinner table. In one of her often repeated stories Charlotte recounted the jealousy of her young classmates who complained when she was commended for her skill in reading literature. Charlotte read Brutus's lines from John Howard Payne's play, *Brutus,* so well that she was moved to the head of the class. The other children protested that Charlotte's exposure to the theater had given her an advantage over them.[15] From her early life Charlotte saw the theater as an avenue to self improvement. Rather than a source of vice, vanity, and licentiousness, as it was depicted in many contemporary religious quarters,[16] in Charlotte's narratives the theater was associated with family, education, and upward mobility. Those who were disparaging of her histrionic talents were merely jealous.

Charlotte Cushman's visits to the theater influenced her playtime as well as her studies. After hearing the operetta *Bluebeard,* she organized a group of neighborhood children and performed it in her attic for an audience of family and neighbors. Outfitted in white Turkish trousers, close-fitting jacket, red sash, and wooden sword, she chose to sing the leading part of the male lover, Selim. Years later, reminiscing with a woman who as a childhood friend had shared in these home theatricals, Charlotte enjoined her to remember when "we were boys together." Whereas her friend claimed to have had "no such penchant for a masculine masquerade as [Charlotte],"[17] it seems clear that in Charlotte Cushman's earliest experiences of performing, playing for herself or with friends, she eagerly traversed conventional gender roles. In Charlotte's anecdotes of her childhood she unselfconsciously represented herself as "boyish," adventurous, and inquisitive; acting afforded her the opportunity and freedom to play whatever parts she chose.

Choosing a Career on the Stage

In the mid-nineteenth century the predominant image of the actress in popular discourse was as an abject character, a woman generally considered "impure" and therefore cut off from polite middle-class society by her "unwomanly" behavior, offstage as well as on. Because a theatrical career was "socially and morally suspect in Puritanical middle-class America"[18]— particularly for women, Charlotte was required to tell and retell the story of how and why she first sought a career on the stage. Despite Augustus Babbit's encouragement of her interest in the theater and Charlotte's pleasure in playacting as well as watching professional productions, published accounts of her choice to pursue a professional stage career all center not on her own desires but on her family's tenuous economic condition. By 1828 the Cushman family finances were so low that Elkanah Cushman was forced into bankruptcy. The family had moved six times before Charlotte's fourteenth birthday. After one move from Boston to Charlestown, Mary Eliza opened a rooming house under her own name.[19] Elkanah's connection to the family grew increasingly tenuous, and soon they practically lost touch with him altogether.[20] Charlotte was forced to leave school at the age of thirteen, after completing the basic courses in reading, writing, and arithmetic.

Carolyn Heilbrun has remarked that "for women who want to live a quest plot, as men's stories . . . encourage them to do, some event must be invented to transform their lives . . . apparently 'accidentally' from a conventional to an eccentric story."[21] In Charlotte Cushman's life the event was her father's business loss and abandonment of his family—and Charlotte's subsequent "duty" to support them. According to Charlotte, "the circumstances in my Father's life which made it necessary that his children should be placed under conditions looking toward their future self-support obliged us to take early advantage of every opportunity for self-sustainment."[22] She began to study singing and sang in the choir at the church tended by young pastor Ralph Waldo Emerson. Charlotte made it clear in her earliest stories explaining her performance career that she had undertaken such a public occupation to support her family, not because she enjoyed performing or longed for the independence it offered.

During the early- and mid-nineteenth century few occupations of any sort were available to respectable women, and those that required women's visibility in public were most socially suspect. Yet, just as women like Charlotte's own mother had had few options, beyond teaching schoolchildren, to be both respectable and self-supporting, middle-class women of Charlotte's generation found virtually all professions closed to them. The ideology that assigned middle-class women to the domestic sphere of the home and men to the public sphere of work and commerce influenced Charlotte's narratives about her background, her motivations, and her life choices, however much her own experience, and that of the women in her family, departed from these commonly expressed expectations. Each of her stories was, to some extent, in dialogue with this ideology.

White, middle-class women of the time were brought up to accept an image of themselves that has since been referred to as "the true woman."[23] Barbara Welter described the rhetoric of "true womanhood" as an articulation of four attributes "by which a woman judged herself and was judged by her husband, her neighbors, and society." According to Welter, these were expressed as "four cardinal virtues—piety, purity, submissiveness, and domesticity— . . . without them, no matter whether there was fame, achievement or wealth, all was ashes."[24] While this image was predominantly produced by and for the middle-class, women whose life circumstances or choices called into question a strict allegiance to the "cardinal virtues" often strove to refer to themselves, and be referred to, as "true women"—even women like Charlotte Cushman.

Cultural artifacts such as women's magazines, religious literature, and personal correspondence—including Charlotte's and that of her family, friends, and partners—were replete with references to true women. And yet, although *true* meant respectable and virtuous, the modifier *true* contains the possibility of its opposite, "false." If only *some* women were true, then the mere biological fact of being female was not enough to guarantee as "natural" the womanly virtues advocates of true womanhood claimed represented all women.

How might women like Charlotte Cushman come to accept in theory such an apparently restricted view of female behavior, an ideology that their lived experience as independent, successful, and powerful women refuted? Historians Nancy Cott and Elizabeth H. Pleck claim that "even women who have purposely evaded the domestic sphere or family ties and have lived independently or sought public careers, find that the attitudes toward them are still shaped by the family norm. The 'deviance' attributed to non-domestic women exposes how strong that norm is."[25] And so Charlotte's earliest narratives, and those of her favorable critics and friends, as cultural productions of this ideology, are replete with references to her family. The economic needs of the Cushman family were called upon to explain and legitimate Charlotte's ambition; in this way her ambition never overtly refuted "appropriate" norms for women. Charlotte's pursuit of a stage career was depicted as a sacrifice, as her pious duty toward her family, not motivated either by the pleasure she might derive from expressing her talents nor by any "right" to economic independence. In fact, at the height of her career, in 1858, Charlotte led a Mrs. J. H. Hanaford of the *Boston Jour-*

nal to believe that she initially "went to work for the sake of a widowed mother and her fatherless children," even though Elkanah Cushman was certainly still living at the time of Charlotte's first performances. Hanaford reported that Charlotte Cushman had "struggled with manly energy and womanly endurance"[26] to fulfill her responsibilities to her "widowed" mother well.

The Cushman family's economic circumstances *had* changed radically after Elkanah Cushman's business disaster, yet, despite their continued desire for respectability, Charlotte was allowed, even encouraged, to violate gender norms and pursue her livelihood. And ultimately Charlotte's family, rather than attempting to curtail her aspirations, *depended upon* them. After all, working-class women, and women with no men on whom to depend, had to find a way to earn their own living.[27] Charlotte's *need* to work—as the "savior" of her family—would, later in life, open a space for her to become a model for women's *right* to work.

Charlotte Cushman's first public appearance was on 25 March 1830, in a recital arranged by her singing teacher, George Farmer. She was just four-teen years old. On the program she was listed anonymously as "A Young Lady." Shortly after this, while singing in Emerson's choir, Cushman's vocal talent came to the attention of Robert D. Sheppard, a friend of Elka-nah Cushman's. Sheppard was said to be so moved by her voice that he offered to be her patron and arranged for John Paddon, George Farmer's singing teacher, to take her on as a pupil. In this endeavor Charlotte, like her neighbor Mary Peabody, another young Boston Unitarian who studied with Paddon after singing in the church choir, was engaging herself in a most "respectable" undertaking. Paddon had advertised that his "mode of instruction in singing belongs to the first European school."[28] Unlike other forms of artistic expression tinged by association with theatricality, singing offered the imprimatur of European culture and reinforced the qualities of pleasing, "womanly" refinements so desired by Charlotte's middle-class peers. The cultivation of a woman's singing voice was well within the bounds of genteel femininity.[29] Mary Peabody (the future wife of educator Horace Mann) and many of the more privileged young women in the parish who studied with Paddon were *amateurs,* young women with talent, eager for the self-confidence they might gain in being able to sing an oper-atic aria for private gatherings. Charlotte, however, was seeking her liveli-hood. With few other financial options open to her, Charlotte agreed to serve for three years as an apprentice to Paddon. It was arranged that she would work in his home in exchange for singing lessons. For months she followed Paddon's demanding routine.

While still under obligation to Paddon, in early 1833 Charlotte was invited by relatives from New York, the Samuel Judd family, for a two-week visit. The two weeks stretched into three months, and the Judds offered to adopt seventeen-year-old Charlotte. Mary Eliza refused. Charlotte had become, in the words of journalist George Ferris years later, her mother's "chief helpmate and confidante in the struggle to live."[30] When Mary Eliza called her daughter home, Charlotte went back to Boston. On her return Charlotte found her singing teacher infuriated that she had stayed away so long and her contract with him canceled. Fortunately, however, the celebrated English singers Joseph and Mary Ann Wood had come to Boston to perform and were looking for a local contralto to sing duets with Mary Ann. They and their coach, James G. Maeder, were impressed with Charlotte Cushman when she sang for them, and Maeder encouraged her to cultivate her voice for the operatic stage, where she might reach "any height of fortune" she coveted.[31] Among the earliest of Charlotte's letters, one she cherished throughout her life is an encouraging note from Mary Ann Wood, in which she advises "dear Charlotte" to practice "steadily so as to be prepared for me when that time arrives, as I am most anxious for your success." Charlotte penciled in the notation "recvd the 23rd Jan. The happiest moment in my life."[32] Although some criticized Mary Ann Wood's "excessive familiarity" with the "ballet-girls" and "stage hands" who surrounded her,[33] Charlotte was enthralled with her and spent as much time as she could in Wood's company. She sang with the Woods during their Boston engagement, but even more fortuitously for her, Maeder decided to stay on in Boston and take Charlotte on as a pupil. Once again she signed a professional agreement, accepting that for the three years she was to serve as Maeder's student she would sing when and how he chose and pay him half of any monies she might earn.[34]

For Charlotte Cushman's official professional debut, Maeder chose the part of Countess Almaviva in Mozart's *Marriage of Figaro*. The debut was scheduled for 8 April 1835. Charlotte was filled with apprehension, for the part of Almaviva was a soprano role, considerably higher than her natural contralto range. Years later, after she had become successful, stories published about her debut claimed that her mother and a young man named Charles Wiggin were less than enthusiastic about Charlotte's embarking on a stage career.[35]

Charlie Wiggin, whose older brother, James Simon Wiggin, had been in business with Charlotte's father, met Charlotte when, at the age of fifteen, he came to room at her family's boardinghouse. Only three years older than Charlotte, Charlie became a close friend and watched her develop from a scrappy young schoolgirl to a determined novice performer. Charlie knew of Charlotte's aspirations as a singer, and he may also have noticed Charlotte's reaction to beautiful British actress Fanny Kemble, who,

Mary Eliza Cushman. Charlotte Cushman's mother was often
disapproving of Charlotte's choice of career and companions.
*(Charlotte Cushman Photo Album. Prints and Photographs
Division. Library of Congress.)*

according to Charlotte, "burst like a meteor upon the American public."
Charlotte was so drawn to the actress, experiencing such "hero-worship for
her," that she "would walk for hours in Tremont Street—only to get the
opportunity of seeing [Fanny] pass from the Hotel to the Theatre"[36] when
Fanny appeared in Boston in the spring of 1833. Now, two years later, Charlotte was to debut there herself. In articles published many years later about
Charlotte's debut Charlie Wiggin was quoted as saying he had hoped that
nineteen-year-old Charlotte would have given up this "unwomanly pro-
ceeding" and marry him.[37]

Whether or not there was any truth to these depictions of the reactions of Charlotte's most intimate associates, such anecdotes locate Charlotte solidly within acceptable bourgeois values: they reinforce her mother's professed concern for propriety and the expectation that young men would be dismayed to have a woman of their acquaintance pursue a stage career. By repeating them, the popular periodicals of the day granted Charlotte a "conventional" background, but they also exposed the limits of those conventions. Later reprinted, these same stories about Charlotte's professional debut position her as rebelling against societal constraints, choosing to perform despite the obstacles against her, and triumphing in the endeavor. But Charlie's interest or desire had not been enough reason for Charlotte to put aside her own aspirations. On 8 April, at Boston's Tremont Theatre, Charlotte Cushman's "first performance on any stage" (as it was announced) took place. Although not unanimous in their praise, the critics were more than favorable, and Charlotte's theatrical debut was deemed a "great success."[38] Enthusiastically, the Boston Daily Atlas of 11 April 1835 reported that:

> There is but one opinion expressed in and out of the house, and that is, that Miss Cushman's success was brilliant . . . the lady evinced much timidity at her first entrance and was not wholly assured throughout the piece . . . [but her voice] even at present . . . is far superior to that of any American performer who has trod our boards.[39]

From as far away as New York, the Spirit of the Times reported that "a Miss Cushman is doing wonders at the Tremont, in opera."[40]

And the press—the arbiter of the public opinion it both reflected and created—was not only a forum for tributes; it could also be a minefield of innuendo and insult. Annoyed that Cushman's sudden success would be attributed to Maeder's coaching, John Paddon wrote a letter to the Boston Transcript claiming that Cushman's skill was a result of his instruction, which she received years before Maeder's name "was heard of in this city."[41] Charlotte responded immediately and vociferously to this charge with a letter asserting that Paddon, doubting her talent, had canceled their agreement. The credit, she claimed, was all Maeder's. This was only the first instance of Charlotte's willingness to use the popular press to deal with criticism head on. Rather than back down when confronted, or let others speak for her—however "womanly" that might appear—she responded immediately and publicly to criticism directed at her or at those she cared about. This earned her a lifelong reputation as someone not to be trifled with. Ironically, in calling attention to the slights against her as presented and debated in the court of public opinion, Charlotte Cushman both revealed the impropriety of Paddon's public discussion of the professional ethics and reputation of a "lady" like herself and, in defending herself, defied those very standards of propriety.

Charlotte performed several more times during the season under James Maeder's direction. Although her performance in *Cinderella* was criticized in both the Boston *Pearl* and the *Literary Gazette* as lacking in "grace," she generally pleased the audiences "concerned in the success of a native of our city."[42] The published accounts of Charlotte's performances, like those of any popular entertainer, served functions not just for herself but also for the particular communities and social groups with which she was identified. At first Charlotte was lauded as a native Bostonian; before long she would be heralded as a national icon.

Turning from Singing to Acting

In the winter of 1835 Charlotte Cushman accompanied James Maeder and his new wife, Clara Fisher Maeder, on a singing engagement in New Orleans. Charlotte knew Clara Fisher well; the former child star had for years been an acclaimed leading melodramatic actress at Boston's Tremont Theatre. Now, in the company of the Maeders, Charlotte's luck and talent appeared at first to have run out. Her New Orleans operatic debut was a failure. James H. Caldwell's four thousand–seat St. Charles Theatre was larger than any other place in which Charlotte had performed. Once again Maeder scheduled her to sing the part of Countess Almaviva, a soprano role, since his wife was to assume the contralto part. In later years Cushman claimed that she had lost her singing voice as a result of the great strain of attempting to project in so large a theater in a role for which she was not suited.[43] In virtually every biographical sketch of Charlotte Cushman some version of this story of Charlotte losing her voice was repeated, and it served many purposes. First, it provided an explanation for her dismal New Orleans reviews. Being forced to assume the highest-pitched, most "feminine-sounding" role, she claimed, harmed her health. The story illustrated, by analogy, a theme that was to run through many of the narratives told about her and offered as explanations for her "natural" inclinations: Charlotte could not be made into a soprano any more than she could be cast successfully in *any* traditionally feminine role, on- or offstage. The fault was attributed to those who directed her to disregard her own leanings. Second, this story served to explain Charlotte's choice to become an actress, a career considered even more socially suspect than that of an opera singer, who, by performing, simply shared what many would deem her god-given talents.

According to the *New Orleans Bee,* however, Charlotte did not lose her voice gradually over the course of her run; she was an almost immediate failure. A reviewer on the second night of her performance stated that "Miss Cushman made the worst Countess we have had the honor of seeing."[44] Clara Fisher Maeder later maintained that Charlotte had found the work of practicing for opera too arduous, that she was "badly 'stage struck'" and *preferred* the idea of acting to singing.[45] In either event, despite her bad reviews, she had a contract to fulfill. She struggled on throughout the season, performing a number of other roles. It was the custom for members of a company to alternate singing and dramatic parts. On the few occasions during which Charlotte performed a minor acting role, her critics seemed mollified. But when she attempted a singing role in *Cinderella* again the reviewer from the *Bee* panned her, suggesting that, since "Miss Cushman can sing nothing," she should limit herself to acting parts.[46] Cushman approached manager James Caldwell about doing just that, and he concurred.

Caldwell introduced Charlotte to James Barton, the British-born leading actor at the St. Charles. With his personal coaching, Charlotte prepared for a 23 April opening as Lady Macbeth. This performance, on the anniversary of Shakespeare's birth, proved an auspicious beginning, although her interpretation of the part was a radical departure from most popular renditions. Many critics expected an embodiment of the role like that Sarah Siddons had made famous in England. Charlotte Cushman's Lady Macbeth, instead of being a feminine helpmate to her husband, was the more powerful of the pair. Charlotte's indomitable energy resounded with the audience and critics, and she later claimed that this performance was the turning point at which she knew that she had found her calling. Despite the biases she would inevitably encounter, Charlotte Cushman would be an actress. She went on to perform other dramatic roles throughout the next month. In early June 1836, when the New Orleans season drew to a close, she set off for New York, determined to pursue a career on the dramatic stage.

Positive reviews in hand, Charlotte's first step after returning to New York was to contact Edmund Simpson, comanager of the Park Theatre, and apply for a position. The Park was the most prestigious of the New York theaters, considered the "Old Drury" of America by those who likened it to London's fashionable Drury Lane Theatre. Simpson replied that the unknown actress could act on trial for him, but he wouldn't offer her a job immediately until he was familiar with her work. Fresh from her sudden dramatic success in New Orleans, the ambitious Charlotte perceived Simpson's response as an insult and applied instead to Thomas Hamblin, manager of the less prestigious Bowery Theatre. Unlike the Park—which catered to elite audiences—at the Bowery, Hamblin was cultivating a working-class audience by promoting indigenous American talent and staging performances of what theater historian Bruce McConachie has termed heroic and apocalyptic "blood-and-guts melodrama."[47] Immediately after hearing of Cushman's talents from James Barton, Hamblin offered her a three-year contract, which she accepted.

Charlotte Cushman's position at the Bowery was that of a "walking lady" in the stock company. While starring actors toured from theater to theater, the regular stock company attached to a given theater filled the supporting roles and any others for which there were no stars. As a member of the stock company, Charlotte was required to play a multitude of different characters as needed, male and female, young and old, servants and soldiers, walk-on parts and leading roles. It was at that time customary that performers supply their own wardrobe. Since Charlotte had neither a wardrobe nor the funds to pay for one, Hamblin supplied her with costumes, for which she would pay over time from her salary. With an apparently secure job to look forward to, Charlotte encouraged her mother to give up their Boston roominghouse and move to New York. Charlotte's brothers, Charles and Augustus, would accompany their mother, but Susan was to stay in Boston in the care of her married half-sister, Isabella Weld, Elkanah's daughter from his first marriage.

On 27 August 1836, several days before Charlotte's scheduled opening, E. Burke Fisher, editor of the *New Yorker,* published a notice of "Miss Cushman . . . [who] will in a few days make her debut before the patrons of the Bowery Theatre." Fisher was evidently familiar with Charlotte; in his brief article he informed his readers, "We have had the pleasure of hearing Miss Cushman and must confess, that despite our bachelorism, we felt inclined to indulge in a trifle of sentiment."[48] Assuring readers of Charlotte Cushman's "private virtues," despite her public profession, and acknowledging his own "sentimental" feelings for her, Fisher's article located her within the competing value systems that framed gender expectations at the time. The formality of Fisher's use of *we* was more than an affectation of the press; Fisher and his colleagues saw themselves as the arbiters of high culture in the United States, speaking to and for those sophisticated New Yorkers whose tastes they attempted to influence.[49]

Unfortunately, the debut did not go as smoothly as planned. Charlotte was stricken with rheumatic fever, and three of the four weeks set aside for her first New York engagement were spent convalescing. Finally, on 12 September, she debuted as Lady Macbeth. The next morning Fisher sent her a personal note:

> You more than exceeded my warmest desires last night, and have now a double claim to the worship of him who now addresses you. If you go on as you have begun, the mind cannot compass an idea of the histrionic triumph you must achieve. Beyond even the wildest dream of Hope will be

your success, until seated upon the lofty eminence of a people's admiration, you become the American Siddons . . . as might be gathered from the attention paid you by the general audience, and the gush of good feeling that beamed in the countenances and twinkled in the eye of those who Came to Criticise [*sic*].[50]

As the reviewer for the *New Yorker,* Fisher had himself come prepared to criticize, but, as he described to Cushman his reactions to her performance, he assured her that other New York critics had shared his estimate of her performance as well.

The stern brow relaxed, the heart expanded, *the soul felt,* and the mind became subdued as Lady Macbeth enacted the thousand passions which Shakespeare has embodied in his most exquisite and *difficult* creation. Everyone was delighted, and I, exalted to the seventh Heaven of beatitude, stood witnessing the divinity of the social circle, conquering all hearts by the splendour of her genius. . . . You may safely depend upon the press—It is one great point gained.[51]

The press, and initially Fisher in particular, were to be instrumental in Charlotte Cushman's career. Fisher went on to assure the novice actress that she had "*carte blanche* of my interests, services and myself." As Fisher explained, "Your correspondent recognizes you, the star of the American Stage, and his pen is governed by that deference, and courtesy, which he feels it to be his duty to pay to the Sovereign in *the Ascendant.*"[52]

Whether or not Charlotte reciprocated his personal admiration is unknown, but undoubtedly she recognized that E. Burke Fisher's regard for her could serve her career well. For, as Charlotte became more professional, she became increasingly aware of her need to negotiate her career and offstage activities very carefully, to have some say in the public persona she was presenting. Governing the pen of one of New York's leading critics was bound to be advantageous for her career; however, Charlotte's self-fashioning was displayed on the pages of other New York papers as well. Fisher's associate, Mordecai Noah, editor of the *Evening Star,* wrote of Charlotte's "fine tall figure and masculine features, and the grace and dignity of her movements and gestures."[53] The press was an important platform for creating as well as reporting public opinion. And theatrical careers, which depended on public support and sanction, were made and broken in the press.

Charlotte Cushman was entering the field at a tumultuous time in the development of the American theater. The period between the end of the War of 1812 and the beginning of the Civil War has been seen by some theater historians as a significant point in American theater history; more theaters were built throughout the United States than ever before.[54] In the sec-

ond half of the nineteenth century, as the new western territories were settled and railroads developed, theatrical enterprises reached almost every
town and village in America.[55] But vestiges of the Puritan prejudice against
the theater were still widely felt. Some people objected to the theater on
religious grounds, believing the very nature of theatrical performance to be
an exercise in artifice and deception and, therefore, inimical to a pious life.
Others objected on moral grounds to the sexual license they associated with
many performers' lifestyles and to the drinking and prostitution that were
indulged in openly in theaters. For some critics the playhouse and the surrounding neighborhood and ancillary businesses that were associated with
the whole enterprise constituted an abject zone, an area apart from respectable society. Other critics condemned the "immodesty" they associated
with the very notion of self-display. Still others objected to the texts themselves, finding the plot or the language in particular scripts distasteful or
indecent. Charlotte, of course, was familiar with all of these objections.
Despite the theater's growing popularity, she and her contemporaries knew
of people who felt their own respectability would be threatened if they associated with performers. Even *attending* the theater was looked down upon
by many of the more evangelical and moralizing American critics. Clergymen as renowned as Lyman Beecher were convinced that the theater was
"the centre of the valley of pollution."[56]

One of the most indicted forms of "pollution" was prostitution. Since
the Restoration prostitutes plied their trade in theaters, and this tradition
continued into the nineteenth century.[57] Recognizing that many "unes-
corted gentlewomen with lodgings to let" frequented the theater, managers
and audiences as a matter of custom quietly set aside the third tier of boxes,
where these women might make assignations with prospective customers.
Thus, "socially respectable" patrons tended to avoid this section of the theater. Many of the more moralizing critics, like Beecher, objected to the
drama functioning as an accessory to "the indecent traffic of impures."[58]
Indeed, at the time of Charlotte's professional debut in New Orleans the
New Orleans Bee noted that the Camp Theatre, "like all others, has its roost
for ladies of a certain class" as well as "its dramshop for drunkards and
smokers."[59]

And women *on* the stage, who exhibited their talents in front of the
audience, for a fee, were considered by many members of the public as little better than the prostitutes who occupied the third tier. As Tracy Davis
has remarked in her study of Victorian actresses as working women, "no
matter how consummate the artist, pre-eminent the favorite, and modest
the woman, the actress could not supersede the fact that she lived a public
life and consented to be 'hired' for amusement by all who could command
the price."[60] Charlotte Cushman could use all the support she could get to

assure that her reputation remained untarnished in this most public of occupations.

Theatrical entertainments of the period featured a repertoire of "classics" and contemporary melodramas. Melodramas presented spectators with a world infused with "the hidden power and significance of virtue," a world in which virtue was rewarded and vice punished; both virtue and vice were closely bound to nineteenth-century ethical and social considerations.[61] In clearly legible terms, supported by the machinery of theatrical lighting and music to encourage spectators' emotional responses, audience members saw the predominant values of their age underscored in the plight of good against evil, and they recognized these standard tropes as the plot unfolded before them. Writing of the moral lessons melodramas offered audiences, Mark Twain asserted that "the Church taught Christian morality to one tenth of mankind while the stage taught it to nine tenths, and taught it more effectively."[62] Charlotte was beginning her acting career during a time that spanned transformations in the melodramatic genre. The emergence of popular heroic melodramas afforded actors the opportunity to thrill and terrify their audiences with passionate physical and emotional expression, effects at which Charlotte excelled. And in this climate classic texts, such as the plays of Shakespeare, were not primarily directed to highbrow or elite audiences either; instead, they were produced in extensively revised editions that emphasized the same oratory, heroism, and violence that characterized the melodramatic productions of the period.[63]

Charlotte saw immediately that the Bowery Theatre's repertory would require considerable versatility of the stock actors. Actors performed numerous roles that changed nightly, sometimes playing several different parts in the same evening, each of which had to be learned, rehearsed, and memorized. In the very week of her success as Lady Macbeth, Charlotte Cushman starred in two contemporary melodramas, as Mrs. Haller in Kotzebue's *The Stranger* and Helen MacGregor in *Rob Roy,* based on the novel by Sir Walter Scott. As Helen MacGregor, Charlotte played a bold Scotswoman who wears a man's hat and carries "a brace of pistols in her belt."[64] These performances, like that of Lady Macbeth, were also immensely popular with Charlotte's spectators.

With their relatively meager salaries performers in acting companies relied for the greater part of their income on the share of receipts they might earn on their specifically designated "benefit night" performances. On Saturday, 17 September, for her benefit night performance, Charlotte appeared in parts calculated to show her range and highlight her androgynous talents: Alicia in a tragedy entitled *Jane Shore* and, hoping to draw a large audience and therefore earn as much as possible, her first male role on the New York stage, Patrick in the operatic farce *The Poor Soldier*. In between the two Charlotte sang "The Sea," a ballad written in the voice of a fifty-year-old sailor. From her earliest observations of actresses like Clara Fisher on the Boston stage, Charlotte had seen how the relatively common practice of women playing male roles, or "breeches parts," offered the promise of a fuller house, a promise she was to exploit in the coming months.[65] Perhaps, as Charlotte's Bowery audience applauded her "manly efforts" to take the male role in a popular farce or to sing a song in the standard repertoire of male vocalists, some in that audience had indications of the direction her career would take.

Coping with Crises

By late September 1836 it seemed as if Charlotte Cushman's New York theatrical career was finally taking off, but she soon suffered another setback. On 22 September, the Bowery Theatre burned down. Charlotte's unpaid-for costumes and her three-year contract literally went up in smoke. The actors in the Bowery company were in desperate straits. In a show of concern for their fellow players the Franklin Theatre and Park Theatre companies performed benefits for the Bowery actors.

Biographical sketches of Charlotte Cushman frequently refer to the Bowery fire as a significant and defining incident in her life, with all the makings of a real-life melodrama. An unexpected disaster, just as Charlotte was attempting to get a foothold in her career, fire was an occupational hazard in the nineteenth century.[66] Between the spectacular (and potentially explosive) effects onstage and the range of lighting (by gaslight and by candles) needed in the auditorium, all performers, managers, and even patrons were at risk. The fire at the Bowery Theatre illustrated the particular vulnerability of performers, whose whole livelihood could be wiped out in one incendiary instant, as painted "flats" and wooden frames were reduced to ashes. In debt for her borrowed costumes, with no immediate employment, and with her family completely dependent on her income, Charlotte's circumstances were particularly desperate. Here again, Charlotte's friend E. Burke Fisher interceded on her behalf. Fisher wrote letters about her to Louis Godey, publisher of the popular women's magazine *Godey's Lady's Book*, and to Francis Wemyss, manager of the American Theatre in Philadelphia, asking if either man could "come to the aid of a young lady with a dependent family to support"[67] and supply her with acting or writing work. In his letter to Wemyss, Fisher apologized for "thrust[ing] myself upon your attention on behalf of a lady connected with your profession, who has requested me to write to you with a view to open a negotiation for an engagement at the American Theatre," and mentioned the urgency of Charlotte's needs: "having a mother & sister to support."[68]

But Fisher had a clear preference about which course of action Charlotte should follow. Although writing as well as acting was a public career, like many of his contemporaries Fisher evidently preferred the notion of a woman he knew personally supporting herself as a writer rather than an actress. In a letter on 7 October, just two weeks after the Bowery fire, Fisher suggested, "You have within you all the materials of a great mind in a higher rank than the one you have chosen . . . so long as you stand connected with the stage you cannot devote your time to study of an advantagizing [sic] character. . . . I could worship you as a poetess."[69] While generally supportive of her acting, Fisher shared some of the antitheatrical biases that cast women performers to the margins of respectability. Nineteenth-century female performers who were told to conduct themselves as "true women" were caught in a bind that their male counterparts did not have to transcend.[70] Although women were, in ever increasing numbers, attempting a career on the stage, they were, as Christopher Kent notes, "caught between Victorian dictates of modesty and the public display that the theatre demanded."[71] Charlotte was more pragmatic than Fisher: while she would gladly supplement her income by writing, acting was potentially the highest paid profession a woman could enter. However much she enjoyed writing poetry and short pieces of fiction, with her entire family dependent upon her income, she could hardly afford to devote time to developing her "character," despite the fact that Fisher's "admiration" for her had made him, for eighteen months, he said, go to bed each night "the victim of [his] monomania."[72] Besides, Charlotte *enjoyed* performing and its promise for financial and social independence. Furthermore, whether she ever shared Fisher's feelings for her is open to question. The tone of her letters to him, far from referring to "monomania" or reciprocal attachment, are merely matter-of-fact. And so, having had a taste of the theater, Charlotte Cushman was determined to continue.

Yet Charlotte's ability with words was a marketable resource she could draw upon when she needed. Reflecting back on these first years of their acquaintance, manager Francis Wemyss claimed that her "*masculine* mind at once perceived that the only means of success was to cultivate the acquaintance of the gentlemen conducting the newspapers; fugitive pieces of poetry appeared in the papers, and in the popular periodical magazines, under the signature of 'Charlotte Cushman.' These answered the double purpose of placing her name before the public as a lady of literary talent, and securing the notice of the publishers to her dramatic career."[73] Although Wemyss depicted Cushman's knack for self-promotion and her business acumen as masculine, her use of the popular press and literary forms to provide a social context for her self-fashionings enabled her to transform some of the predominant attitudes about women performers. Following Fisher's suggestion, Charlotte started a correspondence that grew into a friendship with *Godey's Lady's Book* editor Sarah Josepha Hale. Soon Cushman's poetry and short stories appeared on the pages of *Godey's* and of the *Ladies Companion* magazine.

The virtues and vices of actual performers (and their fictional counterparts) were featured regularly in the columns of contemporary periodicals and in novels. Fiction and the popular periodical press were, therefore, sites in which images of "the actress" were being shaped and debated. While Charlotte was "constructing" herself onstage, her poetry and short stories would feed the popular interest in actors' lives and put her name before a wider audience.[74] The demure, "ladylike" pieces she published under her name could help create a public persona audiences might recognize and equate with the actress.

Charlotte Cushman had been well aware of the debates over the social propriety of actresses, and she attempted to mobilize these competing discourses about women performers in a fictional short story, "The Actress," which she wrote for *Godey's Lady's Book*.[75] She subtitled her story "Extracts from My Journal" and presented it as a tale of a tragic young actress named Leoline, who, in "an hour of agonized confidence" before her untimely death, told the narrator "this true yet mournful story." In "The Actress" Charlotte created a protagonist most likely to win acceptance from "respectable" readers who might have been disparaging of women onstage. Readers were told that Leoline, "gifted in the intellectual accomplishments of her sex," was, prior to her father's death, a member of a family so respectable and wealthy that members of the audience for her debut had "but a few months since . . . welcomed her coming in their social circles."[76] In other words, Leoline was much like *Godey's* readers might be in less fortunate circumstances. Charlotte knew that her readers would identify her—as an actress herself—with Leoline, and she maximized any circumstances which might cast her, or Leoline, as their social equals while simultaneously attempting to challenge their prejudices against the theater.

In her fiction Charlotte set out to refute the assumption that acting was a form of dissembling; she confronted directly the belief that actresses, whose jobs are to pretend to be that which they are not, were duplicitous and therefore morally suspect. Cleverly reversing the conventional terms of the argument, Charlotte's unnamed narrator began by telling *Godey's* readers that "they who can . . . make their features the defensive barriers, behind which their griefs may be screened from vulgar observation," are exercising an "excusable moral deception."[77] It is thus *spectators* who are rude, intrusive, and "vulgar," prying into the lives of the grief-stricken unfortunate, not the performers whose "spirits [are] so constituted, as to wreathe the lip with smiles, even when despair battens upon its fibres." Masking one's true emotions, then, was excusable; it was even a matter of courage and strength, showing proper reserve and decorum. A young woman unfortunate enough to become the "victim of a perverse destiny," like Leoline, had only two choices: to incur "the world's scorn" by openly expressing her misfortune or to govern her features and enact "a mask."[78] Either alternative, the display or the masking of one's true feelings, subjected such a woman to social censure.

The "perverse destiny" to which women were particularly vulnerable was often the need to find an honorable way to support themselves in the absence or refusal of husbands or male family members. In Charlotte's fictional tale, as in the narratives she was to tell repeatedly about her own life, Leoline did not pursue a stage career because of her desire for public fame or her pleasure in acting but because negligent male family members left her family dependent upon her. Charlotte was determined to represent the theater as a respectable occupation for women like herself, who had to support themselves, and she used this story to address those who questioned a woman's motive for appearing onstage. The death of Leoline's father, a wealthy and respected merchant, and the refusal of her brother to support her mother and herself led Leoline to attempt to win "from a liberal public the support for her parent which her selfish kindred seemed unwilling to afford."[79] Charlotte's story did not directly challenge domestic ideology, but she underscored its failure to deal adequately with the plight of unmarried women without the support of male relatives.

Most important, in Charlotte Cushman's tale the actress's ultimate downfall was blamed not on her own immorality or that of the "congenial spirits" in her profession but on men and the dangers women faced in conventional marriage. After young Leoline married, "giving her young and unsullied heart" to an unreliable husband, she retired from the stage. It was not on the public stage but in the private, patriarchal home that the honorable young actress was exposed to a man "with the habits of a bacchanal" who "treated her with coarse and unfeeling rudeness" and "drown[ed] his reason in the inebriating element" of alcohol. This was a fate to which all women were vulnerable, but Charlotte's heroine, having no other family to support her, left the abusive, alcoholic husband, "who had violated every claim to her respect," and returned to the stage, knowing that "to forsake him would . . . open the floodgate of calumny, and expose her to the censures of the unfeeling and misjudging."[80] For Leoline pursuing an acting career required strength and courage; marriage was only a "delusion . . . a pleasant, but too brief dream." Exhausted, despairing as she struggled to appear composed and happy to audiences who did not appreciate her, disillusioned with marriage and social condemnation, Leoline died "ere twenty summers had kissed her brow."[81] Charlotte, who was exactly the same age as her fictional heroine, had constructed a story to win the sympathy of women readers who might hear of or see her onstage. Since the particular venues in which Charlotte published her writing were the very forums that shaped and reflected middle-class domestic ideology, women reading these respectable publications were forced to rethink assumptions that actresses were unfeminine, immodest, or immoral.

So, while availing herself of E. Burke Fisher's help, the twenty-year-old actress was taking her own career firmly in hand. In addition to writing to editor Sarah Josepha Hale and theatrical manager Francis Wemyss herself, Charlotte appealed also to William Dinneford, the manager of the Franklin Theatre in New York, and to his partner, William Rufus Blake, manager of the Pearl Street Theatre in Albany. When Blake offered her a five-week engagement in Albany that would begin almost immediately, on 11 October, she accepted without hesitation.

Immediately following the Franklin Theatre benefit for the Bowery actors, on 7 October, Charlotte, her mother, and her younger brother, Augustus, set off for Albany. The details of whatever transpired between Cushman and Fisher are unknown, but on the day after she left, Fisher wrote to her asking that "henceforth we be as strangers to each other."[82] Although Fisher claimed that his intentions and interest in Charlotte had been "but trifling," the actual reason for severing the relationship may have had more to do with Fisher's pride coupled with his feelings about the stage as a career. He wrote: "I should only know you again, again to lose you and gather renewed thorns around the pathway of my life. . . . It is better that we should meet no more."[83] The tone of Charlotte's letter to him, written on the same day, but probably before she received his, was merely formal and polite.[84]

Whether or not Cushman was actually hurt by Fisher's rejection, it provided her and her later biographers with a convenient narrative to "explain" her decision to remain unmarried and unattached emotionally to any other future male suitors.[85] After her death, when Charlotte Cushman's choice to live in passionate relationships with women came to be regarded with suspicion, the suggestion that Charlotte had been "jilted" by an unnamed suitor with dishonorable intentions—a story Charlotte repeated to her friend, the novelist Geraldine Jewsbury—was frequently reprinted as a justification for Charlotte's avoidance of relationships with men. Although the "young man" in the incident Jewsbury recounted was not identified, the time and relationship described correspond with this incident with Fisher. Charlotte Cushman's "dishonorable suitor" story unmasked most powerfully the myth of male chivalry and protection. In this narrative, as in her own fiction, men were depicted as untrustworthy; women were best off, and in least danger—as she had seen in her own family—if, instead of looking for male protectors and advocates, they took care of themselves.

Many of the most commonly repeated stories about Charlotte's early life attempt to domesticate her, to diffuse her power by providing excuses for her independence. Yet only several months after the Bowery Theatre crises, when Charlotte met the witty British travel writer Captain Frederick Marryat, he evidently recognized a connection between Cushman's striking assertiveness, her professional ambitions, and her indifference to heterosexual romance. Marryat wrote approvingly of her "determination to remain single and not to be the slave of one when she could reign despotic over thousands."[86] The life of an unmarried woman with her own extremely public career seemed considerably more attractive to her than the marriages she had witnessed thus far and promised a degree of power and autonomy unimaginable to most women in Cushman's milieu.[87]

And so, despite the possible wound to her pride issued by Fisher's ending their association, Cushman wasn't deterred. On 11 October 1836 she opened at Albany's Pearl Street Theatre as Lady Macbeth. Her Macbeth on this occasion was the well-known actor Junius Brutus Booth. The run in Albany was to be more socially and professionally successful than she imagined.

Playing Male Roles

It was in Albany that Charlotte Cushman really learned her craft. Her original five-week contract was extended to six months. During these months she performed a wide variety of roles, among them many male characters. For her first benefit night she appeared as Count Belino in the melodrama *The Devil's Bridge,* drawing a large crowd and favorable reviews. As critic Henry Dickinson Stone remembered: "At the time Miss Cushman generally assumed male characters—her stately form, rather masculine contour of countenance, and powerful voice admirably adapting her to the line of male characters. They were invariably rendered most acceptably; she also acquitted herself equally well in female characters."[88] With Cushman's female portrayals mentioned almost as an afterthought, Stone demonstrated that his fellow "Albanians," as he called them, apparently had little or no difficulty accepting the convention of women playing male roles.

Some theater historians attribute the widespread acceptance of this performance practice in the nineteenth century to an appreciation of youthful beauty or an androgynous aesthetic (although why youth or androgyny should best be embodied in a woman is debatable). Others claim the popularity of women playing male characters was encouraged by male spectators' heterosexual desire. After all, this was an age when women's clothing modestly shielded the lower half of female bodies from view. A young woman in a man's tight breeches would display to viewers more of the female body than would be visible in any other guise. From her earliest performances Charlotte demonstrated her fondness for playing male roles, yet her characterizations seemed to complicate the expected picture, since they were as popular with *female* spectators as with men in the audience. Charlotte's cross-dressed performances allowed for and invited a "potentially subversive consciousness"[89]—a homoerotic response—that might animate both the performer and her audience. The erotic feelings she may have displayed for and aroused in other women who witnessed her depictions were more than a titillating novelty; as we shall see in chapter 5, they were to become Charlotte's calling card. Although later in her career many conflicting stories would come to be told to explain or justify Charlotte's proclivity for male impersonations, her choice and ability to play with (and against) gender conventions were among the earliest features of her success.

Yet Charlotte was savvy enough to attempt to structure her public "self" to encourage a range of possible associations for her audience. Perhaps if they saw her as somehow "like" them, if the audiences identified with her, they would be more likely to patronize the theater—particularly on her benefit nights. Immediately following Charlotte's first benefit performance as the heroic Count Belino, on 31 October 1836, she chose to deliver an original poem she had written in honor of the city's firefighters. Theater historian Bruce McConachie has noted that the "curtain speech," or epilogue, delivered by a starring actor after a performance was becoming institutionalized in the American theater at this time and that the practice served an audience hungry to see actors as they "really were."[90] Charlotte's reading of a poem out of character in which she shared her "sincere sentiments" served to bond her and her Albany audience. Since she herself had been materially affected by the Bowery fire, she could empathize with the life-threatening risk firefighters experience. By now Charlotte was well aware that displaying her skills as a writer could do much to forward her career. And it worked. It was the *literary* critic of *Ladies Companion* magazine who publicized her achievement, stating that

> we are by no means departing from our given provinces in noticing Miss Charlotte Cushman, new of the Albany stage . . . As an instance of her remarkable talent, we will state that on the occasion of her benefit at Albany . . . she wrote and delivered an address, complimentary to the Firemen of Albany, in which she had inserted the names of the different Foremans [*sic*], Engineers, Engines, etc., without injuring the harmony of

the verse. The address gained her much popularity, and for several nights the theatre was thronged. It was delivered some three or four nights successively.[91]

Her poem, and her appearance at Albany's Fireman's Ball, did much to endear Charlotte to the residents of that city. Henry Dickinson Stone described the impression Charlotte made as "magnificently attired, her head adorned with an immense and beautiful Bird of Paradise, as she threaded the mazes of the dance, or moved gracefully in the promenade, her stately form towering above her companions"; she was the "Belle of the Ball."[92] And Charlotte's efforts to present herself as a member of Albany society reached into other quarters as well: when it became known that her mother was distantly related to New York's Senator Marcy, it was jokingly remarked that "more members of both (legislative) houses" could be found at her benefit performances "than at the capitol."[93] Charlotte Cushman—powerful, stately, proudly towering over male companions—made a strong impression and secured the support of both the firefighters and their families, who were honored by her acknowledgment, and the more privileged politicians, whom she claimed as relations.

While Charlotte was performing in Albany, another actor dear to the hearts of Albany's citizens was making his debut in England. Edwin Forrest was "first appreciated and encouraged"[94] in the very same theater in which Cushman was now performing. Although the young actress had not met Forrest personally, she seized upon his current success abroad as the occasion for another original "eulogy." As Lesley Ferris has observed, the delivery of a spoken epilogue or prologue served female performers in a particular way. By addressing audiences directly, in the intimacy of the first person, actresses—who were often viewed as sexual objects by spectators—were able to play upon the notion that a female performer was "playing herself" in the interests of promoting and celebrating her own personality.[95] And so, at another Albany benefit night, after her performance as breeches character George Fairman in Joseph Stevens Jones's patriotic drama The Liberty Tree,[96] Charlotte delivered her poem honoring Forrest. Her poetic tribute to Forrest appeared to celebrate the work of her countryman, however, rather than herself, and, through him, to honor indigenous American talent. Charlotte ended her poem with the lines:

He sought to grasp the sceptre of his art
That he deserved to win all know full well
That he has won it, England's praises tell.[97]

Ironically, these final lines of Charlotte's poem would forecast her own success nine years later: when in England playing opposite America's most famous male performer, praises for her would outshine even those for him. But that story would be told later.

For the time being, however, Charlotte was doing well enough in Albany to merit "notice of her remarkable talent" in the *Ladies Companion* as the recent "bright particular star" of the Bowery Theatre, now of the Albany stage.[98] Unfortunately, however, her run was marred by two disturbing family events. While Charlotte, her mother, and her younger brother were in Albany, fourteen-year-old Susan had remained in Boston with her half-sister, Isabella. Elkanah Cushman's friend Nelson Merriman offered to provide for Susan but claimed that, as he was deathly ill, they would have to marry legally in order for her to inherit the monies promised. In the various stories that attempt to account for this potential blot on the respectability of the Cushman family, it is usually reported that, against her better judgment, Mary Eliza acquiesced to the marriage. Whatever the circumstances of the arrangement, on 4 November 1836 Merriman married the unhappy young girl and then "miraculously" recovered. Susan was thus trapped in a loveless marriage to a man old enough to be her father or—given Elkanah's advanced age—her grandfather.

Even more tragically, in early April 1837, at the end of Charlotte's Albany run, her brother Augustus was killed in a riding accident, in a fall from the horse that Charlotte, a devoted rider, had bought for him with her earnings in Albany. Planning to capitalize on her resounding success in Albany, Charlotte had already decided to return to New York when she received the crushing news. Charlotte had planned a stunning farewell benefit night performance. She closed her Albany run in a role she was to make uniquely her own: Romeo. Despite the "enthusiastic applause" and warm wishes of the Albanians, immediately following her final benefit night Charlotte Cushman and her mother hurried back to New York in despair.[99] The family Charlotte had gone onstage to support was rapidly dispersing before her eyes.

Upon her return to New York Charlotte again wrote to Edmund Simpson of the Park Theatre. Now convinced of her talent, Simpson offered the twenty-one-year-old actress twenty dollars per week, a fair wage for a "walking lady" in his stock company. In that capacity Charlotte would hone her skill by performing a multitude of different roles. While waiting to begin this job in September 1837, she undertook a short run at the less prestigious National Theatre in New York. At the National, throwing herself into work while grieving the loss of her young brother, Charlotte once again played Romeo, Patrick, and Count Belino, among her other melodramatic and classic parts. And it was at the National Theatre, just a month after Augustus's death, that Charlotte first played what was to become her most famous role.

Playing Meg Merrilies

On 8 May 1837 a last-minute illness in the cast thrust Charlotte into the role of the old Gypsy Meg Merrilies in Sir Walter Scott's melodrama *Guy Mannering*. She had originally been cast in a minor role as a Gypsy girl who sings a song in Meg's big recognition scene. In a story Charlotte later often repeated, she claimed that she had been told early in the day that because of the illness of her fellow actor, Mrs. Chippendale, she would play Meg that very evening. With less than a day's notice she hunted through the text for a key to the Gypsy's character. As she recalled, it was another character's description of Meg that suggested her interpretation:

> In much trepidation, I listened at the wings trying to catch some inspiration from the progress of the play, when I heard the closing words . . . just preceding the appearance of Meg on the scene—when one says of her, "oh, she doats." To which the other replies, "But she rules the tribe." These sentences gave me sudden clew [*sic*] to the situation of the decrepit but still powerful queen, and a full conception of the character flashed before me.[100]

When hearing the line "she doats,"[101] Charlotte arrived at her conception. She would play Meg as a shriveled crone whose almost supernatural powers and selfless attachment to the young boy she had nursed appeared insane. The character she created "doated" with a hint of madness and ruled the Gypsy tribe through the singular force of her personal power. Spectators might be horrified, but they would be moved as well. Charlotte's surprising portrayal also excited her fellow actors. John Braham, the English tenor cast opposite her, was so shocked to see an old, withered Gypsy instead of the young actress he met backstage that "a cold chill ran all over [him]." After the performance he thanked her for "the most veritable sensation" that he had experienced in a long time.[102]

In her account of the events that led to this characterization Charlotte Cushman represented herself as creative and resourceful, taking advantage of a fortuitous opportunity, transforming what was essentially a minor part into her trademark through her intellectual and interpretative skills. And the fact that she repeatedly asserted that she had not "planned" to play the Gypsy but was merely making the best of her circumstances strengthened the image of Cushman's unique and unexpected talent and her willingness to take on risks. As I discuss in chapter 4, Meg, like all of Cushman's major characters, came to be seen as a popular cultural artifact, imbued with meanings that exceeded the part she served in the play. The story of the "accidental" origins of this larger-than-life character helped mitigate criticism she might receive for creating this bold, unconventional woman.

Charlotte Cushman as Meg Merrilies in *Guy Mannering*. Meg Merrilies was clothed in rags, but her raised scepterlike stick became emblematic of the character's eerie power. *(Harvard Theatre Collection. Houghton Library.)*

Just as Charlotte was beginning her tenure at the Park Theatre, she and her mother received word that Susan was pregnant and that the conniving Nelson Merriman had abandoned his child-wife in Boston. Except for the article Charlotte's friend Mary Howitt would publish in 1846 about "The Miss Cushmans"—perhaps to offset rumors that Susan Cushman had not been married and that her child was therefore illegitimate—the circumstances of Susan Cushman Merriman's marriage, pregnancy, and her desertion by Merriman were rarely, if ever, alluded to publicly in stories about either of the Cushman sisters.[103] But even in Howitt's account these events would be glossed over and the predominant narrative of Charlotte's role as the family breadwinner enlarged; in a short time there were two more mouths for Charlotte to feed, Susan and her newborn baby. Susan arrived in New York to live with Charlotte, their mother, and their brother, Charles. While Charlotte and her mother were in Albany, Charles had stayed behind in New York, working as a clerk in a shop. Now they would all be together again. And, once again, Charlotte would assume the bulk of the responsibility for their support.

On 26 August 1837 twenty-one-year-old Charlotte Cushman opened at the Park Theatre. Excitedly, she took on all sorts of roles as she was needed, once again playing minor and major characters of both sexes and all ages— as well as appearing in her old standby roles. Her opening role was her popular breeches part Patrick in *The Poor Soldier.* In mid-September Edwin Forrest arrived to fulfill an engagement at the Park, and Cushman had her first opportunity to act opposite the fiery star whom she had eulogized in Albany. In person she did not think much of Forrest, mostly staying clear of him and his explosive temper, while onstage she acted on different occasions Cordelia and Goneril to Forrest's Lear and Nahmeokee to his Metamora in the melodrama of the same name.

Metamora (1829), which Forrest had premiered at the Park six years earlier, was one of the best known of the plays with an "Indian" theme then currently in vogue. Forrest had commissioned the play, paid its author John Augustus Stone 500 dollars for rights to the work, and parlayed his impersonation of the "noble savage" into a starring vehicle, which he would play throughout his career and which would earn him a fortune. Although Cushman was disdainful about the artistic value of Forrest's starring vehicle, she recognized the popularity of Indian plays with audiences.[104] She herself would, in little more than a month, follow Forrest and perform the male role of John Rolfe in another "Native" drama, Robert Dale Owen's new version of *Pocahontas.* Owen's "historical drama," as he called it, featured ample opportunity for Rolfe (Cushman) to express "ardent passion" for the beautiful Pocahontas.[105] This was just the beginning of what would soon become open competition between Cushman and Forrest.

The variety of the parts Charlotte Cushman played at the Park, while demanding, proved to be an excellent training ground and kept her occupied throughout the season. At home the Cushman family was kept busy with Susan's infant son, Edwin "Ned" Merriman, born on 4 March 1838, scarcely more than two weeks before his mother's sixteenth birthday. In May Forrest returned to the Park, starring as the lover Claude Melnotte in Edward Bulwer-Lytton's extremely popular new melodrama, *The Lady of Lyons.* Charlotte played a supporting role as Claude's widowed mother. While critic Walt Whitman wrote of her "genius" in the part,[106] on 28 June she attempted a greater challenge, that of Forrest's own role of Claude.

Whatever pleasure Charlotte derived from taking on the leading male

Edwin Forrest as King Lear. Forrest signaled Lear's
prowess with an upraised scepter. Cushman, who competed openly with Forrest for some roles, used a similar
visual sign in playing Meg Merrilies. *(Author's collection.)*

roles herself—rather than merely supporting male colleagues in their starring vehicles—may have been fed in part by a desire to compete directly
with men.[107] In her portrayal of Claude Melnotte so soon after Forrest's she
was certainly challenging and competing with America's most highly
acclaimed male tragedian and a man particularly renowned for his virility.[108] Charlotte would be no less powerful a hero onstage. Comparing the
two performers, the critic from the *Spirit of the Times* questioned whether

Forrest had received louder applause for *his* Claude. Charlotte was, if not superior, at least a worthy competitor as the male romantic lead.[109] Although she did not know it at the time, comparisons between her and Forrest, and the ways each embodied a particular version of virility, would take on a new resonance six years later, in England.[110] But at this point Charlotte was still expanding her acting range.

Playing Nancy Sykes

Charlotte Cushman performed another memorable role for the first time that season: the character of Nancy Sykes in a dramatic version of Charles Dickens's *Oliver Twist*. In her recounting of the story—or, rather, in the version reported by her intimate friend Anne Hampton Brewster—when the casting for *Oliver Twist* was announced in February 1839, Charlotte had been annoyed to find herself slated to portray the ragged Nancy. Dickens's novel had just been adapted for the stage. Charlotte felt that Stephen Price, Edmund Simpson's partner at the Park, did not like her and had cast her in the role to spite her, since the character of the impoverished woman of the streets was considered vulgar. She was determined to make the best of it, however, and set out to impress the spectators, so that Nancy would dominate every scene in which she appeared. "I meant to get the better of my enemy," Brewster remembered Cushman saying, "What he designed for my mortification shall be my triumph."[111] To prepare for the role she put on her plainest clothes and went to live for several days in Five Points, the slum neighborhood on New York's Lower East Side. There, surrounded by people whose material circumstances were as close as possible to those of Dickens's Nancy, Charlotte Cushman developed her character. As she explained to Brewster, she even acquired the clothes she wore onstage and the rusty key she carried for the part from a dying old woman she met in Five Points. When the play opened on 7 February, Walt Whitman called her performance "appallingly" real and the most "intense acting ever felt on the Park boards."[112] In every scene, as Nancy hovered over other characters or rudely thrust her tongue into her cheek, Charlotte attempted to replicate the movements and mannerisms she had observed in Five Points. Audience members couldn't take their eyes off her. Philadelphia manager Francis Wemyss was in attendance and recalled Nancy as a painfully accurate "portrait of female depravity"; he believed it to be her strongest part.[113] Fellow actor Lawrence Barrett remembered Charlotte's superlative handling of Nancy's death scene:

> She dragged herself on to the stage . . . and, keeping her face away from the audience, produced a feeling of chilly horror by the management of

her voice as she called for Bill, and begged him to kiss her. It sounded as if she spoke through blood, and the whole effect was far greater than that which any other actress has ever made, with the sight of the face and all the horrors which can be added.[114]

Charlotte Cushman was not afraid to take risks; in her account to Anne Brewster she—or Brewster—illustrated Cushman's ingenuity in overcoming those who had not appreciated her talents. Saddled with a demeaning part perhaps calculated to embarrass her, Charlotte had turned it into one of her most noteworthy achievements.

Unlike the vast majority of actresses who were eager to be seen as attractive, feminine, and desirable to male spectators, no matter what part they were playing, Charlotte Cushman was one of the first female performers who let herself be seen as *unattractive* if the role required. As Brewster remembered: "Her makeup was a marvel. There was not the sign of feminine vanity about Miss Cushman. She was always ready to sacrifice her appearance at any time to the dresses required by her parts."[115] Brewster's story emphasized Cushman's lack of vanity and downplayed the questionable propriety of a young woman going on her own to live among thieves and prostitutes in the slums in order to depict them "realistically" onstage. Instead, Brewster depicted her friend as ingenious, courageous, and honest, uninterested in artifice. Of course, Anne Brewster, who admired Charlotte's depiction of Nancy and was to become extremely close to Charlotte, learned the details of this story from Charlotte herself. And, as always, Charlotte shaped her stories to present herself in a positive light. Yet prejudice against characters such as Nancy persisted. Just before she left for England actor Junius Booth warned Charlotte not to portray Nancy when she appeared in England. Charlotte told Anne Brewster: "He is right. . . . But I know what I will do, I will act Meg Merrilies just as I do Nancy and I'll make a hit."[116] Nancy's startling appearance and blood-curdling groans could enhance her portrayal of Sir Walter Scott's Gypsy. Rather than refute the prejudices, Charlotte used them. Once again in Charlotte's narratives her resourcefulness triumphed, and, as she faced conditions and circumstances that would limit others, she used them to her advantage.

Playing the Hero of the Family, On- and Offstage

While Charlotte was busy establishing a name for herself at the Park, young Susan began to feel restless. In answer to Susan's restlessness and boredom and—as journalist George Ferris reported after an interview with Charlotte many years later—to aid her sister in getting over her "terrible misfortune" through "the sense of active employment,"[117] Charlotte helped Susan to prepare to join her on the stage. "Active employment," one of the cardinal virtues for Charlotte's Puritan forebears, was an effective way to position Charlotte's role in encouraging her young sister in a theatrical career. On 8 June 1839 Susan Cushman made her stage debut as Laura to Charlotte's Montaldo in Epes Sargent's romantic tragedy, *The Genoese*.[118] Throughout the season Susan and Charlotte Cushman appeared together regularly in a variety of plays. Often Charlotte would play the male leads, such as the impassioned Claude Melnotte, while Susan played more traditional "feminine" parts such as Pauline, the proud young woman to whom Claude is betrothed.

Susan became a perfect foil for Charlotte, who later claimed that she had only played male roles in order to give her sister the support and encouragement she needed.[119] As we have seen, and as her early audiences could attest, Charlotte Cushman had a decided preference for breeches roles long before Susan ever appeared on the stage. Even when both sisters portrayed female characters, they gravitated toward playing decidedly different types of women. Susan was Desdemona while Charlotte played Emilia in *Othello;* similarly, Susan appeared as Ophelia while Charlotte portrayed Gertrude in *Hamlet*. Susan assumed the romantic ingenue roles that called for an actress who was modest, pretty, and graceful. Charlotte continued to portray strong, assertive, and intellectual characters, male and female.

In July 1840 Charlotte's contract at the Park expired. She had played more than one hundred different roles and now felt entitled to a higher salary. When she asked Simpson and Price for a salary increase to twenty-five dollars a week for herself and twelve dollars for Susan, they refused, so Charlotte and Susan Cushman left the Park and left New York City. Charlotte became the leading lady at William E. Burton's newly outfitted National Theatre in Philadelphia. Wherever Charlotte Cushman went, the entire family followed, and so mother, brother, sister, and nephew all moved to Philadelphia. As the leading stock actress at the National, Charlotte was kept busy nightly, playing her proven successes and taking on new roles, such as Smike in Dickens's *Nicholas Nickleby*. On many nights Susan appeared with her more famous sister. But economic conditions were tenuous in the country at large and in the theater in particular. Just four months into her National Theatre run Charlotte wrote to friends in Boston that every day's mail seemed to bring news of another theater closing its doors. Theaters in New York as well as Philadelphia were struggling. With her own finances and the current dismal state of the American theater in mind, Charlotte was eager to enlist her friends and fellow actors, the Creswicks of Boston, in her plans: "I am seriously in hopes that I shall be able to go to England in the Spring. What do you think of going? What if we should go together? I think that we should have a delightful frolic in crossing."[120] But England was still a few years away.

Burton's National Theatre was doing so poorly that Burton was threatened with bankruptcy, so he attempted to encourage greater audience attendance by mounting a spectacular pageant, the *Naiad Queen*. It was a bold scheme. Audiences were used to watching "spectacles," from dramatic equestrian feats to tableaux vivants in which performers posed and froze into positions that would silently tell a story to viewers. But the *Naiad Queen* was different. Along with Charlotte Cushman over a hundred women were onstage, sometimes lolling about on enormous prop seashells, like mythological creatures rising from the sea, other times marching in formation, wearing scanty costumes and baring their legs. Wearing a helmet of white ostrich plumes, a breastplate of gold scales, beige tights, and red sandals, Charlotte appeared commandingly "Amazonian" as she led her female warriors through an orchestrated display of military-like maneuvers.[121]

The scheme was so successful in Philadelphia that Burton moved the show and the entire company to New York. While the critic from the *Spirit of the Times* regretted that "a clever woman like Miss Cushman should be wasting time and a strong intellect in showpieces,"[122] the production had served her well in that it placed her again before the eyes of the New York public and the popular press. Before long she was displaying her talents in more substantial pieces once more. Manager Simpson now offered Cushman fifty dollars a week if she would return to the Park Theatre for the 1841–42 season. Her tenacity had paid off, and she accepted.

Not long afterward, on 13 June 1841, Charlotte received word from Winthrop Babbit, a relative in Boston, that her father had "departed this life" and would be buried immediately.[123] Babbit, recognizing Charlotte's position as head of the family, directed the bad news to her, rather than to her mother. Her parents had grown so estranged from each other that her mother wasn't even present for Charlotte's father's burial. In none of Charlotte's public narratives does this final announcement of her father's death appear. Charlotte's self-presentation as a member of a respectable Victorian family with Puritan forebears would be difficult to maintain if the circumstances of her father's last several years were generally known. Instead, Charlotte buried all references to her father and was intentionally ambiguous about the exact dates of his business failure and his death. But she saved Babbit's letter. Whatever her father had meant to her, this final mention of him would still be among her papers when *she* died thirty-five years later.

With her job at the Park, Charlotte, the head of the Cushman household, was steadily becoming a good provider. Upon their return to the Park

Theatre, Charlotte and Susan Cushman opened the 1841–42 season in a play not seen in New York for the previous fifteen years. The play was Shakespeare's *A Midsummer Night's Dream*, with Charlotte in a male role as Oberon and Susan as Helena. The critics applauded both Cushman sisters and the manner in which they handled Shakespeare's poetry, but the poor notices another cast member received would soon create an unexpected problem for them. Park Benjamin, editor of the *New World*, was friendly with an actress named Miss Clarendon, also of the Park Theatre company and formerly of the National. She and Susan Cushman were often in direct competition for many of the same "ingenue" roles, and Clarendon had been panned for her efforts in *A Midsummer Night's Dream*. When Simpson was pressured by Benjamin into substituting Clarendon for Susan Cushman in the upcoming American premiere of Dion Boucicault's new play *London Assurance*, which was sure to be the hit of the season, Charlotte threatened to quit.

But realizing that leaving would not accomplish anything, either for her sister or for herself, Charlotte reconsidered. Her performance as Lady Gay Spanker, the leading role in *London Assurance*, led Walt Whitman to write that he could not "conceive anything finer."[124] One reason for the production's tremendous success was the realistic detail of set and scenery in this production, which surpassed anything ever seen at that time on the American stage. In addition, the role of Lady Gay Spanker was one in which sexual and gender stereotypes were explored with humor. The character Charlotte created in the American production has been described as "a dominant, horsey woman who drags her gentle husband around" and "offer[s] a potentially challenging vision of strong women, enjoying [their] own sexuality."[125] The etchings of Cushman in this part depict her in tailored riding apparel, with a crop in her hand. For an authoritative, vigorous woman who loved horseback riding, the role was a natural.

Clarendon, however, received some poor reviews as Grace Harkaway. Incensed, Benjamin wrote in the *New World* that Charlotte's Lady Gay was "a blustering hoyden . . . an ill-bred . . . loud talking Amazonian."[126] Benjamin held her responsible for Clarendon's bad notices and publicly suggested Cushman be hissed from the stage. Once again disapproval of Charlotte Cushman was expressed in terms of her violating feminine norms. For those who did not like her, Charlotte's forcefulness—even in a character like Lady Gay—seemed excessive. She responded to Benjamin's charges immediately in a strongly worded note displaying both her tact and her refusal to be intimidated. Rather than defend her own assertiveness from Benjamin's allegations of Amazonian behavior, Cushman complained of Clarendon's "*rude* and un*lady*like behavior" to *her*. "With regard to being 'hissed from the stage,'" she told Benjamin in response to his threat, "that is a matter requiring some time and trouble and when done no satisfaction would accrue to yourself and I think you have business of more importance. With sentiments of deep regret that you should have so misjudged *my* feelings as a woman—and compromised yourself, I remain, Yours in haste."[127]

Charlotte Cushman's personal power and resolution may have appeared Amazonian to one accustomed to passive, modest women. Yet her refutation of Benjamin's charges displayed more than righteous indignation; she had again employed predominant cultural norms about women on *her* behalf. Clarendon, not Cushman, was depicted as "unladylike" and unappreciative, and, in attacking a woman, Benjamin was seen as compromising his own "manliness." Charlotte Cushman's implication—that "real" men have "business of more importance"—rendered Benjamin's actions even more socially suspect. As with many of the stories that she told, Charlotte had not objected that conventional notions of ladylike behavior be the measure against which women were judged; she just routinely redefined that term to include her own actions and refused to be limited by anyone else's interpretations. At her next performance, immediately following the controversy carried out in the press, she drew cheers rather than hisses from the audience. Once again Charlotte had deployed conventional gender tropes to defend her own unconventional position. And it worked. As with other stories Charlotte would tell and reconfigure in years to come, how she would be "read" and understood by her public was largely a matter of how she was represented and what she was believed to represent for others. Whether in the stories she told to a friend, a professional colleague, or the public, through the popular press, Charlotte Cushman was masterful at shaping tales that would serve her desired ends, representing herself in whatever light she chose to be seen.

At the end of the Park season twenty-six-year-old Charlotte Cushman was made a tempting offer, one even more uncharacteristic for a woman. E. A. Marshall, lessee of the Walnut Street Theatre in Philadelphia, offered her the position of manager. In August 1842 the Cushman family moved back to Philadelphia. Soon Charlotte would have an even larger hand in positioning herself.

"Is Such Love Wrong?"

Can a feeling which seemed to elevate and refine my nature as
did that love for her be wicked?

—Anne Hampton Brewster

In early October 1842, several days after the opening of the season, Charlotte Cushman delivered her first address as actress-manager of the Walnut
Street Theatre. The twenty-six-year-old actress stood before the Philadelphia audience and stated that she aimed to encourage the patronage of "a
respectable and *cultivated* audience . . . not merely the people of fashion."[1]
In an attempt to woo "settled and domestic citizens" to the theater, Cushman alluded to a time in the past when, she claimed, "the boxes presented
the smiling and happy faces of whole families while the pit contained the
artisan and man of leisure listening with delight." Whether or not such
audiences were ever regular patrons of Philadelphia theaters, "thus it shall
be, if my efforts can make it so," Charlotte promised.

Looking out over the recently refitted playhouse, newly cleaned and
painted bright white, Charlotte directed the audience's attention to the
atmosphere that pervaded their surroundings. "The theatre I now have
under my charge has been thoroughly repaired and decorated . . . [and]
those who have visited the house since it has been under my management
can bear witness to the *order* and *quiet* with which it is conducted," she
maintained, pledging to "offer this community those good old plays that
have secured the approval of the public, and which may be seen with
advantage and pleasure as they excite a *healthy* tone of feeling by their
morality and generous sentiments."[2] Charlotte's underlines in her manuscript copy of this address unmistakably reveal her emphases; by invoking
and appealing to such contemporary nineteenth-century values as morality, orderliness, decorum, and respectability, she hoped to purge from her
theater any associations with impropriety. In uttering this speech from the
stage, Charlotte was transforming the space around her, and she was giving
her word—"address[ing] the public in person"—so that they would associate her personally with this undertaking and support her attempt to provide "innocent amusement" for the "settled and domestic citizens" of

Philadelphia.³ Charlotte had her work cut out for her. Just a year earlier, in another city, William T. Hamilton had warned the public in his *Sermon on Theatrical Entertainments* about "the presence in the theater of prostitutes and liquor dealers, hyenas of humanity who leap upon the grave of innocence and revel in the very vitals of modesty and worth."⁴ Charlotte's theater was to be a refutation of these associations.

Up until this point Charlotte Cushman had impressed those who noticed her as a solidly dependable, talented actress and a singularly determined and ambitious professional woman. But Charlotte was now at a crossroads, at a point of transition from one stage in her life to another, and in the personal and professional relationships she would forge in the next few years she would come to experience and represent herself differently— more decisively—as a performer, as a woman, and as a woman who loved other women.⁵ These relationships, with writer Anne Brewster, performers William Charles Macready and Fanny Kemble, and painter Rosalie Sully, would serve as the arenas that would shape Charlotte, delineating the outlines of her already "liminal" character. And all would take place against the backdrop of, and in dialogue with, "respectable" middle-class values; values she had referred to in her opening address. Seizing upon the popular discourse of the day, which idealized middle-class women as moralizing influences, Charlotte started her term as manager by presenting herself as the ideal agent for this task; Charlotte would "elevate" the reputation of the theater.

Although she was in a distinct minority, Charlotte Cushman was not the only woman to undertake theatrical management, hopeful that patrons would equate her "womanly" values with the entertainments under her supervision. Right in Philadelphia, Mary Elizabeth Maywood had been recently appointed to manage the competing Chestnut Street Theatre, although Charlotte claimed that Maywood's father, an established theatrical manager, had merely rented the theater in his daughter's name "to prevent being held responsible for anything."⁶ E. A. Marshall, lessee of the Walnut, may have assumed that, by placing Charlotte Cushman at the helm, Philadelphians would have two competing reputable theaters to patronize. Whatever motivated Marshall, it seemed to be smart business. Wherever they were employed, women managers as well as performers were helping to institute changes that would make theatergoing more acceptable to "proper" middle-class audiences. Increasingly, programs were shortened to allow for a later start and earlier finish to accommodate theater attendance after the family dinner hour. Audience members were encouraged to wear fancy evening dress for an outing to the theater. And the rowdy behavior of spectators in the "pit" was suppressed.⁷ In addition to adopting these innovations, Charlotte, particularly conscious of Philadelphia's "blue" laws, made it her business as well to end Saturday evening performances by eleven o'clock, so that all patrons would be home before Sunday morning.

It was a complex and contradictory time for female performers, and these new trends were to have important implications for actresses' social status. Just months earlier, when Anna Cora Ogden Mowatt, the married daughter of successful merchant Samuel Ogden and Eliza Lewis Ogden (whose great grandfather had been one of the signers of the Declaration of Independence), debuted as a public reader in Boston and New York, relatives and friends turned from her, "shocked by my temerity in appearing before the public,"[8] Mowatt painfully recalled. What rankled the moralizers most was the notion of a woman presenting herself to be seen by a "mixed" audience of men and women. It was the commingling of women and men in public venues and the potential presence of prostitutes and their prospective patrons in the notorious third tier that, in the minds of many, presented the greatest threat to public morals. Mowatt noted that one of her critics in the *Ladies Companion* had "suggest[ed] that if public readings must be given, I should read before an audience entirely of my own sex!"[9] As Mowatt was soon to discover in her years as an actress and playwright, "the prejudices of the world against the [theatrical] profession," while often unfounded, were still deeply felt. But women of "high moral character" could "help to elevate the stage" and use the drama as an instrument to "sway the multitude even as [do] the preacher and the orator."[10] As Mowatt and Cushman knew, the more proper it was for genteel women and whole families to patronize the theater, the less actresses themselves might be considered improper. In Philadelphia even more than New York—where a quiet, decorous display of good breeding was valued more highly than the ostentatious display of material wealth and success—to be accepted socially, actresses such as Charlotte Cushman and Anna Cora Mowatt would have to appear to embody, to a greater or lesser degree, some of the virtues of "true womanhood" and attempt to use the dramatic medium to present an ennobling influence onstage.[11]

On the one hand, Charlotte Cushman was an unlikely candidate to be a moral reformer. She was an intensely pragmatic, independent, unmarried woman, supporting herself in one of the most dubious of public professions. But on the other hand, in her own self-fashionings Charlotte was clearly attuned to the popular beliefs about gender and propriety.[12] As long as she drew upon these to account for her life choices, her path would be relatively unobstructed, and she would prosper, often while straddling the boundaries of the very ideologies she deployed.

While the predominant beliefs of Charlotte's era shaped *her* fully as much as she would affect them, one of the reasons she was considered so appropriate a spokeswoman for transforming the attitudes toward the American stage and female performers may have been that Charlotte's already marked disinterest in romantic relationships with men defied the popular notion of actresses as unchaste women who displayed themselves in public, like the prostitutes seated in the third tier. Despite her choice of career, in the eyes of most of her peers Charlotte Cushman was considered a moral paragon, a "true woman." For Charlotte and many of her contemporaries the belief that respectable women lacked "carnal motivation," that women were somehow innately pure and more "moral" than men, was advantageous for women in several ways. This belief created a certain sexual solidarity among women, and it allowed women into the public sphere to discharge their "purifying" influence. And an area of society that many Americans felt in particular need of purifying was the stage.

As Charlotte assured the Walnut Street Theatre audience, the representations she was determined to present onstage were the epitome of the socially acceptable "old plays." Yet, even with these self-imposed restrictions, Charlotte's decisive role in selecting, casting, managing, and performing in standard melodramas and classical dramatic fare would afford her an opportunity to exercise remarkable power.[13] And, while Charlotte poured her energy into the season with the resident company at the Walnut and negotiated with other visiting actors who might appear in Philadelphia, her absence was sorely felt on the Park Theatre boards. In September 1842, when British newcomer George Vandenhoff first came to the United States to debut at the Park Theatre, he found no available leading lady in the stock company to play the "heavy parts" opposite him. In his memoir Vandenhoff remembered the Park's manager Edmund Simpson curtly remarking: "We have no one for those parts. I tried to get Miss Cushman to play with you; but she's at the Walnut, Philadelphia—stage manager there."[14] To Vandenhoff's surprise he found that the company led by Charlotte Cushman, then a promising but "rude, strong, uncultivated talent,"[15] was in many ways superior to that at New York's premiere theater.

Charlotte Cushman enjoyed this newfound power and growing reputation, and she set about building a life in Philadelphia. And, aside from her career, the women who had come to mean so much to Charlotte constituted the emotional center of that life. While her obligations as manager, actress, and breadwinner for her family left her little free time, she did manage to cultivate deep friendships and infatuations with several women and have at least one love affair. While as manager and actress Charlotte acted before and interacted with men on a daily basis, her offstage life was in many ways typical of that of her day, grounded in a predominantly "female world" in which close emotional ties between women, while customarily accepted as womanly behavior, could nonetheless threaten to upset the worlds of the women involved.[16]

Rosalie Sully, whose image was to sustain Charlotte through the long voyage to Liverpool two years later, was not the first woman with whom Charlotte forged a deep emotional bond. In fact, in the years and months just before her voyage to England, Rosalie was not the only woman in Charlotte's life; their relationship, however, was to be the most intense and reciprocal of this period. But, even before Charlotte and Rosalie met, Charlotte's diary records her early years in Philadelphia as being filled with relationships with other women, most notably writer Anne Brewster and actress Fanny Kemble.

Reading Aloud with Anne Brewster

Not long after accepting the position at the Walnut, Charlotte's initial optimism and desire for independence had led her to rent a house for herself on Clover Hill, on the outskirts of Philadelphia, separate from the residence that she maintained for her family at 277 South Eighth Street. In the mornings, as she headed downtown to the theater, Charlotte would often stop and visit with Anne Hampton Brewster at the home where Anne lived with her brother and mother. Anne was only two years younger than Charlotte, but her life was strikingly different and much more in keeping with the expectations and limitations of their era than was Charlotte's. An intelligent, unmarried woman, shackled by both conventional, middle-class ideals of respectability and an overbearing brother—each of which kept her trapped in her "comfortable" home, with no meaningful work to occupy her—Anne was an inveterate reader and diarist, puzzling out her thoughts and feelings in the numerous leather-bound journals that she kept religiously throughout her life. When Charlotte and Anne Brewster were first acquainted, Charlotte reawakened Anne's love of literature and introduced her to the joy of sharing together a life of the mind. Charlotte's presence had a dramatic impact on Anne, who described this "happy time" in the early years of their friendship as "a glorious beam of sunshine in my existence."[17]

Women were not generally encouraged to develop their intellect, let alone to study classical poetic texts and discuss their interpretations with like-minded friends. In fact, Benjamin Brewster, Anne's brother, regarded the whole genre of poetry as suspect. Yet, with Charlotte, Anne "luxuriated" in their favorite authors.[18] For the better part of two years Charlotte Cushman and Anne Brewster would regularly spend their mornings reading poetry together, enjoying the language of Shakespeare, Ben Jonson, and

Beaumont and Fletcher and discussing passages from G. E. Lessing's *Dramaturgie*. Charlotte and Anne's sharing of their pleasure in texts took on an almost erotic component as the two women read aloud to each other, uttering the words of great writers, uncovering the meanings of the texts that Charlotte would embody on the stage in the evenings after their discussions. In the article she published almost forty years later, after Charlotte's death, Anne recalled:

> When she came to me of a morning for a few hours, an invisible curtain rose: a curious existence appeared . . . full of fascination; of sweet songs; perfect passages of poesy and music. . . . When she left, the curtain fell: but the real was beautified by something that hung around it like a subtle perfume; the haunting of a melody; the faint memory of a dream.[19]

Even offstage Charlotte represented previously unimagined possibilities to the women who knew her. In Anne's metaphor the "curtain" that framed Charlotte's appearance in her life separated the "real" from fantasy, but, with Charlotte, Anne could sense that these categories were permeable. The dreams that Charlotte aroused lingered, remaining after the curtain fell. Sharing with Charlotte an appreciation for poetry, which Anne regarded as "elevating to [her] mind and spirit," Anne Brewster came to feel a deeper attachment to Charlotte than she may have understood and one for which she had no other words but the accepted discourse of women's "friendship." Yet the sensuous, ephemeral feelings were palpably different than any other friendship Anne Brewster had ever known. Anne was fascinated with her independent friend, who literally opened up a whole world to her. But how could she describe the bodily sensations of wanting to inhale the "subtle perfume" of the rhapsodic, romantic atmosphere she associated with these times spent in another woman's company? Anne Brewster seized upon the language of spirituality to describe feelings she experienced as separate from the real day-to-day material world. In her diary years later Anne confided:

> How pure and lovely was our friendship, never shall I love another as I loved her. . . . [M]y love for C. was a love that is felt but once in one's lifetime—it was the love of the spirit—When with her I felt elevated above mortal things—so purely intellectual[,] so spiritual was our intercourse—We read together and with care and affection she pointed out to me passages of rare beauty in the old writers we delighted in.[20]

According to historian Nancy Cott, the generally accepted notion of innate female passionlessness allowed women the latitude to consider their love relationships with one another of a higher character than heterosexual relationships because these female friendships were thought to exclude the possibility of carnal passion.[21] For Anne the stirrings she felt as Charlotte initiated her into the shared beauties—and the dangers—of language were characterized as "intellectual" and "spiritual" in her diary; she could not express them as carnal. Although in her own diary Anne Brewster claimed that this intense, loving friendship "elevated and refined" her nature, eventually her brother made his disapproval known.[22] Benjamin Brewster came to consider the closeness between the two women as "wicked" and ultimately forced Anne to end her association with Charlotte.

It is tempting to ponder what so unsettled Benjamin Brewster about his sister "luxuriating" in reading literature with the woman she loved or listening as Charlotte "related to me incidents of her artistic career" and rehearsed and practiced before her first performance of Lady Macbeth with William Charles Macready later in 1843. Perhaps Charlotte's career on the stage was sufficient excuse for Brewster to insist that his sister limit her relationship with the actress. Or Charlotte's customary expressions of vehemence and passion may have appeared unseemly or vulgar to the staid and more conservative Benjamin Brewster.

Anne indeed had protested that, although Charlotte "was said to be violent in temper and rough in language at times, with me she was always gentle and lovely—I never heard from her lips a sentiment or thought or a word that was not perfectly pure and elevated." In fact, as Anne recalled, "Once in a while if I displayed captiousness or a little temper—she would say in loving accents and caressingly—'Do not so dearest one. I want to think of you always as perfect, as gentle and lovely as the ideal image I have of you in my mind.' "[23] However she may have appeared to others and whatever social rules she may have transgressed herself, Charlotte's ideal of womanly perfection was conventional—at least in Anne's account. Charlotte wanted the women closest to her to be feminine, gentle, and "ladylike." Although Charlotte might choose to express *herself* in a more "masculine" fashion, claiming her prerogative either as an independent working woman or as the head of her household, she seemed to prefer that the women to whom she was attracted be more traditionally feminine.

The "rough" language and sentiment of her adored friend that Anne Brewster went to such lengths to deny was considered "crude" or "vulgar," a violation of accepted middle-class "ladylike" behavior. In defending Charlotte from her critics, Anne attested to Charlotte's "purity," calling on her "elevated sentiments" to refute the charges of roughness, of what might be read as either aspects of "mannishness" and "commonness" in Cushman or a conflation of both. The very stereotypes of "passionlessness" to which Nancy Cott refers are, after all, classed notions—ways middle-class women, like Brewster, differentiated themselves from their more working-class contemporaries.

But, however much these charges may have factored in Benjamin Brewster's disdain, there were other reasons beyond Charlotte's occupation or social standing that brought him to forbid her relationship with his sister. Perhaps the intensity of the pleasure the women shared threatened Benjamin Brewster, who may have recognized something in the ardor of these two unmarried women that excluded all interest in men, rendering men superfluous, unnecessary. While Anne Brewster proudly described Charlotte Cushman as "the only being I ever truly loved or shall ever love," she disputed her brother's "wicked" characterization of that love. In her diary years later Anne Brewster was still asking herself the plaintive and rhetorical question her brother's reaction had provoked: "Oh Father above, is such love wrong? Can a feeling which seemed to elevate and refine my nature as did that love for her be wicked? Oh! No it cannot be, my inner self whispers, and I feel assured though separated in this life in another world we shall meet and never know the wretchedness of separation."[24]

Anne attributed her eventual separation from Charlotte to her brother's "interference" and even in her diary felt the need to deny intimations that the two women's "intercourse" was "wrong" and "wicked." By invoking what she described as the pure, spiritual nature of their relationship, Anne enlisted the language of the popular values of the day to justify her feelings for Charlotte. Yet, if women's relationships were regarded so routinely as passionless and pure, why would Benjamin Brewster be so disapproving? If the possibility of passion between women did not occur to most of Charlotte's contemporaries, as some historians claim, how can we account for the contradictory degrees of awareness and acceptance Charlotte's relationship with Anne engendered in her friend and in her friend's brother? As we can see, what Benjamin Brewster's condemnation reveals most clearly, in light of his sister's description of the nature of her feelings for Charlotte, is how very contingent beliefs in women's inherent innocence and passionlessness were. Despite the fact that there was no agreed-upon terminology in the mid-nineteenth century with which to distinguish those passions between women that Benjamin Brewster felt were wicked from the general expressions of affection that were considered socially acceptable, consciousness of the *possibility* of lesbian desire seems to have figured in his discomfort with their friendship. Something struck him as "wrong" in the intensity of his sister's feelings for Charlotte and inspired his determination to legislate Anne's behavior.

Yet, upset as Anne Brewster was and continued to be for years at her brother's interference, and as much as she might disavow his depiction of her relationship with Charlotte as wrong, she never overtly questioned either his right as a male family member to determine how she could conduct her emotional life or his motivations for doing so. Heartbroken, Anne still had to believe that her brother "meant well . . . though at the time I required all the duty bindings of my strict conventional culture to discipline me to obedience."[25] As a true woman, obedience was one of the necessary components of the self-image Anne Brewster constructed and narrated to herself in her diary.

For all the impact Charlotte made on Anne Brewster, it is not clear how Charlotte felt about her friend during these formative years or what effect Benjamin Brewster's disapproval had on Charlotte. Although her own diary lists letters sent and visits paid to "A. B.," there is little trace in Charlotte's remaining letters of the intensity of emotion that Anne Brewster described. And, even as their friendship cooled, Charlotte continued to consult with Benjamin Brewster about her business affairs in Philadelphia and her finances once she was abroad, although she seemed increasingly disinclined to trust him. Perhaps Benjamin Brewster's disdain was a warning to Charlotte. From this time forward she would watch herself much more vigilantly and leave few traces of "feelings" others might condemn. Whether or not Charlotte had initially reciprocated the same degree of attachment as Anne had expressed, by the summer of 1843 the promise of a close emotional connection with another woman living in Philadelphia was to prove even more captivating to her. When Charlotte's former idol, Fanny Kemble, returned to the United States after an extended stay in England with her American husband, Pierce Butler, and their children and took up residence nearby, Charlotte was thrilled.

Meanwhile, for all the pleasant hours she shared with Anne Brewster and the excitement of getting to know Fanny Kemble, Charlotte Cushman had other troubles on her mind. The Walnut Street Theatre was doing poorly. When Charlotte originally called the company together on 15 September 1842 it had all seemed quite promising. Among the members of the company were actors William Wheatley, William Fredericks, Susan Cushman, and Charlotte's former mentor Clara Fisher Maeder. At first visiting leading performers such as George Vandenhoff appeared to be drawing sizable audiences to the theater, but soon it appeared that the economy was so bad that even Edwin Forrest could not bring in enough business to fill the house. Philadelphia was Forrest's home turf, and, as Vandenhoff remarked, "If *he* could not draw in Philadelphia, who could?"[26] Theaters throughout the country were suffering one of the worst seasons ever known. By the end of the 1842–43 season finances were so low at the Walnut that Charlotte resigned as full manager. To preserve appearances that things were going well William Rufus Blake, Cushman's former manager in Albany, was named as her "assistant" to help with management, and she continued to act with the company. Cushman and Blake disliked each other; actor Walter Leman and other members of the Walnut Street company observed that at times their relations were "almost belligerent." Blake resented and made fun of Cushman's personal and social ambitions, and she was peeved that Blake, of all people, was chosen to replace her.[27] But, while Charlotte Cushman may have failed as a manager, her continued exposure at the Walnut provided her with her biggest opportunity as an actress: an offer from the "eminent tragedian" Macready to act with him.

Playing with Macready

William Charles Macready had begun his return trip to the United States with a series of performances at the Park Theatre in New York. Like Vandenhoff, he found no woman there in the stock company to support him satisfactorily. The very actor whose performance had first inspired the young Charlotte Cushman on his last American tour in Boston seventeen years before now sent word that, when he appeared in Philadelphia on 23 October 1843, he wished her to play Lady Macbeth opposite him. Charlotte was excited and nervous. Anne Brewster, then still in close contact with her, recalled her friend's fear and anticipation:

> Some weeks before he came to act with her, she was much excited and expressed her anxiety as an unaffected schoolgirl. . . . "I am dreadfully afraid of him!" she would say. Every day she brought me some news of his mode of acting, his artistic peculiarities, his temper and manners. She was to act Lady Macbeth on his first night. Her repetitions of the tragedy were untiring. We read and re-read it. We consulted everything that had been written on the play and character upon which we could lay our hands. . . . One day she came to me looking unusually serious and resolute. "You will not see me for some days," she said.[28]

Charlotte Cushman had heard that Macready practiced his parts in front of a mirror, and she determined to rehearse in a similar fashion. When she played the part with another actor prior to Macready's arrival and the technique failed miserably, Charlotte was worried. Instead, Anne suggested that she and Charlotte read and study *Two Noble Kinsmen* and Chaucer's *Knight's Tale* to help her form her conception of the powerful Lady Macbeth. Later Anne claimed their discussions were instrumental in helping Charlotte interpret the role. By the time Macready came, according to Anne, Charlotte was prepared.[29]

Macready was obviously impressed with Cushman's performance. On the night of their first *Macbeth,* the star of the British stage was moved to write in his journal: "The Miss Cushman who acted Lady Macbeth interested me much. She has to learn her art, but she showed mind and sympathy with me; a novelty so refreshing to me on the stage."[30] Charlotte was elated by his reaction. Macready was a notoriously hard person to please,

Miss Charlotte Cushman as Lady Macbeth

Charlotte Cushman as Lady Macbeth. Cushman's interpretation of Lady Macbeth emphasized the character's forcefulness and will. *(Harvard Theatre Collection. Houghton Library.)*

MR MACREADY AS MACBETH.

*MACB: Two truths are told, as happy prologues to
the swelling act of the imperial theme.
Act 1.S. 3*

William Charles Macready. The famous British tragedian, seen
here as Macbeth, offered Cushman the biggest break of her
career when he invited her to perform opposite him. *(Author's
collection.)*

and the whole company had been anxious about his reactions. George Vandenhoff, who played Duncan for this performance, was struck by his countryman's "intense devotion to the work of his profession, as a business, and his equally intense *egoism;* which imperiously subjected, as far as he was able, everything and every body, to the sole purpose of making himself the one mark for all eyes to look at . . . the one name for all mouths to repeat and eulogize."[31] Macready orchestrated every aspect of the productions in which he appeared to heighten his own prominence, cutting other characters' lines and even demanding that important dramatic moments like climactic death scenes be played off to the side so that the audience would continuously focus on him. Vandenhoff believed that in Macready's "tyrannical self-aggrandizement" other actors were "mere scaffoldings to support his [Macready's] artistic designs."[32] But, unlike Vandenhoff, Charlotte Cushman was initially so excited to be performing with the eminent tragedian, and so eager to learn all she could from him that she had no objection to affording him center stage. And Macready was so pleased to have a reliable female costar in America that he spoke to her about accompanying him when he performed in Boston in November.

It would be wonderful to return to her native city and perform opposite Macready. Now that she was "released" from the obligations of theater management, it seemed that nothing would stand in her way. Unknown to Macready, she had already anticipated the possibility of performing with him in Boston and had written to William Pelby, the manager of the Boston theater, and offered her services to perform when Macready appeared there. But Pelby refused, preferring to cast his daughter opposite the British star. Cushman traveled to Boston anyway, hoping to change his mind, but Pelby was annoyed and unwavering. Nonetheless, when Cushman arrived in Boston, Macready felt obligated to pay her the fifty dollars he had agreed to, and she determined to stay on in town during his run. Even if she could not act with Macready, she could at least attend his performances, after which she sent him extravagant, gushing notes complimenting every aspect of his acting. But Macready was wary; although flattered by her attentiveness, he became increasingly circumspect in his dealings with her.

Perhaps it was her dramatic flare or an intense desire to please, but Charlotte had a tendency to be effusive and overwhelm whomever was the object of her admiration. Macready noted in his diary that, since he had "not the slightest purpose, dream, or intent of wrong or folly," he made it a point to meet with her only in public venues, and he remarked after one visit that "she kissed my hand, but I was only kind."[33] During his free time in Boston—then considered the intellectual capital, or the "Athens," of America[34]—Macready, who was always more at home with friends among the literati than with fellow performers, kept busy visiting writers Ralph Waldo

Emerson and Henry Wadsworth Longfellow, whom he had met in England, and British writer and journalist Thomas Colley Grattan, who was at that time British consul in Boston (and a special friend of Charlotte's). Grattan put in a good word for the American actress, and, when Macready returned to New York in December 1843 for several more weeks of performances at the Park Theatre, again he asked Charlotte to perform opposite him.

Years later Charlotte claimed that it had been this invitation to perform with Macready in New York that prompted her to give up management of her theater,[35] but, as we have seen, she had already resigned her management responsibilities—or been replaced—several months earlier. In any event it was fortunate that she was not so encumbered, because throughout Macready's New York run that December, Cushman made the grueling commute between Philadelphia and New York every other day to act opposite him at the Park Theatre. At Macready's request she had prepared several new parts for her New York appearances. This time, however, Macready was initially less pleased with her performance, complaining that he felt she was reading, rather than acting, her part in *The Bridal*, Sheridan Knowles's adaptation of Beaumont and Fletcher's *Maid's Tragedy* (a play in which Macready had created the role of the brave soldier Melantius).[36] Yet ultimately all the traveling, memorization, and study were worth her effort. With Macready as a model, she began to perfect her own style, and, after her first attempt, she prepared for each part more rigorously than ever.

Performing every other night with Macready on the boards of New York's most prestigious theater, Charlotte Cushman was enthusiastically received,[37] somewhat to Macready's chagrin. In his diary Macready wrote, "They called for Miss Cushman here, who gets puffed up in the papers, very absurdly."[38] Apparently, the positive reviews she received from friendly critics in the press when the two actors performed together had begun to irritate him—especially when her talent was compared with his own. Then Macready read an erroneous allegation printed, or planted, in a New York paper stating that he was planning to have Charlotte Cushman accompany him on his upcoming Southern tour "and then go to London and appear under [his] auspices." Annoyed, the British actor recorded in his diary that this claim was "without a shadow of truth";[39] still, the New York journalists were apparently eager to report Macready's support for one of their own. Whether or not Charlotte herself had a hand in feeding this hopeful, but inaccurate, notice to the press, the plan backfired.

The December 1843 New York run closed on a disappointing note for Charlotte. Macready refused to act at her benefit night performance. As the visiting star performer, he was insulted at the mere suggestion that such a lesser-known actress would ask him to perform for *her* financial gain. Instead, Macready noted that he had "fixed Miss Cushman" by explaining that he had refused to act at the benefit nights for other cast members as well.[40] Apparently, Charlotte felt slighted by his manner toward her. For all the attention she had received she had earned hardly any money from her regular performances with Macready in New York and would have stood to make a considerable sum from a benefit performance that featured the British star. But without him Charlotte's share of the profits for her benefit night was meager, and she was "more closely quartered in money matters than [she had] been in the last two years."[41] In addition to the financial disappointment, Macready had wounded her pride.

Characteristically, Cushman would not let the matter drop, and she sent Macready a note confronting him directly. Several days later Macready wrote in his diary that he had received a letter from her "on the subject of her Benefit in New York. It is too bad that I am to be tormented thus."[42] The "great" tragedian's attitude of condescension toward the young American actress is clear in his diary. But, as much as he privately resented her temerity, he responded immediately in a letter with quite a different tone. Macready replied that he had "never by word or act been wanting . . . in . . . kindly feeling since [he had] had the pleasure of knowing [her]."[43] What did the British star *really* think of Charlotte Cushman? The contradictions between the tone of his letter and the sentiments expressed in his diary reveal a discrepancy between his confidential protests of annoyance and his carefully honed more public face. Here was a young, relatively inexperienced American woman who was being compared with him in the press and who expected to be treated practically as his equal. However audacious Macready may have considered her privately, he evidently felt the need to represent himself as a "gentleman," and he had the good business sense not to wish to offend one of the strongest performers and potential costars he had encountered. And Charlotte, for her part, had to admit that, despite any feelings of resentment between them, she had learned much about rehearsal techniques and elocution from Macready, and performing with him had helped her career immeasurably.

Nevertheless, when Macready did not invite her to accompany him on his Southern tour, Charlotte was disheartened. She wrote of her disappointment to Thomas Colley Grattan, who had just seen Macready in Boston. Grattan "was quite grieved and disappointed" by the tone of her letter. "What on earth can have come over Mr. Macready's mind to make him less satisfied with you? He spoke of you to me on several occasions in terms the most flattering."[44] Grattan wondered if she suffered from "over anxiety to please those whom the ardor of your temper leads you to overestimate."[45] Maybe she *had* overestimated Macready. Or perhaps the intensity of her admiration had overwhelmed him. In any event Charlotte had insisted upon an explanation from him: not something a star of William

Charles Macready's magnitude—and ego—was accustomed to encountering in supporting performers, let alone in a woman. And "Miss Cushman," as Macready was later to remark, was "full of the idea of her own importance, and will not listen to any other notion."[46]

Charlotte Cushman took another tack. Immediately after their New York run she wrote a poem about her famous costar that she published in the January 1844 issue of the *Anglo American,* in which she praised Macready's "all matchless skill." While paying tribute to the esteemed actor, Cushman was engaging in her own form of self-promotion. All who read her laudatory poem would remember *her* as the actress who had recently performed with the British star, and her name would continue to be linked with his even while he toured without her. Macready may have been irritated with her nerviness, but he responded graciously, writing to thank her "for the beauty of the lines, and for the kind feeling that suggested myself as a subject worthy of them."[47]

In January 1844, while Macready toured the South, Charlotte, concerned about the ever-diminishing finances in Philadelphia, embarked on a short tour through New England, occasionally playing with resident companies so "drunken and ignorant" that she despaired.[48] After having performed at the Park Theatre with Macready, the prospect of traveling from town to town, acting with small, rural stock companies, seemed particularly bleak that winter. In this mood of despondency, while performing in Providence, Charlotte mused in her diary:

> Jan 12, 1844 . . . Another awful performance . . . Alas, alas was it for this I left my home, my family, my friends. . . . I wonder if it will be a lesson to me. How often have I censured F.B. [Fanny Butler] for expressing her feelings of disgust at a profession which she loathed and how unjust I was . . . how I hated myself tonight—as I felt that I formed one of a miserable group and why should I not be considered as bad as they?[49]

Macready and Fanny Kemble Butler, the most admired of Charlotte Cushman's theatrical colleagues, were both known to disavow and depreciate the very occupation that had made each so successful. Shortly before her marriage, and perhaps influenced by her future husband's prejudices, Fanny had written, "How I do loathe the stage, those wretched tawdry, glittering rags flung over the forms of ideal loveliness, pitiful substitutes for the glories of poetry."[50] Occasionally, in anguished moments on tour Charlotte also participated in this characterization of the theater. The constant travel and frequently uncertain transportation, the relentless arrangements to be made, and dubious conditions once one arrived—all this took an inevitable toll. Every encounter Charlotte had with unprofessional, unprepared, or inebriated local stock actors reinforced the societal prejudice against all performers. It would be more than a decade before Anna Cora Mowatt would admit in print that, contrary to those performers who "affect[ed]" to "detest their own vocation," she "received intense delight from the presentation of some characters"; for her "the power of swaying the emotions of a crowd [was] one of the most thrilling sensations that [she] ever experienced."[51] As Charlotte well appreciated even at this early point in her career, the potential financial gain and autonomy the theater afforded her were frequently rewarding, despite the demands and uncertainties of the itinerant life. If she could only exert her "moral" influence and raise the standards as well as the social estimation of the theater, so that others wouldn't look down upon those who worked on the stage, Charlotte might be able to arrive at a coherent response to the contradictory impulses she recorded in her diary.

One of the most decided advantages of such a public career to a woman of Charlotte's emotional proclivities was the opportunity to come into contact with other women outside of a set circle of acquaintances and friends. On this same tour to Providence, despite her misgivings about her fellow performers, Charlotte could not help noting the beauty of one of the women with whom she dined. In her diary she ruminated over her reaction to

> the loveliest woman I ever looked upon[,] in the wife of an editor named Church—Such eyes[,] such hair[,] such eyebrows: mouth[,] nose[,] chin and *tout ensemble* I never saw in my life before—She is a Carolinian I hear and has a sister more lovely than herself. What a lucky thing I am not of the other sex, for a heavy mortgage would have been made upon me from this hour. As it was it almost deprived me of appetite for my dinner.[52]

Although Charlotte made it a point to differentiate herself from "the other sex" when describing her reaction to this beautiful woman, clearly she could and did identify with the perspective of a person who uncontrollably finds other women attractive. Rather than describing a distanced aesthetic appreciation of her dinner companion, in Charlotte's impassioned account she was so moved by the other woman's beauty as to feel physically affected. Charlotte knew from her own bodily excitement that other women could be more than close friends and intellectual companions; occasionally, they excited palpable sensual responses as well.

But there were women who interested her and compelled her admiration closer to home. Back in Philadelphia, at the Walnut Street Theatre in February 1844, Charlotte resumed her whirl of social activities along with her accustomed roles. Most eagerly, she looked forward to any opportunity to see and, hopefully, to spend time with Fanny Kemble Butler. Both Charlotte and Macready were mutual friends with Fanny, but the intimacy that Charlotte had been cultivating with Fanny these past few months was far different from the professional and social connections she had sought with Macready.

Little more than two months earlier, on 27 November 1843, while Charlotte and Macready were performing together in New York, Charlotte had sent Fanny flowers for her thirty-fourth birthday. Fanny, distraught in her marriage, had written to thank Charlotte "for [her] sweet flowers[;] they are the *only* bright things which will belong to this birthday of mine save for the thought that one year more of trial and difficulty is past."[53] And, despite Fanny's obvious unhappiness, Charlotte had saved her note, as she had saved all of the notes she received from the beautiful former actress, pleased to be the bearer of any pleasure she could. Now when Charlotte hurried home to Philadelphia it meant she would have further occasions to visit with Fanny, to enjoy her company, maybe even to be of help, if she could.

Following Fanny Kemble

Charlotte Cushman's relationship with Fanny Kemble Butler, however, was to be more problematic than she imagined. At first, when Fanny and her family returned to Philadelphia in the late spring of 1843, after months abroad, Charlotte was so smitten with the cultivated, graceful woman seven years her senior, so excited about the possibility of a friendship with her, that she showered Fanny with gifts and invitations to go riding. Fanny, like Charlotte, was an inveterate horsewoman, and, though Fanny's riding displeased her husband, Pierce Butler, it was one of the few pleasures available to her as their marriage grew increasingly strained. At first Charlotte had been a valuable distraction. Fanny informed Charlotte when she was at home "and either morning or evening [I] shall be very glad to receive you any day and every day as often as your inclination prompts."[54] Fanny responded to Charlotte's overtures with notes and gifts of "some old theatrical properties" that Charlotte could use as she liked or "toss . . . into the Walnut St. wardrobe."[55]

Charlotte was thrilled with Fanny's attention and support and so infatuated with her that the early portions of Charlotte's 1844 diary are replete with mention of Fanny. "Yesterday evening F.B. sang me that exquisite ballad. . . . What an expressive face and figure are hers—it possesses me like enchantment," Charlotte recollected.[56] And Charlotte *was* "possessed"; she used this term as she would in the future, to convey the all-consuming, hypnotic quality that another woman excited in her. Charlotte recorded every note she received from Fanny and made particular mention when Fanny commended her singing voice and her acting, feeling that "it is much to be praised by her."[57] Fanny was her idol; the mix of attraction, admiration, and urge to emulate her—feelings of both identification and desire—were complex for Charlotte. The beautiful Fanny had been the leading actress in the United States and England until her retirement at the time of her marriage to Pierce Butler. Fanny's success in many of the roles Charlotte played were the standards by which Charlotte was judged and judged herself.

Throughout the winter Charlotte continued to visit Fanny, and Charlotte could not help noting how distressed Fanny was as she "talked much to me of her sorrows. What a terrible fate she has."[58] Fanny's fate was indeed terrible. Brought up in cosmopolitan London, Fanny had married into an American slaveholding family, and she was horrified when she saw the conditions of life on the Butler family's Georgia plantation. She soon found herself in profound disagreement with her autocratic husband and utterly powerless to influence him—particularly with regard to the institution of slavery, which she despised. Fanny's earliest and closest American friends, the Sedgwicks, were ardent abolitionists, and Fanny shared their views. Pierce Butler made no secret of the fact that he resented any show of independence on the part of his formerly professional wife and that he actively enjoyed the company of other women (including their children's governess). The rift between him and his wife had grown irreconcilable. By now Fanny Kemble was eager to be divorced from Butler but desperate lest she lose custody of her daughters, as was usual for divorced women at the time. Fanny confided in Charlotte, encouraging at first Charlotte's eagerness to be near and to be useful to Fanny.

In the back of Charlotte's diary was a draft of a letter that Charlotte prepared to send Fanny, probably written early in 1844, while Charlotte was on tour in New England.

> You would almost consider me foolish could you know the deprivation it is to me not to be able to see you. . . . I hope to see you wear a more cheerful look than the one you wore on Sunday: for indeed, indeed—dearly as I love your presence—I had rather never see you—than with that sad and fearful expression. . . . Don't despair or despond, you have friends ready to stake everything for your happiness.[59]

Charlotte Cushman was more than willing to help rescue Fanny. Charlotte enjoyed being the savior, and here was a chance to right a great wrong against a woman she adored and render herself indispensable. She offered to help Fanny amass proof of Pierce Butler's infidelities so that Fanny could divorce him and retain custody of her children. But none of Charlotte's overzealous attempts to help were successful. And any slight waning of Fanny's interest was painful to Charlotte. More like a lover than a colleague, an interested friend, or an admiring fan, Charlotte continued to inundate Fanny with flowers, although Fanny was rapidly becoming overwhelmed by Charlotte's intensity. If Fanny mentioned a desire to speak with someone, Charlotte brought that person to Fanny's door, only to be reproved for her efforts.[60] Soon even Charlotte's efforts at demonstrative affection were met with crushing notes refusing Charlotte's "flower bounties" and begging her "not to waste [her] money so terribly for indeed it gives me annoyance rather than pleasure to have you do so." Dismissively, Fanny thanked Charlotte for her verses and a book, but noted, "I *believe* I have a whole library of yours already."[61]

Fanny Kemble Butler's anguish over her marriage and fear of being separated from her children was taking its toll on all her relationships. Soon Charlotte's efforts seemed to irritate her more than offer relief. Perhaps Fanny was embarrassed by Charlotte's effusiveness or by the plainly romantic quality of her attachment. Fanny had only one thing on her mind—retaining her children—and Charlotte's flowers and poetry were of no help or solace. Fanny had been informed that "there is but *one means* by which I am to be helped and that is by the providing of evidence such as would furnish me w/a plea for a divorce *in the event* of Mr. Butler's taking my children from me."[62] Charlotte, with her characteristic determination, had assured Fanny that she could provide such evidence. When this proved to be a more difficult and embarrassing task than Fanny anticipated, she finally asked Charlotte to stop interceding on her behalf. Whatever Charlotte *was* able to ascertain about Pierce Butler's escapades with other women—while sufficiently convincing to give Fanny considerable pain—was not enough to stand up in a court of law. Only "specific and incontrovertible evidence of adultery—[which] you have I presume by this time discovered that it is not possible to obtain"—would help Fanny's case; "therefore the only chance I had (that I would take) of retaining my children is at an end."[63]

But Charlotte persisted, serving only to further estrange Fanny from her. Charlotte Cushman could not reconcile herself to failure, and she could not accept Fanny's willingness to let the matter drop. Fanny's notes to her grew increasingly cold. Finally, Fanny wrote: "From the tenor of my last two notes to you, you must have perceived that I had entirely given up all expectation of arriving at the evidence which you have so positively held out to me as within your power to obtain for some time past." Fanny told Charlotte she had "only one more request to make of you—from this time forth consider that I no longer desire or authorise you to pursue the enquiry for me—it exposes you to malevolent and revengeful feelings and keeps my mind in a perpetual torment by reports of the grossest & most harmful kind which subsequently cannot be substantiated."[64] Charlotte was deeply insulted. She had gladly, willingly, offered her assistance, and, now that she was deemed no longer of use, she was being dismissed. Charlotte would harbor ill feelings about Fanny Kemble for years.[65] But from this Charlotte had learned an important lesson: that she needed to be in an emotional relationship where *she* was appreciated and admired as well as admiring. It wasn't enough just to follow after Fanny. Despite Charlotte's remarkable self-possession onstage, in the company of someone she deeply revered Charlotte felt at an acute disadvantage unless she could "lose herself" as she did in the characters she embodied onstage.[66] From this time on Charlotte would gravitate to relationships in which she was the more visible, more public partner.

Getting to Know Rosalie

Charlotte's career was gaining momentum, and with her growing popular success she decided to record her increased prominence in some tangible way. She commissioned a portrait of herself by Thomas Sully, Rosalie's father, an artist prominent in the cultural life of Philadelphia and known for his portraits of celebrated performers and politicians.[67] Ironically, it is almost certainly through Fanny Kemble that Charlotte Cushman came to know the Sullys. In 1832, when Fanny and her father, actor Charles Kemble, arrived in the United States on a performance tour, Sully, a distant relative of Pierce Butler, painted the first of his numerous portraits of Fanny. And, as with so many of Charlotte's early professional choices, she followed the example that Fanny had set. In the spring of 1843 Charlotte came to Thomas Sully's studio in his home at 11 South Fifth Street to sit for her portrait. She soon grew as fond of Thomas Sully and his family as had Fanny. As Charlotte sat in Thomas Sully's studio during the day watching the light change through the large floor-to-ceiling window or, along with Fanny Kemble, socialized with the Sully family in the evening, Charlotte felt a particular fondness developing for one of Sully's daughters, Rosalie, who was just two years younger than she. By February 1844, along with her diary notations of letters to and from Anne Brewster, Fanny Kemble, and others, Charlotte noted for the first time that she wrote to "R. Sully." Here was a woman who would come to match the intensity of Charlotte's feelings and respond in kind.

On 6 March Rosalie acknowledged what had been Charlotte's fascination with Fanny Kemble and responded to Charlotte's overtures of friendship with a gift for Charlotte; a miniature Rosalie had painted of Fanny

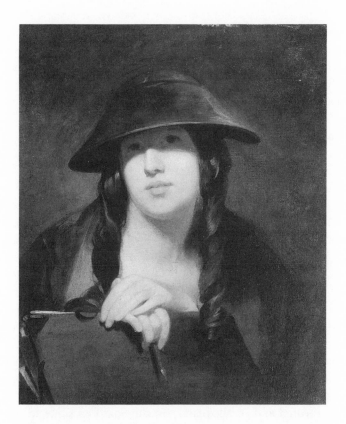

The Student (Rosalie Kemble Sully, 1818–47), by Thomas Sully, 1839. Portraitist Thomas Sully recognized his daughter Rosalie's talent and ambition as an artist by choosing to depict her as an art student with her portfolio in hand. *(Oil on canvas, 23 1/2 x 19 1/2 in. The Metropolitan Museum of Art. Bequest of Francis T. S. Darley, 1914 [14.126.4]. All rights reserved, Metropolitan Museum of Art.)*

Kemble Butler. At one time this recognition of the woman she idolized would have delighted Charlotte, but by now the rift between the two was irreparable. Still, Charlotte evidently sent the miniature to Fanny, but it was returned to her with a note that, while denying any ill will on Fanny's part, made it apparent that any relationship between them was completely severed. "My dear Miss Cushman, I send you back the locket with my miniature which I think does our friend Rose great credit." Whatever other words of affection or concern Charlotte sent along with the locket, Fanny did not deign to respond to, protesting instead that "there is one thing in your note, one alone bearing reference to my affairs which I will answer."

Fanny assured Charlotte that "lawyers and friends one and all" had told Fanny that her case against Pierce Butler was impossible.[68] And with this cool rejection Fanny was clearly no longer including Charlotte in her category of friends.

Fortunately for Charlotte, the close of this relationship opened the way for the deep, mutual love she was soon to find with Rosalie Sully. At the same time as their relationship was growing in intensity, Charlotte's career was growing in prominence. In her own cryptic diary notations for the next six months Charlotte chronicled the roles she played, the money she spent, letters she sent and received, and the nights she "slept with Rose."[69] And, with her growing love attachment to Rosalie, Charlotte was constructing an extended family. Although Charlotte continued to seek out Benjamin Brewster's opinions when she needed financial advice, Thomas Sully became, in Charlotte's diary, "Father." When on the road performing out of town, Charlotte now noted the times she "wrote to Rosalie" and "father," as well as the letters she received from them. Rosalie's visits to Charlotte's home on Clover Hill were particularly pleasurable times, as on 23 August, when Charlotte jotted in her diary, "Happy day Rose rode out and came home hungry." What made Charlotte happy on that hot August day? Was it her pleasure in Rosalie's company, her enjoyment in her partner coming to *her* home, where they could be alone, or their riding horseback together? Was it other passions they excited in each other, feelings Charlotte savored and recalled later, on shipboard en route to England? Whatever else transpired between the two women is not known, since all but one of the letters between them, which Charlotte faithfully recorded sending and receiving, have been destroyed. Yet in her brief diary notations Charlotte recorded the existence of their growing relationship.

In May 1844 Macready returned to the Northeast and, at Edmund Simpson's suggestion, once more asked Charlotte to perform with him. In May and again in September and October she acted with him in New York, Philadelphia, and finally even in Boston. Although Macready was outwardly complimentary, Charlotte was increasingly aware of his feelings of superiority over most Americans and his wariness with her.[70] Macready had long been a supporter of the United States and the ideal of democracy and a critic of British aristocracy to such an extent that he had even considered retiring in America.[71] But at heart he ultimately considered British sensibilities and British audiences more judicious and better able than Americans to differentiate between ranting emotionalism and talent.[72] The general belief in British cultural supremacy was shared by many on both sides of the Atlantic. And Charlotte also sensed the acknowledgment that might result from British success.

For years, in letters to friends Thomas Colley Grattan, the Creswicks, and others, Charlotte Cushman had contemplated going to England to try her talents there, as Edwin Forrest had. Apparently, she had even corresponded with and received offers from British theaters. In December 1842— ten months before she ever appeared with Macready—Grattan had written in response to one of her letters that he was "sincerely glad that you have made up your mind to go to England next summer. It must do you infinite good, if you go there in a mood of true philosophy, not expecting too much, & resolved not to be discouraged if things fall short of your hopes."[73]

Now, almost two years later, after another series of successful and critically acclaimed performances on her home turf with Macready, Charlotte resolved eventually to earn star billing and a salary commensurate with his. To achieve this level of success she would have to follow what she later reported had been *Macready's* advice to "go to England where your talents will be appreciated at their true value."[74] Why would Charlotte retroactively credit one of the most significant career choices of her life to Macready? Although she had been planning a tour of England for years, it served her purposes well to attribute her decision to the prompting of this older, successful, professional, and, most important, male actor.

Early accounts of Charlotte Cushman's success draw heavily upon the fact that her talent was recognized by so reputable and highly acclaimed a performer as Macready and that *his* estimation of her talents encouraged her to take actions that furthered her career. Yet, as much as she was helped professionally from appearing with Macready, Cushman's aspirations were clearly her own. Whether or not Macready actually encouraged her, this anecdote has been repeated in virtually every biographical sketch of Cushman and is part of the accepted story of her life as she told it.

Charlotte was determined to leave shortly after her final Boston tour with Macready. But, as Emma Stebbins has reported, Macready acted up until "the last available hour, and the morning of . . . Miss Cushman's scheduled benefit he sailed for England."[75] Once again, without Macready, a disappointed Charlotte Cushman found attendance poor for her benefit performance. With a packet of letters of introduction Charlotte set off for Philadelphia, to pack up her belongings, bid farewell to friends and family, and prepare for her departure. Yet, as talented as Charlotte clearly was, American audiences had yet to fully appreciate her, and her farewell performance in New York on 25 October 1844, just before she set sail, was played to a half-full house. Charlotte was performing as Beatrice to George Vandenhoff's Benedick in a production of *Much Ado about Nothing* at the Park Theatre. As Vandenhoff remembered, Charlotte was so anxious about the step she was about to take—or so careless—that she confused her lines, "knocking the fourth and fifth acts together, extemporaneously."[76] Every penny that she earned was needed to tide her over as she marshaled her resources for England, and the disappointingly small turnout for her last performance on American soil didn't auger well for the step Charlotte was about to take. Still, as always, she was determined.

Rosalie and Thomas Sully accompanied Charlotte, her mother, and her brother to New York to see her off. Although the two women shared the intimacy and commitment that already passed between them and their hopes of Charlotte achieving enough success so that someday they might have a life together, neither knew when, if ever, they would meet again. Perhaps Rosalie was optimistic. Her father had made this long voyage several times; no matter how far afield or long away his work kept him, Thomas Sully had always returned to his family in Philadelphia.

In addition to his gift of books to read on the long voyage, Thomas Sully supplied his surrogate daughter with advice. As she was leaving, Charlotte noted with pleasure that "my father said the other day that I was much altered in the last six months . . . altered for the better and surely nothing could do that in one whose character was so forward as mine but an affection the most sincere and devoted and such I feel it to be; it possesses me entirely and on lying down at night, rising in the morning at every moment of the day she [Rosalie] haunts me."[77] Charlotte's relationship with Rosalie Sully *had* changed her. In Charlotte's mind her "devoted affection" for Rosalie had rendered Rosalie's family her own. Charlotte's father had been dead for several years and absent from her life for considerably longer. Charlotte's use of "my father" to refer to Thomas Sully reflected the commitment she and Rosalie had forged, a passionate connection that, curiously, Charlotte felt had *tempered* her too "forward" nature, rather than *resulted from* it. As with her earlier intimate relationships with women, Charlotte felt "haunted" and "possessed" by her desire, but this attachment was significantly different than any she had experienced before. With Anne Brewster, she had learned the pleasure of sharing an intense connection with another woman and the danger and ostracism that could result from others' reactions to such intensity. From her infatuation with Fanny Kemble Butler, Charlotte had seen the power such desire might wield over her and the necessity that it be reciprocal. She had also moved in that relationship from seeing herself as an adoring fan, revering the object of her desire, to recognizing herself as an equal professional in her own right. Similarly, in her professional dealings with Macready, Charlotte had learned to stand up for herself and place her career second to none. Now, with Rosalie, secure in the knowledge of the affection they shared, the general acceptance of her by Rosalie's family, and the two women's determination to pursue their respective talents, Charlotte was filled with the possibilities such passion opened up for her. Out of these relationships Charlotte had forged the beginnings of a new sense of herself. Whatever individual women meant to Charlotte, for her female spectators Charlotte Cushman would come to stand for both desire and agency, object and subject, simultaneous positions unprecedented in her day.

On parting from the Sullys, Charlotte's only wish was "a last word to her on whom my soul doats." She went on to say, "I wanted to have written a longer note on the morning of my leaving—but was in a corner of the wheelhouse with my brother & had only time to write on the back of my book just a 'good bye,' but my letter of the night before was then on its way."[78] However acceptable her relationship with Rosalie was believed to be, Charlotte knew that she still had need to be circumspect, and so her public farewell to her brother was given primacy over the fervent sentiments she wanted to express to Rosalie. But she had written her lover a deeply passionate note the night before she left and could sail away knowing that letter was, even then, en route to Rosalie.

Traveling along with Charlotte Cushman was Sallie Mercer, a fourteen-year-old African American young woman newly hired to serve as the actress's personal maid. Over the previous few months, Charlotte's diary had included mention of travel arrangements made for Sallie as she accompanied Charlotte throughout most of her recent tours. The young woman Charlotte called "my right hand"[79] was originally hired because of her earnestness and intelligence. Charlotte was first struck by what she described as young Sallie's "conscientious eyebrows" and "anxious forehead."[80] It is not clear exactly how Sallie came to find herself employed as Charlotte's maid, dresser, and assistant nor how she felt about it at the time. Emma Stebbins, writing years later, after having lived with Charlotte and Sallie Mercer for almost two decades, with all the conscious and unacknowledged racism of the era, wrote that: "There was some difficulty in taking her [Sallie] away from her mother, who also had her ideas of the child's value; but it was one of the things fated to be, and so it was accomplished."[81] While it is extremely unlikely that Sallie Mercer received any more formal education than had Charlotte, who left school at thirteen, it is apparent that from the beginning that Charlotte depended upon Sallie Mercer's intelligence as well as her practical good sense and gave Sallie ample opportunities to exercise both. For months before their voyage, whenever she was out of town without Sallie, Charlotte would write her young maid lengthy letters filled with instructions for errands to be run, merchants to negotiate with, costumes to prepare. However Sallie felt about her numerous obligations, given the limited options available to a free black woman living in Philadelphia in 1844, Sallie may well have been

Sallie Mercer. Joining Cushman's household at the age of fourteen, Sallie Mercer was to live with Cushman and her family for the remainder of her life. This *carte de visite* of Mercer, ca. 1858, appears among those of other members of Cushman's family and close friends in Cushman's photograph album. *(Charlotte Cushman Photo Album. Prints and Photographs Division. Library of Congress.)*

content with her lot.[82] There are no extant letters of Sallie's from this early period to suggest how she felt, but Sallie was to spend the remainder of her life (including her "retirement") with Charlotte and Charlotte's family, living with them in her old age, even after Charlotte's death. In later years Sallie's letters attest to her devotion to Charlotte, but the complexity of the two women's relationship as maid and mistress, trusted servant and international celebrity, woman of African descent and woman of European descent, must be foregrounded by the meanings and construction of race operative during their era. Whatever the circumstances of their first meeting, on 26 October 1844, the devoted fourteen-year-old maid and her mistress, an apprehensive twenty-eight-year-old actress, bade goodbye to their respective friends and family members, boarded a ship aptly named the *Garrick,* and sailed for England.

With Sallie to assist her, friends she had made on board for company, an armful of letters of introduction, and a notebook from Rosalie in which she was recording her thoughts, the resolute Charlotte Cushman first stepped onto British soil. Eleven months earlier, in response to one of Charlotte's letters at a low point, Thomas Colley Grattan had written to her: "You talk of quitting the profession in a year. I expect to see you stand very high in it indeed by that time."[83] Now, within a few months, on the other side of the Atlantic, Charlotte was to more than exceed her friend's prediction.

Embodying
Strong(-minded) Women

The Shapes Charlotte Cushman Wore Onstage

[Charlotte Cushman's] masculine personal appearance entirely
unfitted her for many parts. . . . her true forte is . . . in characters where, roused by passion or incited by some earnest and
long cherished determination, the woman, for the time being,
assumes all the power of manhood.
—Joseph N. Ireland, *Records of the New York Stage*

For a female, her genius is peculiar. The blandishments of the
softer sex have not been her histrionic study, but her masculine
genius aims at the startling expression of violent emotions.
—*Dispatch* (London)

When Charlotte Cushman and her fourteen-year-old maid, Sallie Mercer,
first arrived in England, on 18 November 1844, Charlotte described herself
in a letter to her mother as being "in exile," where her only relief would be
"to get letters from home."[1] But Charlotte had come to England determined to perform—and succeed—on the British dramatic stage, as she had
in the United States. Although she had brought with her seventy letters of
introduction and found "on arriving at the hotel here that Macready had
sent . . . three times to see if I had arrived," Charlotte was apprehensive and
lonely. Pleased overall with Charlotte's performance during his successful
tour in the United States, Macready was inviting her to perform with him
in Paris. But his company included the beautiful, popular British actress
Helena Faucit, and Macready told Cushman that, as he was playing opposite Faucit, he could not promise her starring roles, but at least she could
make a beginning. Charlotte, however, had determined that to be successful she must debut in nothing but a leading role, all of which were presumably going to Faucit, so she refused. Although finances were certainly a concern, Charlotte had the resolve, and the ambition, to hold out for the best.

She turned down the eminent British tragedian's offer and chose instead to accept an invitation to visit Scotland with the Blisses, the American couple she had met on shipboard.

Throughout Scotland Charlotte was received at the homes of the most socially prominent citizens. As she knew, acceptance into elite social circles could only help her career, and she cultivated those associations she made. With pride Charlotte wrote her mother that she had been treated "like a princess" by people who lived in "such splendor" and "elegance of manner . . . the right kind of people to make me in every way respected."[2] After the trip she headed to London to try to arrange an opportunity to demonstrate her talents before British audiences, aiming, as she had in the United States, to secure both respectability and professional success. Charlotte had to chart her course of action carefully. She was an *actress,* a member of a profession as largely considered disreputable in England as in the United States because of the sexual license and freedom many equated with the lifestyle of a female performer. Yet, as America's leading breeches actress, Charlotte's performance of gender in her portrayal of male characters, while within the conventions of the nineteenth-century stage, illustrated the fluidity of discrete gender roles. And, the twenty-eight-year-old actress was an *American.* Americans of both sexes were seen as the personification of the youthful vigor and "muscularity" of their proud, young nation.[3] On this side of the Atlantic each of these variables would continue to shape Charlotte's choices and the ways she would come to be seen by others.

But at first, despite her notices and letters, Charlotte could not secure a starring engagement with any of the managers to whom she applied in England, so she did travel to Paris. Macready was still performing with Faucit, but he had begun to think that Faucit was undermining him, so he offered Charlotte some "leading business." Although she later claimed that she refused because she "disdained to build her own promotion on the downfall of another,"[4] Charlotte may have determined that replacing the popular, beautiful, and socially prominent Helena Faucit might alienate her from, rather than endear her to, British audiences.[5]

Charlotte returned to London without having performed at all. Her American colleague Edwin Forrest, eager to fuel the growing competition between himself and his British rival, Macready, was looking for acting work in England, hoping to repeat the success of his 1835–36 tour and challenge the British actor on his own turf, as he felt Macready had challenged him in the United States. In London J. M. Maddox, theatrical manager of the Princess Theatre, was booking performers for the new theater that he had assumed control of the previous year. Eager to build an audience, he hired Forrest for a run. Cushman had also applied to Maddox for work. But, as Maddox later told actor George Vandenhoff, when Charlotte Cushman had first approached the British manager for work, he refused, thinking she was not attractive enough to be a successful actress, despite her many letters of introduction and recommendation. Vandenhoff admired Charlotte's spirit and "pluck," as he called it, for Maddox told him that, when Charlotte turned to leave Maddox's office after being turned down, she suddenly threw herself on the floor like a quintessential melodramatic heroine and, raising her clenched fist shuddered, "I know I have enemies in this country, but so help me—! I'll defeat them!"[6]

According to Peter Brooks, "melodrama is more than a genre; it is a mode of conception and expression."[7] Charlotte used such public and everyday life performances of gestures of excess and overstatement to make sense of her experience and present it to others. In her outburst she drew upon the ambivalent attitudes many Britons held toward Americans—likening their former colonists either to rebellious children or independent thinkers, uncultured "savages" or powerful democratic idealists. These complex attitudes could fill theaters with interested spectators eager to see for themselves what an American woman might accomplish on the stage. Based upon her "performance" of earnest determination and desperation in his office, Maddox reconsidered Charlotte's ability to move an audience. This, coupled with his need to secure a costar for Edwin Forrest, apparently led Maddox to her door the following morning. Ever watchful of Charlotte's interests, Sallie Mercer, standing at the window, had observed Maddox pacing in front of their lodgings very early in the day. Speculating that he might be waiting to call upon her with an offer, Charlotte reportedly concluded that, since Maddox seemed "anxious, I can make my own terms."[8] And she did. She agreed to play opposite Forrest only if she could debut *without* him, the evening before, in a play of her own choice. As a shrewd businesswoman, she was aware that the novelty of the two Americans performing together in London would probably draw a British audience, but she did not want her success seen as dependent upon Forrest's support. If she proved herself successful on her own terms, Charlotte—who was by now fiercely and openly competitive with her male colleagues—would not be "second" to anyone. Although it is impossible to verify these stories of Charlotte's first British engagement, they illustrate how her temerity was rewarded.[9]

The narratives Charlotte told and authorized were constructions, shaped in response to dominant values of the time and repeated later in the press or by Charlotte herself to account for the very choices that exceeded conventional life scripts available to most women in her era. Charlotte was on the verge of becoming an icon for many of her contemporaries, a personification of the changing and contradictory messages about performers, about middle-class respectability, about women, about women performers, about women who loved other women, about Americans. And now, in England, her career would come to fruition. The roles that Charlotte Cushman played in Britain not only brought her acclaim; they also drew on and called into question beliefs about gender, sexuality, nationality, power. What did Charlotte, onstage, come to signify for her first British audiences? In this chapter I explore the major female characters Charlotte Cushman portrayed throughout her career, starting with her first British performances. Since Charlotte's performance of gender was a noteworthy feature in her characterizations and a significant component of her audience's response to her, I will discuss separately, in chapter 5, the male characters Charlotte portrayed.

Bianca

Actor Lawrence Barrett has identified Lady Macbeth, Romeo, Queen Katharine, and Meg Merrilies as Charlotte Cushman's great characters.[10] Of the almost 190 characters that she portrayed throughout her career, she performed these 4 the most often. But for her debut in England Charlotte selected the part of Bianca in Henry Hart Milman's *Fazio*. She had only one opportunity before performing opposite Edwin Forrest to demonstrate what she could accomplish on her own, and in this part she succeeded famously. As the critic from the London *Sun* proclaimed:

> Since the memorable first appearance of Edmund Kean in 1814, never has there been such a debut on the boards of an English theatre. She is, without exception, the very finest actress we have. True, we have *lady-like,* accomplished finished artistes, but there is a wide gulf between them and Miss Cushman—the gulf that divides talent, even of the highest order, from genius.[11]

Charlotte had chosen the play that would introduce her to the British audiences and press wisely. She needed to appear in a part that would gain her British audience's sympathy and respect. Melodramas, according to Peter Brooks, reach their climax by making the world "morally legible"; the signs spectators "read" and recognize in the expressionistic vehicles of actors' bodies serve as unambiguous renderings of characters' virtue or villainy.[12] At the time of Charlotte's British debut, *Fazio* was an established melodramatic standard in which Fazio, a poor, ambitious, unscrupulous man, steals the gold of a "rascally old usurer" who has died accidentally. At first Fazio's wife, Bianca, shares in his ill-gotten wealth, but, when Fazio is unfaithful to her and turns his attentions to the beautiful Aldabella, Bianca denounces her husband as a thief.

Fazio exploited one of the key motifs of melodrama: the audience's witnessing of characters' discovery and recognition of the moral universe of the play unfolding before them. Charlotte masterfully conveyed Bianca's dawning realization of her husband's unfaithfulness. "The early part of the play affords an audience no criterion of what an actress can do," claimed the critic from the *Times*, "but from the instant where she suspects that her husband's affections are wavering, and with a flash of horrible excitement exclaims, 'Fazio, thou hast seen Aldabella!' Miss Cushman's career was certain."[13]

Yet for all her vengeful jealousy Bianca does not want her husband to be executed for his crimes. To save him from that fate she sacrifices her pride and sinks, "'huddled into a heap' at the feet of her rival, imploring [Aldabella] to save the life of Fazio."[14] Written by a respected minister and Oxford don, the play offered Charlotte as Bianca, the wronged wife, an opportunity to demonstrate what the *Times* called "her power to dart from emotion to emotion with the greatest rapidity, as if carried on by impulse alone."[15] By turns Bianca is rejected, tender, jealous, remorseful, and despairing, and Charlotte literally threw herself into an intense display of agonizing emotional virtuosity.

As an experienced performer, Charlotte knew that her face and body would be scrutinized and commented upon. But moving an audience in the emotional tour-de-force of *Fazio* would not depend on "ladylike talent," or conventional attractiveness. As the spurned wife whose husband has betrayed her for her more attractive rival, Charlotte's "unfeminine" physical appearance could be made to work to her advantage. Commending the intensity of Charlotte's melodramatic performances, the reviewer from the *English Gentleman* noted that Charlotte "so thoroughly identifies herself with the part entrusted to her as to entirely overcome disadvantages, which, to an individual less gifted, might mar the intended effect. We allude to the lady's personal appearance. Her face and figure are not, by any means favorable to her success." Despite the compliment to her talent, this blunt assessment of her appearance must have disturbed Charlotte; in her scrapbook copy of this review she had crossed out "by any means."[16]

Yet in Charlotte's case, with British audiences as well as American, "feminine" beauty would ultimately be considered less valuable than "masculine" intellect; the same anonymous critic claimed:

> The intelligence which beams in her face banishes every thought of "plainness." We are carried away by the superiority of mind over matter— ... acknowledging no influence, but that of intellect. The charms of form and feature ... are for those who possess nought else, while Miss Cushman, with a single-handed but all-powerful genius, needs no such corporeal and questionable auxiliaries.[17]

Thus, paradoxically for Charlotte, the *absence* of feminine attractiveness in both her personal aspect and in the part she played was, rather than a detriment, read by this reviewer as a sign that she possessed *more than* "auxiliary" "charms of form and feature." Feminine attractiveness was located exclusively in the body, and, while more immediately discernible to an audience, it was considered of lesser value than Charlotte's intellectual qualities and the province of the mind. There were, of course, a few negative voices, criticizing Charlotte's "inelegancies" and "mannerisms" as Bianca, but these were the exception.[18] Spectators who could see beyond surface appeal recognized Charlotte's value.[19]

The day after Charlotte's debut, manager Maddox appeared at her door again, now with a note of congratulations and newspapers filled with the critics' glowing reviews. Most laudatory was the critic from the *Sun*, who wrote: "America has long owed us a heavy debt for enticing away from us so many of our best actors. She has now more than repaid it by giving us the greatest of actresses, Miss Cushman."[20] Charlotte wrote to her mother of her *"brilliant* and *triumphant* success in London . . . far far beyond [her] most *sanguine expectations!"* and sent newspaper clippings that "could tell . . . in much better language than [she] could" how well she had been received. *"No American has ever succeeded as I have,"*[21] Charlotte bragged. She proudly shared the reactions she received from the British critics and spectators, who treated her "with much more kindness than [she] ever was [treated] at home."[22] In fact, within two years of her debut Charlotte's new friend, British novelist Geraldine Jewsbury, would publish her novel, *The Half Sisters,* which featured an actress named Bianca, based largely on Charlotte.[23]

Why were the British so receptive to Charlotte's Bianca? In the critical responses that she received, ideologies of nationalism, class, and gender were consistently invoked. It was at this time that modern notions of nationalism first emerged, and class-identified manners, morals, and gender-inflected interpretations of behavior were changing significantly. As Eve Sedgwick describes, throughout this period these "critical nodes of culture" were being "definitively reshaped."[24] In her interpretation of the character of the passionate Italian Bianca, Charlotte Cushman—the American, the foreigner—was rewarded for her intense emotional expression and her paroxysms of despair, even though such violent sentiments were not commonly displayed by "proper" Englishwomen.

For British critics Charlotte's vehement expressiveness as Bianca was conflated with her identity as an American; Bianca's heightened emotionalism was acceptable largely *because* Charlotte was American. Although the critic from the *Dispatch* felt that Charlotte was "without the means of fascinating an audience by the display of feminine tenderness[,] . . . the Rembrandtish relief of her soul-torturing passion throws almost into the shade the gentle traits which adorn the female character."[25] Once again Charlotte's characterizations—while not gentle and feminine—were likened to masterpieces of pictorial representation, to genius. Other actresses had played Bianca successfully, but Charlotte's interpretation was remarkable because such forceful, masculine emotional displays were unusual for a female artist. And, curiously, it was Charlotte's "*masculine* genius," as the London *Dispatch* described it some years later, that was believed responsible for her "startling expression of violent emotions" in this role.[26] The writer from the *Dispatch* recorded that "the violence of her excitement, and the mental anguish produced by its effect, caused the blood to rush through the veins, the heart to beat with sympathy."[27]

Just as Charlotte's body was "read" by spectators looking for indications of her character, critics' physical responses to the melodramatic spectacles they witnessed were frequently their barometer of a performer's success. Watching Charlotte play Bianca moved her spectators to experience the thrills and horrors they witnessed as bodily sensations. For playwright John Westland Marston, in the audience for Charlotte's first London performance, her Bianca was unforgettable, from her "display of the passion of jealousy writhing under the torture of betrayal . . . to that [point] when the doom of the husband she has adored and betrayed arrests and petrifies her, till horror subsides in death, her performance carried away the spectators by a torrent of emotion."[28] Actor John Coleman remembered sitting languidly in the stage box during the first two acts of *Fazio* and then suddenly being stunned by Charlotte's tone, look, and action in the third act. "A mist rose before my eyes; a thrill, half-pleasure, half-pain, passed through the spinal column; a lump rose in my throat; and I sat shivering and shuddering till the fatal bell, which heralded the death of Fazio, sounded the death-knell of his hapless wife."[29] Coleman, moved to tears, rose to his feet cheering and waving his handkerchief. Charlotte had thawed the iceberg, hypnotizing the "insolent" young actor who had initially regarded her dismissively from the audience. Whenever she played this role, Charlotte would garner her audiences' sympathy for Bianca—a sympathy they projected onto her as well.

In later years Charlotte continued to play Bianca, although *Fazio* itself increasingly suffered from judgments of "bad morals and false sentiment"; its moral universe was becoming troubling to spectators who questioned the absence of purely virtuous motives and behaviors in any of the characters. After all, it was Bianca's vengeful jealousy that led her to turn her husband over to the authorities. And seeing the wronged and repentant wife prostrating herself before her husband's mistress was unsettling for some audiences. By 1854, when new popular expectations for women's emotional display were gaining favor, some critics would not only question the virtue of Bianca's character but suggest, as did the reviewer from the *Morning Post,* that Charlotte's performance of the part, while "generally excellent," would benefit from some toning down. "A little more *feminine* softness, pathos, and naturalness would have improved her delivery of certain passages." Although Charlotte excelled in "vigour and phrenetic ebullitions . . . her poetic fury might well have been slightly mitigated."[30]

Whether appreciated or criticized, from the time of her first British performance Charlotte's emotional displays onstage—the intense, fervent depictions of powerful feelings—were generally read as masculine attributes. The self-directed agency of a desiring character, rather than the gentle portrayals of traits that might please others, became Charlotte's hallmark on- and offstage. Satisfied with the largely positive reactions she received, Charlotte followed her initial triumph in February 1845 with the supporting parts she had agreed to perform with Edwin Forrest.

Americans Abroad

Two days after her successful British debut Charlotte played the secondary role of Emilia to Edwin Forrest's *Othello.* Again, happily, the English press commended her work. Forrest, however, was treated mercilessly by reviewers who would repeatedly compare the two American performers. The *Times'* reviewer criticized Forrest's "sudden and impetuous bursts" and "that slowness of enunciation which, we have heard, is customary in the United States."[31] With a decided anti-American and classist bias, the critic from the *Examiner* reviewing Forrest's Othello claimed: "Mr. Forrest cannot appreciate, even if he understands, the language . . . of the bard of Avon; his reading was defective in every line, and betrayed an ignorance, . . . disgraceful and distressing." Forrest's pronunciation was filled with "vulgarisms" that would be "unpardonable on the boards of a provincial theatre," the critic complained: "If this American mummer be engaged to pamper the vitiated taste for witnessing foreign performers, the public are in fault for supporting such absurdity."[32] Although the reviews in the *Examiner* were unsigned, they are almost definitely the work of one of Macready's dearest friends, critic and editor John Forster. Forster, in addition to being the dramatic critic for the *Weekly Examiner* and later its editor, was an essayist, historian, loyal friend to Macready, and amateur actor. In a conflation of class, national, and ethnic chauvinism Forster described Forrest's Othello, in which the actor apparently used ochre body paint, as having "more the appearance of a Red Indian than a Moor," asserting that Forrest "has been flattered and encouraged by his own ignorant, ill-judging countrymen, who know no more of Shakespeare than of Hebrew or Sanskrit, and who mistake rapt and outrageous gestures for expression and feeling." Yet of Charlotte Cushman—one of those *same* countrypeople—the same reviewer stated, "It is impossible to speak too highly."[33] If most Americans were ignorant, vulgar, "savage," Charlotte was the exception.

The reviewer from the *English Gentleman* went even further, describing Cushman's success "such as no other American ever merited" and claiming that it took audiences of *British* sensibilities to appreciate her talents—"for that lady's abilities have never been appreciated on the other side of the Atlantic." He went on to contend that Americans were "slow to discover anything approaching real genuine and native genius among [their] dramatic sons and daughters."[34] Not only were most Americans not thought up to the standards Charlotte displayed; they were considered incapable of perceiving or valuing her strengths. The American actress's newfound acclaim with British audiences was curiously enlisted as evidence of the superiority of *British* taste and sensibility, over that of its former colony.

Complimenting Charlotte by raising her above her countrypeople, critics also drew upon her as a refutation of gender stereotypes. In the popular press Charlotte Cushman was commended throughout her first British season for the masculine "intelligence and force"[35] of her performances as well as the excellence of her "thorough comprehension of [Shakespeare]" and her "clear, distinct, and sustained utterance," qualities generally marked for, or indicative of, class privilege, particularly to the British. Yet, as popular as she was becoming with the British, Charlotte saw herself as fundamentally American, and she wanted to be acclaimed on *both* continents. "The very idea of being thought so much of here will make me much more valuable at home,"[36] she wrote to her mother after these first few performances, never imagining how prophetic those words would prove to be.

With her professional success came much welcome social approbation. In a whirl of parties and glittering receptions after these first performances, she was toasted and cheered—as much for what she represented to those who conflated the actress with the parts she played as for herself. In each of her major roles Charlotte Cushman was seen to embody a constellation of gender, national, and class identifications for her audiences. Each of these factors would contribute to the complex construction of Charlotte's personae on- and offstage and challenge spectators' established attitudes about any one of these interrelated elements. From her first weeks in Britain Charlotte wrote to her sister, "I have been introduced into some of the best society in London and am fitting in famously."[37] Charlotte's American male costar did not fit in, however, socially or professionally. As the embodiment of the vigorous, physical, democratic common-man-as-hero, Forrest did not fit the particular image of masculinity expected by British audiences, particularly when he appeared in their most revered canonical texts: the plays of Shakespeare. As Charlotte confided in a letter home, Forrest "failed most dreadfully" in the second major play they attempted together, *Macbeth*. "In *Macbeth* they shouted with laughter and hissed him [Forrest] to death. . . . The papers cut him all to pieces." Always conscious of her reputation, Charlotte added, "but don't say this from me—*it would sound badly*."[38] Especially since her portrayal of Lady Macbeth was such a triumph.

Lady Macbeth

Charlotte's first dramatic success in 1836 had been as Lady Macbeth, and this was one of the roles with which she would be identified for the rest of her career. When British actor James Barton had first helped her prepare for this role at the St. Charles Theatre in New Orleans, a decade before her London debut, he recognized in Cushman's interpretation a very different conception of the part than that of the esteemed Sarah Siddons, the late beloved "queen" of the British stage and aunt of Charlotte's friend Fanny Kemble Butler. In her essay on Siddons, Charlotte's new friend, critic Anna Jameson, had discussed the earlier actress's "feminine grace and grandeur" and the "magnificence of her deportment," particularly as she glided through Lady Macbeth's sleepwalking scene.[39]

Performing opposite Edwin Forrest in her first English season, Charlotte Cushman, now known as the "American Siddons," was to give her own characteristically forceful and physically vigorous interpretation of the part. Unlike Sarah Siddons's fair, feminine, even fragile Lady Macbeth, Cushman appeared "robust; . . . her performance of Lady Macbeth was masculine, and she governed her pliant lord . . . by the force of a superior will rather than by blandishment or personal attractions."[40] Even so, the British audiences who saw Forrest and Cushman in *Macbeth* in March 1845 lauded her fresh interpretation.

Charlotte's Lady Macbeth was commanding and imperious from the start of the play. She entered, reading the letter from Macbeth, and took her text literally; in an attempt to "lay" her husband's letter "to [her] heart," she placed the missive into the bodice of her gown. With her stern jaw set against any opposition, she was implacable. As he had with Charlotte's display of emotional intensity in the characters of Bianca and Emilia, critic William Winter later felt that "whenever the occasion arrived for liberated power, passionate feeling, poetic significance, dramatic effect, she rose to that occasion and made it superb."[41] In Lady Macbeth Charlotte performed with the broad strokes of her other characterizations, infusing the role with the melodramatic register she brought to all her work. In this signature part she drew upon the resources of her powerful, energetic body and her deep, resonant voice to convey the range of Lady Macbeth's emotions. Winter described her "sinister force," her "thrilling, pitiless tones," as she said, ominously, "He that's coming must be provided for": "[when] with wild, roving inspired glances, . . . she invoked the angels of crime, . . . the blood of the listener was chilled with the horror of her infernal purpose."[42]

As Lady Macbeth, Charlotte greeted Duncan as an equal, to whom, even in their first encounter, she refused to acquiesce. She shrank from Duncan's hand when he offered to lead her into the castle. As the play progressed, she demonstrated Lady Macbeth's "will" and "boldness."[43] In later years Lawrence Barrett, who often performed with Cushman, felt that in this role "her own indomitable purpose was well illustrated in the fine scorn of Lady Macbeth when her vacillating lord hints at failure. She knew not that beast word. Her success was immediate."[44]

In fact, in February 1845, when Forrest played Macbeth opposite Cushman, her success with the British press and public served to highlight the depths of her countryman's failure. While critics described Forrest's Macbeth as "one of the most incomplete, the most unsatisfactory, the most inconclusive performances at present known to the higher drama of this country,"[45] Charlotte was extolled for her "boldness" and "zeal." As with their reviews of *Othello*, the more elitist English critics were particularly dismissive of what they regarded as the violence of Forrest's emotional displays coupled with his noticeably American pronunciation. To British ears attuned to associating class privilege, education, and intellect with particular accents and speech patterns, Forrest sounded uncouth. After very few performances "the tragedy was not announced for repetition, probably on account of the general disapprobation that Mr. Forrest's peculiarities elicited, in spite of the unanimous applause awarded to Miss Cushman."[46]

Yet *both* performers were large, forceful, emotionally expressive, and American. In Forrest's display of heroic virility—a quality he brought to all of his performances—he personified and articulated a particularly *American* democratic and rugged individualistic ideal of masculinity and one he was eager to distinguish from the British representations of refined and decorous gentility. As a champion of "indigenous" American values, Forrest cultivated heroic roles like Spartacus and the "Native" American Metamora, roles that epitomized his muscular bravado.[47]

Charlotte Cushman was also seen as a "virile" American, given to intense and melodramatic emotional displays. As positively as she had been received in the United States, the occasional negative criticisms had invariably focused on her "unfeminine" demeanor or her large body size. Although more spectators supported and enjoyed her bold characters than had dismissed her, some of Cushman's male costars had reacted negatively to her and would continue to, particularly when she played Lady Macbeth. Actor George Vandenhoff complained that she bullied Macbeth instead of delicately chiding him into action. Vandenhoff, who described Charlotte's Lady Macbeth as "too animal" because of her reliance on her "physical energy," wrote in his memoir that, "as one sees her large clenched hand and muscular arm threatening him, in alarming proximity, one feels that if other arguments fail with her husband, she will have recourse to blows."[48] Similarly, Edwin Booth would later remark to friends that, when her Lady Macbeth urged his Macbeth on to murder, he felt like crying out: "Why don't you kill him? You're a great deal bigger than I am."[49] Charlotte's strength, power, and physicality in her female roles were inevitably contrasted not only with other women's portrayals of these roles but also with the performances of her *male* costars, most of whom were taken aback at such direct challenge to their physical prowess.

But, if her vigorous manner disturbed those male performers who regarded her as unfeminine, Charlotte had, likewise, a cause to complain. She would later tell William Winter, "The actors who come on for Macbeth are usually such little men I have to look down at them." Winter took this remark to mean that the actors were not just of small stature "but that their presentment of the great part was, to her apprehension, puny."[50] Macready was the one actor whom Cushman felt really understood the part. Not only did they have a similar conception of the play—seeing Macbeth and Lady Macbeth as literally drunk with power—but Charlotte Cushman was even said to resemble her British former costar in talent as well as appearance (see, e.g., the illustrations on pp. 62–63). Forrest was not pleased.

Although Forrest was large, imposing, and rugged, even an actor of his size and strength was resentful of Cushman's tall and indomitable Lady Macbeth. Charlotte Cushman was a woman with the audacity to be as powerful as he, and now it appeared that the British public preferred her interpretations to his. In fact, her reception so overshadowed his that he held her personally responsible and was never to forgive her. He went so far as to allege that she must be plotting with Macready against him. The enmity between the two American performers became so severe that Charlotte resolved never to act with him again. A few months later, in Edinburgh— where Forrest was again a commercial failure—the indignant Forrest described Cushman to a fellow actor as "an epicene thing . . . hideous as Sycorax," "a Macready in petticoats." Forrest regarded her success as "an outrage upon common sense and his nationality."[51] In later years Forrest witnessed a production of *Macbeth* starring Charlotte Cushman and Edwin Booth. When Charlotte, as the sleepwalking Lady Macbeth, said, "All the perfumes of Arabia will not sweeten this little hand," Forrest remarked

Charlotte Cushman as Lady Macbeth. Actual photographs of
Cushman as Lady Macbeth reveal even more clearly than
artists' renderings Cushman's large physique, which prompted
Forrest's spiteful comment that her hand was "as big as a
codfish." In this photograph the chinstrap of Lady Macbeth's
crown almost resembles a beard, thus giving more ammuni-
tion to those critics who damned Cushman as "epicene." *(Harvard Theatre Collection. Houghton Library.)*

spitefully—and loud enough for other audience members to hear—"Little hand! Why it's as big as a codfish."[52]

Charlotte's choice to portray a forceful rather than feminine Lady Macbeth was guided by her body as much as by her temperament. And her body shaped others' reactions to her. Years later, interviewing Charlotte for the *Boston Journal,* Mrs. J. A. Hanaford reported being "engrossed . . . as the blaze of those dark eyes flashed out from beneath that noble and over-arching brow." Charlotte's "whole physique spoke of energy" to Hanaford, who "drank in eagerly her every word."[53] At five feet six inches—quite tall by nineteenth-century standards—Charlotte was actually taller than many of the men who played opposite her. Although for some fellow actors and audience alike it was hard to accept such a large, ambitious woman dominating her male costar with the force of her body and her will, for others, particularly *female* spectators, this was the quality that most drew their admiration and, occasionally, desire. Throughout their lives women who, like feminist publisher and orator Emily Faithfull, experienced their own passionate connections to other women would continue to find themselves "spellbound" by Charlotte's "powerful intellect and passionate nature, combined with her personal magnetism and wonderful, deep-toned voice" in parts like Lady Macbeth.[54]

For her first British audiences the very forceful "masculine" elements Charlotte brought to her interpretation of this character were accepted because they were seen to reflect her identity as an *American.* There, to audiences for whom Americans were already regarded as peculiar, rebellious, passionate and, in the words of her contemporaries, "queer" or "weird," Charlotte's so-called masculine qualities were not merely an acceptable *violation* of gender expectations on the part of a great actress but, rather, a *reinforcement* of a particular variety of national identity the British had come to expect—and what they had come to the theater to see—and so played a significant part in her extraordinary popular success. Part of the "spectacle" Charlotte Cushman provided her British audiences was the opportunity of witnessing "foreigners" on their stage. In the minds of many Britons power, forcefulness, and virility were equated with America, and Americans of both sexes were assumed to represent, in their bodies and bearing, the independence, physicality, and forthrightness of their nation.[55]

If Charlotte Cushman was, to some extent, celebrated by the British for her masculine attributes, how do we account for the negative reactions of the British press to the hypermasculine Forrest? Historian George L. Mosse has explored some of the ways that bourgeois respectability and sexual mores came to be allied with nationalism. Mosse contends that in nineteenth-century England "manliness" was equated with "the restraint and the self-control so dear to the middle class. Manliness, for the British, "meant freedom from sexual passion, the sublimation of sensuality into leadership of society and nation; . . . not just a matter of courage, it was a pattern of manners and morals . . . exemplified [in] the transcendence of the so-called lower passions."[56] Forrest—"democratic," explosive, unrestrained—appeared vulgar and uncouth, rather than "manly," to British audiences. Cushman, on the other hand, was seen as chaste and respectable as well as powerfully masculine. So, in labeling her "manly," British critics were implying that she lived up to the genteel, intellectual, and stalwart self-control of British ideals, although she was a woman. Since she was an American, they would not hold her up to British standards of "femininity," and, since she was an actress, they might have expected uncouth, loose morals—so her lack of vulgarity and women's "lower passions" made her appear manly.

While both performers were seen as vigorously emotional, muscular Americans, Cushman, unlike Forrest, was not only considered intellectual but also moral and dignified. During this first British tour one critic assured his readers that Charlotte Cushman was "an esteemed member of the Unitarian congregation at Philadelphia" and so their "moral taste, instead of being offended . . . will be improved by the parts she assumes."[57] In her bearing, in her voice, even in her lack of interest in heterosexual passions, Charlotte seemed to epitomize a perfect blend of middle-class British manners and forceful American initiative.

Articulation was one of the identifiable markers of both intellect and prestige for many Britons. Although many British critics did not feel that the new American actress was quite up to the standards Sarah Siddons had set as Lady Macbeth, nonetheless Charlotte was complimented for the clarity of her "utterances" and her comprehension of the play. In other words, her speech wasn't marked by the American accent that so marred Forrest's delivery. Charlotte, an excellent mimic and quick study, had "fallen into" British "habits of articulation and enunciation" from her very first performance as Lady Macbeth in 1836. When British actor James Barton had coached Charlotte in New Orleans for that performance, he modeled the speech patterns that would do her great stead in the years to come. Later, performing opposite Macready in the United States had reinforced Charlotte's notions of effective stage delivery.[58] So, by the time she appeared before British audiences, each of the papers that mentioned Forrest's overdrawn pauses and faulty articulation spoke positively of Charlotte and commended her for her decorum, vocal restraint, and "intellect"—the very class-inflected qualities they found lacking in Forrest. The same critic who accused Forrest of mangling and murdering Shakespeare with his mispronunciations "regret[ted] that Mr. Forrest has not taken a few hints from his accomplished countrywoman." As an example, the reviewer noted Charlotte's "very judicious alteration on the common mode of reciting . . . 'Out! Out! damn'd spot!' " Most actresses emphasized the *damn'd*, but Cushman, "by pronouncing the last syllable at full length and raising the voice . . . converted a profane expression, not likely to fall from the lips of a lady . . . into one of fervent remorse of conscience."[59]

And Charlotte Cushman wanted to be seen as a lady, albeit an androgynous one. Because she knew that her professional advancement was tied to social success offstage, she cultivated societal acceptance. "One cannot be too careful of popular interest," Charlotte confided to James Murdoch years later.[60] Throughout her career reviewers discussed her conception of Lady Macbeth in terms of accepted standards of nineteenth-century middle-class womanly behavior. In later years Cushman's American critics would increasingly grapple with the "masculinity" of her interpretation and try to justify her choices. A critic for the *Chicago Times* would claim that "it is the intense love of a wife for her husband, her woman's ambition for *his* supreme greatness," that motivated this "powerful," "resolute" portrayal of Lady Macbeth. After Duncan's murder "what strength remains is consecrated to the purest womanly purpose, ignoring herself entirely."[61] One of Charlotte's contemporary biographers would claim that when Lady Macbeth asks, "How now my lord, why do you keep alone?," and pleads, "Come on, gentle my lord," she demonstrated "loving tenderness and solicitude," which "relieved" the "masculine elements" in her interpretation.[62] Similarly, while in the early scenes of *Macbeth* it appeared to critic Henry Augustin Clapp that Charlotte's Lady Macbeth was motivated purely by her own ambition, he claimed that as the play progressed "Miss Cushman represent[ed] the womanly nature of Lady Macbeth as succumbing in anguish before her own conscience, while her whole heart is turned in tender compassion to the suffering of her husband."[63] In an era when being womanly meant "succumbing" and "ignoring oneself entirely," rather than being ambitious, for Charlotte's Lady Macbeth to appear to uphold conventional values, her own self-directed agency had to be mitigated, explained away, or reconfigured so as to support a conventional patriarchal marital relationship.

Not everyone was willing to accept Charlotte's strong-willed Lady Macbeth even on those terms, however. In a review of Charlotte's 1858 American tour, Forrest's intimate friend, journalist James Oakes, wrote a particularly dismissive review of her characterization. According to Oakes, although Charlotte's depiction was a "startling piece of acting, and has gained for her much fame, both in Europe and in this country," it was "not in accordance with [his] conception of the character."[64] What he objected to was not merely the power and masculinity of Charlotte's Lady Macbeth but the impossibility of reading Charlotte—and hence, her character—as a woman capable of, or motivated by, heterosexual love.

> It would seem necessary that a woman should gain the love and affection of a man before she could have the influence over him that Lady Macbeth exercised over her husband . . . [but] instead of inspiring love in the heart of a man, the Lady Macbeth of Miss Cushman would excite quite a different passion, as she seems to bully Macbeth into the commission of the murder of Duncan, and divests the character of all those little womanly characteristics which is [sic] innate to the nature of the gentler sex.[65]

Yet Oakes intimated that such characteristics were *not* "innate" in Charlotte, a woman with no known attachments to men. Like Charlotte, Oakes felt "Shakespeare's Lady Macbeth is an ambitious woman, with extraordinary intellectual powers." But, unlike Charlotte, Lady Macbeth, "having been a mother," Oakes alleged, "must have possessed some tenderness of feeling and gentleness of disposition, neither of which is very apparent in Miss Cushman's interpretation of the character."[66] In this thinly veiled attack on what he implied was Charlotte's own "disposition," Oakes raised the specter of the "unnaturalness" of Charlotte's lack of so-called tender characteristics.

Both her supporters and her detractors conflated Charlotte with the characters she played. Much of Charlotte's abiding success as Lady Macbeth was due to what William Winter called "the infusion of her own great personality into the character." Fans like Winter saw in Charlotte's characterization "the regal mind, the indomitable will, the burning passion, the colossal courage,"[67] and saw these traits as belonging *both* to Charlotte Cushman *and* to Lady Macbeth. As Lady Macbeth, Charlotte had the opportunity to portray a woman of strength and ambition. In 1845 one of her earliest British critics claimed that "there is much in the constitution of [Charlotte's] mind to fit her for the part."[68] While her power and will may not have been feminine, they were appropriately "regal" and, therefore, in keeping with her character. And the emotional intensity and thrills Charlotte brought to her personification of the murderous, ambitious monarch was a consistent feature in the melodramas and sensation plays audiences were flocking to see.

Charlotte's Lady Macbeth was described as "melodrama 'in excelsis'" by critic John Ranken Towse,[69] and it was *as* melodrama that Charlotte exceeded the conventional boundaries of gender. Charlotte was not unique in performing Shakespeare as a melodrama, but critics were particularly responsive to her efforts.[70] For Towse her "Lady Macbeth was a splendid virago, more than masculine in ambition, courage and will, more bloody, bold, and resolute than she wished her husband to be. She was the source and mainspring of the whole tragedy. She was inhuman, terrible, incredible, and horribly fascinating."[71] Small wonder then, that British playgoers would be equally responsive to Charlotte in the part she had most made her own—Meg Merrilies.

Meg Merrilies

Despite the popularity of her Shakespearean roles, Charlotte Cushman was to be most strongly identified with the part of Meg Merrilies, the Gypsy witch of Sir Walter Scott's *Guy Mannering*. Director George Pierce Baker recalled the effects of having seen Charlotte as Meg when he was a young boy: "I knew the theater first, I think, at the age of six. Then in early but intense recognition of the genius of Charlotte Cushman in Meg Merrilies, I was, for the good of the public, removed shrieking from the theatre."[72]

During the spring of 1845, after Charlotte's first flush of success in England, she realized that, since she was doing so well professionally and would likely not return to America for years, it would help to have her family with her. Besides, her brother, Charlie, "was doing nothing" at home, as she dismissively put it, and could be of service to her in London. At the end of April, when Charlie Cushman arrived in England, he found Charlotte praised as "the greatest creature in the greatest city in the civilized world."[73] As one of his first tasks, Charlie was to represent her, to act as a booking agent of sorts. What she was absolutely certain about that first season was that she would not yet play Romeo. She would wait until her mother and sister arrived from America and then follow her successful first season with a spectacular debut of the Cushman sisters as Romeo and Juliet. So Charlotte was alarmed when Maddox scheduled her as Romeo a season ahead of her plans. She sent Charlie to negotiate a substitution. The one role Charlotte implored him *not* to suggest was Meg Merrilies. Charlotte's social and professional acclaim were dependent upon the seriousness and respectability of her characterizations, and she was not yet sure how Meg would be received in England. But, forgetting her request, Charlie *did* commit her to play Meg. As Charlie Cushman remembered, after his sister's initial dismay her response was, "Well I will do it as it never has been done before." Into the role of the Gypsy queen Charlotte was to infuse all the poignant passion and shuddering death scenes she had employed in the characters of the

Charles Cushman. The only extant photograph of Charlotte
Cushman's brother, Charles, dates from a later period when
Charlotte's financial, critical, and social success had measur-
ably improved the material conditions of the Cushman family.
*(Charlotte Cushman Photo Album. Prints and Photographs Divi-
sion. Library of Congress.)*

betrayed wife Bianca and the downtrodden prostitute Nancy Sykes,
blended with the haughty majesty of her Lady Macbeth. She would create a
sensation.

On the sweltering night of 10 June 1845, toward the end of her first London season, a crowded audience at the Princess Theatre witnessed Charlotte's London debut as Meg. Waiting in the wings, Charlie was relieved
and gratified when he heard "the sounds of acclamations," the screeches of
applause, and saw hats and handkerchiefs waved as the audience went
"almost mad with enthusiasm."[74] By now it appeared to Charlie that most
of the London theatergoing public and the literati had "caught the prevail-

ing epidemic"[75] of a worshipful championing of his sister's talents. Although Charlie was himself caught up in her success, his metaphor of sickness and contagion to account for the responses Charlotte was receiving is very curious. Did he feel that there was something "unhealthy" about the devotion Charlotte's new friends were expressing for her?

British audiences loved Charlotte as the mysterious Gypsy queen. As Sir Walter Scott's creation, she was both *of* them and otherworldly—given leave to assume unusually powerful dimensions and yet sympathetic as the "foreign," caring, maternal figure who watches over the hero. Playwright Westland Marston believed Charlotte "derived her conception from a study of the great novelist himself, and had . . . expanded and raised a sketch of the dramatic version to something like the fulness [*sic*] of Scott's creation in *Guy Mannering*."[76] Madame Eliza Vestris, herself a noted performer and theatrical manager, felt her blood turn cold upon witnessing Cushman as the haggard old woman.[77]

Why did Meg have such a strong impact on spectators? William Winter explained that, as Meg, Cushman was "a veritable incarnation of all that is ominous, fateful and strangely beautiful . . . a vision to register itself at once in the memory and there to remain forever."[78] While Daniel Terry's dramatized version of Scott's novel had been popular since 1816, the character of Meg had never been the fulcrum of the story until Charlotte played it. The part is not a large one, but Charlotte's interpretation highlighted the character out of all proportion to its original importance in the play or novel. Meg Merrilies does not appear until late in the second act; however, from that point on Charlotte's Meg dominated the remainder of the play.

At the opening of *Guy Mannering* the audience learns of the death of Lord Bertram and of the kidnaping and disappearance, twenty years earlier, of Bertram's six-year-old son, Henry. As the melodrama progresses, it becomes apparent that a Gypsy tribe is responsible for the kidnaping of young Henry Bertram. Bertram, who has grown up unaware of his true identity, has escaped and returned to Scotland. The important action of the play commences when Bertram's old Gypsy nurse, Meg Merrilies, appears and recognizes him after he and his friend Dinmont, lost and hungry, wander into a Gypsy camp. A young Gypsy girl has prepared food for them, which they began to eat, thereby focusing the audience's attention on them. Suddenly, apparently out of nowhere, spectators saw a "creature of the ideal world and not of earth." At this moment, unbeknownst to Dinmont and Bertram, Charlotte's Meg sprang onto the stage from a cave in the moonlight and stood "with a towering figure and extended arms, tense, rigid and terribly beautiful, glaring at the form of Henry Bertram."[79] With this entrance Charlotte, in her rags and heavy makeup, startled spectators in England as she had, and would continue to, in the United States.

Geraldine Jewsbury, Charlotte's novelist friend, recalled that from Charlotte's first London performances of the part, "Meg Merrilies, and that strange silent spring to the middle of the stage, which was her entrance on it, can never be forgotten."[80] Charlotte, as Meg, with what actress Kate Reignolds Winslow called her hurricane-like swooping, rushed to the middle of the stage, stopped, and froze in that position, constructing a tableau that suspended the action. "She stood at her topmost height, as it seemed, without drawing her breath. . . . Though the attitude strained every muscle, she was absolutely motionless."[81] Years later William Winter marveled at her sudden projection into the "dusky, romantic stage picture before any except an expert observer could discern whence she came or how she got there."[82] The pictorial effect of Charlotte's abrupt, almost supernatural, entrance and then her dramatic freeze was the essence of melodrama. Peter Brooks has suggested that melodramas are dependent upon heightened moments of visibility and recognition. *Guy Mannering* offered spectators the opportunity to read along with the characters the available clues as the plot unfolded, unearthing the meanings in hidden and obscured details and relationships and participating in the dramatic tension of discovery.

According to Charlotte's promptbook, as Bertram continued to speak, with his back to Meg, unaware of her presence, Meg crept softly a step or two toward him and gazed intently on him. Dinmont, catching sight of Meg, suddenly stopped eating. He tried to distract Bertram from his reverie by kicking him under the table. After a long pause, he said, "But lord, Capt'n . . . did you ever in your life see a woman stand staring as that old gipsey [*sic*] woman has been staring at you?"[83]

Bertram then turned around and saw Meg hovering over him. When he had played Bertram opposite Charlotte seven years earlier, John Braham had "started in sudden fright at the wizened face, the demented eyes glaring at him through shredded grey wisps of hair, the wrinkled chin and twisted bones held rigid."[84] As with Charlotte's American performances as Nancy Sykes, she was not concerned that the audience perceive her as attractive. Instead, she painted on eerie makeup and assumed a crouched gait and quirky mannerisms to produce the startling effects of the old Gypsy. Actress Mary Anderson remembered that Charlotte's audiences were frightened "every whit as much" as Bertram and Dinmont. Charlotte's Meg was "an apparition," an ominously "tall sybil-like figure" with "blazing eyes and snaky locks."[85] With a hollow voice she crooned the lullaby that she had often sung to Bertram as a child, before the kidnaping. Moved by this memory from his childhood, Bertram was bent almost onto the table by the end of Meg's song.

In other productions of this play the actress playing Meg summoned a Gypsy girl to sing the plaintive lullaby. In Charlotte's promptbook there is a note that she delivers this song herself. At the time of her first performance as Meg in America, when Charlotte stepped in at the last minute to play the part, replacing the ill Mrs. Chippendale, she had originally been cast as the Gypsy girl who was called in to sing the lullaby. Since no one had replaced her as the young Gypsy, she had to improvise, and so Charlotte incorporated the song into Meg's role. Her rendition was so successful that she continued to sing the tremulous lullaby whenever she played the part.

After Meg's song she called for another Gypsy to guide Dinmont and Bertram safely on their way. Then, suddenly doubting the guide's trustworthiness, Charlotte's Meg used her robust physical prowess to protect Bertram. Gripping the other Gypsy's arm, Meg literally threw him toward the footlights. Charlotte's authoritative physicality was put to use later in the play as well when the villainous Hatteraick and his gang threatened Bertram. Meg stood over the villains, intimidating them, and asked them once more to "forgo their foul design." When one villain refused, Meg exclaimed, "Bear witness, heaven and earth!" Dramatically, she let her stick fall. To signify Meg's supernatural power, Charlotte threw a little flax dipped in wine onto the fire, which then blazed towards the roof. Meg appeared omnipotent; even the fire obeyed her commands. As soon as she gave this signal, Hatteraick fired his gun at her. Meg staggered forward and fell precisely at center stage. Bertram's friend Dinmont went over to help the dying Meg, who refused his efforts, claiming that she wanted only to see justice done. In virtuous, melodramatic fashion she had sacrificed herself to restore Bertram to his rightful place in the family.

During her protracted death scene Meg suddenly raised herself up and, with her last words, implored the townspeople to shout their repeated acknowledgment of Bertram as lord of Ellangowan. Charlotte's Meg died slowly, with "terrible writhing" and quivering. Some critics considered her death scenes to be in bad taste because they were so shudderingly literal, so extremely realistic.[86] Finally Meg sunk into Dinmont's arms, and he gently bore her offstage.

For some spectators, like Queen Victoria, who attended an 1854 production of *Guy Mannering,* Charlotte's choices to defy expectations of conventional feminine attractiveness were disturbing and incomprehensible. In her diary Queen Victoria noted that, as Meg Merrilies, "Miss Cushman acted in quite a wrong, unconvincing manner. She looked like the most frightful witch in *Macbeth* and was quite hideous to behold."[87] The last time the queen had seen a production of *Guy Mannering* was twenty years earlier, and Charlotte's interpretation was considerably different, especially since she had *intentionally* made herself look "frightful" in this part. The sensations Charlotte Cushman sought to provoke in her audience were horror and pathos.

Charlotte Cushman as Meg Merrilies in *Guy Mannering.*
Cushman's use of makeup and costume led to a portrayal of
Meg Merrilies as a withered crone that shocked and horrified
audiences. *(Harvard Theatre Collection. Houghton Library.)*

For Charlotte's first appearances as Meg she had improvised a costume
of rags. As her success in the role grew, she strengthened her conception of
the part and codified the costume and makeup that, for many, were to
become her trademark. Drawings of Cushman as Meg at different periods
of her career show the evolution of this garment from a simple loose-fitting
shift to an elaborate collection of scraps of material, scarves, and rags that
she collected over the years. From Sallie Mercer's first year as Charlotte's
dresser one of her important tasks was to attend to the mysterious collection of rags and scraps that she fashioned into Meg's vestments. From their
earliest years in England Sallie was "the guardian and custodian" of all
Charlotte's theatrical properties. "She knew to a pin whatever was necessary to each costume, and no matter how many were the changes, nothing
was ever missing."[88] Only Sallie ever knew the secrets of how to put
together what became the famous "Meg" costume. Emma Stebbins later
contended that this apparent bundle of rags assumed an almost majestic
quality on the old Gypsy queen: "Every scrap of it was put together with reference to antecedent experiences—the wind, the storm, the out-door life of

hardship, the tossing and tempering it had received through its long wanderings."[89] Meg's "battered head-dress was arranged in vague and shadowy semblance to a crown," and the gnarled and twisted branch she carried "suggested a scepter" (see, e.g., the illustration on p. 43). Striving for the perfect pictorial effect, Charlotte even took it upon herself to dye the stockings that she wore as Meg so as to attain "the exact tint of age and dirt."[90]

Charlotte was as particular about Meg's makeup as she was her costume. For each performance as the old Gypsy she carefully painted the lines and shadows of age. When asked by a portrait painter how she knew where to draw the lines and creases for such frightening detail, Charlotte responded, "I don't *know*, I only *feel* where they ought to come."[91] The makeup was considered "singularly successful," and, together with her "excessively appropriate voice and manner," it enabled Charlotte to "invest the old weird woman with both power and pathos."[92] In almost all of Charlotte Cushman's portrayals of Meg the last scene of the play was followed by a chorus and finale. During this interval she removed the heavy makeup and gray wig that she wore as Meg. When Charlotte came out for her curtain call "the contrast between the wild, weird, intense face of Meg and the genial aspect of the actress was a veritable sensation."[93]

Although Charlotte may have been loath to admit it, Meg Merrilies was probably her most popular role and her largest financial success. She preferred playing Lady Macbeth, Romeo, and Queen Katharine in *Henry VIII,* but the public continued to clamor for Meg. Charlotte recognized the drawing power of Meg and lamented, "with an outlandish dress and a trick or two, I can bring more money to the theatre than when I give the public my heart's blood in my finest characters."[94]

No matter how crude or coarse Charlotte might feel the role to be, her success as Meg reached cultlike proportions. In later years fans in each city where she played collected as a prized souvenir the staff she wielded as Meg. The character was to become so popular that toward the end of Charlotte's life Augustin Daly would beseech her to take on a New York run in 1874 in a production of *Guy Mannering* in which he would extend Meg's role throughout the play.[95] But Charlotte, ill with breast cancer, refused.

Although Meg was a short part, consisting of less than five hundred words, it was an enormous strain on Charlotte's vocal organs. Her husky, hollow tone of voice, however, made her "capable of effects which few players could duplicate." Late in her career, when she played this character, Cushman would have to resort to constant gargles to keep her from losing her voice completely, a problem that had plagued her since her days as an opera singer. Her vocal work had always been a significant aspect in her performances, but the "weird, prophetic, tones" she employed as Meg were achieved at the price of real physical pain. Charlotte forced her voice to express intense, sustained grief and anger or denunciation,[96] making her voice thicken as though she were dying, crack with advanced age, or sound hollow and despairing. And she used, and abused, her body as well if it would help her characterization. Actress Mary Anderson reported that when Charlotte was still performing, despite her suffering from the ravages of breast cancer, she would strike her breast while playing Meg Merrilies, to enhance the performance with real shrieks of pain.[97] As Meg, from her crooning lullaby to her anguished death scene, Charlotte used her voice and body to further strengthen the character which, according to Lawrence Barrett, "will be forever associated with her name."[98]

Charlotte added to the vocal effects her physical energy. Like the characters of Lady Macbeth and Queen Katharine, Meg possessed an imperious, commanding quality. By her strength of will and conviction as well as her physical prowess, she ruled the Gypsy tribe. Cushman's personal style, as we have seen, was similarly dynamic and imposing.

In other roles Charlotte had been criticized for being too forceful or too emotional or not attractive and feminine enough, but for the character of Meg Merrilies these criticisms did not hold. Charlotte created the old Gypsy as the embodiment of what the critic from the Boston *Prompter* called "all we have seen or known, or had presented to us in the stage or closet—of wild women-crazed prophetesses—strange in attire—sore distraught in spirit—and borne above the common flight of their sex by something demoniac [*sic*] and supernatural."[99] For over thirty years, when Meg died her "horribly realistic," shuddering death, audiences on both continents were wildly enthusiastic.

Queen Katharine

Of all Charlotte Cushman's major roles Queen Katharine in Shakespeare's *Henry VIII* was described as the most "womanly." Near the end of her career a critic from the New York *Herald* claimed that "perhaps in no other of her impersonations has Miss Cushman so happily blended the tenderness and force of womanhood."[100]

As we have seen, the conventional nineteenth-century conception of "true womanhood" called for women to be chaste, pious, and submissive. Being powerful and strong-willed in her own self-representations, Charlotte seemed to contradict the last of these attributes, yet, as the majestic Shakespearean queen, Charlotte was playing a part that could be read either as upholding or calling into question women's submission to men. As with the character of Bianca, Charlotte portrayed in Queen Katharine another tragically wronged woman shunted aside by her husband's voracious appetites and desire for another woman. But, unlike Bianca, this character, who comes to a shattering, melodramatic end, was wholly sympathetic.

The faithful, chaste Katharine has been a good wife, although she failed to produce a male heir. As Henry plots to divorce her, Katharine refuses to be a meek victim but, rather, retains her regal bearing. In this character some critics and spectators read Charlotte's portrayal of Katharine's strength and "indomitable will" as womanly perseverance rather than manly power. The righteous indignation of a good woman wronged was a theme that even the most conservative playgoers might point to as uplifting and instructive: one critic wrote that this role "enables [Charlotte] to show us how a woman of inconquerable spirit and pride, yet of intense sweetness, can behave when overwhelmed in grief and misery."[101]

On 13 October 1847, when Charlotte began playing Queen Katharine opposite Macready as Cardinal Wolsey, it was not hard for her to conjure up images of a woman "overwhelmed in grief." Just months earlier Charlotte had been exhausted from overwork when news of Rosalie Sully's death in the United States reached her. Charlotte plummeted into what she described as "nervous prostration." As we shall see in chapter 6, by this time much in Charlotte's life had changed and other women had come to mean much to her, yet the finality of this loss was overwhelming, and Charlotte undertook a rest cure at Malvern for several weeks.

Queen Katharine was the first major part Charlotte played after her convalescence. In what would become a pattern for her, Charlotte devoted herself to work whenever she felt pain or despair, and so into this new role she poured all her personal grief over Rosalie's death.[102] Charlotte had expressed her concern about her abilities in this part to her new friend, Henry Chorley, the musical critic for the *Athenaeum*. Chorley's friendship, as well as his generous reviews, had come to be a regular feature in Charlotte's London life. After viewing the performance on 28 October, Chorley allayed Cushman's fears. He wrote to her: "You are wholly wrong to fancy that the part does not do you good, and you good to the part. It has given me a higher idea of your powers than any I have yet seen you act[.] I am truly glad for your own sake you played the part."[103] Apparently, Charlotte's audience, other critics, and costar agreed. On 10 July 1848 Macready asked her to repeat the role for his farewell benefit at Drury Lane. This command performance was attended by Queen Victoria and Prince Albert, the Queen Dowager, and other members of the royal family. One critic wrote of Cushman's Queen Katharine: "Not a Queen on earth but could have learned a lesson of dignity and nobility as well as deportment from the modest and truly womanly, yet equally majestic stateliness of her carriage, utterance and act."[104]

As Katharine, Charlotte portrayed a queen and a daughter of a king, "a woman accustomed to command," "vehement for outraged justice." When she appealed to the king on behalf of his subjects, her plea was "grand yet gentle." In later years critics commented on the "righteous fearlessness with which she striked [sic] directly at the potent Cardinal at the root of the mischief."[105] Katharine was a woman who had always behaved honorably and was slow to realize that her husband intended to preempt her in favor of a woman he found more attractive. For Charlotte, Henry's line to Ann Boleyn, "O beauty, till now I never knew thee," had a poignant resonance. Once again Charlotte was playing a plain woman whose husband preferred her more attractive rival.

In Charlotte's depiction the dignified and rejected Queen Katharine was forceful, contemptuous, and fearless as she refused to submit herself to the court of which Cardinal Wolsey, architect of her undoing, was judge. Spectators and critics mention her passion and prideful challenge to authority in this role as most memorable. "With one swift motion of her right arm and pointing forefinger, but without turning her head or body," Charlotte's Katharine challenged her adversary with defiance and scorn—"Lord Cardinal, to *you* I speak"—completely "electrifying" her audience. Clara Erskine Clement declared, "The sudden transition from almost humbleness to imperious command was one of the finest things I have ever witnessed on the stage."[106] George William Bell, an actor friend of Charlotte's, recalled "the sternness of her electric reply to [Wolsey's] entreaty to 'be patient,' 'I will, when you are humble!'"[107]

According to critic William Winter, the quintessential moment in Charlotte's portrayal of Katharine came at the close of the trial scene, "after the heartbreaking delivery of her noble and pathetic appeal to King Henry." As Winter remembered, "I, an auditor, was sitting, alone, in a lower box, almost on the stage. As the Queen turned to make her exit from the trial . . . —she advanced directly toward the box in which I sat, and, looking straight forward . . . seemed to fix her gaze steadfastly upon *me*." When the queen is summoned by one of her attendants, she exclaims indignantly, "When *you* are called, return!" When Cushman delivered this line, "so tremendous was the majesty of her presence and so awful the mingled anguish, dignity and passion in her countenance that, with involuntary motion," Winter said, he "fairly shrunk away to the rear of the box, overwhelmed, astounded and quite oblivious that this was a dramatic performance and not a reality."[108]

Winter responded positively to the power and passion with which Charlotte imbued Katharine. Other critics favored her in this role because for them it confirmed the tragic consequences of "appropriate" female behavior. The critic from the *World* claimed that "the beauty of the trial scene lay not so much in the defiance of a queenly woman as in the dominance of the woman's helplessness . . . the pathos and pitiableness of a *true womanly* nature beset by the artful designers of court were made the dominant notes in the music of her acting."[109] Obviously, not all critics found beauty in "woman's helplessness," but most audience members could empathize with the tragedy of a woman who behaves in ways her society would consider exemplary yet is rejected nonetheless. Advocates of "true womanhood" saw this as a genuine, heartrending tragedy; individuals who found the ideology too restrictive heard in this play the ironic message that passivity and submission do not guarantee a woman the love and admiration she deserves.

The "ghastly realism"[110] of Katharine's death scene afforded Charlotte Cushman's nineteenth-century audiences the vicarious experience of watching a good, "true woman" suffer in melodramatic fashion and still maintain her dignity. Charlotte's graphic portrayal of Katharine's resignation, like her depiction of the queen's moral superiority, was in keeping with contemporary values. As Sarah Stickney Ellis, a popular nineteenth-century author of advice books, counseled, an unhappily married woman must remember that "her highest duty is so often to suffer and be still."[111] And so, as in Charlotte's melodramatic renderings of Meg Merrilies's graphic death scene, as Katharine her suffering was "even painful in its artistic power, leaving the audience almost powerless to express its admiration."[112] Yet Edwin Forrest's friend James Oakes, writing for the *Spirit of the Times*, complained that Charlotte's death scene "thrilled the senses rather than touched the cord of sympathy in the hearts of her audience."[113] Imagining Katharine to be dying of consumption, she had worked up the "business" of the whole scene so that her voice would become increasingly querulous and thick.[114] In Charlotte's hands *Henry VIII* was a sensational melodrama, with all the vehement intensity, rage, pathos, and despair characteristic of the genre.

But, as the suffering queen, Charlotte Cushman was also finally playing a part that could be read as sufficiently feminine to satisfy most of her more conservative critics. Late in her career a reviewer from the *World* asserted that, "unlike the strong masculine outlines" with which Cushman rendered her other major roles, Queen Katharine has "a womanly and noble type of dignity, moderation and kindly virtue." These "feminine revelations" of the actress the writer ascribed to "the softening and ripening influence of a studious experience," thus implying that her feminine demeanor was the result of much time and practice: Charlotte had learned well how to act a woman.[115] As they did with all Charlotte's major roles, critics once again read her onstage persona as a sign of her offstage personality. While for many actresses such a conflation might threaten their social status, in this case Charlotte benefited from the association with her character. A reviewer from the *Daily Advertiser* asserted that "none but a true, noble, and great natured woman could ever give such a rendering of such a part."[116] Another critic claimed to "doubt if there is any woman who treads the stage in queenly robes who can assume with a higher degree of perfection the dignity and majesty of the character."[117]

Nobility and *majesty* are terms that have multiple valences, simultaneously invoking the powerful and privileged state into which one may have been born and an admirable personality trait one may possess. There was about Cushman a sense of personal power that her supporters saw as majestic self-assurance and her detractors saw as dominating, masculine, and haughty. Playwright Westland Marston, who became Charlotte's friend during her first London season, called her "'Captain Charlotte' . . . a designation which her enterprise and straightforwardness had caused some of us to give her in intimate talk."[118] "I can tell you at once the sort of character I should like," Captain Charlotte told Marston, hoping he would write a play for her. "I long to play a woman of strong ambition, who is at the same time very wily and diplomatic, and who has the opportunity of a great outburst when her plans are successful—in short, a female Richelieu."[119] Marston never wrote the play she had in mind, but as Queen Katharine, just as with Bianca, Meg Merrilies, and Lady Macbeth, Charlotte could be both majestic and scornful, dignified and imperious. As British audiences perceived from her first performance, Charlotte was playing a character much like herself; one determined to maintain her power over those around her, to assume a commanding presence regardless of the circumstances, performing her self-possession and fearless perseverance in face of all challenges.

In her portrayal of each of her major female characters Charlotte Cushman was physically strong, agile, intelligent, and often, in the vernacular of her day, "strong-minded." The women she represented onstage knew their own minds and were determined to act accordingly, regardless of the obstacles they faced in the stage worlds they inhabited. I contend that with Charlotte's active physical style, her large body came to be seen as a metonym for her characters' power, rather than an impediment she had to overcome. Unlike contemporary actresses who courted the gaze of male spectators, doing little more than posing, "carry[ing] expensive costumes upon an attractive body, and wander[ing] through a play the subject only of the lorgnette and the eyeglasses,"[120] Charlotte's representations depicted women's agency. As her costar Lawrence Barrett remembered, when Charlotte was "reproached" for her "constant action, which defied repose," she explained that beautiful women might be "content to stand still and be gazed at. But it was not so with herself; she must occupy the eye with action and movement."[121] Because she appeared not to be interested in being "gazed at," Charlotte managed to escape some of the stigma associated with actresses. Friends and acquaintances observed how *unlike* an actress Charlotte appeared. Elizabeth Barrett Browning commented, "Never was a woman in the world less like an actress. I can't conceive how such a woman would look onstage, or speak, or gesticulate—she has just the look of a sensible woman, not at all young."[122] Charlotte's active female characters were cultural constructions that, like "strong-minded" women in the social and political realm outside the theater, dramatized new potentials for those audience members who witnessed or read about them.

Onstage Charlotte's independence and forthrightness registered as "truthfulness" when compared with the coy, flirtatious behavior calculated to engage and interest men. In fact, her refusal to exhibit deferential behavior or demonstrate care in being regarded as attractive or desirable by male spectators were some of her most notable characteristics. Some believed these qualities of directness of word and demeanor to be national traits of Americans; others gravitated to her as either a model of female chastity or a symbol of female power. In either case, from her first successful British performances Charlotte Cushman had been acclaimed for embodying powerful women onstage.

Although it was possible for many of her spectators to read Charlotte's characters as manly and masculine, these qualities when applied to women could be complimentary *or* derogatory. And Charlotte's characters were open to multiple and contradictory interpretations, like the gender-marked terms that described them. For admiring audience members, particularly other women, Charlotte's larger-than-life representations could be regarded as strong, courageous, and assertive—virile as her countrymen, regal as the female monarch on the British throne, or respectable as the bourgeois true women who were singing her praises. Yet at the margins of such female agency and strength was the prospect that the large, masculine female characters Charlotte embodied were monstrously "unnatural," capable of unnameable passions. In dialogue with the possibilities made "flesh" in the parts Charlotte played, spectators were confronted with tangible representations of unprecedented female power, of physical and vocal dimensions—a resonant, active force that spectators could feel in their own bodies as Charlotte's leaps, shrieks, and writhing deaths onstage changed the air around them, enabling them to witness and condemn, applaud or even possibly desire, her embodiment of strong women.

Wearing the Breeches

Charlotte Cushman's Male Roles

It is open to question whether Romeo may not best be
impersonated by a woman, for it is thus only that in actual
representation can we view the passionate love of this play
made real and palpable. . . . Females may together give us
an image of the desire of the lovers of Verona, without
suggesting a thought of vice.

—*Brittania*, 3 January 1846

Sitting in London's Haymarket Theatre audience in December 1845, playwright Westland Marston saw "the house roused to the wildest excitement,
as if by some tragic event in actual life." Onstage, playing Romeo for the
first time in London, Charlotte Cushman had given "full scope to her
impetuosity in emotion and to the virile force of her style." In fact, she was
so passionate that Marston—who was also a critic—believed that, "as a
lover, the ardour of her devotion exceeded that of any male actor I have
ever seen in the part." For a moment the audience was silent. Had they
accepted her in the part? "There was a pause before the recollection that
Romeo's misery was but feigned, enabled [the audience] to thank the
impassioned performer in volley after volley of applause."[1] She was a hit.

A year earlier, in late 1844, Charlotte had come to England armed with
letters and reviews that had identified her as the premiere breeches actress
in the United States. As we have seen, in her first season abroad Charlotte
had been highly acclaimed for embodying powerful women onstage, and
many critics and fans found her force and self-possession captivating, but
she had yet to appear before British audiences in any male roles. Romeo
would become her signature part, and in later years she would play a range
of male characters, from the young Hamlet to the stately and manipulative
Cardinal Wolsey.

During the nineteenth century many popular actresses in England and
the United States attempted male roles. Charlotte had no doubt been

influenced by the success of earlier female Romeos such as Ellen Tree Kean, who had appeared in the role at Convent Garden in 1829. Clara Fisher Maeder, the first actress with whom Charlotte had ever worked, had achieved her greatest acclaim impersonating characters "both male and female . . . where her natural vivacity and charm were exploitable; rollicking boys and girls, saucy chambermaids and coquettish belles."[2] And so Charlotte had observed at close hand from the very start of her career how attractive women in breeches roles were to audiences.[3] In those early years, along with the many other roles Charlotte played, she had appeared as Romeo at least three times: at the close of her successful stint at the Pearl Street Theatre in Albany, in the summer of 1837 at the National Theatre, and then again on 7 January 1839 at the Park Theatre, both in New York City. From her very first attempts at the role, she was well received.

Yet from the start it had been clear to her critics and audiences that Cushman's interpretations of male roles were different from those of most of her contemporaries. Unlike actresses who played up the possibility of titillating the predominantly male audience by displaying shapely bodies and legs, Charlotte Cushman, who by most accounts neither excited the passions of men nor wished to be seen as desirable to them, could actually attempt to *personify* male characters.[4] Of her 1837 performance as Romeo at New York's National Theatre the critic from the *Courier* had remarked, "a casual observer would have found some difficulty . . . in realizing the fact that Romeo was played by a girl."[5] Charlotte, it seems, "could assume male characters with less incongruity than almost any other woman."[6] And the "Lady Correspondent" of the *Spirit of the Times* would later declare that Charlotte was "the only woman on the stage who *can* play Romeo." This writer bemoaned the fact that "a pair of handsome legs has oftener been the instigation to 'get up' in Romeo than any impression of intellectual capacity to do justice to the part," yet she maintained that Charlotte was "in face, form and general make-up a most perfect specimen of the impetuous and yet loving Romeo."[7] What had the audience seen in her "ardor" as Shakespeare's preeminent male lover?

"Sapphic" Romeo

Once Charlotte recognized that she was a hit in her first British theater season, she forged a plan. Since she intended to stay in England for several more years, she would encourage her mother and sister to join her, as her brother had. Then the following winter she would play Romeo opposite Susan as Juliet. Six months before their London debut Charlotte had written home, instructing her mother to have Susan study the part of Juliet, "for when she comes I will bring her out under such auspices as nobody ever had in that part."[8] Should there be any objections, she could claim, as she later did to squelch criticism in Edinburgh, that she had only taken on the role of Romeo to give her sister Susan "the support I knew she required, and would never get from any gentleman that could be got to act with her."[9] Like Charlotte's earlier narrative that she went on the stage merely to support her family, this deployment of her sister's straitened material circumstances would allow Charlotte to represent herself as the protector of her sister's respectability, rather than as a possible transgressor of gender norms in her own right.

Swept up with her own social and professional success, Charlotte confided to her new friend, writer Mary Howitt, that she was "getting quite nervous as the time draws near to expect my mother and sister."[10] In mid-July 1845 the rest of the Cushman family arrived in England. There had always been considerable tension between the assertive, domineering Charlotte and her passive, attractive, sister, but now Charlotte was determined that "hereafter we shall be very happy together. She shall find that I am not the witch I have been represented."[11] Although Charlotte and Susan Cushman were never very close, Charlotte resumed her responsibilities as head of her household with renewed determination to make her family life as harmonious as possible.

Throughout the summer Charlotte and Susan prepared for a winter opening of *Romeo and Juliet* at the Haymarket Theatre in London. Together they practiced in the small cottage Charlotte had rented for herself and her family—including, of course, Sallie Mercer—on Garway Road, in Bayswater. Later they tried out their parts before audiences in Edinburgh and Southampton. In Edinburgh Charlotte may have paused to reconsider the wisdom of risking all her newfound British acclaim on this upcoming performance with Susan. Here she encountered some initial resistance to her portrayal of the prototypical male lover. Charlotte had met noted phrenologist George Combe and his wife, Cecilia—daughter of esteemed British actress Sarah Siddons and cousin of Fanny Kemble—on an earlier visit some months before. She had been a guest in their home, introduced to their friends. Now, appearing in Edinburgh with her younger divorced sister, whose own past was the subject of speculation and gossip, Charlotte attempted to ward off aspersions on her or Susan's character that Combe reported to her. In response to his objections, Charlotte wrote Combe that, since her goal in playing Romeo had been merely to support her sister, "a thought of indelicacy in the assumption never cross'd my mind. I see however, that a *gross* motive *might* be attributed to it and can only hope that those who know me will acquit me of an intentional immodesty." Besides, as Combe knew, in recent years Ellen Tree Kean had acted Romeo and Ion repeatedly "without bringing upon herself the charge of indelicacy."[12] Neither Cushman nor Combe named the "indelicacy" her Romeo might signify. While he may have merely objected to the self-display of an actress appearing in revealing breeches, given the tone of the rest of the correspondence and the fact that Combe's mother-in-law had also played Hamlet, I believe that intimations of lesbianism, or at the least a display of "inappropriate" female sexual desire, rather than disapproval with breeches acting, were the grounds for his objections.[13]

Combe persisted in trying to dissuade Charlotte from performing Romeo. Something was visibly different about the spectacle of Charlotte, a "masculine woman," portraying a male lover of women when compared with breeches performances by Ellen Tree Kean, Eliza Vestris, or Clara Fisher Maeder—all married women whose breeches characters were familiar on the Victorian stage and whose form-fitting costumes frequently appealed to the heterosexual men in their audience. Without a husband to attest to her modesty and morality, the performance of respectability Charlotte strove to enact offstage was momentarily threatened by Combe's reaction. Combe implored her repeatedly to provide evidence of her propriety and good breeding, which he would then make public: "Put me in possession of a narrative which I may show to all your friends and which they and I may probe to the bottom. When you do this, and satisfy them, you may rely on their using every means in their power for your vindication."[14]

Believing that, as a public woman, Charlotte owed an account of her life to those acquaintances who had personally befriended her, Combe wrote letters to Fanny Kemble Butler and to anyone else he could find to inquire whether Charlotte and her family were above reproach. To Charlotte he wrote that her friends could not support her "unless you admit one and all of them to your confidence," and he admitted that, as Charlotte had suspected, Edwin Forrest had been the source of the most damaging innuendoes.[15] As much as she strove to present herself as "well-bred," Charlotte was annoyed.

While Charlotte was exonerated from unspecified charges of indelicacy, Forrest's allegations led "some of the *hospitable* people of Edinburgh," as she sarcastically complained to her new friend Mrs. Darbishire, to believe that Susan was not married. The husband of twenty-three-year-old Susan Cushman had abandoned her years before, but her seven-year-old son, Ned, was very much in evidence. "We have been obliged to send for marriage certificates, bills, and papers to prove our respectability." It was "galling" to Charlotte's pride and "mortifying" to Susan. They "met the slander boldly," she announced to Darbishire, who had welcomed the

Cushmans into her circle of Unitarian friends, but Charlotte had also learned how tenuous respectability was—and how easily the threat of scandal could destroy all her hard work.[16]

Mary Jean Corbett has asserted that the movement toward professionalization of the Victorian theater took "bourgeois values as its standard at every level of theatrical life." The self-definitions of actresses of Charlotte's era, whether onstage, in autobiographies, or in their personal letters, were, in Corbett's terms, "contingent less on the 'facts' of their private lives, and more on how well they c[ould] publicly imitate and produce the signs and attitudes that mark individuals as belonging to a certain class and gender."[17] By now Charlotte Cushman was masterful at imitating and producing signs of bourgeois respectability, and in her written responses to Combe and others she represented her beliefs and behavior in terms of her readers' most conventional values.

In London as well there were minor complications before Charlotte and Susan's opening. During rehearsals the Haymarket company had expressed their reservations, though not because a woman was to be Romeo or because young Susan's marital status raised eyebrows. It was Charlotte's presumptuousness as an *American* that rankled the Haymarket actors. In Charlotte's performance of *Romeo and Juliet,* in addition to presenting British spectators with a woman's interpretation of the passionate, youthful Romeo, she planned to restore to the stage Shakespeare's original text. By presenting a Romeo who differentiated between his attraction to Rosaline—which was usually cut in contemporary stage versions—and the passion he, or she, feels for Juliet, Charlotte portrayed what one critic was to call the character's "ardent passionate disposition, that waited for the opportunity to break forth with irresistible violence, so that the first scenes contained the whole possibility of the tragedy."[18] The British company expressed their dissatisfaction with the "impudent" "American Indians" who insisted on following Shakespeare's original text instead of the familiar, watered-down David Garrick version of the play that they were accustomed to performing.[19]

Before their premiere the Haymarket cast was so outspoken that she almost abandoned the plan. Rather tentatively, Charlotte wrote to manager Benjamin Webster, apologizing for "annoy[ing] you which I fear I am likely to do." Charlotte had heard that when some of the actors "expressed in no very measured terms their displeasure at the trouble this 'original text' was giving them, the stage manager informed them that it was 'because one Miss Cushman could not bring another Miss Cushman out of the tomb'"—as though her intention to restore the text reflected a weakness on her part. Charlotte acknowledged the insults and the implication that she was both outdated in preferring Shakespeare's version and somehow not capable of performing David Garrick's more simplistic adaptation. But, while Charlotte was *"thoroughly prepared to do whatever you wish,"* as she emphatically underscored in her letter to Webster, and "quite prepared to act Romeo in any way that *shall please you,"*[20] Webster went along with her plan. And, once the accolades poured in from both critics and fans pleased to see the restored text, the Haymarket actors were mollified.

And accolades did pour in. As positively as Charlotte's previous season had been received by the British critics and audiences, when the Cushman sisters first performed *Romeo and Juliet* for London audiences, on 29 December 1845, critics were overwhelmed. Charlotte's friends evidently anticipated her spectacular success. At the conclusion of the opening performance Charlie Cushman recalled that a "grand supper" was planned in his sisters' honor, given by their friends Frank and Louisa Beard. Invited to meet Charlotte and Susan and celebrate what was expected to be a remarkable debut were such literary notables as Charles Dickens, William Thackeray, and "heaps of newspaper writers."[21] The following day's papers heralded her achievement.

The critic from the London *Times* stated enthusiastically that "it is enough to say that the Romeo of Miss Cushman is far superior to any Romeo that has been seen for years. . . . Miss Cushman's Romeo is a creative, living, breathing, animated, ardent human being."[22] A human being—not a caricature or a freak; this passionate woman publicly professing erotic love for another woman was regarded as superior to other *male* British actors as Romeo. The acclaim that was lavished upon Charlotte's Romeo by the London press was in no way qualified by her sex. Critics from the *Times,* the *Era,* and the *Britannia* found Charlotte exciting and captivating as well as believable as Romeo, not merely as a "female Romeo." As the *Atlas* reported on 3 January 1846: "The appearance of Miss Cushman at the Haymarket, and the debut of her sister, Miss Susan Cushman, has been the theatrical event of the week. . . . Miss Cushman as Romeo has created no small sensation. . . . Perhaps a more intellectual and at the same time a more theatrically effective performance has never been witnessed."[23]

Susan Cushman's Juliet also received positive reviews. Although critics were quick to note that "she does not possess the powers of her sister," Susan Cushman was said to "strongly resemble" Charlotte, "with the addition of a pleasing and feminine expression."[24] If Susan's traditional femininity pleased the general public, Charlotte's masculine impersonation pleased reviewers even more. What did spectators and critics see in Charlotte's Romeo to account for this remarkable reception? In what ways did what Marjorie Garber has called the "complex and often unconscious eroticism" of cross-dressed performance shape audience responses to Charlotte—allowing her to serve as the personification of Shakespeare's romantic lover for some spectators and as a transgressive erotic force for others?[25]

Curiously, it was the general perception of Charlotte's "realism," or authenticity, as the male lover that seemed to resonate with spectators of both types. The critic from the *Britannia* declared that "Miss Cushman as Romeo gave an illustration of the character startlingly real. Singularly masculine in her energy and her decisive action, this lady might pass for a youthful actor with little chance of her sex being detected. She was therefore, the creation of the poet."[26] Jessie Meriton White, one of Charlotte's earliest British female spectators, claimed that, as Romeo, "her figure, her gait, her gestures, are manly. . . . Had I not known that the part was played by a woman, I do not think I should have suspected her sex." White was not merely reacting to Charlotte's appearance. She felt that, as Romeo, Charlotte displayed "all the vehemence, the warmth of passion, the melancholy, the luxuriant imagination, the glowing yet delicate vitality . . . of the Italian boy-lover."[27]

How did Charlotte's contemporaries read an androgynous youth in what today appears to be an obviously female—even buxom—body? Although the only existing photograph of Charlotte as Romeo dates from a later period, when she no longer resembled a lanky, angular lad, apparently her quality of movement, demeanor, and self-assurance—so difficult to capture in a still photograph, examined with twentieth-century eyes—were evidently still legible to live audiences.[28]

Stephen Orgel has suggested that contemporary readers need to understand how an earlier society "construct[ed] the norm of womanliness"—or manliness—in order "to historicize our notions of verisimilitude."[29] In 1846 Charlotte, at thirty years of age, could "pass" for an ardent, agile, young man. Tall, angular, and square-jawed, with a sure stride and a deep voice, she embodied masculinity to an extent that impressed British viewers even more than it had Americans. Henry Chorley, in the *Athenaeum*, likened the audience's response to Charlotte to Romeo's reaction to Juliet in the restored Shakespearean text. For Chorley "it is Love at First sight—but not first love; . . . this is very different from the mere sentimentalism which, under the title of Shakespeare's play, has so long usurped the boards. What there was of the woman just served to indicate juvenility, and no more. . . . Never was courtship more fervent, more apparently sincere, more reverential, and yet more impetuously passionate, than that which on the silent air of night ascended to Juliet's window."[30]

Romeo's youthful impetuosity and ardor were highlighted in Charlotte's interpretation of the character, motivating her passionate embraces and declarations of love for Juliet as well as the certainty and physical prowess of Romeo's duel with Tybalt. Years later Emma Stebbins contended that this appearance of youthfulness especially suited Charlotte to

Charlotte and Susan Cushman as Romeo and Juliet. In 1846 the *Illustrated London News* depicted Charlotte as a visibly masculine and gallant Romeo to Susan's diminutive and submissive Juliet. *(Harvard Theatre Collection. Houghton Library.)*

the role. Stebbins claimed that few male Romeos had looked young and "passionately agile" enough to be convincing in the role if they were mature men. Young male actors may have appeared more suitable, but they lacked the necessary maturity and depth. Charlotte possessed agility, passion, *and* maturity.[31] During London's 1846 season other critics concurred, writing that "Miss Cushman seemed just man enough to be a boy."[32]

In the part of Romeo, as with her earlier Lady Macbeth and Meg Merrilies, Charlotte used to her advantage her forceful physical and vocal style and her own strong temperament to create a character who was androgynous, active, and passionate. Since working with Macready in the United States three years before her London opening, Charlotte's voice had become an instrument of even broader flexibility and range. She had

Charlotte Cushman as Romeo, ca. mid- to late 1850s.
Cushman's visibly female buxom Romeo was often read by
nineteenth-century spectators as convincingly male and
youthful. *(Harvard Theatre Collection. Houghton Library.)*

learned to imitate his deep tones and his sudden alterations from high-
pitched declaration to a deep, hollow whisper.[33] Although Robert Browning—who had met Charlotte at a party hosted by their mutual friend Henry
Chorley—complained of Charlotte's "whining" voice as Romeo,[34] the critic
from the *Theatrical Journal* spoke highly of her skill. Romeo's voice in the
scene when he gave Balthazar the letter haunted the listener, echoing
"through his soul" and ringing "in his ears for weeks after."[35] Charlotte's
voice—deeper, huskier, and breathier than most women's—served her well
in male roles.

Poet Gilbert Abbott á Beckett took the vocal and even physical resemblance between Cushman and Macready one step further in a poem published in the February 1846 *Almanack of the Month*, remarking on the popularity of Charlotte's Romeo:

> But what's the attraction? Why thus do they rush, man?
> Don't you know? 'Tis Romeo, played by Miss Cushman . . .
> What figure is that which appears on the scene?
> 'Tis Madam Macready—Miss Cushman, I mean.
> What wonderous resemblance! The walk on the toes,
> The eloquent, short, intellectual nose—
> The bend of the knee, the slight sneer of the lip,
> The frown on the forehead, the hand on the hip;
> In the chin, in the voice, 'tis the same to a tittle,
> Miss Cushman is Mr. Macready in little.[36]

While this poem may have been more satire than praise, many critics, like Macready's friend the playwright James Sheridan Knowles, sincerely appreciated Charlotte Cushman's performance. After seeing Charlotte as Romeo in this 1846 season, Knowles claimed that, as "unanimous and lavish as were the encomiums of London Press, I was not prepared for a triumph of pure genius." "Genius" was a compliment usually reserved for men. Knowles compared Charlotte's Romeo scene in Friar Lawrence's cell to Edmund Kean's memorable performance of Othello: "Throughout it was a triumph, equal to the proudest of those which I used to witness years ago, and for a repetition of which I have looked in vain till now."[37] According to Knowles, the emotion in Romeo's banishment scene was incomparable, "a scene of topmost passion!—not simulated passion—no such thing—[so] real, palpably real." So much so that Knowles said, "I listened, and gazed, and held my breath, while my blood ran hot and cold." Knowles attributed some of Cushman's success in this scene to her physical energy. Like a contemporary melodramatic hero, as the banished Romeo, Charlotte was so grief-stricken and distraught that, "with unexpected desperation, she dashed herself upon the earth 'taking the measure of an unmade grave.'"[38]

Knowles's praise was reprinted across the Atlantic, and the New York *Spirit of the Times*, although protesting the "unsexing of the mind and heart which she [Charlotte] must undergo in assuming such a character as Romeo," took pride in the American actress's success abroad, asserting that "Charlotte Cushman, whatever she may be, belongs to New York, and whatever triumph she may achieve, in it New York is interested, and of it will be proud."[39] For Americans, as well as for the British, Charlotte had come to represent the United States, and, for Americans who still smarted under the weight of their assumed cultural inferiority when compared with the British, championing the success of one of their own took on a nationalistic fervor. The terms of the cultural competition in which Charlotte found herself, and which she was to help transform, were spelled out explicitly by the *English Gentleman,* a periodical whose very name combined national and class identities.

> Miss Cushman is, *par excellence* the exception to the rule that America cannot produce any theatrical "wonder of the age" and this fact is morally admitted throughout the States, for an English actor or actress of very ordinary abilities is received among them as an extraordinary luminary, and bad performers are patronized in the absence of something better.[40]

Now Charlotte had turned the tables. Her first season had introduced the British audiences to her particularly American talent, but this production of *Romeo and Juliet* placed Charlotte "on the highest pinnacle of fame in London, and was the great feature of the season 1845–1846."[41]

In her first British impersonation of Romeo, Charlotte planned her bold, deliberate movements precisely for maximum effect and involved herself in every detail of their commission. She gave instructions to lower the bedstead in *Romeo and Juliet* by four inches because, she explained, "the bed is awkwardly high to fall upon,"[42] and she wanted nothing to deter her from literally throwing herself into the character. Other reviewers singled out for praise the realism of Charlotte's fencing scenes. Her "electrifying power" as she seized upon Tybalt was so "perfect . . . [an] illusion," reported the *Era,* "that for an instant could we not fancy that the mortal thrust was given by female arm."[43] Rather than engage in a lengthy, protracted duel, Charlotte's Romeo lunged decisively at Tybalt. Years later Walter Herries Pollock of the *Saturday Review* wrote of Charlotte as Romeo, "In the usual version Romeo's fight with Tybalt is a long business, but last night Romeo rushed upon him the moment he appeared, and before he could get well upon his guard, Tybalt was struck dead as lightning strikes the pine."[44] Although Charlotte's Romeo was commendable as a duelist, it was in her embodied depiction as a lover that Charlotte attracted the most attention for her realistic enactment.

Prints of Charlotte and Susan Cushman in the balcony scenes indicate contemporary impressions of Charlotte's gestures and stance as Romeo. Mary Howitt's friend Margaret Gillies etched an illustration to accompany a laudatory article Howitt published about the two "Miss Cushmans" in the *People's Journal.* In Gillies's drawing Charlotte's left hand is protectively placed on Susan's head, while her right hand and arm support her Juliet. Susan looks wistfully up at her Romeo, while Charlotte looks away, as if toward the future she must face. Charlotte's carriage appears strong and

Charlotte and Susan Cushman as Romeo and Juliet. From a
drawing by Margaret Gillies. This drawing of Charlotte and
Susan Cushman was published in the popular *People's Journal*
on 18 July 1846, introducing the Cushman sisters to a broad
English public. *(Author's collection.)*

direct. Her wide stance and raised chin seem to be very much in keeping with both the determination of her romantic male character and her heroic role as a character in the family drama that Howitt drafted.

Another etching of the Cushmans gives a somewhat different picture of the look and mood of the famous balcony scene.[45] The tenderness and surprisingly sexual verve suggested in this drawing may help to explain the complex reactions to Charlotte's performance. Juliet's arms are wrapped around her Romeo in a tender and romantic manner. Charlotte is astride the balcony ledge in a position most uncharacteristic for Victorian women, who even rode horses sidesaddle, but acceptable for the sensual, passionate Romeo. "As a rule, actresses of refinement and sensibility, when they assume male attire, betray their female origin by quaint little movements, the lower limbs are apt to cling helplessly together, the knees instinctively bowed inward." But Charlotte was different, according to actor John Coleman, who had met her during her first season in Edinburgh. Charlotte's demeanor as Romeo "was distinctly masculine," claimed Coleman, who described "her limbs" as "strident, as those of a youth." Furthermore, Coleman remembered that Charlotte's "amorous endearments" toward her sister "were of so erotic a character that no man would have dared indulge in them [in public]."[46]

As Romeo, Charlotte laced arms with her Juliet and closely embraced her. Some critics maintained that the protectiveness and concern that Romeo displayed for Juliet reflected in part Charlotte's own familial feelings toward her sister. Yet, as I have established, not only were Charlotte and Susan not particularly fond of each other, but with other Juliets Charlotte had been—and would be in the future—just as passionate. In 1858, when eighteen-year-old Emma Crow first saw Charlotte perform as Romeo, Charlotte seemed to be "the incarnation of the ideal lover."[47] This female spectator, like numerous others who wrote to and about Charlotte as Romeo over the decades she played the part, was drawn in by the physical depiction of desire manifested in the love story. And those who were offended were so *because* of the vivid passion in the love scenes between the two women.

As with Charlotte's forceful female characters, spectators and critics most receptive to her remarked on her intensity and strength, her commanding presence, her physical agility, and her powerful expression of emotion. The character of Romeo afforded Charlotte a unique opportunity to demonstrate these attributes, but it offered something more as well. As the passionate male lover of another woman, Charlotte's Romeo could, paradoxically, be seen as the chaste embodiment of youthful masculinity and heterosexual love or, given the fact that the ardent lover was *female,* as representative of a possibility of passionate love between two women.

Charlotte and Susan Cushman as Romeo and Juliet. Few images would flout Victorian conventions of womanhood more than this illustration of Cushman, who, while acting within the parameters of a breeches role, is depicted with her legs astride a balcony ledge, holding another woman in a blatently erotic embrace. *(Harvard Theatre Collection. Houghton Library.)*

Moreover, in her very portrayal of male characters Charlotte raised the possibility that if a woman could so convincingly act the man, perhaps being a man was merely an "act."

This act—this performance of gender—which Charlotte's contemporaries saw her brandish with such verisimilitude, was, as we have seen, composed of a series of gestures and expressions that unmistakably signified manliness to her spectators. Current theoretical work in gender studies has been influenced by Judith Butler's notion of "gender performativity," or the concept that individuals are socialized to perform accepted depictions of masculinity or femininity in their everyday lives. Butler has described gender as a "performative act . . . in which bodily gestures, movements, and styles of various kinds constitute the appearance of an abiding gendered self." In Charlotte Cushman's realistic portrayal of male characters, in her gestures, demeanor, and "amorous endearments" she embodied and revealed what Butler refers to as "the imitative structure of gender itself—as well as its contingency."[48]

Ironically, because Charlotte lived in an age when the prescribed expectations of gender display were in flux, a time both of rigid Victorian notions of acceptable female behavior and of theatrical conventions that afforded a few women the ability to transcend traditional mores and portray male characters, in many ways being a female Romeo was an asset. In keeping with the Victorian belief that embodied expressions of passion *between men and women* would be improper and immoral, after seeing Charlotte, the critic from the *Brittania* declared that perhaps a *woman* was better suited to play Romeo, since "females may together give us an image of the desire of the lovers of Verona, *without suggesting a thought of vice.*"[49]

Since nineteenth-century "respectable" women were generally believed to be sexually chaste, the love performed by two women, however ardent, was seen by most as innocent. Yet, in an allusion that may reveal a recognition this critic intuited but could not name, he or she wrote of *Romeo and Juliet,* "The whole play is an illustration of those immortal lines of Sappho, in which love subdues the frame to fainting, relaxes the limbs, shoots forth cold drops upon the brow, and scorches the tongue as with fire."[50] Charlotte was lauded as a "Sapphic Romeo." The *Britannia*'s critic went so far as to state, "To give an adequate embodiment of the true feeling of this play, would certainly outrage the sense of a modern audience, were the performers of *opposite* sex."[51] Within a tradition that largely accepted same-sex love between women—whether as conceived by Shakespeare or Sappho—as passionate, even perhaps erotic, yet still chaste and respectable, Charlotte's male characterizations afforded her a space within which she could express her desire for other women, a desire that animated her offstage as well as on.

When Charlotte returned to Edinburgh with Susan to appear as Romeo and Juliet later in the 1846 season, after her London success, John Coleman witnessed the stir she created. "During her short absence, my eccentric friend had become more eccentric than ever. She had mounted a man's hat and coat, a man's collar and cravat, Wellington boots, which, so far from trying to conceal, she displayed without reticence or restraint as she strode about." According to Coleman, "these masculine proclivities shocked the spinsters of the company and provoked satirical comment amongst admirers or detractors, who incontinently dubbed the new Romeo 'Charley de Boots.'" And "Charley's" "desire to disport herself in masculine attire" led to "speculations" that Coleman found too "indecorous" to repeat.[52] Whatever her fellow performers thought of "Charley's" offstage cross-dressing, by now it was common knowledge that Charlotte spent most of her time in the company of close women friends; some, like poet Eliza Cook, were also inclined to dress in masculine garb.

In public discussions of Charlotte's Romeo, however, no overt connection was made between Charlotte's breeches performance, her offstage "masculine proclivities," and the possibilities of women's sexual desire for one another. Instead, women's desire remained coded, overshadowed by more "acceptable" explanations. According to the critic from the *Era,* it was Charlotte's "consciousness" of her "innate qualification" for the part, "backed by sisterly affection" that induced her "to transmute her sex."[53] In the pages of the *People's Journal* Mary Howitt extolled her friend's "earnestness," "purity of purpose," and "purity of life." Howitt maintained that Cushman's acting was "not acting in its imitative sense, but action; the very action of nature, and therefore it is always true." Rather than associate Charlotte with artifice, Howitt's remarks located her within the sphere of "true" womanhood and commended Charlotte—a woman who loved other women, an actress with no relationships with men to tarnish her reputation—for her "resistance of temptation, self-denial, and purity." And Howitt offered "a few words . . . on a subject which has excited some remarks, as we think, needlessly, to Miss Cushman's disadvantage—we mean on her taking male parts. We can assert it as a fact, and it is a fact full of generosity and affection, that it is solely on her sister's account that she has done so. By taking the male character, for which she was in many cases admirably suited," Charlotte had secured the leading female parts for Susan. Howitt claimed that "the affection of these two noble-hearted sisters" was "the most beautiful feature in this narrative."[54] In Howitt's article Charlotte's proclivity for male roles was reconfigured into a gesture of generous self-sacrifice that appeared to support, rather than subvert, contemporary gender roles.

Despite her friends' assertions that she assumed the role of Romeo solely for her "dear sister's sake,"[55] Charlotte would continue to play the part and other male characters for more than a decade after Susan Cushman's retirement from the stage in 1848. The passion of Charlotte's Romeo for her Juliet was not an expression of sisterly affection but, rather, a decided preference born of her "innate qualifications," an animating desire for which there was no agreed-upon vocabulary but which might now be considered lesbian.

However Charlotte's supporters tried to explain or excuse the visible passion that she expressed for other women in the guise of Romeo, there remained a potential source of excitement that, while palpable to women who recognized it, seemed inexplicable to others. As Romeo, Charlotte played with and against the covert meanings others—particularly other women—might read into her portrayal as the romantic lover of women. For some of Charlotte's female spectators the graphic depiction of one woman's embodiment of desire for another could be the *cause* for Charlotte's critical acclaim. I contend that Charlotte's performance of Romeo produced multiple "meanings" and made available to spectators who could decode it, ways of perceiving and articulating female erotic desire that called into question the heterosexual framework of the texts in which she appeared.[56]

But some male colleagues, particularly in the United States, criticized Cushman's masculine depictions even more than they had her forceful female characters. They found Charlotte's abilities to traverse gender categories and separate gender and biological sex in her breeches performances, her challenge to hard-and-fast categories, and her presentation of unsettling possibilities disturbing, regardless of the audience's approval. In 1843, when Charlotte had played Romeo at the Walnut Street Theatre in Philadelphia, George Vandenhoff had been cast as Mercutio. No matter how common was the practice of women playing breeches parts, Vandenhoff was repelled by the whole idea of a woman performing a masculine role. Vandenhoff, who seemed to detect the homoerotic potential in Charlotte's Romeo, considered this a "*hybrid* performance" in which Charlotte, who borrowed his hat, cloak, and sword for the part, looked "neither man nor woman[;] her passion [was] epicene."[57] Vandenhoff protested that: "Romeo requires a *man*, to feel his passion, and to express his despair. A woman, in attempting it, 'unsexes' herself to no purpose . . . she *denaturalizes* the situations; and sets up a monstrous anomaly. . . . There should be a law against such perversions," which Vandenhoff believed were "offences against propriety, and desecrations of Shakspere [*sic*]."[58] Yet, Vandenhoff was not too repelled in later years, after Cushman's British success, to comment favorably on her skill with a sword and claim credit for teaching her "masculine and effective" swordsmanship.

But the unnatural, the unsexed, the monstrous, the perverted—the lesbian—all of these readings of eroticism between women were always possible just under the surface of Charlotte's interpretation. And, despite the generally accepted belief that male and female characteristics were natural, innate, and distinct from one another, the concern that taking on the clothes and gestures of the other sex could "unsex" a woman points to the contingency of nineteenth-century ideas about sex, gender, the body, and performance. For their most virulent critics women like Charlotte who played male roles were not imitating or even parodying masculinity (and therefore heterosexuality); they were, in effect, transforming their sex. The possibility that gender was in fact *a performance* continued to haunt the edges of the generally positive reactions Charlotte received as Romeo, as did the specter that some women might have innate qualifications to unsex themselves. Charlotte's Romeo became a sign that called into question the boundaries between the sexes.

After Susan's retirement from the stage, Charlotte continued to play Romeo opposite many other Juliets. When family loyalty could no longer be enlisted as an excuse for her male portrayals, the fervent passion of Charlotte's Romeo could not be explained as an expression of sisterly affection. Instead, Charlotte's performative preferences would later be discussed in the press as indications of her virtuosity as an actress or of her great business sense. On the rare occasions that Charlotte's performance of erotic and protective feelings toward other women provoked overt disapproval, other pervasive attitudes about "acceptable" gender behavior were enlisted to explain her choices. In one performance during the 1851–52 season at Boston's National Theatre, Charlotte's Juliet was Sarah Anderton, with whom she had had a romantic connection offstage as well as on. During one of Romeo's most tender speeches an audience member uttered an insulting, derisive snort. Still in the character of the gallant Romeo, Charlotte placed a protective arm around her Juliet and led her offstage. Then, returning to the stage, Charlotte/Romeo faced the audience and commanded, "Some man must put that person out, or I shall be obliged to do it myself!"[59] The audience evicted the heckler and cheered Charlotte as the epitome of chivalry, and the play went on.

Charlotte Cushman's Romeo inhabited that contested borderland between "acceptable" exceptions that proved the general rules about appropriate male and female behavior and those that threatened to topple the norms completely. Although some critics and spectators denounced the "unnaturalness" of Charlotte's passionate Romeo, far more attempted to find a way to read her Romeo as an *exemplar* rather than a refutation of predominant values. So, for the British, for example, if as Romeo or in her masculine interpretation of female characters Charlotte violated their expectations about women, she *reinforced* their beliefs about powerful, dynamic Americans. For Americans different constructions of national identities were seized upon to explain Charlotte's performance as the male lover, and these constructions shifted as the nineteenth century progressed.

By 1860 the reviewer for the *New York Times* pronounced to American readers that "generally mankind do not love to see a woman acting the part and wearing the garb of a man. And this instinct, like all popular instincts, is correct." But in the case of Romeo, Charlotte's cross-dressing was warranted, the critic claimed, because "there is in the delicacy of Romeo's character something which requires a woman to represent it, and unfits almost every man for its impersonation. The luscious language which draws its rich, lascivious color from the fiery blood of Young Italy, sounds ridiculous alongside of the rather blasé sensible style of love-making of Young New York, and here seems strange on the lips of a man."[60] Thus, for this critic men—particularly American men—were too pragmatic and sensible, too masculine, in effect, to portray Romeo. But *Italian* men were considered by Americans to be as romantic and emotional as women; therefore, *women* could best portray them. Once again gender and nationality were conflated in Charlotte's embodiment of a cultural text. As the *Times* proclaimed:

> We know of no one who *can* play the part but Miss Cushman. At times she may seem too restless and full of action. But it is necessary to be so to relieve the character from that languid, sickly hue, so falsely given to it. In Miss Cushman's picture of Romeo there is nothing sickly, or subtle or morbid. It is the love of a young glowing, unreflecting Italian, rich in passion and tenderness, and yet in its hottest glow chastened with delicacy—a love not of mere sensuality, but of sensuality spiritualized by imagination, and reveling in the frankness of unhesitating trust.[61]

Paradoxically, as Romeo, Charlotte would be commended by this critic for her active interpretation of a male role described as potentially too weak, sickly, or effeminate to be played by a man. And lest any of her spectators condemn her depiction as "morbid" or unhealthy in its same-sex erotic appeal, the *Times* explained, Charlotte was not portraying the desire of a character who might today be called lesbian; she was merely playing an Italian, and Italians of both sexes were as "unreflecting," emotional, and sensual as women—and frequently as delicate and spiritual as well.

Throughout her long career Charlotte knew that women responded strongly to her as Romeo. Strangers as well as friends admired and were attracted to her androgynous force and passion. Spectators like Martha Le Baron explicitly described to Charlotte the impassioned response they felt to her, which rendered this fan unable to "hold . . . down my impulse to write to you," as she sent "a woman's love and admiration." Likening the feeling she had for Charlotte with that she had once experienced "when I came into the presence of the bravest man I ever saw," Le Baron, who had met the actress briefly after a performance of Romeo, "felt it once more when I laid my hand in yours yesterday morning." In an attempt to understand her own desire Le Baron wrote of "the strange pleasure of the half-hour I spent with you[;] I longed to lay my head in your lap and cry out the over-fullness of my content . . . [to] feel that absolute sense of rest in a woman's power and calmness and wise tenderness, that perhaps I shall never feel again."

Le Baron also compared the passion she felt for Charlotte with her feelings for other women. "There are women whom I love intensely, but no one of them stretches out for me an almost boundless horizon . . . as you did for me."[62] Charlotte had sprained her ankle between the first and second acts of *Romeo and Juliet* the night Le Baron attended the theater, but "would not let the play be stopped in consequence."[63] Concerned about Charlotte's sprained ankle, Le Baron said that "it was very hard not to be able to help you in any way" and that she "could not help being very absurdly jealous of pretty Juliet when you drew her head against your bosom & kissed her."[64] How do we interpret these fan letters, keeping in mind that they were written to a woman playing a man making love to a woman? One possibility is that these fans responded to Charlotte's Romeo as a man they were attracted to and longed to find in real life. Another—far more operative in many cases, it seems to me—is that some women responded to Charlotte in all her androgynous splendor as a captivating woman making love to another woman. When female spectators witnessed Charlotte press another woman to her breast, they could see enacted before them in such gestures possibilities that they may have longed for but never consciously considered.[65] Charlotte was a woman they might both desire to *be* or be *desired by*.

Charlotte recognized and basked in the response she evoked in her female fans, writing, at one point, to her devoted "little lover" Emma Crow that she was "visiting a friend who has two grown daughters who fell so in love with Romeo last night . . . I fear my moments of leisure . . . will be very few and far between." Charlotte enjoyed women's reactions to her as Romeo and playfully announced that her hostess had "loved me in years gone by, and the rising generation seem to emulate the examples of their parents."[66] In another letter to Emma Crow, Charlotte wrote more specifically about the connections between spectatorship and desire. After mentioning that she had been "acting Romeo for the last six nights with such a pretty Juliet . . . that I am inclined to think I never acted it so well before," Charlotte mused, "I wonder if you would be very jealous if you were to see the performance; . . . she acts Juliet charmingly and would delight you in the abstract idea of Juliet, but as your darling's Juliet, I don't know."[67] Evidently, it was the beauty of Charlotte's female costar that inspired Charlotte's impassioned performance as her lover, and Charlotte knew that the desire she exhibited onstage could be read not just as an "abstract idea" but as a real possibility—so real, in fact, that an offstage lover might be jealous.

Charlotte's Juliets also seemed satisfied to act opposite a female Romeo. During the years Charlotte Cushman and Mary Devlin corresponded, Devlin signed her letters, "Your Juliet." And even in the decades of her semi-retirement from the stage the female friends with whom Charlotte associated continued to identify her as Romeo and referred to Emma Stebbins, Charlotte's acknowledged companion at the time, as "her Juliet," underscoring not only Charlotte's cross-dressed characterization but also her identity as a romantic lover of women offstage.[68]

In Charlotte's first British season as Romeo one of her female fans was heard to remark, "Miss Cushman is a very dangerous young man," and others concurred. Agreeing that Charlotte was "unfeminine"—but, that whatever else the term implied, unfeminine in Charlotte's case also meant "that she is grand, large-souled, and strong passioned"—Charlotte's critic proclaimed "Miss Cushman's Romeo" roused feelings of "wonder" and "mystery" in a "fit audience."[69] As forceful and determined as she was as Romeo, he was not the only male character she attempted that season. At the height of their success as the Shakespearean lovers, for variety Charlotte and Susan Cushman performed in Thomas Noon Talfourd's *Ion,* with Charlotte as the male lover, taking on the title role Talfourd had originally written for Macready in 1835.[70] Although Charlotte received some positive notices, critics were not nearly as enthusiastic as they had been about her Romeo. In recent years audiences had seen Ellen Tree Kean and Macready as Ion, and both had been quite successful in the part. Talfourd's classically inspired story of Ion and Clemanthe afforded "few opportunities for the display of those bursts of energy and passion which constitute the most striking points of Miss Cushman's performances," proclaimed one of Charlotte's London critics.[71] Although her admiring young friend Sarah Anderton was apparently drawn to Charlotte in this role, and Charlotte signed some of her most romantic letters to Sarah "your Ion," by March 1846 Charlotte anxiously admitted to Benjamin Webster that she feared "all novelty of my acting Romeo and Ion is rubbed off. . . . I must act in parts where comparisons cannot be instituted or . . . in some such out of the way thing as Romeo."[72] It is impossible to determine whether Charlotte actually considered Romeo and Ion merely "novelties" and "out of the way things" or whether she represented these parts in this manner to her manager for some other strategic purpose; after all, she was to continue playing Romeo for decades. But in any event the new part she proposed was yet another male character, the Prince in Mary Mitford's new play *Inez de Castro*. Despite Charlotte's hopes for a new part that she would originate, one that might set her apart from other actors, none of her male characters was to resound with audiences to the same degree as Romeo. And no season would be as remarkable as 1846—when Charlotte and Susan Cushman's Romeo and Juliet took London by storm. Nonetheless, throughout her career she would continue to perform in breeches roles, most notably as the Shakespearean characters of Hamlet and Cardinal Wolsey.

"Gentleman" Hamlet

It was on 24 November 1851, on a return trip to the United States, that Charlotte first played Hamlet at Brougham's Lyceum in New York. Emma Stebbins accounted for her partner's Hamlet as she had her Romeo, professing that "an old Hamlet is . . . incongruous" and claiming that "in this respect Miss Cushman satisfied the eye, in all others she gratified the mind." For Stebbins, as for many other women who enjoyed seeing Charlotte in breeches, Charlotte "looked the part of Hamlet as well as she did that of Romeo. Her commanding and well-made figure appeared to advantage in the dress of the princely Dane, and her long experience in the assumption of male parts took from her appearance all sense of incongruity."[73] In other words, the more Charlotte played a man, the less incongruous her male impersonations appeared.

For many actors Hamlet is the quintessential character in dramatic literature—the part they most relish performing and, consequently, the male character most frequently played by women. Throughout the eighteenth and nineteenth centuries scores of actresses appeared as Hamlet and were acclaimed for their portrayals.[74] Sarah Siddons first appeared in the part in 1776 and last played the brooding Danish prince twenty-six years later. Although Hamlet as written is a young man still in school, mature actors frequently played the part. In the few times Charlotte performed this role she would be competing directly with the leading contemporary male actors, particularly Edwin Booth, who had married one of her most passionate and beautiful Juliets, Mary Devlin. As Booth confided to his friend Richard Cary before Charlotte's Boston performance in 1861, "Cushman . . . is down on me as an actor; says I don't know anything at all about 'Hamlet,' so she is going to play here in February."[75] And when she did she demonstrated that she could literally fill his pants; she had the audacity to borrow his costume. To Booth's wife Charlotte noted that she would "never have been able to act Hamlet so well but in [Booth's] mantle and draperies . . . [she] looked so splendid in it."[76]

Charlotte enjoyed playing Hamlet, and she relished the challenge it presented. As she explained to her most devoted fan, Emma Crow, after a performance in Philadelphia: "Hamlet is the most awfully exhausting part as you will see when you come to see me act it in Boston. . . . Mentally and physically it is exhausting . . . but darling, it is such a magnificent character and I can assure you that though I was nervous lest all the words should not be right, I acted the part as much better than anything else I have done here, that I am amazed at myself and wonder whether the spirit of the Dane was not with me and around me last night."[77] Some members of the Philadelphia press evidently agreed, claiming to be "not a little astonished." "It was to be expected that Miss Cushman's Hamlet . . . would be very fine for a woman; but we at least were not prepared for a performance of such great absolute excellence." This reviewer raved that Charlotte's "conception of the part is far more complete and subtle than that usually seen upon the stage. She appreciates the influence of the supernatural upon his mind, and does not therefore, fall into the error of representing him as one who is merely playing a part, while throughout she enters into his melancholy, his poetic philosophy, his resolution and his impulsiveness."[78]

Charlotte's acclaim as Hamlet had preceded her to Washington, where an announcement of her 1857 engagement at the Washington Theatre was accompanied by a well-publicized request: "We the undersigned respectfully solicit you to appear some evening as Hamlet, a part where you have lately created such a profound sensation, and one so beautifully suited to your refined mind and undoubted genius."[79] The thirty distinguished names that followed this petition attested to the "respectability" of Charlotte's undertaking. It took "refinement" as well as intellect and talent to portray Hamlet. Charlotte, a woman, possessed all three. In Washington critics were even more enthusiastic than they had been in Philadelphia, again conflating gender, sex, and class, as one announced rapturously: "We never saw *Hamlet* until it was done by Cushman. Charlotte Cushman is a perfect gentleman, and was therefore in her *Hamlet* the true prince."[80]

Once again women spectators seemed most intrigued by Charlotte's Hamlet. In the Boston audience in the 1851 season was young sculptor Harriet Hosmer. Hosmer, then twenty-one years old, wrote enthusiastically to her dear friend Cornelia Crow after she had seen Charlotte in her best-known parts: "I used to think Lady Macbeth the finest of anything that could be done but Queen Katharine shook my foundation and Hamlet overturned it—Oh it was most glorious."[81] Yet as much as Charlotte liked playing the part and as decidedly as some female fans, especially ambitious young women like Hosmer, might gravitate to Charlotte's male impersonations, seeing in the characters she played possibilities previously unimaginable for women, not everyone agreed about her effectiveness as the young prince. Others found that her male performances opened up deep-seated anxieties about sexual ambiguity.

In the United States as well as in Britain there had been female Hamlets before Charlotte—"mongrel Hamlets," Charlotte's contemporary Laurence Hutton called them dismissively, conceding that "the most daring and successful of these . . . was unquestionably Miss Charlotte Cushman." Hutton argued, however, that "even the genius of a Cushman was not great enough to crown the effort with success."[82] While actor Lawrence Barrett, who played Laertes to Charlotte's Hamlet in Boston, claimed that, when she wore the "borrowed mantle" of their colleague Edwin Booth, Charlotte "gave novel color to that complex character," he believed Booth to be superior in the role.[83]

The threat Charlotte—as Hamlet as in her other breeches roles—posed to her male colleagues was most marked in the reaction of Edwin Forrest. Forrest continued to be so unsettled by Charlotte's ability and determination to act male roles, and perhaps by her success in them as well, that years later he stated derisively that not only wasn't she womanly; she wasn't even a woman. Charlotte, enraged with Forrest since her first British season, described him as a "butcher."[84]

Cardinal Wolsey

Charlotte Cushman's fluidity in the performance of gender was particularly striking when she took on the part of Cardinal Wolsey in *Henry VIII*. As we have seen, Charlotte's characterization of Queen Katharine in that play was already one of her most highly acclaimed roles by the time she decided occasionally to alternate and play the *male* lead. How permeable might the borders be between male and female when the same performer could just as easily be seen as Katharine one night and as Wolsey the next? Interestingly, in 1851, for novelty Charlotte had offered to alternate performances as Romeo and Juliet, speculating that, "if Fanny Kemble was not too big, old, or fat to [play Juliet], I am sure I am not."[85] But her friend manager William Fredericks apparently discouraged her from the attempt; Charlotte just would not be believable as the feminine Juliet. Wolsey, however, was another matter.

Unlike Romeo or Hamlet, there was no established tradition of women performing this part. Wolsey is not a romantic hero. For much of the play he is not even a sympathetic character. Rather, he is, in the words of one of Charlotte's reviewers, "a remarkable mixture of nobility and meanness, of high and noble aims which are sought to be promoted by craft and cunning."[86] At first Wolsey is a haughty, ambitious man, grand and imposing. In her interpretation of the part Charlotte "contrive[d], with subtle skill, to give just emphasis to that petty malice and that keen fondness for unworthy intrigue which disfigure the character of the man."[87] But the third act, when Wolsey was old, defeated, and heartbroken, provided Charlotte an opportunity to pour out her emotional virtuosity. She depicted Wolsey's misery and self-abasement; when grief-stricken, Wolsey exclaims: "Had I but served my God with half the zeal / I served the King, He would not in my age / Have left me naked to mine enemies."[88] Charlotte loved displaying the range of emotion the part required.

When Charlotte Cushman first played Wolsey, on 13 November 1857, at Burton's New Theatre in New York, no one could recall another actress who had ever undertaken the part. But Charlotte was starting to get too old to play Romeo, and Wolsey offered new challenges. Lawrence Barrett, who was in the cast for this "unique performance," claimed that in this part "she copied faithfully the style of Macready—a very remarkable achievement for a woman."[89] Some of her critics at this and subsequent performances commented on her "robustness" as Wolsey, claiming that "it was a magnificent piece of acting, which fairly carried away her audience; even for a man it is an arduous character, and we had doubts of the success which would attend it; but she knew her own powers, and commanded a great success."[90] And others asserted that "Miss Cushman is the only living actress who could undertake such a character with success, for intensely feminine as are some of the characteristics of her acting, she has a masculine vigor of style and masculine power of voice that render it possible for her, in a great degree, to sink the woman in assuming a male role."[91] Although few others ever described Charlotte Cushman as having "intensely feminine" characteristics, for this reviewer gender was a set of behaviors that could be willfully submerged, or "sunk," if a performer chose.

As with her other major roles, Charlotte demonstrated her ability to present rapidly changing emotions and the deep pathos of a character who ranges from dominating power to profound misery. Some critics likened her work as Wolsey to her other famous characters, favorably comparing the piteous "picture of desolation, of forlorn helplessness and bitter disappointment" in this part to that of her death scene as Queen Katharine. Others, particularly late in Charlotte's life, used this part to comment on the appropriateness of her cross-gender personifications.

"As a general thing the unsexed representatives of females are not successes," announced one critic after Charlotte's performance as Wolsey at the Walnut Street Theatre in Philadelphia. "They may be strong, but they are unnatural. The female Hamlets and Romeos and Richards that have trod the boards are remembered only as curiosities. . . . Their efforts shed no new or additional light upon the characters they assumed."[92] Believing the sexes to be so "essentially" distinct from each other they are incapable of comprehending the world from the vantage point of the other, this critic claimed that "women look at the acts of man from their own standpoint, and hence the picture is wrong in drawing and false in color. The audience will remember who is playing a part, and when a woman dons male attire, wields a sceptre, or exercises male prerogatives, they feel the position is not proper and the dramatic situations lose half their power."[93] But ironically, despite those caveats, this reviewer felt that Charlotte was not only "better fitted" to play the part of Wolsey "than any other female now on the stage"; she even *looked* like the cardinal. "She has the calm, strong face, the quiet manner and the sedate deportment which marked the churchly man who measured power with bluff Henry, of England."[94]

Thus, in the character of Wolsey, as with Hamlet and Romeo, Charlotte's body was regarded by those who supported her performance in breeches parts as *justification for* the appropriateness of her male portrayals. In male roles, as in her female characterizations, many claimed that Charlotte was just doing what came "naturally"; she was merely playing roles for which, given her body, she was well "suited"—characters who were in some crucial ways like herself. But, for those spectators for whom a woman donning male attire was too direct a threat to male privilege, Charlotte's wielding of a phallic scepter or even the degree to which she might naturally look male, pointed out a disturbing incoherence. If the so-called masculine features associated with Charlotte's face and body were, by implication, deviant, then they might become, as Sidonie Smith suggests of bodies categorized as abnormal, "associated with those forces threatening the stability of the body politic" as a whole.[95] And the body politic that largely accepted Charlotte's male characterizations nonetheless frequently believed, as Horace Mann wrote in 1853, that "between the sexes . . . there are innate and connate distinctions, which nature never loses sight of, unless occasionally in the production of a monster."[96]

Paradoxically, although gender was most frequently seen as the outward display of an essential, biologically determined identity, and the body was believed to reflect an individual's inherent personality characteristics, Charlotte embodied characters who appeared to confound these assumed inborn differences between men and women. The popularity of Charlotte's breeches characterizations attests to the multiple readings audience members brought to the images Charlotte created and embodied onstage. In male personae the masculine qualities that were so pronounced even in Charlotte's female roles were now given a purpose, an intention. As I have established, Charlotte's enormous acclaim and acceptance in the role of Romeo by British audiences was, to some extent, shaped by the virility they saw in all Americans, but the *fact* of that acceptance—and the source of pride it offered other Americans—would give more significance to her male portrayals in the United States in years to come, granting her "permission" to do at home what she was so lauded for abroad. On one level all Charlotte's major roles appeared to uphold and contribute to dominant cultural narratives: the idealization of women's chastity and respectability; the muscularity of Americans; the grandeur of nobility. But at the same time Charlotte's characters also contained the possibility of reinforcing meanings and values that exceeded and called into question the status quo, offering pleasures and critiques to those who resisted conventional readings.

In her cross-dressed roles Charlotte was the mediator on the contested borderland of competing social discourses about what constitutes the natural and the unnatural, the respectable and the immoral, the American and the British, the heterosexual and the homosexual. As we have seen in the reactions she received, notions of what it means to be feminine or masculine, to love others of the same sex, to act in a manner appropriate to one's class, to reflect the values of one's nation, were all interrelated variables. Although some few spectators and critics might regard her as monstrous, or unnatural, Charlotte's characterizations also could be seized upon to justify or explain the very specific gradations and resonances called up by maleness or femaleness in different national or cultural settings. The lived experiences of women in her audiences were most directly implicated with the characters Charlotte created. If the contours of Charlotte's female body could be imaginatively reshaped, re-presented to form male characters, to claim male privilege, so might their own.

Charlotte's representations illuminated as well the contradictory space for female spectators whose own erotic responses allowed them to read the covert meanings possible when they saw and recognized the woman's body clothed in the guise of a male character. In her breeches parts, particularly as Romeo, Charlotte epitomized Marjorie Garber's observation that "clothing as a system of signification . . . speak[s] in a number of registers" to observers, calling up associations with class, gender, sexuality, and erotic style. While some spectators saw only Shakespeare's youthful lover, for others—particularly those women who, seeing Charlotte declaring her love for another woman, recognized some of their own desire—there could be both "pleasure and danger" in decoding what they saw enacted before them.[97] Underneath Charlotte's disguise, or because of it, her desiring sexual subjectivity, her lesbianism, was visible to anyone who could read the code. But she was also ambiguous enough in her on- and offstage gender display so that spectators and critics who did not share in the "referential context"[98] could decode her performances as merely *reinforcing* nineteenth-century ideologies of female sexlessness—since she so clearly did not direct her body to male spectators' desire—as well as those of nationality and of class.

In male guise this animated force that ushered forth from a female body challenged the terms under which many understood the most classical and popularly accepted texts of the day: Charlotte as the star-crossed fe/male lover of women; Charlotte as the prince of Denmark, robbed of his—or her—rightful throne by a father's murder; Charlotte as the cleric who could make or break royalty. Charlotte was both the representation and the actor who constructed the image, seemingly able willfully to transform herself into whatever characterization she chose. Out of each of her major roles Charlotte forged images of forceful and compelling women and men to whom fans responded—expanding their vocabulary of possibilities while *simultaneously* appearing to uphold some of her era's most cherished traditional values. In the years that followed Charlotte's British debut as Romeo, fans like poet Sallie Bridges would see in Charlotte's characterizations a model of female strength that enlarged the concept of true womanhood without contradicting it. Bridges, who followed Charlotte's career for years, wrote:

How often in youth's sweet remembered day,
Your genius has thrilled my conquered heart!
At every vision of each chosen part
Admiring thoughts bestow'd new leaves of bay!
For then I only saw the shapes you wore.
King Henry's Queen when Cromwell wept beside,
Unruly Katharine as a fractious bride,
Romeo raving by the tomb's clos'd door!
Or listened to Meg's weird prophetic tones,
Fair Rosalind's laugh and Portia's judgement meet;
Heard Lady Macbeth's awful midnight groans
Or wept to Pathos of the London Street,
Now mind and soul even higher homage send,
True woman hail you and a faithful friend.[99]

The "shapes Charlotte wore" onstage were representations charged with multiple and contested meanings. And while Charlotte was first donning them, tailoring them, crafting them for the British public, she came in contact with other women who plied their artistry in different professional venues, creating characters on the page who echoed what Charlotte was doing on the stage.

Scribbling Circles and Strange Sympathies

Charlotte Cushman's London Circle of Lovers and Friends

> I gazed with joy upon thy open brow,
> And Faith sprung up between us—firm and sound;
> We were good, earnest friends at first, and now
> Where is the hand by which could be unbound
> The mingled threads of Feeling's fairest hues,
> That hold us captive in Affection's thrall?
> —Eliza Cook, "To Charlotte Cushman"

In Charlotte Cushman's diary for her first months in England are names of women—particularly women writers—who met, befriended, and championed the "new American actress" in their midst. What would these women come to mean to Charlotte and she to them? At first they were just names to her: art critic Anna Jameson, essayist Mary Howitt, poet Eliza Cook. She had read their books, poems, and essays. From Charlotte's first arrival in England and her earliest performances there, she found herself welcomed by and drawn to a number of other professional women. In England, as in the United States, many women found Cushman's forcefulness and self-possession captivating. Their letters to Charlotte and to one another and their published texts survive, offering a view of this extended circle of writers and reformers who shaped themselves into an informal network of friends and lovers. Soon Charlotte Cushman herself, and her professional achievements, would be drawn upon by these and other women writers as "material" that could be shaped into their own poetry, fictional narratives, and essays. For her literary friends and partners Charlotte would become a "text" they could fashion and use in their own work to represent a range of different attitudes about women and performance. These fictional depictions would extend her circle of friends and give rise to a virtual community of female readers and spectators joined in their recognition of desire—Charlotte's and their own—for autonomy, for success, and, often, for other women.

Nineteenth-century women writers, like women performers, were frequently seen as transgressors of male authority in their attempt to wrest for themselves paid, public careers. Although women writers didn't risk the same degree of social ostracism that women performers did, many of their contemporaries who disapproved of careers for women regarded their endeavors as a violation of Victorian dictates of appropriate feminine behavior because, as Norma Clarke notes, "writing women . . . occupied the printed page with words which might attain the power of definition and they competed with male writers in the marketplace, earning money and potentially acquiring economic independence."[1] Precisely for this reason, some male writers, such as Nathaniel Hawthorne, complained about the increasing numbers of "damned scribbling women" now popular on both sides of the Atlantic.[2] Yet, many others admired women writers in spite or because of their transgressions. And Charlotte Cushman, striving to maintain her economic independence as a professional woman, in a foreign country, was particularly pleased with the social cachet of being associated with Britain's literati in their politically progressive and artistic circles.

One of the first women writers to usher Charlotte into her group of friends was Mary Howitt. Mary and her husband, writer and editor William, were Quaker radicals whose periodical the *People's Journal* was advertised as "an international publication . . . for every class and condition . . . devoted to the advocacy of the broad principle of Human Brotherhood."[3] The Howitts had enthusiastically welcomed other American women writers and activists, such as Lucretia Mott, whom they met when she was in London in 1840 attending the World Anti-Slavery Convention, and transcendentalist writer Margaret Fuller. To Mary Howitt, Charlotte Cushman was yet another independent American woman, a representative of a democratic ideal and the embodiment of the struggles faced by all women who sought to earn their own living in the arts. As one of the Howitts' biographers noted, Charlotte "enchanted Mary who extolled her self-denial, and purity of life."[4] As I have established, Mary Howitt's article about the American actress in the *People's Journal* helped construct the image by which Charlotte would be known in England.

Shortly after Charlotte arrived in London, Mary Howitt generously opened up her circle of acquaintances to the young actress and introduced Charlotte to other women writers, including Mary Mitford and Geraldine Jewsbury, whose social standing and intellectual interests might be helpful and sympathetic to Charlotte.[5] After a series of performances in Manchester, Charlotte wrote to thank Mary Howitt for her kindness in providing letters of introduction: "Miss Jewsbury came to see me and I am charmed with her. She is very clever and talks most admirably."[6] And Geraldine Jewsbury was similarly charmed with her new American friend, particularly in the role of

Bianca in Milman's *Fazio*. As this growing circle of British women writers embraced the American actress and applauded her efforts, Charlotte was more than pleased to find herself so frequently in the company of other intelligent women as dedicated to their careers as she was to her own. Happily, Charlotte remarked in a letter to her mother, "I have been crowded with company since I've acted. . . . My reputation abroad is as somewhat clever and it keeps me in a constant excitement to keep that up."[7]

Most flattering to her was the acceptance by women whose writing she had long admired. On 19 May 1845 Charlotte noted in her diary that she had met the feminist writer Anna Jameson, whose cultural criticism, such as her enormously influential *Characteristics of Women* (1832), based on female characters in Shakespeare's plays, had been dedicated to Charlotte's old friend Fanny Kemble.[8] Shortly after their first meeting Charlotte told Jameson, "I hardly know how to tell you at what a high rate I esteem your good opinion and am only sorry that you have been so situated that I have seen comparatively little of you, for I could wish you to find reason for liking me."[9] Anna Jameson *did* like Charlotte Cushman. Jameson was a prolific and popular writer who, by the 1840s, was known for several books she had written about celebrated women. In *Characteristics of Women* Jameson had described acting as a noble profession for women and argued that classic female dramatic characters and their embodiment onstage could serve as suitable models of women's "moral" characteristics. Jameson's friendship, like Mary Howitt's, was not only personally rewarding but also strategically advantageous to Charlotte. Her association with these accomplished and respectable women afforded Charlotte visibility while placing her within a milieu that was much more socially desirable than that most theatrical performers frequented. As an actress among other female creative artists and social reformers, Charlotte found herself among women who championed socially progressive causes and depicted the stage as "an instrument of human advance[ment] and enlightenment," requiring "devotion of heart, earnestness, purity of purpose, and purity of life."[10] And women like Jameson, Howitt, and Jewsbury were fascinated with the forthright American actress.

Once she found herself welcomed into this circle, from her first season on the British stage Charlotte's life in London was filled with parties and receptions. One of her most helpful supporters was critic Henry Fothergill Chorley, the music and dramatic critic for the *Athenaeum*. Charlotte met Chorley shortly after she arrived in London, and he soon became a close friend. In addition to being a highly respected critic Chorley was a well-regarded social host. At Chorley's regular gatherings Charlotte met such literary notables as Robert Browning and kept up her acquaintance with Jameson and the Howitts. At first the warm reactions she received sur-

prised even herself. Knowing that her popularity baffled, even discon-
certed, her own family, Charlotte remarked to her mother, "I hesitate to
write even to you the complimentary things that are said and done to me
here, for it looks monstrously like boasting."[11] Her brother, Charles, somewhat sardonically related that among "the many devotees to her shrine at
this period . . . [were] the literati of the day, and from a good many of them
very kind attentions were received."[12]

For Americans at home, however, Charlotte's acceptance into this
esteemed artistic circle was a source of national pride. The New York *News*
announced that:

> It will be gratifying to the friends of our favorite Charlotte to learn that
> the last steamer brought good intelligence of her progress, and the man-
> ner in which she is appreciated in England. She is a welcome guest in the
> societies of the learned and the distinguished. In literary circles she is par-
> ticularly an object of interest.[13]

Yet of all the literary friendships Charlotte cultivated, her growing relationship with the woman the *News* described as "Eliza Cook, the charming
poetess" was more than a supportive friendship; it was to become a romantic love, much closer in emotion and substance to Charlotte's earlier attachment to Rosalie Sully.

"Red-hot" Eliza Cook

Charlotte Cushman and Eliza Cook met in May 1845, as Charlotte was
completing her first London season. Sitting in the audience during a production of *Fazio*, Eliza Cook had been so moved by Charlotte's representation of Bianca that she later sent Charlotte a poem:

> I had seen many "fret and strut their hour";
> But my brain never had become such slave
> To fiction, as it did beneath thy power,
> Nor owned such homage as to thee it gave.[14]

By the beginning of Charlotte's second season, Eliza was paying "homage"
to Charlotte in other ways as well, showering her with other poems and a
sketch of Charlotte Cushman in the role of Meg Merrilies, entitled "Yankee
holding out her banner."[15] In the drawing Meg was literally "blowing her
own horn." Out of the trumpet Eliza Cook had written the names of the
various characters Charlotte had performed in London thus far. In-
terspersed with these names was the word *ego* written several times. In this
drawing Eliza depicted Charlotte literally declaring herself to *be* her

characters; it is as if she were saying, "I am Romeo," "I am Bianca." Eliza recognized that in Charlotte's utterance of herself as these characters she was constructing her offstage self as well. Eliza expressed pride in her new American friend's accomplishments and in her own. In Eliza's drawing Meg holds a banner that resembles the American flag; on each of the stripes are listed the names of periodicals in which Eliza Cook had published poetry proclaiming her feelings for Charlotte.

In her published poetry Cook represented the two women's growing attachment to each other in language describing powerful attractions, shared vows, and secret understandings despite the efforts of others to separate them. Cook wrote:

> So thou hast come, all absolute, to rule my inmost soul;
> But yet how calm, how dream-like, is the strength of thy control.
> There are sealed pages in my heart, traced with illumined hand,
> That none can see, and if they did, oh! who would understand?
> But thou, by some strange sympathy, hast thrown a searching look,
> And read at sight the hardest scroll indorsed [sic] within the book.
> I love thee with a free-born will, that no rude force can break—
> Thou lovest me—I know thou dost—and for my own poor sake;
> And though the coward's barb is launched, it can but vainly flit,
> While we may smile to watch the aim too meanly weak to hit.
> ... I've staked my faith upon thy heart—it will not cheat my hope—
> I cling to it as trustingly as sailor to the rope.[16]

Eliza Cook's poetry to Charlotte is replete with sensual (and sexual) imagery that suggests bodily responses to the erotic desires they aroused in each other. In this poem, Eliza's heart, or body, is likened to a book with "sealed pages" that Charlotte, with her "strange sympathy," has understood, seen, and opened with her "illumined hand," "read[ing] at sight the hardest scroll" within the book. "Cowards" may have "launched barbs" against the women's relationship, whether in the form of social censure or the disapproval of specific friends or family members, but in this poem Eliza proclaims that she trusts and clings to the woman who has "come . . . to rule my inmost soul."

Many outsiders could not "read at sight" or understand the growing passionate connection between Charlotte and Eliza. Although Charles Cushman apparently thought quite highly of Eliza Cook, asserting that "not a more deserving—upright—honorable—woman ever walked the earth,"[17] others, particularly Charlotte's mother and sister, were no more supportive of the "strange sympathy" and the love between the two women than they had been about Charlotte's closeness with other women to whom she was passionately connected.[18]

"Yankee Hanging Out Her Banner," by Eliza Cook. Charlotte
Cushman's companion, poet Eliza Cook, championed her
lover's British triumph in this sketch, in which Cushman's
nationality is highlighted as well as her performance as the
supernaturally powerful Gypsy queen Meg Merrilies.
*(Charlotte Cushman Papers. Manuscript Division, Library
of Congress.)*

Yet Eliza was, in many ways, a suitable companion for Charlotte. She
was as renowned in her profession as Charlotte was rapidly becoming on
the stage. Like Charlotte, she came from a middle-class family of modest
means. Eliza was the daughter of a tradesman, a brazier, who had allowed
his children to educate themselves according to their interests. Before she
was twenty years old Eliza Cook had published her first volume of poetry[19]
and written regularly for periodicals, most notably the *Weekly Dispatch.*
Eliza had become so close with the family of Alderman Harmer, the principal proprietor of the *Weekly Dispatch,* that she spent much time with them
at their home, Ingress Abbey, in Kent. As much as Eliza Cook was commended in some quarters for the moral and sentimental tone and themes

of her poetry, her intimate relations with other women even before she met Charlotte Cushman, and her unconventional demeanor, left her vulnerable to scandal. There had been whispers about Eliza's having become "warmly attached" to the granddaughter of Alderman Harmer. Critics ridiculed "the poetess's intimacy with the family of the Alderman" and "indulged in insinuations of the most absurd kind."[20]

Yet, despite these intriguing (but never explained) "absurd insinuations," Eliza Cook's poetry, which emphasized the simple love of hearth and home, led her, in the words of this same memoirist, to be considered "one of the most popular women in England."[21] By the time she met Charlotte, Eliza had already enjoyed years of popular acclaim among the "masses."[22] But arbiters of literary quality on both sides of the Atlantic were clearly critical of both Cook's poetry and her demeanor. As one reviewer wrote in the literary section of the *New York Daily Times,* "Miss Eliza Cook, whose poetry must be familiar to thousands . . . is popular, but she is not a poetess for all that." Instead, the critic expressed the opinion that "Miss Cook has written a vast amount of silly verses." But much of this journalist's patronizing criticism of "our rhyming subject" was directed at "the half Bloomerish appearance of the lady." When he met her Eliza was "dressed . . . in a staring red plaid dress; . . . her hair was dressed in a man-ish fashion," and "she rather sauntered than walked into the drawing room" looking "red hot." Equally remarkable was Eliza's audacity as she was observed to "tilt back her chair, plant her feet on the fender and bluffly call for a glass of beer"[23]—not typical behavior for a "respectable" nineteenth-century "poetess."

Unlike the more socially prominent women writers with whom Charlotte associated, Eliza Cook explicitly wrote her poetry to and for the lower middle classes. Charles Cushman recognized Eliza Cook's principled character and noted that she was "a very popular writer among a certain class of people but . . . amongst another and more snobbish set was vilified & abused."[24] Eliza was forthright about her politics, her unconventional clothing, and her deep love for Charlotte, who was intrigued by her. Soon Charlotte, and occasionally Charles, were accompanying Eliza on visits to Ingress Abbey.

And Charlotte took pleasure in doing whatever she could to further Eliza's career. Just a few months after Charlotte established herself in London and first met Eliza, she attempted to intercede on Eliza's behalf. Charlotte discovered that Eliza had written to Henry Langley, an American publisher whom Charlotte knew, but that Langley had never replied to her. Describing Eliza Cook's situation to Langley, Charlotte implored him to negotiate with Eliza directly: "She is the most kind and gentle creature in the world—and I sure felt hurt that you had taken no notice of her letter—

Will you think of it?"[25] Apparently, Charlotte's effort on Eliza's behalf was successful, for shortly afterward a notice in the New York *News* announced that Langley was republishing a "splendid volume" of Cook's poems. In the same newspaper article (possibly supplied by Langley to promote sales of Eliza Cook's poetry) Eliza professed to "admire and estimate your countrywoman, Miss Cushman. We are friends, and I trust will long be such. She is gathering golden opinions from the English, and will take a high standing in her profession."[26]

Several years later, when Charlotte's friend Sarah Josepha Hale, the influential American editor of *Godey's Lady's Book,* decided to edit a biographical volume cataloging a record of women's achievements, she wanted to include mention of both Charlotte Cushman and Eliza Cook. In the years since *Godey's* had published Charlotte's short story, "The Actress," Charlotte had been aware that a connection with *Godey's Lady's Book* (and its editor) could offer an imprimatur of respectability, affording a degree of acceptance that she continued to value and one she wished for Eliza as well. In order to help secure Eliza Cook's name as a poet before *Godey's* solidly middle-class American female readership, Cushman wrote to Hale, "I should be glad to have a *true woman* like yourself give to the world a true account of her."[27] Charlotte happily served as defender, promoter, literary agent, and social intermediary for the woman who had "staked [her] faith upon [Charlotte's] heart."

But, for all the good an association with Charlotte might bring about in some quarters, in others actresses, even those as highly regarded as Charlotte Cushman, were of still questionable social status, and many of their contemporaries did not hold women performers in the same esteem as they did women writers. For example, while Mary Howitt's elderly mother approved of the Howitts' "literary productions, . . . she took exception to [their] advocacy of the stage." As Mary Howitt explained, her Quaker mother believed "that virtuous persons, assuming fictitious characters, became ultimately what they simulated. She consequently eschewed some exemplary actresses—our familiar associates—terming them 'stage girls,' whom she pitied, but whose accomplishments she abhorred."[28]

On both sides of the Atlantic Charlotte's very public profession was deemed less reputable by many than Eliza Cook's vocation as a poet, yet of the two women Cook was the more politically radical and nonconformist because of her championing of the poor and disenfranchised and because of her practical decision to forgo such "feminine" finery as tight-laced corsets and frilly women's dresses. Charlotte Cushman was clearly influenced by Eliza, and soon the two women were seen dressing alike. Mary Howitt noted approvingly in her diary that her two friends signaled their attachment to each other, and the intimacy of their relationship, in

Eliza Cook, frontispiece to *Poems by Eliza Cook* (London: Simpkin, Marshall, 1848). Eliza Cook's hair, described as short and "mannish," and her plain shirt collar and tailored jacket excited much comment among her contemporaries.

the clothing that they wore. Having received a bolt of cloth while visiting friends in Yorkshire, Charlotte had matching clothing made for herself and Eliza Cook, whom Mary Howitt described as "dressed in a very masculine style, which was considered strange at that time, with short hair parted on one side, and a tight-fitting, lapelled bodice, showing a shirtfront and ruffle." Seeing the two women together, Mary Howitt thought that Eliza Cook "looked well in her dark steel-blue alpaca, and Miss Cushman, who possessed a strongly-built, heroic figure, not the less so."[29]

Inevitably, word of Charlotte's newfound closeness had gotten back to Philadelphia and to Rosalie Sully. Now that Charlotte had moved her entire family to England, it was clear that the six-month separation that Rosalie had encouraged might be permanent. How did Charlotte feel about her unprecedented acclaim and her growing closeness to Eliza Cook? Charlotte had left her pet birds and books and Thomas Sully's portrait of her with

Charlotte Cushman, by Wilhelm Trautschold, ca. 1847. Cushman's relationship with Eliza Cook is indicated in this painting
both by Cushman's increasingly "masculine" attire and the fact
that Trautschold, who met Cook along with Cushman, painted
Charlotte Cushman holding her lover's book, *Poems by Eliza
Cook. (From the Art Collection of the Folger Shakespeare
Library.)*

Rosalie, all in the expectation that she would be returning soon. But every
day was taking her further from the life she remembered with Rosalie.
Charlotte's priorities had clearly shifted from the previous year. While it is
not certain to what degree her relationship with Rosalie cooled once Charlotte encouraged her family to join her in England, press reports of her very
public closeness with Eliza Cook did not help matters. Although only one
letter from Rosalie exists, as early as 10 May 1845 Charlotte noted in her
diary that she had received a letter from Rosalie, breaking her heart. Whatever happened between them, the love Charlotte had shared with Rosalie

seemed to fade in the flush of Charlotte's British success. As hard as it might be to admit to her American lover, there was much about this new British life to recommend it. Certainly, Charlotte had never been so professionally or socially successful before. In England she could earn a fortune. Charlotte determined that she would stay three years more. By then, at the rate she was going, she expected to have earned fifty thousand dollars—an extraordinary amount of money at the time—and have enough money to retire and live comfortably wherever and with whomever she chose.[30]

In what would eventually become something of a pattern in Charlotte's life, the attachment she enjoyed with Eliza Cook, while intimate, was not exclusive. Despite the two women's closeness, Charlotte continued to write to and spend time with other women who were her passionate friends. For Eliza Cook the degree of erotic desire she felt with Charlotte was unprecedented; Charlotte's glances aroused "a flushing ray into my breast it never felt before."[31] Yet, by November 1845, while Charlotte was on tour in Sheffield, she met a much younger woman, an eighteen-year-old music teacher and devotee who was known as Sarah Anderton.

Initially, Sarah, a theatrical hopeful, wrote Charlotte asking advice. She had been barely eking out a living as a piano teacher, and Charlotte advised her to consider the stage. Soon they began exchanging particularly passionate letters.[32] "Dearest," Charlotte wrote, "you are held among the dearest things to me and I long for Saturday like a young lover." Charlotte had been ill on the road, and she mused that "in your love I should have been happier—I am strangely dependent for affection and looks of love have a more healing power w/me than all the doctor's stuff in the world."[33] There is no question but that Sarah's infatuation with Charlotte had an erotic component—one Charlotte encouraged, despite her attachment to Eliza Cook and to any lingering sense of loyalty she may have felt toward Rosalie Sully.

Despite the predominant ideology of women's passionlessness that allowed women's love for each other to be generally accepted—often likened to the sentimental attachment of sisters or close friends—Charlotte, as she had in her earlier relationships, recognized her own erotic desire and was keenly aware of the disapproval such feelings between women might engender. Charlotte wrote cautiously to Anderton: "The postscript of your last dear note reached me on Wednesday, dearest, and I . . . felt *most certain that you were not writing freely to me*. . . . I asked you a question in one of my notes . . . which would set my mind at ease. . . . I asked you if *any* one saw your letters (written or recd) but yourself. I know a great difference exists in families with regard to this."[34] Charlotte clearly felt that some expressions of sentiment between the two women would not meet their families' approval. Perhaps Benjamin Brewster's insistence that his sister end her relationship with Charlotte was still fresh in her mind, or the numerous scowls and comments her own mother and sister displayed when confronted with other women in her life may have served as a warning to her.

On her way to a return engagement in Sheffield, Charlotte confided to Sarah: "I wish my sister was not going to be w/me, for I wish to have you all to myself. I want to talk to you a great deal, and my sister has cold eyes and may frighten you."[35] Although Mary Eliza Cushman complained about Charlotte's plan to stop in Sheffield, Charlotte assured Sarah, "My heart is there and I must look after everything that belongs to me or no one else will."[36] Sarah, whom Charlotte claimed "belonged" to her, had evidently written of her love for Charlotte in familial terms, likening the two women's intimacy to that of sisters. But the embodied passion that Charlotte Cushman desired—in fact, depended upon—from some of the women closest to her was differentiated in her mind from the sisterly affection she felt for others. In this same letter Charlotte offered: "You wish I was your sister. I wish you were mine—but I shall tell you things when I see you which will make you believe that a stranger love is often dearer than a sister."[37]

Charlotte encouraged the erotic reactions female friends and fans expressed. When Sarah Anderton regaled her idol with "dear notes and poetry," Charlotte seductively confided to her, with at least an unconscious resonance, that while she was playing Bianca she had placed Anderton's note into her bodice, "next to my heart and went to work rejoicing," feeling the love note between her breasts. Backstage, between scenes, Charlotte read it and then "placed it where I had taken it from [and] . . . placed my hand upon my heart to assure myself your dear note was safe, and then drew it forth to comfort me in my weariness."[38] Anderton's note could touch the great actress's "heart" while she acted, even if Anderton herself were far away.

Yet, despite her flirtatious assurances of love, Charlotte asked her "little pet," as she called Sarah, for a favor, to obtain a copy of the Sheffield paper "containing Miss Cook's lines to me."[39] Even in her letters to other women who adored her, Charlotte frequently mentioned the woman whom she now acknowledged as most significant in her life. "I do speak of you often to Eliza Cook who wishes to see you and you shall meet one of these days," Charlotte wrote Sarah. "You would like her exceedingly. She is shy at first but the best and truest of women."[40] Charlotte even "took the liberty" of sending her accomplished lover copies of the effusive love poems young Sarah sent her, for Eliza to correct and comment on, to help "improve" Sarah's writing. Regardless of how Charlotte's "little pet" felt when told by the woman she revered that her lover "could give you hints" to help develop your "great poetic talent,"[41] Charlotte was reminding Sarah of Eliza Cook's priority in her affections.

Charlotte was so thrilled with Eliza Cook's poetry and with her public declarations of affection in print that she shared copies of Eliza's poems with another woman admirer, Geraldine Jewsbury. Charlotte seemed not to consider the jealousy and awkwardness actions like this might provoke. In her attempt to create communities of women and networks of support Charlotte, who loved being the center of attention, introduced her friends, admirers, and lovers to one another. Throughout her life she usually maintained a relationship with one primary partner who was a peer, while she explored the attraction and erotic appeal of a much younger devotee. At times the competition for her time and affection clouded the already ambiguous distinctions between degrees of attachment Charlotte encouraged. The lack of available language to distinguish clearly relationships between close female friends from those between women who felt erotic and emotional desire for each other further complicated matters for them. Yet language is all that remains now, and it is only through the ephemeral clues left in the public texts and private correspondence of the women with whom Charlotte was most intimate that we can glimpse the contours of their relationships. Although there are no existing letters between Charlotte and Eliza, in Eliza Cook's poetry and in letters in which they mention each other to other friends, the emotional intensity of Charlotte and Eliza's relationship is clearly evident. And one of the friends with whom Charlotte most candidly discussed her feelings for Eliza was Geraldine Jewsbury.

Geraldine Jewsbury: "In a Blaze of Enthusiasm"

Geraldine Jewsbury had been attracted to Charlotte Cushman since their first meeting in Manchester, during Charlotte's provincial tour. In her letters Geraldine expressed the tensions often present among Charlotte's overlapping relationships, particularly the growing jealousy Geraldine felt about Charlotte's closeness to Eliza Cook. Geraldine and Charlotte met after Jane Carlyle, the witty and acerbic wife of writer Thomas Carlyle, had become the passionate center of Geraldine's life. But, as Geraldine's admiration for Charlotte grew stronger, Geraldine's relationship with Jane Carlyle became temporarily estranged. Jane Carlyle confided her jealousy of Geraldine's affection for Charlotte in a letter to her cousin:

> Geraldine, by the way, is all in a blaze of enthusiasm about Miss Cushman the Actress—with whom she swore everlasting friendship at Manchester just when she had got jealous of me and Mrs. Paulet. Ever since her [Geraldine Jewsbury's] letters have been filled with lyrics about this woman [Charlotte Cushman],—till I could stand it no longer—I have written her such a screed of my mind.[42]

Many women, like Geraldine Jewsbury and Jane Carlyle, whether married or not, frequently made pacts indicating the emotional preeminence of their relationships with each other. The performative nature of these literal declarations of closeness between women, like the "swearing of everlasting friendship," created a bond by its very articulation. Just as Jane Carlyle could not stand to see in writing the "lyrical" expressions of Geraldine's enthusiasm for Charlotte, reading Eliza Cook's letters and love poems to Charlotte unsettled Geraldine, and she wrote to Charlotte: "this time last year I cd have written passionate things *myself* to another—and to see that poem and to read E.C.'s letters seems like meeting my own ghost."[43] Furthermore, as Geraldine noted critically, "I do not care much about the poem as a whole—When people *feel* a great deal they cannot put it into either prose or poetry and that is the case here—if you ever quarrel, she will write a much finer *poem* on you. . . . I wish I did not care about *you* as I do for I know full well I shall be made miserable for it someday."[44]

Infatuated, and "puzzled" by Charlotte's "neglect," Geraldine warned Charlotte that "I am *not* an angel but a wild cat and I'll scratch you if I can't *beat* you. . . . Miss Cooke [*sic*] would think me very good if she could *believe* that another person might love you as well as she does." Geraldine Jewsbury's struggle to recognize the fact that the love Charlotte shared with Eliza differed both in degree and kind from her own friendship with and infatuation for the actress demonstrates some of the ways women who loved other women understood, represented, and differentiated between their relationships with one another. Charlotte and Eliza Cook clearly experienced themselves as a "couple"; Eliza Cook told a mutual friend "I need not say I am very happy with my companion."[45] Geraldine attempted to reconcile herself to the intensity of Charlotte's attachment to Eliza, even as she flirted teasingly:

> I have got something else to tell you only I am like a baby and want you to give me a kiss before I can find grace to get it said. . . . It is about E. Cooke [*sic*]. . . . I feel quite glad that I have got into sympathy with you about her and I think I shall get to like her on my own account in time. . . . I don't want to be separated from you by want of sympathy for anybody you care for; I am jealous enough myself.[46]

Despite Geraldine Jewsbury's observation that great affection could not be captured in either prose or poetry, in 1848, while Eliza Cook was still writing poetry expressing her love for Charlotte, Geraldine channeled her admiration for Charlotte into her second novel, *The Half Sisters,* in which the protagonist is an actress named Bianca, bearing the name of the first character Charlotte played in England.[47]

In *The Half Sisters* Bianca—like Charlotte's own fictional heroine Leoline and, or so Charlotte claimed, like Charlotte herself—had gone onstage only because "she was face to face with destitution . . . with nothing but her own hands to stave it off herself and her mother." But, as Geraldine and her readers knew, actresses were frequently condemned, especially by the social elite, as "dissipated disorderly vagabonds, whom it would not have been creditable to know, or altogether safe to admit to the neighborhood of their silver spoons,"[48] regardless of their reasons for going onstage. Yet Bianca, like Charlotte, was too complex a character to be reduced to either an abject, social outcast threatening to disrupt the social order or a dutiful Victorian daughter determined to uphold it. Bianca was described, as Charlotte Cushman frequently was, as a liminal character just over the edge of conventional femininity—a respectable woman who possessed "manly" traits such as "a strong and indomitable resolution—an energy that would shrink from nothing" once it "was roused."[49] Even Bianca's desire for stardom was motivated by higher and nobler ends, such as her desire to purify the theatrical profession "from the sensualism that has defaced it."[50] And at the same time Bianca could experience the sense of purpose that was missing from her conventional half-sister's marriage. In words that mirror Charlotte's in other contexts Bianca proclaims: "The stage is to me like a *passion*, as well as a profession . . . it possesses one like a demon; it is a sacred necessity laid upon me, which I cannot help obeying."[51]

While Bianca is initially a social outcast, ultimately she becomes a star like Charlotte who exercises "sovereign sway and masterdom" over her audience, "wielding their souls as she chooses, producing what emotions she will, playing upon them as upon some curious instrument."[52] In *The Half Sisters* Jewsbury raises and disposes of one of the most damning claims about women who performed onstage: the claim that acting "unsexed" a woman,[53] leaving her with "neither the softness of a woman, nor the firm, well-proportioned principles of a man."[54] According to Conrad, Bianca's high-born but false lover, as a result of acting a masculine part in her everyday life by pursuing a profession, Bianca "loves like a man, and yet expects to be adored as a woman."[55] Yet Jewsbury's novel exposed the contradictions implicit in these prejudices against masculine women. If one could be "unsexed" by engaging in a given public behavior, then one's sex was not an intrinsic and "natural" part of an individual. While Conrad lambasted "women who follow *their own desire* and insist on being *strong-minded* women" as being "decidedly disagreeable," other sympathetic characters, like Lord Melton, claim that women need a "vent for . . . the vitality that is in them," which they can only find if "they have a definite profession." Bianca's honor and chastity is a result of her "serv[ing] [her] art with that singleness of mind and oneness of purpose which all art required."[56] Charlotte, however, still had to contend with the actual abhorrence some people felt for "unsexed" professional women, particularly those who chose to spend their lives with other women.

If Charlotte's friends had difficulty integrating her relationship with Eliza Cook into their own friendship with Charlotte, she had an even more difficult time escaping the cold eyes in her own family.[57] As she confided to Geraldine, Mary Eliza and Susan Cushman's disapproval of Charlotte's relationships with other women continued to cast a pall over Charlotte's most cherished attachments. Despite her own jealousy, Geraldine told Charlotte to "*follow your own instinct.* You need love to keep you up in your daily course more even than most women."[58]

And Charlotte did. But she felt that need most poignantly in the summer of 1847, after she received word that Rosalie Sully had died, on 8 July, at the age of twenty-nine in Philadelphia. I have been unable to determine the cause of her death. Since one of her brothers died in the same year, it is possible that she died of either an infectious disease or an inherited disorder. But Rosalie was also clearly brokenhearted about Charlotte's not returning to her and about rumors of Charlotte's closeness with other women, so I can't help conjecturing that Rosalie's despondency contributed to her untimely death. She said in her sole existing letter to Charlotte that she was "praying fervently for death to end my misery."[59]

Charlotte, at the edge of collapse from overwork and emotional distress, followed Geraldine's advice to go to Malvern, a well-known spa, where she might mourn, rest, and try the "water cure" to help raise her flagging spirits. Did Charlotte regret not having done more for Rosalie? Maybe she was saddened that she had outgrown her dearest friend or that she may have been the cause of Rosalie's unhappiness. Whatever brooding thoughts occupied Charlotte's mind, Geraldine Jewsbury advised that, if the women presently in Charlotte's life were "worthy, cling to them."[60] Charlotte clung to Eliza Cook.

Things did not work smoothly for Charlotte and Eliza, however, despite their intense feelings and the mutual admiration they felt for each other's professional achievements. Eliza was aware of the adulation that her partner was receiving from masses of spectators, many of them adoring female fans, who saw Charlotte as their idol. While Eliza Cook refused to compete for Charlotte's attention, Eliza wrote:

I will not praise as others praise—thou need'st it not from me,
Thy Genius has won its meed, and Fame is crowning thee;
. . . I held thee closely ere I knew thy gift was rare and great,
My being was enlinked with thine, by some entrancing fate.
And now I bow not to thee as the million gazers nod,
To them thou art an incense pyre—to me a 'household god.' "[61]

Ultimately, Charlotte and Eliza's dreams of a "household" together succumbed not to the intoxicating heat or passion, the "incense pyre" that Charlotte inspired in her "million gazers," but to far more pragmatic concerns. Charlotte loved to travel and fully intended to return to the United States, victorious, once she had made her mark in England. Eliza Cook was deathly afraid of the sea and was unwilling to travel with Charlotte to the Continent or later to the United States. Yet Eliza Cook was, according to Charles Cushman, "sincerely and devotedly fond of Charlotte."[62] And Charlotte continued to spend time with Eliza, but increasingly they found themselves "agreeing to differ."[63]

At this time Charlotte's circle of women writers was expanding, and she began to develop other friendships. In the years to come Charlotte would continue to surround herself with other women whose livelihoods she would promote. As Charles Cushman remembered, before the final break in Charlotte and Eliza's relationship, "for a short time a Miss Lynn—a lady of some literary merit,"[64] was a member of Charlotte's London circle.

Eliza Lynn lived in a rooming house near the British Museum and not far from the small house on Garway Road, in Bayswater, that Charlotte had rented for herself and her family when they joined her in England. Also living nearby was Lynn's friend, Samuel Laurence, a portraitist whose regular Sunday evening gatherings were attended by an intellectual, progressive, and "insurgent" collection of writers and reformers, according to Eliza Lynn.[65] Charlotte Cushman was also acquainted with this group, whom she met just months after her arrival in London, when she sat for a portrait by Laurence in April 1845.[66] In addition to Eliza Lynn, regular visitors to this unconventional household included philanthropists committed to social reform such as Robert Owen, Edmund Larken, a Mrs. Milner-Gibson, Ellen Braysher (whom Lynn described as "a woman of large means holding advanced views"),[67] and William James Linton (whom Eliza Lynn later married), and writers George Henry Lewes, Amelia Edwards, and Matilda Mary Hays, novelist and translator of George Sand and soon to become Charlotte Cushman's long-term partner.

Charles Cushman remembered that Charlotte's relationship to Eliza Lynn "was not a lengthy one for the lack I suppose of sympathy between them."[68] Perhaps the "lack of sympathy" between Charlotte Cushman and Eliza Lynn was ideological as well as emotional. It appears that Lynn recognized and then recanted the nature of her early attraction to Cushman, just as she did her early progressive political bent. "In those days," Lynn later claimed, "I was as much an insurgent as the rest, and despised all that was old and proved in favour of all that was new and untried. We take this moral sickness in our ardent youth as we take measles and scarlet fever in childhood. Experience and time bring in their counteracting influences."[69] What Eliza Lynn felt to be a "moral sickness" a half-century later may have, in part, been a veiled acknowledgment of Charlotte Cushman's (and probably her own) passionate feelings toward other women. Years later Eliza Lynn hinted suggestively in her autobiographical novel, *Christopher Kirkland*, written in the voice of a male narrator, that "things cling about her [Charlotte Cushman's] name which it is well not to disturb."[70]

In the 1840s, while Charlotte was getting to know members of Laurence's radical bohemian circle, she was gaining accolades and becoming increasingly well-known throughout Britain. After witnessing Charlotte playing Romeo and Claude Melnotte opposite her sister's Juliet and Pauline, the critic from the *Mercury* commented that, compared with Charlotte Cushman's ardent expression, "lovemaking, as practiced by the other sex" would "appear a very stale, flat, and unprofitable affair."[71] Highlighting Charlotte's onstage ardor for a woman, this critic seems to have captured some of the appeal Charlotte's performances had for female spectators. What spectators saw demonstrated before them were possibilities for women's lives other than conventional marriage plots: satisfying, independent lives filled with passion shared with other women.

In a letter written shortly after *The Half Sisters* was published, Geraldine Jewsbury told Jane Carlyle—in answer to Jane's accounts of her daily domestic drudgery—that "I believe we are touching on better days, when women will have a genuine, normal life of their own to lead. There perhaps, will not be as many marriages, and women will be taught not to feel their destiny *manqué* if they remain single. They will be able to be friends and companions in a way they cannot be now."[72] Women who read texts like *The Half Sisters* that featured powerful, self-supporting women and female spectators and fans who admired Charlotte Cushman "read" Charlotte as the personification of a life previously unimagined. And their shared readings of her became a common thread, uniting them. In later years even Jane Carlyle felt a "sudden affection" for Charlotte that was not merely a result of their personal relationship and the "elective affinities" they shared but, rather, of the *idea* of Charlotte Cushman, of what she had come to represent for Jane and their mutual friends as well as for her spectators and those who read about her. Even "without seeing you," Jane wrote to Charlotte, "without interchanging words with you, it is a pleasure to know of you in the same world with me. The influence of a strong, brave, loving, true woman may be felt at any distance."[73] Wherever they were, members of Charlotte Cushman's real and virtual communities felt her influence.

Although she meant different things to different women, her spectators could summon Charlotte's image as a lodestone for those particular qualities they might have no other way to represent.

Despite her empowering example, Charlotte recognized the possibility that the life of a woman independent of marriage was fraught with peril. As successful as she was becoming in her theatrical career, Charlotte empathized with the plight of women in her midst striving to pursue literary careers. A few women writers, like Eliza Lynn, had influential families or friends who could contribute to their support as they struggled against convention to write and publish their work. Others, like Mary Howitt's and Eliza Lynn's friend Eliza Meteyard (known by her pseudonym "Silverpen"), were nearly destitute. To Eliza Meteyard, Charlotte noted, "I have been made acquainted with more wickedness and heartlessness since I have known literary people and their sufferings through publishers than I believed existed out from my own profession . . . but publishers are greater rascals than managers—and God knows the latter are bad enough."[74] Charlotte Cushman had stood up to unethical managers and dishonest agents, but having witnessed Eliza Cook's efforts, she was now aware of how desperately women writers struggled and how completely they depended upon publishers to get their work before the public. Whenever she could, Cushman offered to exert influence on behalf of her growing network of friends.

After four remarkably successful years in England Charlotte could well afford to assist those women she championed. Her eagerness to help women writers was tied to more, however, than a general appreciation for their struggles as professional women. In all likelihood, by the time she came to know Eliza Meteyard's plight Charlotte had made the acquaintance of a woman writer passionately involved in women's rights, the woman with whom she would spend the next decade of her life, Matilda Hays.

Enter Matilda Hays: "English Editrix" and "Juliet to Miss Cushman's Romeo"

It is not certain how Charlotte Cushman and Matilda Hays first met. They were both acquainted with other members of Laurence's Bayswater circle, and they had numerous close friends in common, including Mary Howitt, Geraldine Jewsbury, Eliza Meteyard, and William Charles Macready. Even Eliza Cook and Matilda Hays knew each other.[75] Sometime, probably after 1846, Charlotte Cushman's and Matilda Hays's paths crossed. Matilda Hays was already a novelist and journalist determined to use her writing to improve the condition of women. At eighteen she had been a regular contributor to numerous periodicals, and in 1846, at the age of twenty-six, she published her first novel, *Helen Stanley*. Dedicated to an anonymous "Her, whose love has for years endeared life and filled it with Belief in the true and the beautiful,"[76] *Helen Stanley* is a tale of a talented young woman artist whose father's business failure leaves her faced with the dismal prospect of a loveless marriage or a life as a paid companion to another woman. Hays's novel is also a polemic representing the lack of options available to women. As Matilda Hays wrote in *Helen Stanley*, women's social and economic conditions would not improve "till women teach their daughters to respect themselves, . . . to work for their daily bread, rather than prostitute their persons and hearts" in loveless marriages.[77]

Matilda Hays's writing was undoubtedly influenced by French novelist George Sand. In 1847 Hays and Eliza Ashurst, daughter of solicitor and radical reformer William Ashurst, turned their attention to an even larger project, the publication of the first series of English translations of George Sand's novels. Matilda Hays had been encouraged to undertake this project by George Henry Lewes and William Charles Macready, each of whom knew Sand and wrote to her on Hays's behalf. The series was partially funded by Edmund Larken,[78] the chaplain to Hays's friend Lady Theodosia Monson[79] and a member of Laurence's Bayswater circle. Larken also took an active literary interest in the project, translating Sand's *Miller of Angibault* for the series.

To many of her contemporaries George Sand was the epitome of the passionate, independent nineteenth-century woman: a believer in free love who dressed in male attire and lived as she pleased with whomever she chose. In Matilda Hays's and Eliza Ashurst's broad-minded milieu such sentiments were laudable, as was the employment of a popular form, like the novel, to address questions of social and political inequities between rich and poor and men and women.[80] Many people in England, however, considered Sand's novels scandalous, and independent women and women novelists who dealt with social issues of the day were frequently accused of "George Sandism."[81] While Hays's desire was to make Sand's work available to English readers, Lewes suggested she translate the works so as to make their unconventional messages palatable to English sensibilities. The series, introduced into a somewhat hostile climate, floundered after four volumes. The reasons for its termination, however, are mixed. The conservative *Quarterly Review* denounced the attempt "by an English editrix, assisted among others by a beneficed clergyman of the English Church, to circulate [Sand's work] . . . in an English translation" as "a smuggler's attempt to conceal the real nature of his infamous cargo."[82] Larken and Hays were disparaged both for "procuring" these forbidden goods and misrepresenting the character of their "merchandise." Larken was further chastised by the Anglican Church hierarchy. Hays's translation was also criticized by Sand's friend Italian revolutionary Giuseppe Mazzini, who felt her attempt to impose "English taste" upon Sand's work had stripped it of its power.[83] But Eliza Ashurst claimed that she and Hays "met with great literary success, but lost a great deal of money—as Miss Hays had chosen a bad business publisher,"[84] the same publisher who had published *Helen Stanley*.

It may have been through the Ashurst family that Charlotte Cushman and Matilda Hays were first acquainted. The Ashursts' Muswell Hill home was often a meeting place for radicals and reformers where the leading thinkers, writers, and political activists of the day socialized. At the time the Ashursts were also devoted friends of the Howitts and well acquainted with Geraldine Jewsbury, who came down from Manchester for long visits and stayed with them in London. Early in her first provincial tour Charlotte had benefited from William Ashurst's services as a solicitor. She had been misled by the unscrupulous manager of a theater in Norwich, who, though he had advertised his place of business as a theater "Royal," managed what Charlotte determined was a "low" place of amusement. Concerned that she would damage her reputation if she were to perform there, Charlotte wisely canceled her engagement but needed a legal advisor to get out of her commitment. The solicitor she hired was Eliza Ashurst's father.

By the fall of 1847, with friends like Ashurst, Howitt, and Jewsbury publicizing her performances and helping to protect—or create—her reputation, Charlotte Cushman had come to be known to the British public as the "native genius" of "the young country."[85] Following her successful season with Susan in *Romeo and Juliet*, Charlotte was now appearing with Macready at the Princess Theatre in London. In another highly acclaimed run of performances she played Emilia and Lady Macbeth to Macready's Othello and Macbeth, and for the first time she was seen as Queen Katharine to his Wolsey.

While Charlotte Cushman was busy portraying powerful women and men onstage, Matilda Hays had seized upon yet another plan to represent women's interests. In 1847 she had the idea of publishing and editing a periodical to further the cause for women's rights and to serve as a platform for the work of women writers. Years later, in her application for a pension from the governmental literary fund, Matilda declared, "having always advocated the better education and training of girls and young women, and their admission into fresh fields of remunerative labour, I endeavored to secure the co-operation of literary friends with a view of starting a *Woman's Journal* therebye [*sic*] affording free discussion of a subject for which at that time it was impossible to obtain a hearing through ordinary channels of the Press."[86] Increasingly, women were joining the ranks of paid contributors to the periodical press. But what Hays was proposing was a journal expressly directed to women readers, edited by women, and serving as a vehicle for discourse about broadening notions of acceptable women's employment. To help in this effort Mary Howitt offered her assistance. Howitt contacted Sarah Josepha Hale on Matilda Hays's behalf, thinking that *Godey's Lady's Book* might serve as a model for Hays to emulate. Mary Howitt told Hale she would be "greatly obliged if you can give an impetus to our friend."[87] Despite Howitt's help and that of Charlotte Cushman, who contacted Eliza Meteyard, inviting her to work for "our journal" and asking her for information about payments for articles,[88] Matilda Hays was not to launch her journal then, after all. "The time . . . was not considered ripe for the experiment," she later declared, "and I was obliged to content myself with such advocacy as opportunity presented."[89]

Instead, faced with the dilemma of supporting herself that Charlotte had encountered a decade earlier, Matilda considered the stage. Perhaps Charlotte encouraged the intense and fiery Matilda. Certainly, Matilda Hays's financial situation had taken a sudden turn for the worse when, she claimed, "the embarrassed circumstances of my father, in whose hands the small fortune I possessed lay, induced me, in 1848 to accede to a proposition from Miss Charlotte Cushman, the American Actress, to try the stage as a more remunerative profession than the one I had chosen, and to fit myself to take the place of her sister—Susan Cushman—then about to marry and retire into private life."[90] By now Nelson Merriman, Susan's husband, who had abandoned her and Ned, the child he had never seen, was presumed dead. With Charlotte's support Susan had managed to construct a career and livelihood for herself and young Ned. But once James Sheridan Muspratt, a prosperous Liverpool scientist, indicated an interest in Susan, Mary Eliza urged her younger daughter to marry Muspratt, whom Charlotte claimed Susan did not love, "and so let her sell her soul."[91] With Susan retiring from the stage, Charlotte would need a reliable new Juliet.

Charlotte started giving Matilda acting lessons, to prepare her for their work together, but the effort to start a journal was not completely in vain. Less than year later, as Charlotte and Matilda rehearsed for their debut performances as *Romeo and Juliet,* Eliza Cook turned her attention from poetry to journalism and soon launched *her* new periodical, *Eliza Cook's Journal.* Although Eliza Cook wrote most of the material in the weekly journal herself, Eliza Meteyard and other popular journalists were frequent contributors, as, most likely, was Matilda Hays. With its decidedly feminist stance *Eliza Cook's Journal* was a compendium of essays, poetry, reviews, and fiction that particularly addressed issues such as women's education, dress reform, temperance, and the plight of the working class and domestic servants.

While work on *Eliza Cook's Journal* was getting under way, Charlotte and Matilda prepared for Matilda Hays's debut in the most public of all professions—a career on the stage. As always, Charlotte's social contacts helped offset any potential criticism. The duke of Devonshire offered his Yorkshire estate to Charlotte and Matilda, where they rehearsed for their upcoming performance, scheduled for 6 October 1848, at Bath. Together they performed for several months in various parts of the country, with Matilda chiefly playing Juliet in *Romeo and Juliet* and, occasionally, Pauline to Charlotte's Claude Melnotte in *The Lady of Lyons.* Witnessing Charlotte and Matilda in the roles of romantic partners, the critics at Brighton, Bristol, and Dublin commented on Matilda's "fine, tall figure" and "her force of expression" and predicted her success in her new career—when she overcame "the terrors of a stage fright."[92]

By this time the two women were living as romantic partners offstage as well as on. It was becoming increasingly clear to all of Charlotte's associates that her emotions were tied up with Matilda, whom friends frequently called "Max" or "Mathew."[93] After seeing Charlotte with Matilda, Elizabeth Barrett Browning explained to her sisters, "I understand that she and Miss Hays have made vows of celibacy and of eternal attachment to each other— they live together, dress alike, . . . it is a female marriage."[94] By the mid-nineteenth century increasing numbers of women lived with other women in what Browning and others referred to as a "female marriage," or romantic friendship. Yet, women who, like Charlotte Cushman, elected to live in long-term emotional partnerships with other women for no expedient, monetary reason, who dressed as Cushman, Cook, and Hays did, in skirts and tailored shirts and jackets (a fashion considered androgynous at the time) rather than in frilly dresses, and who referred to themselves or their partners with male nicknames—these women embodied an alternative to heterosexuality for which there was no distinct label, but which today would be considered lesbian.

Charlotte Cushman and Matilda Hays were living together as partners— emotionally and perhaps sexually—although their professional theatrical career together lasted for just a few months. Performing on the British stage was increasingly lucrative and usually enjoyable for Charlotte, who was becoming accustomed to being a star. Women in her life, whether accomplished equals like Eliza Cook, or much younger, idolizing colleagues and fans like Sarah Anderton, were frequently deferential to her and dependent upon her assistance and advice. Eliza Cook had written lovingly of the "strength of [Cushman's] control" and that her own talent "lies only at the feet of thy dear self."[95] Whereas these women supported Charlotte's acting career, Matilda was somewhat conflicted, sharing as she did many of the

Charlotte Cushman (seated) and Matilda Hays (standing), ca. 1851. Charlotte Cushman and her lover Matilda Hays posed in matching clothing for this cabinet photo taken during Cushman's return trip to the United States. A short time later Elizabeth Barrett Browning would comment on their "female marriage." *(Harvard Theatre Collection. Houghton Library.)*

mid-Victorian prejudices about the theater. And, unlike many other women in Charlotte Cushman's life, she was not used to playing such a subordinate role. Years later Matilda described her own brief attempt at acting as "acceding" to Charlotte's proposition, depicting the decision to take over Susan Cushman's supporting roles as helping Charlotte. That is, in Matilda's narrative it was *Charlotte's* needs, not her own desires, that led Matilda to abandon her writing for a career on the stage. Of course, Matilda Hays expressed these sentiments in an application for a pension, so they may not necessarily reflect her actual feelings but may have been constructed to depict accepted attitudes and prejudices about the theater, to gain the sympathy of the officials determining whether or not she would receive the funds for which she applied.

Whatever Matilda did feel at the time about acting with her famous partner, it seems clear that Matilda's theatrical career with Charlotte was troubled from the start. Two months after their debut together, in the middle of a regional tour in Birmingham, Charlotte sent an urgent note to Sarah Anderton, asking Sarah to join Charlotte, who found herself "awkwardly placed by some unforeseen circumstances occurring which will prevent Miss Hays from acting in Chester." Charlotte repeatedly implored the younger actress who had been so devoted to her to "pray come to me if you possibly can,"[96] and she asked if Anderton were free to perform for the rest of the engagements Charlotte had scheduled with Matilda in Ireland and Scotland. Whatever the "unforseen circumstances," Matilda *did* eventually resume the tour, and in Dublin a month later all seemed well. Charlotte wrote to Sarah Anderton that "Miss Hays sends her best love to you."[97] Yet there were signs of more trouble brewing.

Whether because of her own nervousness, her ultimate disdain for the stage, or the difficulties of working with a partner who was so visibly celebrated, Matilda Hays's theatrical career was short-lived. Years later she asserted that "the strain of so arduous a part as Juliet to Miss Cushman's Romeo, constantly repeated, brought on a condition of health which after a short time obliged me to give up the stage altogether."[98] Although Matilda decided to stop acting, she stayed with Charlotte as her partner. Matilda's invoking of her onstage role as Juliet (which was, after all, only one of the characters she played opposite Charlotte) was metonymic for the emotional part she played as Charlotte's lover, companion, and "wife" in their day-to-day lives together. For almost a decade Matilda would continue to play Juliet to Charlotte's Romeo *offstage,* a role that may also have proved "arduous" for her, as we shall see.

With Matilda to accompany her, Charlotte made plans to return to America in the fall of 1849. Five years earlier she had left the United States an eager young actress. Now she was returning as a star. The British press and Charlotte's literary circle had recognized her, lauded her, and claimed her as their own. Charlotte carried their high estimation with her as part of the multiple and often contradictory values she embodied for spectators on both continents. To the British critics she had become a symbol "marked with the most brilliant and permanent success." On her return visit to the United States, "to the scenes of her earliest struggles," they noted that she bore "not alone the stamp of European fame upon her genius" but also "the warm admiration and respect of enlightened circles, who, seeking the artist, found the woman yet more worthy of homage and esteem." This same anonymous journalist noted that on this return trip "Miss Cushman will be accompanied by her friend, novelist and translator, Matilda M. Hays."[99] While Matilda was firmly identified with her own literary pursuits, journalists always mentioned her relationship with her more highly acclaimed partner.

For the press and the public by this time, whenever Charlotte Cushman was mentioned she was seen as a symbol who was a unique blend of two previously opposed discursive categories, those of both "woman" and "artist." To Eliza Ashurst and other members of Cushman's London circle "Miss Cushman, the celebrated American actress"[100] was, as Ashurst advised an American friend, "worth going out of the way to see not only as an actress, but as a woman."[101] Now an internationally acclaimed performing artist in her public persona, Cushman was sought out by the masses. But to those theatergoers who were drawn to her "as a woman," rather than "as an actress," she represented a curious amalgam of professional talent and one of the most highly esteemed character traits for a Victorian woman—a seeming disinterest in emotional or sexual allegiances with men. Charlotte's British fame helped her straddle these apparent inconsistencies, as did, ironically, the curious ways in which Charlotte—a woman who passionately loved other women—served as a refutation of stereotypical images of actresses' "promiscuousness."[102]

Back in the United States, before Charlotte launched into a series of performances, she negotiated with her old actor friend William Chippendale, now a theatrical manager, demanding something unprecedented for women in any other career in her day: absolute parity with the highest paid *men* in her field. The theater was probably the only career open to women in which those who had achieved the highest levels of acclaim could earn as much as their male colleagues. And Charlotte demanded her due. "My terms must be the same as those given to Mr. Macready and Mr. Forrest, in other words, a clear half the house on each night."[103] And she got it, for American audiences were eager to see the actress the British had regarded so highly. As journalist George G. Foster announced in *New York by Gas-Light*, Charlotte Cushman was now "the rage." In the "puffing and panting criticisms" of the hyperbolic press: "everything about her is either tremendous, terrific or magnificent." After "receiv[ing] the stamp of foreign approbation," Charlotte was "return[ing] to her countrymen an empress, nodding but to be obeyed, smiling but to be worshipped."[104]

Traveling throughout the East and the Midwest, Charlotte performed her familiar and successful roles. The only part she hesitated to recreate was Nancy Sykes in Dickens's *Oliver Twist*. Although some of Charlotte's American fans and friends, like Anne Brewster, had thought Nancy one of

MISS CHARLOTTE CUSHMAN.

The rise and progress of this distinguished American actress, is a strong evidence of what perseverance, steadily directed to one object, will accomplish. She first made her debut in public life as a vocalist, but finding that she could scarcely hope to excel in this line, she soon after adopted the stage as her future field of action. Her first attempts upon the stage were far from giving promise of her future ability; indeed, she was considered as having made a signal failure of it; but nothing daunted, she still strove on, hoped on, watching, studying, and improving, until at last, slowly, but steadily, she rose to the distinguished position which she holds, as the queen of tragedy. Miss Cushman has earned a very high European reputation, and her present tour through this country, we are gratified to know, has been eminently successful and profitable. We understand that she is soon to return to England. The picture by our artist, given herewith, is no less peculiar in the expression, than faithful as a likeness, evincing much of the strong masculine will and purpose that forms so prominent a part of this lady's moral character. Miss Cushman has indicated her right to the name of poetess, by some very beautiful and feeling productions.

OUTWARD BEAUTY.

I cannot understand the importance which certain people set upon outward beauty or plainness. I am of opinion that all true education must infuse a noble calm, a wholesome coldness or indifference, or whatever people may call it, towards such-like outward gifts, or the want of them. And who has not experienced of how little consequence they are, in fact, for the weal or woe of life? Who has not experienced how, on nearer acquaintance, plainness becomes beautified, and beauty loses its charm, exactly according to the quality of the heart and mind?
—*Fredericka Bremer.*

MISS CHARLOTTE CUSHMAN.

"Miss Charlotte Cushman," *Gleason's Pictorial Drawing Room Companion*, 1851. This American periodical published during Charlotte Cushman's return tour lauded her "European reputation" as well as her "strong masculine will and purpose" and claimed that Cushman's appearance was indicative of her moral character. The illustration that accompanies the text is coupled with an additional quote on the unimportance of outward beauty.

the best and most powerful of her parts, Anne Brewster noted with some sarcasm: "C[harlotte] could not play Nancy Sykes in England. They were too fine and fastidious there—it would have given her the Bowery stamp."[105] Now Charlotte instructed her friend, actor and theatrical manager William Fredericks, to "see if you can borrow, beg, or steal for me a copy of *Oliver Twist*," because, Charlotte informed him, "Miss Hays wants to read it to see if she will allow me to act it."[106] Charlotte trusted Matilda Hays's taste and sensibility, and she looked to Matilda as a barometer of the British refinement to which Charlotte now aspired.

Wherever Charlotte performed in the United States, theater critics generally wrote glowing reviews of the American performer who had represented her countrypeople so ably abroad, but some of Charlotte's old friends, like Anne Brewster, were initially put off by her spectacular success and unsure about how to relate to the woman they once knew, now raised to the status of national and cultural icon. Charlotte's old Philadelphia circle was not the same, either. Rosalie Sully was dead, and, though Anne Brewster had never stopped thinking about Charlotte and musing about their relationship in her diary, Anne, now a professional writer herself, was nervous about seeing Charlotte again. Anne was unsure how she was "expected to act towards [Charlotte]" and "expected to find her quiet, self-possessed and perfectly satisfied with her position and attainments."[107] As important as their relationship had been to Anne Brewster, she was afraid that, now that Charlotte had become so famous, "four years of such a life as she has led may have effaced all recollection of our past intercourse."[108] Charlotte was a fantasy figure for Anne, as she had become for many of her female fans, the cherished object of their desire and an emblem of what women might achieve as successful, independent artists. In the years since they had seen each other last Anne Brewster had "felt out at sea without rudder or compass. For a long while she had been 'my star.'"[109]

But Anne's initial reaction after seeing Charlotte again was disappointment. She found Charlotte affected, *"pronouncée."* Charlotte's European success could be read in her facial expressions and the words she now uttered: "her tongue strikes attitudes and her mouth is filled with proper nouns like a letter to the *Home Journal* from its European correspondent," Anne concluded sadly.[110] With her success Charlotte had become a stranger.

Charlotte *did* remember their former intimacy, however, and, after several more visits while Charlotte was performing in Philadelphia, Anne acknowledged that the awkwardness between them could have been due, in part, to her own nervousness. Finally, during a visit on 21 November, "one word after another seemed to melt us both—ceremony was forgotten, the inexplicable chasm between us was bridged over and for the first time in many years our hearts met in a warm loving union." Or, rather, as Anne clarified, "of this one thing I am sure, *my* heart was true—*my* love real . . . sentences, expressions, looks, come before me hourly like the memory of sweet melodies and oh so lovingly are they treasured so foolishly it may be."[111] Even in her own fervent account of the feelings summoned up by her loving reunion with Charlotte, Anne Brewster admitted the sad fact that the intensity of her feelings might not be reciprocated. Perhaps, she mused in her journal, she should rip out the pages where she gave space to the "foolish" feelings she still harbored about Charlotte—or else she might leave them as a warning to steel herself against more disappointment. The surrounding pages are missing now, torn from the tightly bound journal. What did Anne, or someone else after her death, ultimately decide to eliminate from her account, I wonder? Which of Anne's feelings for Charlotte could not be safely contained in the neat, brown leather diaries in which Brewster carefully recorded, narrated, and constructed her life?

Back in England the woman Charlotte had left behind was also pining for her and fondly remembering their time together. In the 26 January 1850 issue of *Eliza Cook's Journal,* Eliza published a poem entitled "Our Rambles by the Dove: Addressed to C.C. in America," in answer to the letters Charlotte was sending, telling "of the glories of the West." Eliza wanted to remind Charlotte of a favorite place of theirs in England, a tiny river, the Dove, where the two women had spent some of their closest time together.

> Oh, no indeed, I know *thy* land will never chase away
> The happiness we found in *mine* on that long, sunny day;
> I know thy great White Mountains cannot dim the winding steep
> That lured us dreamily along to gain the "Lover's Leap."

And Eliza Cook, missing Charlotte, sought to remind her of these favorite, shared experiences, and her hope that Charlotte would return, "that thou wilt come with all thy olden love, / And let my prayers be answered by the waters of the 'Dove.'"[112]

While Eliza was struggling to keep her spirits up and edit her popular journal and Charlotte was performing to great acclaim in America, Matilda Hays was dividing her time and energy between accompanying Charlotte on tour and, "from time to time," attempting to "renew" her "literary labours" by contributing articles to journals and "art-letters" to newspapers.[113] She was also busy translating George Sand's *Fadette.* Matilda dedicated her newest work:

> To Charlotte Cushman,
> true artist, and yet truer woman,
> the translation of this beautiful little tale is inscribed
> in affectionate remembrance
> of our travels in the country honored by her birth.[114]

The return tour was going well. Then Charlotte received the news, in the summer of 1850, that Eliza Cook was deathly ill. Without hesitating, Charlotte canceled her tour and immediately sailed back to England. Some of the critics in the popular press, for whom Charlotte was now "news," were suspicious about this sudden turn of events. The critic from the *Prompter* noted that "to the surprise of all people interested in the movements of eminent performers, Miss Charlotte Cushman, who, it was supposed, would continue her series of engagements in this country through the coming year, was suddenly announced one day last week to leave the United States, in the steamer of Wednesday the 12th." The anonymous critic intimated that, although

> the public attributed this sudden departure to the news of the illness of a distinguished friend in England, there have been speculators, however, ready to ascribe the abrupt retirement to dissatisfactions here and to various annoyances which had been thrown in her path by certain portions of the American Press and by professional competition. A general charge has been laid against Miss Cushman, that she has not been as friendly and familiar with her countrypeople on her return, as she was expected to be.[115]

Regardless of professional jealousies or allegations perpetuated by the *Prompter* that Charlotte was somehow less loyal and "friendly" to America, the initial report of a friend's illness was accurate. Charlotte *was* rushing back to see Eliza Cook, who, in her illness, was staying at the Muswell Hill home of the Ashurst family. That summer Eliza Ashurst had returned home from Paris, where she lived with her new husband, and "found Eliza Cook, the poetess staying with my mother—She was a most dreadful sufferer from some internal complaint, her paroxysms of suffering were terrible to see." As Eliza Ashurst explained to an American friend, "Miss Cushman, your countrywoman, who is the most attached friend of Eliza Cook's came over for a month to see her."[116]

Charlotte stayed with her former partner long enough to assure herself that Eliza Cook's illness was not, in fact, fatal and then, after visiting briefly with her sister Susan's family in Liverpool, hurried back to the United States to resume her tour. Eliza Cook was never to fully recover from the unnamed illness; although she lived, mostly as an invalid, for almost four more decades, Charles Cushman speculated that the "rupture" between his sister and Eliza Cook was "in a great measure the cause of the illness she had greatly suffered from almost ever since."[117] It was perhaps with this visit that Eliza Cook realized that, despite her dreams by the "Dove," the two women would never again share the same degree of affection they once had. Matilda Hays was now the primary person in Charlotte's life.

Once back in the United States Charlotte launched into another round of performances. As she arranged her itinerary and negotiated with theatrical managers, she realized that she had come to represent a variety of qualities for different segments of the American public and attempted to market her appeal. While her British acclaim may have appealed to more elite audiences at home, as we have seen, Charlotte was accused by the critic from the *Prompter* of no longer being "American" enough. And Edwin Forrest's intimate friend, James Oakes, was writing unflattering notices of her in the *Atlas*. Nonetheless, Charlotte's portrayals continued to be extremely successful, and managers knew her male characterizations were a particularly large part of her appeal.

As she toured from city to city with Matilda Hays, intimations of gender transgressions in Charlotte's *offstage* persona were cited by commentators who read her clothing and her demeanor as a statement, a sign of her advocacy for expanding women's options and mobility in the society at large. A correspondent from the *Cleveland Plain Dealer* remarked, perhaps satirically, that offstage Charlotte "appear[ed] in masculine attire, hat, coat, unmentionables and all. . . . If a woman of her acknowledged genius, taste, virtue, and social position sees no indelicacy in wearing every rag of male attire when the urgency of the case—as fishing, for example—points it out as the most suitable, we see no reason why so many ladies should be squeamish about adopting the Bloomer costume."[118] The combination of Charlotte's increasing social acceptance as a successful—yet "virtuous"—single woman and her "acknowledged genius," or talent, afforded her the possibility of dressing as she pleased; her unconventional attire could be read as a triumph of pragmatism over conventionally feminine squeamishness. But the anonymous Ohio critic encouraged voyeuristic readers to speculate, nonetheless, on Charlotte's donning of masculine "unmentionables." What might be underneath the skirts of a woman who wore breeches?

The meanings that images of Charlotte called up in others were shifting and unstable. Some of the women who avidly read articles like these about her and the female fans who saw her onstage and followed her career devoutly shared a sense of belonging to a "virtual" community. Some fans may have been hard-pressed to explain their response to Charlotte, but they were nonetheless brought together in the shared experience of watching enacted before them, or reading about, an embodiment of female power, assertiveness, and passion. While members of this extended virtual community of women readers, spectators, and fans were often geographically separate from and unknown to one another, invoking Charlotte they all belonged to some faction of the same "club." "All true communities are knit together by their codes," Nina Auerbach has claimed, "but a code can range from a dogma to a flexible, private, and often semi-conscious set of beliefs. . . . [I]n female communities, the code seems a whispered and a fleeting thing, more a buried language than a rallying cry."[119] Charlotte Cushman had become a symbol, a code for those who saw or read about her. To female fans who were, as feminist writer Bessie Rayner Parkes wrote, "constituted as she [Charlotte] was"—and particularly for those for whom the emotional center of their lives were other women—Charlotte's wooing of women in her male personifications had been a palpable representation of female desire and one they recognized in themselves. Interestingly, despite the wealth of contemporary responses such as these, in later accounts of this time in Charlotte's career it was reported that she had become briefly attracted to Conrad Clarke, her costar in Cincinnati, and had been "disappointed" to discover that he was married. Given her personality, I believe that Charlotte may have been flattered by Clarke's expressions of admiration and thus annoyed to discover that ambition, not sincere affection, may have motivated his attentiveness.[120]

Among the fans pondering the possibilities of what Charlotte, clothed in male attire, represented to them were some who were moved to become members of her intimate circle of friends. Of the many friendships rekindled and new friendships Charlotte and Matilda made during this tour, one that was to become most significant to both of them was with a young Massachusetts woman who aspired to a career as a sculptor. Twenty-one-year-old Harriet Hosmer was clearly smitten by the mature actress and her partner when she met them in Boston. After meeting Charlotte, "Hatty" spent most of the next three weeks in Charlotte and Matilda's company. "I saw Miss Cushman as Lady Macbeth, Queen Katharine, Romeo, Claude Melnotte, La Tisbe, Meg Merrilies, Hamlet, and in a comedy," Hatty exclaimed enthusiastically to her dear friend and former schoolmate Cornelia Crow. Hamlet particularly impressed her. "Oh it was most glorious . . . I went to rehearsals with Miss Cushman—behind the scenes every night, into the property room, the green room . . . even into her dressing room. You have no idea how much I enjoyed it."[121] Both Charlotte and her partner impressed the spunky and impetuous Hatty Hosmer. "Miss Cushman and Miss Hays have left Boston and you can't tell how lonely I feel. . . . Isn't it queer how we meet people in this world and become attached to them in so short a time—now I feel as if I lost my best friends."[122]

Charlotte and Matilda together embodied a degree of female independence and an alternative style of living that Hatty had never seen before. About this time Charlotte began planning to retire from the stage after her successful performances in the United States. Charlotte, Matilda, and their new friend, journalist Grace Greenwood,[123] were planning to travel to Rome for the winter. They invited Hatty to join their group of "jolly female bachelors."[124] Numerous English and American writers and artists had been drawn to Italy for the climate and the inspiration. Hatty could study her art amid the same antiquities that had inspired the Brownings and sculptors John Gibson and William Wetmore Story. With her father's approval, and his agreement to travel with them, Hatty eagerly accepted: "Miss Cushman and Miss Hays will be there and it will be truly sublime."[125]

While Charlotte acted a series of American performances that she publicized as being her farewell to the stage career that had rewarded her so richly and brought her such celebrity, Charlotte and Matilda looked forward to a life in Rome. Before they left Charlotte finalized one piece of family business. With her sister's approval she filed papers to adopt formally her fourteen-year-old nephew, Ned. Charlotte had supported Ned for the greater part of his life. For the past several years tensions between her nephew and his stepfather threatened to disrupt Susan's Liverpool home. Perhaps Sheridan Muspratt was uncomfortable with a stepson not quite sixteen years younger than his wife. In any case, when her nephew became "Ned Cushman," Charlotte could do even more to help him, although Ned could hardly foresee the impact Charlotte was to have on his life. Grateful now that Charlotte secured a place for him in the United States Naval Academy, he told her of his experiences in the academy and dutifully sent his "love to Miss Hays, Sallie and yourself."[126]

Charlotte Cushman, Matilda Hays, and Sallie Mercer returned to England in the summer of 1852 to plan for the trip to Italy. Charlotte was delighted that Grace Greenwood had come over to England and encouraged her to join them in their "pilgrimage to and sojourn" in Italy. Charlotte Cushman and Matilda Hays were planning their Roman expedition as they had orchestrated their lives together, as a couple. To Grace, Charlotte described Matilda "as my right hand," who "will tell my left all my curiosity asks of you."[127]

Along with the journalists and critics who had been writing about her, chronicling her every movement, the particular resonances called up by the celebrated actress, her stage career, and her love affairs with other women had become part of an ongoing conversation in print about the social position of "the actress" as an independent Victorian working woman. For numerous women writers who knew Charlotte personally, their contributions to this conversation were created against the background of the intense intimate relationships and "strange sympathies" they experienced amid Charlotte's circle of friends. Their texts helped create a virtual community of female readers just as Charlotte's performances had given rise to a virtual community of spectators. But, as much as Charlotte relished the attention, at times she felt herself practically consumed by the needs of the people who surrounded her and claimed she needed to be "away from the thousand mouths that are feeding upon me."[128] She was already more successful than she had ever dreamed. Just before her thirty-seventh birthday, Charlotte made a decision. She would retire and live farther from the public eye. Trading the attentions of the multitudes for the more intimate pleasure of the small group of close friends, Charlotte Cushman and the other "jolly bachelors" set off to Rome. There they would create their own community.

Building a Community
Charlotte Cushman's Roman Salon

Miss Cushman has a profound love of art, a reverence for
genius, originality and character in a woman. She has also, as
those who know her best, best know, strong and generous
affections.
                                    —Grace Greenwood, *Chicagoan*

In late 1852 Charlotte Cushman arrived in Rome with her partner Matilda
Hays, Sallie Mercer, and her new friends a Miss Smith, journalist Grace
Greenwood, young sculptor Harriet Hosmer, Hosmer's father, and Hos-
mer's schoolmate Virginia Vaughan.[1] Shortly after their arrival another
American expatriate, sculptor William Wetmore Story, wrote to poet James
Russell Lowell about the "harem (scarem) . . . [of] emancipated females
who dwell there in heavenly unity—viz the Cushman, Grace Greenwood,
Hosmer-Smith and Co." Although Story was a Boston native like Cushman, and her contemporary, as a wealthy son of a United States Supreme
Court judge he and Charlotte had traveled in different social sets. And the
woman-centered community Charlotte was determined to create in
Rome—his adopted city—was particularly unsettling to him. Story, living
comfortably in Rome with his wife and children, found Charlotte and her
friends' "unity" with other women and their "emancipation" from men
equally notewothy and displeasing. Those expatriates who embraced this
group, such as Story's fellow artist British sculptor Shakspere Wood, were
mocked for "danc[ing] attendance upon them everywhere."[2]

Charlotte Cushman, fresh from her announced "farewell performances" in the United States, was the acknowledged center of this
"harem"; her fame and renowned independence had served as a magnet for
the other women who came to Italy with her. The undercurrent of homoerotic energy that drew her lover, Matilda Hays, and some of the other
women to her also served as a source of female creativity and strength and
was to be an enabling force in their own artistic pursuits. The home Charlotte was constructing in Rome for and with the women in her life would be

the stage on which their accomplishments would be displayed, and her own repertoire of social roles would increase to include host, sponsor, and great artist-at-leisure in this new setting. In her Roman home Charlotte would be giving up an extended, "virtual" community of adoring fans for a small collection of chosen friends. Would it be enough?

Charlotte's initial plan was to explore Rome as a place to retire. Now financially secure, she looked to Rome as many Anglo-American expatriates did, as a place to live economically in a lively setting surrounded by the beauty of the wild *campagna*. Writers came, encouraged by the lives and poetry of Keats and Byron. Artists were drawn to Rome to study classical sculpture and painting. And women of independent means and spirit, encouraged by the Italian adventures of heroines in novels by Madame de Staël, Anna Jameson, and Margaret Fuller, gravitated to Rome looking for freedom from the social constraints of the United States or England. In Rome, as Charlotte said, "the Mrs. Grundies [are] so scarce, [and] the artist society . . . so nice, that it is hard to choose or find any other place so attractive."[3]

Members of the English-speaking colony lived in the same neighborhood as Keats had in earlier decades, at the foot of the Spanish Steps and along the narrow, picturesque cobblestone streets that led to the Bernini Fountain. Cushman, Hays, Hosmer, and Grace Greenwood lodged nearby, at 28 Via del Corso. So many artists resided in the area that would-be models lined up along the Spanish Steps, hopeful that a painter or sculptor might hire them. Some of the wealthy, like the Story family, lived in sumptuous surroundings of former palaces. Struggling artists shared small flats. But for all the expatriates, life in Rome was easier than at home: rents were less expensive, artists' materials cheaper, and the warm weather offered the promise of long afternoons spent in the still rustic *campagna* that surrounded the city and of evenings in bustling artists' cafes or at private receptions and parties. Streets, studios, and galleries were teeming with a steady flow of American and British tourists abroad drawn to "discover" Rome. Many tourists were eager to purchase a painting or sculpture as a memento of their grand tour and to return with an anecdote about the reigning social celebrities. Here, even in her own drawing room, Charlotte Cushman could still be a star. The thriving Anglo-American community seemed a perfect place for Cushman, Hays, Hosmer, and their friends to live.

The "emancipated women" who arrived with Charlotte Cushman this first winter were, apparently, pleased with their joint living arrangement. "We are a jolly party ourselves," Hatty Hosmer explained. Everything about Rome seemed wondrous. Deciding Rome was "grand," Hatty began to picture it as her future home.[4] None of the independent women in Charlotte's company felt compelled to reenact in Rome the middle-class conventions of feminine decorum and deportment they left at home, but Hatty was particularly unconventional. Only twenty-two years old, short, energetic, and routinely described as "boyish," Hatty relished the freedom of her life in the female-centered household and felt empowered by the example of Charlotte's autonomy to live as "wildly" as she pleased. In one frequently repeated anecdote, when the American charge d'affaires stopped Hatty, traveling alone, and offered his protection, she refused and jokingly offered him hers.[5] Whether the "jolly female bachelors" paid social visits and returned home unaccompanied by men or rode at breakneck speed through the *campagna*, Charlotte's friends determined for themselves how they would spend their time and which social rituals they might comfortably disregard.

Their gender transgressions particularly disturbed some of their "fellow" expatriates. To Story, Charlotte was "man-ny," and the men who surrounded her circle of independent women were mocked as well for their feminine qualities. As Story noted with disgust, even Hatty Hosmer's father did not conform to appropriately gendered behavior: "the Dr. was called by them all while he was here by the sobriquet 'Elizabeth' and answered to it quite seriously."[6] Having a father who answered to a female nickname was, indeed, unusual, but Hiram Hosmer was, as Story claimed, almost "*fou*" about his determined young daughter, his only surviving family member, and wanted to see her happily established before he returned to the United States. Hatty's mother and siblings had died of tuberculosis when she was quite young, and—in the narrative most commonly offered to account for Hatty's physical prowess and independent spirit—her physician father determined that the best way to insure his daughter's health was to raise her as a boy, to encourage her to play outdoors and enjoy sports and rigorous physical challenges.

Hatty was known for her good-humored practical jokes and risk-taking adventures. Perhaps Hiram Hosmer's own comfort with flouting gender conventions had influenced his daughter's choice of companions and role models. The first time Hatty had seen Charlotte Cushman perform she had been struck by Charlotte's power and perseverance as well as her "glorious" interpretation of male roles. Seeing Charlotte onstage had "overturned [Hatty's] foundation"[7] of what was possible for women to achieve. And, as Grace Greenwood remembered, from the start Charlotte had been instrumental in encouraging Hatty to come with them to Rome. An assurance from the celebrated actress that she would look after his daughter had weighed heavily in Hiram Hosmer's comfort with his daughter's decision. Grace remembered the excitement of the first days of the autumn of 1852, when she and the Hosmers "joined Miss Cushman, accompanied her to Italy, and resided with her in a private household, of which she was the head, throughout the winter."[8] Soon Hatty's father returned to the United States, leaving his daughter in Charlotte's care.

Although Charlotte Cushman and Matilda Hays had come to Rome to rest and contemplate retirement, Hatty had come to work at her art. William Story claimed that although the "very wilful and too independent" Miss Hosmer was "mixed up with a set I do not like"[9]— Charlotte Cushman's circle—*he* had been responsible for arranging for Hatty to study with the British master sculptor John Gibson. Story was angry that Charlotte and Hatty's new friend Shakspere Wood had taken the credit. Over breakfast coffee at the artists' favorite meeting place, the Cafe Greco, Wood had shown Gibson pictures of Hatty's sculpture of the mythological figure Hesper. Gibson was impressed and agreed to meet Hatty. To the surprise of all members of the artists' community, he took her on as his pupil, despite the fact that he rarely took on any students, much less a young American woman.

Charlotte Cushman's role as support and center of their female household was significant to Hatty. "Miss Cushman loved and admired her clever countrywoman," according to Grace Greenwood, who felt much of Hatty's future success was due to the fact that Charlotte "interested all who frequented her charming house, in the history and character of the young American sculptor, who soon became . . . a lioness in artistic and literary circles." And Grace herself was busily writing, documenting her reactions to their life abroad in a travel volume she would publish as soon as she returned to the United States.[10] For both women Charlotte was more than a sponsor or a benevolent friend; she provided the "womanly sympathy" of a "sister-artist."[11]

Although Charlotte was not practicing *her* art professionally in Rome, much of her identity was still tied up with her reputation as a star. While Charlotte, presumably retired from the professional arena of her very public success, might no longer "need" to work, she still entertained at private gatherings. Walking away from a career that demonstrated her abilities, afforded her great freedom, justified her independence, and provided her with concrete rewards was not easy. If Charlotte Cushman was not a performer, what was she? And would the pleasures she derived from her career be available to her in other, less public settings?

As Charlotte quickly determined, one of the settings in which she could continue to perform was the numerous drawing-room parties and receptions of the Anglo-American community. The most prominent expatriate hostess of the day was Fanny Kemble's sister, the former singer Adelaide Kemble Sartoris. Cushman and the jolly female bachelors saw Sartoris often, and in January Fanny Kemble Butler came to Rome for an extended visit as well. It was the practice at the parties of the artists and social elites for hosts and guests alike to sing or recite. Here Charlotte was in her element. She relished these opportunities to perform informally for friends "at home,"—as did her similarly "retired" colleague Sartoris, who rolled out her piano and charmed the guests she invited to her home.

At these gatherings William Story was particularly hostile to Charlotte. He thought her arrogant and scoffed at what he considered her affectations. Soon after she had arrived in Rome, Story complained, "the Cushman sings savage ballads in a hoarse manny voice, and requests people recitatively to forget her not. I am sure I shall not."[12] While Story and a number of other American men clearly did not appreciate the role Charlotte played at these gatherings, other partygoers were thrilled by her willingness to sing for her friends or regale them with stories told in Irish and Scottish dialects. Charlotte loved to tell droll stories and "set the table in a roar" or to sprawl across the piano and sing one of her signature dialect pieces—"declaiming to music," as she called it.[13]

As much as Charlotte enjoyed these private entertainments, she apparently was not yet ready to settle down. Instead, she decided to return to London and her professional career. Perhaps in that first winter in Italy it had disturbed Charlotte to see the relationship that was brewing between Matilda Hays and Hatty Hosmer. Hatty was effervescent and charming and looked surprisingly like a younger version of Charlotte herself. Whatever the actual dynamics between the women, Charlotte was accustomed to being the center of attention. But that winter and spring of 1853, as she hinted grimly to Grace Greenwood, her relationship with Matilda had begun to break down, although this was not yet clear to the rest of the household. Charlotte had tried to keep most of the details of the volatile relationship between herself and her partner circumspect, and so "no human being could know all the tortures to which I was subjected in Rome—for no one saw but our two selves."[14] Perhaps she hoped a change of scene would heal the breach between them. At any rate, when Charlotte, Matilda, and Sallie Mercer returned to England in the spring, Charlotte had left in place the seeds of the female artist community she had started. Before long she would return there to live.

Hatty Hosmer and, for a time, Grace Greenwood and Virginia Vaughan stayed on in Rome. With their new friend and neighbor at 28 Via del Corso, Isa Blagden, an independent woman whose novels featured the intensity and primacy of women's relationships with each other, they continued their rounds of social visits. Hatty relished the "charming circle of people," which included the Brownings and Pre-Raphaelite painter Frederic Leighton, who was Hatty's age and soon became one of her closest friends. Leighton, whom friends called "Fay," was as comfortable with violating gender conventions as was Hatty. He described the boyish Hatty as the "queerest, best-natured little chap possible," and she found him "very good-looking, suggestive of the young Raphael style."[15] In this privileged, holiday-like climate, where members of the expatriate community entertained themselves and one another, there was a great deal of social freedom as well as artistic exploration. The eccentricities and absence of conventional feminine manner that others labeled "queer" in Hatty were attributed to her artistic temperament, as was Leighton's self-presentation as an attractive aesthete who enjoyed classical art and the company of young men as well as older, married women, like the maternal Adelaide Sartoris. Every Sunday and Wednesday evening Hatty Hosmer joined Leighton at a "family party" at Adelaide Sartoris's, where "Mrs. Sartoris sings and Mrs. Kemble sometimes reads and all in all it is the perfection of all that is charming and sociable."[16] But, having lived in the company of women like Charlotte and Matilda, whose tumultuous life together included elements of sexual passion, Hatty may have occasionally longed for a more physical form of love as well.

As a schoolgirl, Hatty had a warm, sentimental friendship with Cornelia Crow, which may have had an erotic subtext for Hatty. But Cornelia was married now and living thousands of miles away in St. Louis. Cornelia's father, Wayman Crow, a successful businessman and civic leader in St. Louis, had agreed to serve as Hatty's patron, sending her money and encouraging her art. Thanking Wayman Crow for his "never ceasing kindness," Hatty sent one of her early sculptures back to the Crow family. "When Daphne arrives," Hosmer suggested to her intimate friend Cornelia, "kiss her lips and then remember that I kissed her just before she left me."[17] The flirtatious physical connection that Hatty evoked between Cornelia and herself illustrates how ambiguous and slippery the boundaries were between the romantic relationships of female friends and relationships between women who felt sexual desire for each other. And, among the group of women who had formed Charlotte's Roman circle, the subtle erotic energy that pulsed just under the surface of their various relationships with each other occasionally threatened to disrupt long-standing commitments, like that between Charlotte and Matilda.

Whatever tensions had been growing between Charlotte and Matilda in Rome reached a breaking point when they were back in London. That October, while Charlotte was with Sallie Mercer at the spa at Malvern, taking the cold water cures to alleviate the stresses of the troubles with Matilda, Charlotte's lover left her and returned to Rome alone, to be with Hatty Hosmer. Charlotte confided to Grace Greenwood that Matilda's leaving "nearly broke my heart if not my head."[18] Devastated at this turn of events and seeking the only remedy she knew, Charlotte had "suddenly determined that there was something higher and grander" than the pain of her breakup with Matilda. After an extended visit with her sister's family in Liverpool, Charlotte returned to the stage, sorry that she had ever left the one thing that gave her such pleasure. Demonstrating the mixed feelings expressed by her family, from the United States Ned wrote to his mother, "I was perfectly taken aback when I heard of the difficulty between Aunty and Miss Hays, but I suppose it is all for the best."[19]

Back in Italy Matilda endeavored to fit in with the artist community Hatty had cultivated and to renew acquaintances she and Charlotte had made the year before. While Charlotte and Matilda were in England, Robert and Elizabeth Barrett Browning had become extremely close to both Hatty Hosmer and Isa Blagden. As Elizabeth Barrett Browning enthusiastically described the group of spirited women in her midst, "there's a house of what I call emancipated women—a young sculptress—American, Miss Hosmer, a pupil of Gibson's, very clever and very strange—and Miss Hayes [sic] the translator of George Sand."[20]

En route to Rome a year earlier Robert and Elizabeth Barrett Browning had seen Charlotte and Matilda Hays in Paris and had remarked on their "female marriage." Several months later, on their way back to England, Charlotte and Matilda had stopped in Florence and visited with the Brownings again. Elizabeth Barrett Browning "like[d] the 'manly soul' in [Charlotte's] face and manners." She was quick to clarify and attribute her terms: "manly, not masculine—an excellent distinction of Mrs. Jameson's."[21] Although Elizabeth Barrett Browning did not elaborate on the difference Anna Jameson perceived, I can infer that, while *masculine* might refer to the perception of physical virility and the assumption of qualities and privileges that could be read as mimicking male behaviors or usurping male prerogatives, *manly* connoted a more intrinsic and androgynous strength; although nominally associated with males, it would invoke a character trait desirable in either sex. Offstage as well as on, Charlotte Cushman was admirably "manly."

Now Hatty and Matilda were described by the women who admired them in Rome in similarly gendered terms. Elizabeth Barrett Browning explained to her sister that, although Matilda Hays—who "dresses like a man down to the waist"—was "a peculiar person altogether," she was "decided, direct."[22] Elizabeth Barrett Browning even enjoyed the look of the tailored waistcoat Matilda characteristically wore. And Hatty continued to be described by her friends as "the funniest little creature, not at all coarse, rough or slangy, but like a little *boy*."[23] When Bessie Rayner Parkes met the young sculptor, she said she had "never seen anything as innocent as Hatty, nor so very queer."[24] Hatty traveled and dined alone in the cafes just as the

Charlotte Cushman, ca. 1851. Cushman's "manliness" was regarded as a positive attribute by those who admired her strong, direct demeanor. *(Harvard Theatre Collection. Houghton Library.)*

male artists did, moving through Rome with an ease and familiarity uncommon for women. Even her gait was remarkable, as she "manage[d] her petticoats with a certain extraordinary ease suggestive of trousers."[25]

So, while Matilda Hays and Hatty Hosmer were making the rounds of the winter season in Rome, Charlotte threw herself into her "old religion of labour" with a fabulously successful London engagement. As much as she may have missed Matilda, Charlotte reveled in the glowing reception of her 1854 performances as Bianca and Queen Katharine which "immediately accorded [her] the highest place on the rolls of histrionic fame."[26] With her unprecedented professional success came further social success, much of it due to the eroticism other women read into Charlotte's performances. After visiting Charlotte in London, Isa Blagden attempted to explain to another woman in their social set the vehement reactions Charlotte

Harriet Goodhue Hosmer. "Hatty" Hosmer, the young sculptor, so admired Charlotte Cushman that she bragged to her patron Wayman Crow, "It is said that I look uncommonly like her [Cushman]." *(Schlesinger Library. Radcliffe College.)*

inspired in her: "I am sorry you were a little huffed by my expression that I should *attack* Miss Cushman—it was but an expression meant to express the warmth with which I should speak about [her performance of] Bianca to her."[27] Isa Blagden clearly understood the erotic dimensions of the code that linked together members of Charlotte's virtual community, but I am not suggesting that this was true of all Cushman's fans. For Elizabeth Kinney, a married woman whose reaction to Cushman took the form of "hero worship" and was reverential but probably not erotic, Blagden's ardor had needed further clarification.[28] As we have seen, Charlotte Cushman could signify a range of things, with multiple and sometimes contradictory effects for her spectators. However Charlotte may have intended to be "read," she found the support and admiration of her growing social circle as rewarding as her material success. In London, as she had bragged to Grace Greenwood, her Tuesday evening receptions, "for artistic excellence and fashionable friends quite threw our Roman receptions into the shade. . . . I was gratified by being sought out by . . . [p]ainters, poets, scholars, composers, singers,—artists of all kinds honoured me."[29]

Word of the accolades, social and professional, that Charlotte was receiving reached Rome. Although Hatty was contented with her Roman life, Matilda, it seems, was "very miserable, very sorrowful . . . very penitent and wretched," without Charlotte. She remained in Rome for four months, but, "having found and had the generosity to confess her mistake in having left [Charlotte]," Matilda set out for England.[30] Charlotte, at the height of her popularity, was performing as Meg Merrilies to an audience that included Queen Victoria and Prince Albert on 17 February 1854—the very day that Matilda Hays left Rome, alone, to return to her. Although Charlotte was wary, she felt that Matilda was "much improved" by all she had suffered and welcomed her back. With her characteristic pragmatism Charlotte, who was emotionally dependent upon the company of a loving female companion, acknowledged that "in a short time, now, we shall be together again, never again perhaps to be what she once was to me—still, perhaps, better for us both that I am not so dependent upon her and that she has tried others."[31]

What did it mean for Matilda to have "tried others"? Had she and Hatty Hosmer engaged in a brief, passionate love affair of their own? Whatever Matilda "tried," it hadn't worked; perhaps by comparison, she and Charlotte had seemed more compatible, after all. Charlotte chose not to record the details. Even in an extremely self-disclosing letter to Grace Greenwood, Charlotte was aware of how she was representing herself and her relationship with her partner. "If I were seated by your side in Philadelphia I could tell you of these things—but now," Charlotte wrote, "as the man in the play says—'you must go uninformed to your grave.'" Charlotte Cushman knew that even the details she had shared with her friend Grace about the intensity of her feelings for Matilda were potentially damaging. "All that I have told you of myself and my affairs is for your eye alone—and I should be grieved if I thought anyone would ever know the contents of this letter," Charlotte implored.[32] Women who lived as closely as Grace and Hatty had with Charlotte and Matilda could observe the intimacies and the intensity of passions that the two women shared. If they were close enough confidantes, the details of each other's relationships might even be discussed but still not committed to written words. As we have seen, Charlotte's awareness of a censorious public extended even to her most private correspondence, and the self she presented in her letters was as much a conscious construction as were the roles she played onstage or in the drawing rooms in Rome and London.

For the next two years Charlotte continued to be spectacularly successful, acting in London and in the provinces, entertaining, and finding herself routinely admired. Much of this admiration came from new friends and female fans who advocated opening more channels for women's careers and were particularly impressed by Charlotte's example. Bessie Rayner Parkes felt Charlotte possessed "genius," as did "the Brownings . . . and Rachel [the French actress] and George Sand, Currer Bell . . . I sit down in awe before our own sex[;] what will they become."[33] Parkes saw Cushman as performing a valuable service as a representative of the advancement of women, associating her not only with great performers and literary artists of the day but also with other activists "bent on doing the right" for women.[34]

In January 1855 Charlotte and Matilda moved into the lovely home Charlotte purchased in London on Bolton Row, near Berkeley Square. In this elegant Georgian townhouse Sallie Mercer was assisted by a cook and a "proper" British butler named Wilmot. Charlotte's success had brought more comfort to all their lives. For much of the next year, while Charlotte Cushman and Matilda Hays lived together in London, Charlotte was frequently off touring or traveling with other friends, and Matilda spent her time in the company of literary and politically activist friends like Bessie Rayner Parkes when Charlotte was out of town. When they were home together in London, with Matilda by her side, Charlotte hosted immensely popular parties at Bolton Row that were attended by the most celebrated literary and musical notables as well as fans and "lion seekers." But Rome still beckoned.

In the winter of 1856–57 Charlotte and Matilda Hays decided to return to Rome. At first Matilda was glad to be back and see Hatty. Matilda found, delightedly, that Hatty had "developed a charming little waist and figure"; her wardrobe was now "elegant and tasteful," but "she [was] the same frank, unaffected darling, as in old times—her spirits more boisterous and sustained than ever." Whether or not Matilda Hays was still smitten with Hatty, it pleased Matilda to find that the young sculptor's "progress in art [was] wonderful" and that her latest work, a statue of Beatrice Cenci, was "beautiful in conception and execution." For all the praise that Matilda lavished on her friend, at this time she still represented herself as being in a relationship of primary intensity with Charlotte and speculated that, at some point in the next few months, "probably Hatty will cross the Atlantic with Miss Cushman and me."[35]

But Matilda never returned to the United States with Charlotte, for it wasn't long before her relationship with Charlotte was to end irrevocably.

Making a Spectacle: A Tussle before Witnesses

In Charlotte Cushman and Matilda Hays's second attempt to set up a household together in Rome, the impression that Charlotte strove to create of herself as a tasteful, decorous hostess and "lady" at leisure with a similarly respectable companion was put to a crucial test, for in Rome that same winter was a new resident, an American sculptor named Emma Stebbins.

Cushman and Stebbins met at the height of a busy social season in the Anglo-American community. Anna Jameson was in Rome, and Bessie Rayner Parkes had come to visit. During Lenten week in March Charlotte, her friend Margaret Gill, and Emma Stebbins went to Naples. Matilda Hays stayed behind. Bessie Parkes arrived around this time, eager to spend time with Charlotte and Matilda. The day after she arrived Bessie was with Anna Jameson in a "fever of delight; . . . as we were driving full post down the Pincian Hill, I saw a large light figure talking to two other ladies, a Michael Angelique figure it always seems to me—which never belonged to anyone else but Miss Cushman [her]self." Charlotte's large, powerful presence was unmistakable. Matilda introduced Bessie to Rome, taking her to meet Hatty Hosmer in her studio, "to the Via Appia on the mournfullest of misty afternoons where [they] prowled around like two ghouls," and to spend several days in the mountains at Albano and Frascati.[36] Charlotte was also busy entertaining. Although Charlotte also took a hand in showing Bessie her adopted home—inviting her to dine with Hatty, Matilda, and herself and to see the Colosseum by moonlight—Charlotte was frequently occupied with Emma Stebbins. And, consequently, Charlotte and Matilda were spending more of their time apart.

Matilda had been growing increasingly jealous of the time and emotional energy her partner was spending with the new American sculptor. Friends in their company could see, as Hatty Hosmer remembered, that Charlotte and Matilda "fought like cat and dog. They used to throw brushes and combs at each other"; Charlotte could be "tyrannical" toward her companion.[37] The tensions in their relationship excited comments of members of their various circles. Certainly Sallie saw everything, although, as far as the record shows, she kept her opinions to herself. At first Ned chastised his mother for her derogatory characterization of Charlotte and Matilda, since, he wrote, "I don't like to say anything about Aunty's friendships for she has been very kind to me and I suppose it is none of my business . . . but never mind, she will come to the right way of thinking someday."[38] What was "the right way of thinking" to heterosexual family members like Ned and Susan? Was it the volatility of Charlotte and Matilda's attachment that upset them or the visible presence of intense, impassioned feelings—feelings of jealousy and rage—that the two women excited in each other? Soon the two women's relationship would reach a breaking point.

Clearly, something had shifted. Perhaps Matilda sensed the change when she saw the light and pleasure in Charlotte's deep-set, blue-gray eyes—her best feature—when Charlotte was with Emma Stebbins. Matilda had been described as erratic and volatile on other occasions before. But at this point, feeling her place in Charlotte's life changing irreparably, Matilda could not contain her anger and pain. The end of Charlotte and Matilda's relationship came after Matilda violated social convention to a degree unforgivable for Charlotte, by displaying her anger overtly and violently in what Hatty Hosmer described as "a tussle before witnesses"—herself and Margaret Gill. Perhaps Charlotte had gotten tired of Matilda and their frequent arguments. "Seeing Charlotte Cushman angry" was, as a mutual friend reported, "like a storm on the Alps."[39] In all probability Charlotte's attentions had already turned toward Emma Stebbins, with whom she was spending ever more time.

Hatty awoke one afternoon from a nap to see enacted before her what she remembered years later as the "vulgar" scene of Matilda, "beside herself with rage," chasing Charlotte through their home. Hatty "saw Miss H. attacking Miss C. with her fists and Miss C. defending herself." In Hatty's narrative Matilda's outburst was provoked when Charlotte "began to write a note on some business matter and Miss H. thought it was a note to this new object of affection [Emma Stebbins] and grew mad with jealousy. She . . . insisted upon seeing the note." But Charlotte refused, and, rather than show the note to Matilda and either satisfy or justify her jealousy, "C would not say to whom she was writing and refused indignantly to show the note." As Hatty described it years later to Anne Brewster, when Matilda tried to get the note from Charlotte, "Miss C. coolly put the note into her mouth! Then the H. woman beside herself with rage, swore she'd make C. swallow it. . . . Miss H. pursued her from the salon into the dining room and chairs and tables, and clothing and C. flew about together."

Hatty expressed her disgust at the "fisticuffs" she observed, characterizing her friends' quarrel as "equal to two washwomen." Women of their social class were not expected to feel such uncontrollable rage—and certainly not to lower themselves by engaging in a physical altercation. But Charlotte and Matilda Hays "fought like two gladiators," and, when Hatty tried to intercede and enjoin "Max" [as they often called Matilda], "the victorious Amazon," to stop, "the H. woman turned on her, 'Damn you,' she cried like a fishwoman 'You had better not meddle in my affairs.'"[40] Hatty's disillusionment with and consequent revulsion for Matilda Hays appeared, in Brewster's account of the breakup, to be as much a reaction to the "coarse" and "vulgar" language Hatty heard uttered as to the physical violence she observed. And Hatty's disgust, like Charlotte's, was insurmountable. Matilda had gone too far. Rage and violence were not to be experienced or expressed by respectable women, however provoked.

Why were members of their circle so shocked and disturbed by Matilda's actions? The fact that Charlotte and Matilda could have physically hurt each other is not mentioned in this account. Were they concerned that the vehemence of Matilda's behavior threatened to reveal something about *their own* passions? Writers of etiquette manuals of the day counseled that a woman who displayed rage—or other excessive emotions—was "one of the most disgusting sights in nature."[41] By resorting to "violent fisticuffs," Matilda was, in the words of *Miss Leslie's Behavior Book*, "mak[ing] herself a frightful spectacle."[42] Certainly, the potential passion and pain revealed in this episode had always simmered just below the surface in Charlotte and Matilda's intense relationship, but once it was seen, witnessed—rendered *as spectacle*—the emotional content of lesbian desire and the anguish of its frustration could not be hidden. As Eliza Leslie had warned her female readers in 1853, women's "friendships are not always lasting—particularly those that become inordinately violent, and where both parties, by their excessive intimacy put themselves too much into each other's power. Very mortifying disclosures are sometimes made after a quarrel."[43] Matilda's fury was probably provoked at least in part by her feelings of betrayal; the intimacy she had shared with Charlotte for almost a decade made her emotionally dependent on and vulnerable to her lover. And the intense jealousy that Matilda felt was exacerbated by the fact that, financially as well as emotionally, she "was dependent in a great measure" on Charlotte at this time, having given up her writing to build her life around Charlotte. In that time Charlotte had become fabulously successful and acclaimed, but Matilda Hays's own work and the causes she believed in had faded into the background.

Whatever disclosures or accusations Matilda revealed during this furious confrontation disgusted Charlotte and the others who witnessed it. Dangerously out of control with rage as she sensed her female partner turning her attentions to another woman, Matilda shattered for all of them any lingering illusion of a "passionless" romantic friendship by the vehemence of her anger and grief. By her actions Matilda Hays had unintentionally displayed what was, for many of her contemporaries, the "excessive," the "monstrous," the "disgusting"—in fact, the *lesbian*—quality of her relationship with Charlotte. And the spectacle observed by Hosmer and Gill so compromised Matilda Hays that there was no going back. When Matilda left Rome two days later, on 20 April 1857, she "threatened to bring a suit against her [Charlotte] for damages resulting from a broken literary career—she alleged she had sacrificed a certain position to serve CC." In this, arguably one of the earliest of what are now referred to informally as "palimony" suits, Matilda Hays's emotional contribution and material sacrifice in abandoning her own career to assume the role of companion to another woman was recognized, and, according to Brewster, "C[harlotte] had to buy her off with some small sum[,] a thousand or two dollars."[44] By July Charlotte Cushman was living with Emma Stebbins.

Matilda Hays returned to London and to the literary career she now so regretted leaving. With Bessie Rayner Parkes and Barbara Leigh Smith, Matilda formed the women's journal she had intended a decade earlier. In the *English Woman's Journal,* considered the first British feminist periodical,[45] Matilda Hays employed her writing for explicitly feminist ends, calling for better work and educational opportunities for women. For five years after her breakup with Charlotte, she devoted herself both to the journal and the Society for Promoting the Employment of Women, which she helped found, "drawing a small salary as Editor" and giving her services otherwise "gratuitously to the cause."[46]

The "cause" was vital to women like Matilda. Wealthy and successful fathers, husbands, or even long-term female companions like Charlotte Cushman did not guarantee women either financial security or independence. Unmarried middle-class women could only be independent and secure their own livelihood if there were more employment options available to them. With the explosion of a market for periodicals and mass-produced, domestic fiction, writing offered one such venue.

In addition to her work on the *English Woman's Journal,* Matilda Hays started writing a novel, *Adrienne Hope,* partially based on her years with Charlotte Cushman. In the novel, published in 1866, a minor character, Miss Reay—a thinly disguised version of Matilda Hays herself—is described as "a literary woman" who was "engaged in editing a philanthropic journal" similar to the *English Woman's Journal.* Miss Reay "made a fair start in early life in a literary career," but the "best years of [her] life were utterly and uselessly sacrificed . . . through the treachery" of a woman she "loved and trusted." Rather than reverse the sex of the lover who had caused Miss Reay such pain, Matilda describes her as many others had Charlotte: as "a woman of strong intellect, of considerable genius in her walk of art."[47] And, in keeping with her own disdain for the theater, Matilda Hays has her alterego, Miss Reay, assert that the "art" in which her former partner excelled was "not calculated to strengthen the moral character under any circumstances."[48] In this depiction Matilda conflates the image of the actress-as-dissembler with that of a false lover.

Even more significant, however, are the resonances of Charlotte and Matilda's relationship in the main plot line. Adrienne Hope is a vulnerable young woman from a modest background who sacrifices her budding musical career when she marries "Lord Charles." Charles forces Adrienne into a secret marriage because of the difference in their social rank and then abandons her and their child for a bigamous marriage to a wealthy heiress. Coded in this account of a heterosexual "secret" marriage, the events of the novel closely parallel Matilda Hays's life with Charlotte Cushman. The very streets on which they lived in Rome—and where Charlotte now lived with Emma Stebbins—are described in careful detail, and members of their Roman circle, such as Hatty Hosmer, are featured by name. While Lord Charles and his new wife honeymoon in Rome, the abandoned Adrienne remains in England to mourn the death of "Charlie," the child Lord Charles never legally acknowledged. In the details of the death of the child Matilda paints a metaphoric account of the "death" of her life with Charlotte. In the novel the child's tombstone reads: "In Memory of Charlie. Born October 1852. Died March 1857." The first date corresponds with the month Matilda and Charlotte set off to spend their lives together in Rome; the second is the month Charlotte left Matilda to spend a week in Naples with Emma Stebbins. And Lord Charles and Lady Charlotte Luttrell are married in July 1857, the very month Emma Stebbins moved in with Charlotte Cushman.

Emma Stebbins: A Lady Artist

Who was this American woman who had captured Charlotte's fancy? Unlike the emotionally volatile and politically radical Matilda Hays, Emma Stebbins, daughter of a banker and stockbroker, epitomized inherited wealth and social respectability. She was "a lady artist . . . a devotee of Art against the wishes of her aristocratic family." When Stebbins first came to Europe, she was forty-one years old—Charlotte's age—unmarried, and "full of noble aspirations for the spread of true art amongst the people."[49] For years Emma Stebbins had studied painting in New York, but in 1856, perhaps influenced by reports of Hatty Hosmer's remarkable success abroad, she decided to go to Italy and study sculpture. The Anglo-American community was small, and, once introduced into it, new arrivals made acquaintances quickly. Emma Stebbins could not help noticing how Charlotte Cushman's return to Rome had been eagerly anticipated; her acclaim had skyrocketed in the ensuing years, and Hosmer and others were looking forward to her arrival.

Emma Stebbins first met and became attracted to the famous actress who was to become her partner in a round of private receptions in Rome, where "no salon seemed complete without her, and her potent charm enhanced all the delights of the place."[50] As Emma Stebbins remembered, "There was a winning charm about her far above mere beauty of feature," and Charlotte "had, moreover, many of the requisites for real beauty—a fine stately presence, a movement always graceful and impressive, a warm healthy complexion, beautiful wavy chestnut hair, and the finest eyes in the world."[51] Within months the two women would be making arrangements to live together in an apartment at 38 Via Gregoriana. Charlotte planned to be back in the United States performing for several months while renovations were made.

The house was well located, on the street at the top of the Spanish Steps, with a superb, unobstructed view "taking in most of the picturesque outlines of the city, St. Peter's looming large and grand in front, with a limitless expanse of open Campagna, and the marvelous sky of Rome for background."[52] For Emma Stebbins "a glow of warmth and comfort, combined with a certain elegance, pervaded the pleasant rooms."[53] Over time Charlotte would furnish their Roman home "with choice pictures and such sculpture as there was space for, . . . antique carved furniture, [and an] abundance of books." According to Stebbins, who was accustomed to much material wealth, "the reception rooms were not large"; nonetheless, "there was an air of homeiness [sic]" in their apartment that seemed "in harmony with the true hospitable nature of its mistress."[54] Sallie Mercer, by now fluent in Italian, presided over the domestic arrangements in Rome as she did in all of Charlotte's households. Sallie was more than a maid or housekeeper. It was she who always "knew where everything was, who kept a watchful eye over all." The Italian servants reported to her and "looked upon her as a sort of deus ex machina," whose powers and resources were remarkable.[55]

As soon as Charlotte secured and outfitted enough space in her Via Gregoriana home, she earmarked several rooms for Hatty. Charlotte's household was to include her intimate circle, not just her partner and the ever-present Sallie Mercer. Over the years Charlotte invited numerous women friends to come and visit or live with her circle in Rome. In Charlotte's "salone," Hatty explained, she sat in her characteristic place, "vis-à-vis to Charlotte," Emma Stebbins was on her left side, and "the invaluable Sallie" on her right—"and this," Hatty continued, "composes a family party."[56]

As with any other social role, Charlotte Cushman's role as head of the household was fashioned in part by others who were willing to acknowledge and respond to this aspect of her personality. But in order to perform it successfully, those whom Charlotte supported were expected to express

Charlotte Cushman. Her "stately presence" and deepset gray eyes—the "finest eyes in the world"—impressed her new love, sculptor Emma Stebbins. Cushman dressed more conventionally after she met Stebbins. *(Harvard Theatre Collection. Houghton Library.)*

their gratitude for her efforts. For many years Hatty Hosmer was grateful, remarking "how good and thoughtful Miss Cushman is, she thinks of everybody's pleasure and welfare and manages to stretch out a handful of blessings to everybody she knows sooner or later."[57] For Charlotte one of the metaphors available to her for representing—and experiencing—her connection to some of her female friends was that of matriarch. In her letters from this period Hatty, fourteen years younger than Charlotte, began to characterize Charlotte as a surrogate mother, and Charlotte—who addressed her letters to Hatty "Dear Child"—started signing her letters, "Madre Mia," "Minnie," and "Mimmie," to signal the familial relationship she was creating with Hatty, Emma Stebbins, and later other women she brought under her wing. But Charlotte was more than a maternal figure to

Hatty; in addition to providing material help when Hatty's father had stopped sending her money, Charlotte believed in her, believed that the artist life Hatty envisioned for herself was possible, and provided the means to make that happen. The nurturing Charlotte offered her female household was more than parental; she provided an empowering model of female self-sufficiency and strength.

The affinities and contradictions present in a house full of women who love other women were more complex than a mere replica of a heterosexual nuclear family, even if that was the only language available to describe their ties. Witness, for example, some of the ways Hatty used the word *wife*. When Hatty first came to live with the more stereotypically feminine Emma Stebbins, she wrote to Wayman Crow that she had "taken unto myself a wife in the form of Miss Stebbins, another *sculptrice* and we are very happy together."[58] But Emma Stebbins was living with both Hatty and Charlotte. While Hatty's depiction of Charlotte's partner as her own "wife" may have been a reflection of Hatty's (unconscious) feelings of competition with Charlotte, it may have also afforded Hatty a way to differentiate her own professional aspirations within their household from those of Emma Stebbins. Hatty never used the feminine diminutive "sculptrice" to describe herself, and her playful invoking of gender in this letter may imply as much about Hatty's perception of herself as a serious (male), professional sculptor, when compared with the feminine, domestic "wifely" Emma, as it does the closeness of any relationship between them. Although women in their era might unabashedly liken their relationship with other women—whether as friends or as lovers—to heterosexual marriages, secure in the belief that to most readers this allusion would be read as a signal of affectionate friendship rather than sexual passion, still the terms also contained the possibility of invoking "wifely" or "husbandly" sensual and sexual bonds as well as the strictly sentimental.

Like Charlotte, Hatty expressed her comfort with her choice to live in a woman-centered community by embracing some of the very language that was often used against "unmarried" women. Hatty had jokingly described the first Roman home of the "jolly bachelors" as "old maids' hall."[59] To members of their circle these expressions were not pejorative; instead, they were used ironically, as a critique of the heterosexual institution of marriage that Charlotte and her friends resisted. At a later time during one of Charlotte's extended absences from their Roman home, Hatty quipped to Wayman Crow, "Miss Cushman left last Sunday so I am a forlorn old maid once more."[60]

Even in their communal household of "old maids" it was clear that Charlotte Cushman and Emma Stebbins were a couple. Together they shared Charlotte's quarters, while Hatty's rooms were her own. Early on

Charlotte and Emma developed a well-established routine. They awoke at seven o'clock, breakfasted at eight, and then Emma went off to her studio. At eleven Charlotte generally would join her and read or write letters, while Emma worked at her sculpture. At half past one they would lunch together then return home and dress for horseback riding. Starting at half past two, they would "ride hard for two hours" and get home to dine at five, "after which," Charlotte described, "we either stay at home to receive visits or we pay them."[61]

For her part Charlotte savored both the comfort of her life with her chosen partner and the propriety that a relationship with Stebbins represented for her, feeling that "I have ever held it the largest privilege of my life to have known and lived in the association which I have been allowed to do with her." Charlotte valued the "wifely" Emma Stebbins's respectability as well as her determined pursuit of her own art. But it pained Charlotte to admit that Emma's wealthy, socially conscious family did not think highly of her choice to make her home with Charlotte Cushman. Charlotte bristled at the fact that Emma's "whole family utterly disapproved of her life with me," particularly since "they felt that she was morally, socially, and physically injured by it."[62]

When describing how Emma Stebbins "has made me happy," Charlotte elaborated, depicting her partner in language that reflected the values of nineteenth-century "true" women: "She is high, true, noble and self-sacrificing."[63] Others shared Charlotte's estimation of the "soft, gentle, quiet ladylike woman" and thought that by Charlotte's association with Emma Stebbins, Charlotte "grew to be more of a lady."[64] Charlotte, for whom playing the respectable lady both on and offstage was so important, increased her social status through her connection to a woman who was born into the genteel graces that Charlotte had aspired to and learned to perform.

Charlotte's contemporaries recognized the theatrical aspects of "cultivated" society, and popular etiquette manuals of the day, such as *The Art of Conversing*, instructed aspiring middle-class readers to consider their parlors and drawing rooms as "a stage upon which parts are performed before a public, that applauds or hisses, according to the merits of the actor."[65] At their Via Gregoriana home Charlotte could now act the lady in her own drawing room, and she could play host to the expatriate community who had invited her into their homes. Before long so many guests attended Charlotte's popular Saturday evening receptions that "the house could hardly contain the numbers who thronged there." Emma Stebbins proudly noted, "It was delightful to see her in the midst of them, with a kind word, a ready repartee, a hearty laugh."[66] Sue-Ellen Case has discussed women's performances in the domestic domain of the salon as "personal theatres" in which "the audience was composed not of consumers who paid for admittance . . . but of personal friends and interesting acquaintances who came specifically to engage in social dialogue with one another." In her salon-theater, Charlotte served, in Case's terms, as the playwright of witty repartee, the director who cast the production by "creating the guest list . . . making the introductions," and, of course, "helping to create the scenes," as well as the starring actor.[67]

Yet, as William Story had indicated three years earlier, some of their contemporaries found Charlotte vain and egotistical as a society host because she was seen as still "performing." Despite the accepted metaphor of the fashionable home as a "stage" for the display of prosperous middle-class life, the presence of an actual professional actress in their midst continued to be problematic for many members of Charlotte's increasingly rarefied social set. Authors of prescriptive literature reminded their readers that, unlike female writers or visual artists who might "paint scores of pictures, write shelvesful of books" while they lived a "simple and peaceful life," the performing "*artiste* is very different; she needs to be constantly before the public, not only mentally, but physically."[68] Even in retirement Charlotte was liable to be branded an *artiste*—a derogatory term for a professional female performing artist. According to writer Dinah Mulock Craik, "the natural result of this . . . incessant struggle for the public's personal verdict" for a woman who had performed for her livelihood was "intense involuntary egotism."[69] Having intentionally courted the public's attention for so long, women performers might be unable to exist without it. And Charlotte, who was perpetually threatening to retire and then resuming her stage career, appeared to be an illustration of this principle.

The professional stage *had* shaped Charlotte. As much as Charlotte attempted to differentiate her professional labors from her social entertainments at home in Rome, responses to her offstage roles as artist-at-leisure, host, sponsor, mentor, or lover were often contradictory. For, while Charlotte the retired actress might be condemned for her egotism or self-serving behavior as an *artiste*, she was also acting as a generous host. And for many in her immediate circle Charlotte's performance as the host of her own popular salon carried with it as well the implicit obligation to respond appreciatively to her performance as its most featured entertainer.

But not everyone who witnessed Charlotte's dramatic musical renderings was willing to oblige. One of Charlotte's biggest adversaries in Rome was sculptor Randolph Rogers, who was competing for commissions with Emma Stebbins and Hatty Hosmer. Journalist and amateur painter William J. Stillman claimed that, when he first arrived in Rome to serve as American consul, Charlotte offered him her considerable hospitality but expected him to demonstrate his loyalty by undermining the work of Rogers, Story, and other male artists, a request Stillman refused.[70] Although

Charlotte Cushman and Randolph Rogers kept up a veneer of civility whenever they encountered each other, the enmity between them was ferocious and frequently played out before others. Rogers, an excellent mimic, chose to parody Charlotte's very theatrical delivery of her signature songs at every available opportunity. As Stillman remembered, "When the two cordial enemies met in society somebody was sure to ask Rogers to sing 'The Sands of Dee' . . . and Miss Cushman was obliged, to her intense anger, to applaud the caricature of her best performance." Stillman did not like Cushman yet admitted that this public humiliation "was cruel" and that Rogers "was merciless, and spared no exaggeration of her voice, her dramatic manner, and a way she had of sprawling over the piano . . . which made it impossible to hear her again in the same songs without a disposition to laugh."[71]

Thus, while Charlotte was attempting to play the part of the great artist-at-leisure as well as the generous host, Rogers was attempting to impersonate Charlotte Cushman, the dramatic *artiste,* and thereby reveal as unnatural and artificial the very characteristic behaviors by which she was known. If being *Charlotte Cushman* were not so much the expression of her individual identity but, rather, a conglomeration of external gestures and vocal traits that others—like Rogers—could imitate, then Charlotte herself might be seen as inauthentic and "stagy." Stillman, for example, felt Charlotte "never failed to impress the visitors to Rome with her sincerity and benevolence, though she really possessed neither of these qualities." Stillman instead attributed her personal power and influence to her abilities as a *performer,* contending that "she was always on the stage—in the most familiar act and in the presence of strangers she never lost sight of the footlights, and the best acting I ever saw her in was in private and in the representation of some comedy or tragedy of her own interests." And Stillman claimed that women whom Charlotte "chose to fascinate" were especially vulnerable to her charms and thus "completely under her control."[72]

Emma Stebbins, exerting some control of her own, was eager to disassociate Charlotte from any "reminder of the professional in [her] private life." While Stebbins enjoyed her partner's social entertainments, she guarded the categories of "private" and "professional" vigilantly, however much Charlotte's performing in her drawing room or on the stage might complicate matters. Emma Stebbins clearly had her own antitheatrical biases and boasted that "the singular absence from Miss Cushman's personality of any suggestion of the stage—if we may so express it—was most remarkable in one who had lived upon it so long."[73] Stebbins declared, proudly, that from Charlotte's dress and manner others could not detect that she was a "professional," since she was so "beautifully natural and true in her manner,"[74] as though being natural and true were antithetical to being a professional performer.

Just as the home that Charlotte made with Emma Stebbins in Rome can be considered a "salon-theater" in which their relationship and the relationships among other women were played out, it was also a setting made up of carefully chosen objects and domestic routines that were read by others as representative of the character of its hosts. In choosing to make a home with Emma Stebbins, Charlotte was attempting both to guard against whatever erotic meanings might have been read into the earlier impassioned, emotionally tumultuous relationship she had forged with Matilda Hays and to construct a life with another woman that *appeared to be* an acceptable alternative. Taken together, these artifacts, domestic rituals, and ways of relating that guests saw Charlotte Cushman and Emma Stebbins perform were a representation of a form of intimacy between women that others might acknowledge and accept.

Irish feminist Frances Power Cobbe was a guest clearly charmed by Charlotte Cushman's social performances in Rome and was frequently welcomed "at [her] hospitable table" in her "handsome house" in Rome. Cobbe remarked that Charlotte "had, of course, like all actors, the acquired habit of giving outward expression to every emotion, just as we quiet English ladies are taught from our cradles to repress such signs, and to cultivate a calm manner under all emergencies." But, rather than condemn her for excessively emotional, "unfeminine" display, Cobbe recognized that both the outward expression and inward repression of emotions were matters of habit rather than of nature—learned, cultivated ways of displaying or withholding the arbitrary signs of emotional affect. Besides, Charlotte Cushman's "vivacity rendered her all the more interesting."[75] As a close friend, Cobbe was often part of the fabric of Charlotte's household's day-to-day life. For Cobbe "[t]here was a brightness, freedom and joyousness among these gifted Americans which was quite delightful to me."[76]

Charlotte was eager to have old friends as well as new see her in her home with Emma Stebbins. She encouraged Emilie Ashurst Venturi, sister of Matilda Hays's old friend Eliza Ashurst, to visit her in Rome. Venturi had remained close to Charlotte and would continue to be so for decades—their friendship outliving both of Venturi's marriages and several of Cushman's intimate relationships. "I hope I shall not return to England without seeing the 'jolly Bachelors,'" Venturi mused in 1859.[77] After several years of being out of touch, Charlotte wrote to Bessie Rayner Parkes that a room awaited her "with the warmest welcome from all the inmates of 38 Gregoriana" when she next came to Rome. By 1864 Charlotte had secured the entire four-story house, and with Emma Stebbins's help it was now "so much

Charlotte Cushman (seated) and Emma Stebbins (standing),
ca. 1859. With Stebbins at her side as her respectable "better
half," Cushman constructed a picture of domestic harmony.
(Harvard Theatre Collection. Houghton Library.)

improved, so much larger—so much prettier—so much wider and better
able to exhibit hospitalities."[78] Charlotte was eager to show Bessie Parkes
the change in her Roman household now that she was sharing it with her
"true and faithful friend" Emma Stebbins. "Every hour of my life I prize her
more," Charlotte wrote of Emma, "the truest and noblest artist soul that
ever lived."[79] But Bessie Parkes evidently remembered the "shocks" of her
last visit during Charlotte and Matilda's breakup and "had a divided mind"
about staying at Via Gregoriana, fearful it might be "re-opening a closed
book."[80]

In addition to her immediate circle some of the women who surrounded Charlotte Cushman in Rome over the years were friends engaged in exploring their own intense relationships with other women. After her initial visit Kate Field, a young writer whose father had performed with Charlotte and whose aunt was friends with Charlotte, stayed on in Italy with Isa Blagden, whom Field affectionately called "Hubby." Like Charlotte and Hatty, many women of the period unselfconsciously used the metaphor of marriage to describe their connections to the women closest to them. Charlotte frequently described Stebbins as her "other and better half," referring to her as men frequently did to their wives, in a slightly patronizing tone that reflected both the two women's closeness, their "marriage," and Charlotte's position as the more male-identified member of the partnership. Among themselves members of Charlotte and Emma's circle supported this perception. Playfully acknowledging the roles Charlotte played as romantic lover of women and recognizing Emma Stebbins's part as Charlotte's partner, Kate Field addressed her letters to Charlotte Cushman as "Beloved Romeo."[81] Even in letters to others Field wrote in her characteristic teasing tone that she was "very disappointed at not seeing Romeo and her Juliet, Miss Stebbins," and she complained that "Romeo never answered my last billet-doux, just like these men."[82] To Charlotte, Kate quipped that her mother, also a former actress, was "trying to make me a moral woman and forgiving me though I don't profit much by her efforts."[83] Field's mother had soon come to the conclusion that "it [was] useless to attempt alterations or repairs" on Field's character now, "so you see, mother is forgetting her propriety most rapidly and very shortly will be qualified for our set."[84]

It was through Charlotte and her "set"—a largely homosocial extended community of like-minded women artists—that Frances Power Cobbe met sculptor Mary Lloyd. As Cobbe recounted it, "One day when I had been lunching at her house, Miss Cushman asked whether I would drive with her in her brougham to call on a friend."[85] Cobbe was, of course, very willing to meet Mary Lloyd, whom she and Charlotte found "busy in her sculptor's studio over a model of her Arab horse." Like Charlotte Cushman and Hatty Hosmer, Lloyd and Cobbe also shared a love of riding. Frances Cobbe remembered that, "on hearing that I was anxious to ride," Mary Lloyd kindly offered to provide a horse "if I would join her in her rides on the Campagna. Then began an acquaintance, which was further improved two years later . . . and from that time, now more than thirty years ago, she and I have lived together."[86]

In one of her novels Isa Blagden attempted to articulate the intensity of the relationships between women she observed around her in this circle: "I think few writers lay sufficient stress on the large space which a true friendship, such as two minds can feel for each other, holds in the lives of two single women, and what exquisite enjoyments are derived from it. In the personal intimacy which exists in such a relation, there is entire comprehension and knowledge of each other. This is seldom attained, even in the holiest and truest marriage."[87] Writers Isa Blagden, Kate Field, Frances Power Cobbe, and sculptors Hatty Hosmer, Edmonia Lewis, Emma Stebbins, Mary Lloyd, and Margaret Foley were never to marry men. Instead, the women in the homosocial network of Charlotte's Roman circle chose to find "exquisite enjoyments" in their intimacies with other women.

For some of the women in their circle Charlotte Cushman and Emma Stebbins were a visible symbol of this intimacy. One American friend would refer to photographs she had of them whenever she was "assailed by those who believe . . . that women's friendships are like pretty bows of ribbon to be put on or taken off at caprice." In response to such trivializing of intimate committed relationships between women, this correspondent "pointed triumphantly to these pictures and assured [her] antagonists that here, at least, were two whose lives beautifully illustrated the converse of such a malicious assertion—two as firm in their friendship as the Ladies of Llangollen."[88] To modern readers the "Ladies of Llangollen," Lady Eleanor Butler and her lifetime companion and partner, Sarah Ponsonby, are themselves emblematic of the committed lesbian couple. Running away together from their respective families and homes in Ireland at the end of the eighteenth century, Butler and Ponsonby "eloped" to live together in Wales. Many nineteenth-century women saw in Cushman and Stebbins's relationship a similarly exclusive dedication.

What is clearly evident from Charlotte's and her contemporaries' letters is that relationships of primary emotional intensity between women could be seen by some as enduring sentimental friendships, acceptable embodiments of an almost religious, morally uplifting "sisterhood," yet at the same time the exclusive commitment of one woman to another allowed for the possibility of intense romantic *and* erotic pleasure as well as precluding the female partners' relationships to men. Erotic desire was always a possible component of the narrative of sentimental friendship—so possible, in fact, that it often threatened the boundaries of that friendship, as we have seen in Charlotte's relationship with Matilda Hays and others. But, with Emma Stebbins, Charlotte enacted an "idealized view" of women's loving relationships, which, paradoxically, appeared to many people to exemplify conventional societal values rather than challenge them.

Many women who shared the lifestyle Charlotte Cushman and Emma Stebbins presented sought one another out, each couple recognizing in the other a display of gender and affectional options similar to their own. Charlotte's photograph album contained photographs and *cartes de visite* of celebrated women whom Cushman didn't know well,[89] like George Sand, but whose independence and challenge to traditional gender norms she admired, and of acquaintances, like Rosa Bonheur, who also shared their lives with other women. Charlotte bragged that when she and Emma Stebbins met the acclaimed French painter, Bonheur expressed her admiration for Charlotte and "said such lovely things to us . . . that it made me blush."[90] There were decided similarities between Charlotte Cushman's and Rosa Bonheur's prominence in their respective arts and each woman's masculine dress. Bonheur's artistic achievements were regarded as "masterful" and a source of pride to the French, just as Cushman's renowned performances were to Americans. And each lived openly with a female partner whom she considered her "wife." Bonheur wanted to preserve the image of another like-minded female couple, similar to herself and her lifelong partner, Nathalie Micas: "She has made us promise to sit for a photograph," Charlotte explained to Emma Crow, "Aunt Em[ma Stebbins] and I."[91]

A "Flock" of Female Artists

Charlotte Cushman had always been unequivocal in her support of women artists, and with Emma Stebbins in her life Charlotte's role in Rome as "the nucleus of a little clique of women sculptors" became even more clearly defined.[92] Her advocacy for women artists became a mission that gave purpose to her life in Italy. "Accordingly," William Stillman alleged, "she made war on sculptors of the other sex." As if championing the efforts of women necessarily meant denigrating those of men, Stillman claimed she drew upon "all the curious ways of womanly malice" in order to guarantee for "her protegees . . . the exclusive reaping . . . of the golden harvest" of commissions and artistic acclaim.[93] And William Wetmore Story was particularly critical of the fact that so many women artists gravitated toward her, complaining that "Miss Cushman is mouthing it as usual, and has her satellites revolving around her."[94] What led Stillman and Story to consider women sculptors—practitioners of an art markedly different than Charlotte's own—her "protegees" and "satellites"? Perhaps the women who surrounded Charlotte in Italy were seen as her followers to the extent that they modeled their autonomous lives on hers. Charlotte was known to be fiercely ambitious, and she inspired similar determination in other women.

Despite the difficulties women faced competing with men in their chosen form of artistic expression, it had been clear to Charlotte from her first association with Hatty Hosmer that Hosmer had both ambition and talent. Grace Greenwood, who had seen Hosmer hard at work in her studio, commended Hosmer's determination as well as her talent in "bravely chiseling out her own womanly enthusiasms," thereby "giving enduring form . . . to the yearnings and aspirations of feminine genius, which too often by reason of unfriendly conditions, pass away."[95] But Hatty had refused to let "unfriendly conditions" in Rome or elsewhere deter her; within a relatively short time she had won over critics and achieved international fame and prominence as the foremost female sculptor—and the first American woman to achieve such success in this art form. Charlotte attributed much of Hatty's success to the younger artist's self-assurance, a quality Charlotte recognized in herself and fostered in others, believing that "there is no so sure way of making people believe in you as believing in yourself."[96] And, as Charlotte knew, self-confidence was contagious.

At first Hatty had received commissions for public and commemorative sculptures primarily through the help of Wayman Crow. But within a few years even Britain's young Prince of Wales purchased a copy of Hosmer's most commercially successful work, *Puck,* and soon other members of the nobility of various European countries were acquiring her sculptures.[97] Hatty's unprecedented accomplishments were publicized in contemporary periodicals, and this encouraged other women sculptors to come to Rome. As Charlotte Cushman met each of the new arrivals and welcomed them into the female artists' community, she informally took on the role as their sponsor, advocate, and representative. One woman alone might be seen as a singular, exceptional genius, but a community of women could refute the predominate prejudices against women's talents and encourage the efforts of each of its members.

The success of the women in Charlotte's immediate circle continued to inspire others; before long there was, according to Henry James, a "strange sisterhood of American 'lady sculptors' who at one time settled upon the seven hills in a white marmorean flock."[98] James attributed the "odd phenomenon," as he characterized it, of the "practically simultaneous appearance" of Charlotte Cushman and this group of female artists to a "peculiar" form of taste in the "simmering society that produced them."[99] But, despite his dismissive metaphor, it was not merely synchronicity, random circumstance, or a particular fashion for such work as might be produced by women sculptors that drew them all to Rome. Many women came *because of* Charlotte Cushman. Her achievements epitomized the possibility of combining the independent, aggressive pursuit of an artistic career with the fulfillment of a devoted, familial community of women. Charlotte's life with her lovers and friends suggested to other women artists that women could be self-sufficient and have a productive, satisfying life with one another.[100]

Charlotte Cushman worked assiduously to try to use her contacts to arrange commissions, first for Hatty Hosmer and later for Emma Stebbins and other American women, such as Vermont-born cameo cutter Margaret

"Peggy" Foley and African American and Native American sculptor Edmonia Lewis. For each of these artists Charlotte's ready offer of her time, company, and contacts was encouraging and greatly appreciated. If the women artists in her midst were, to some extent, a project Charlotte took up in her leisure, the pleasure she found in their successes confirmed her estimation of their talents. Charlotte's friend Peggy Foley had been a worker in the Lowell, Massachusetts, mills before she turned to cameo cutting. In the mid-1850s, after seven years of practicing her art in Boston, Foley arrived in Rome. From cameos Foley went on to make commemorative medallions and eventually modeled busts and even an elaborate fountain. Charlotte encouraged Foley's work and arranged for Foley to make medallion portraits of Wayman Crow and his daughter, Charlotte's beloved friend Emma Crow.

When Edmonia Lewis, the American-born orphaned daughter of a Chippewa mother and a father of African descent, came to Rome in the mid-1860s to study sculpture, she faced obstacles even greater than those encountered by white women artists. Lydia Maria Child, an abolitionist and friend of Hatty Hosmer, had befriended Lewis in the United States. While the very humanity of persons of color was being violently debated on the battlefield of the United States Civil War, Cushman, Stebbins, and Hosmer welcomed Lewis into their growing social circle. Cushman and Stebbins took an active part in securing commissions for Lewis, whose sculptures often featured Native American subjects, like Hiawatha, or images of enslaved people breaking their chains. The first sculpture Lewis created in Rome was a statue of the biblical figure Hagar. As she explained her choice to depict the plight of rejected, scorned, or tragic women in her work, "I have a strong sympathy for all women who have struggled and suffered."[101]

Hoping to popularize Lewis's work, Charlotte Cushman and Emma Stebbins wrote a letter on behalf of "a number of Americans . . . in Rome [who] have had occasion to know the praiseworthy efforts at improvement of a young colored artist Miss Edmonia Lewis, established here in her profession as a sculptor." Together they had taken up a collection and "in the hope of making her better known at home" purchased one of Lewis's sculptures and then offered it to the Young Men's Christian Association of Boston "as primary proof that a race which hitherto in every age or country has been looked upon with disfavor [was] . . . capable . . . under favorable circumstances, of producing works worthy the admiration of cultivated persons."[102] Charlotte made a similar effort to arrange for Edmonia Lewis's sculptures to be purchased for the Mercantile Library in Boston.[103] As with other female artists whose work she championed, Charlotte advocated support for Lewis not only because of her estimation of the aesthetic value of the artwork Lewis produced but because of her personal association with the artist. In Edmonia Lewis's case race as well as sex was a significant factor in Charlotte's advocacy of the artist and her work. Although in later years Charlotte was credited with unqualified support for Lewis, to modern readers there is a decidedly patronizing tone in the famous white actress's promotion of her countrywoman. The first draft of the letter that Charlotte and Emma Stebbins wrote to garner support for Lewis mentioned Lewis's "estimable character," but the phrase was crossed out and amended to include word of Lewis's "praiseworthy efforts at improvement."[104] Perhaps Charlotte and her circle felt that the recipients of Edmonia Lewis's work would be more receptive to a free woman of color who was attempting to "improve herself," rather than acknowledging that she already possessed those qualities of character this group considered praiseworthy.

During this time Hatty Hosmer's work had continued to attract growing international attention, particularly after her large statue *Zenobia*, completed in 1859, was exhibited to great acclaim at the Crystal Palace in London in 1862 and then in the United States in 1864, where thousands of people paid just to see the colossal statue. Published photographs of the diminutive Hatty at work on the seven-foot statue fueled the lingering prejudice against women sculptors, and many people were incredulous that a woman could accomplish such an enormous work on her own. Derogatory articles appeared in the *Art Journal* and the *Queen*, implying that Hatty did not do her own work but that her "master," Gibson, had actually created the statue. Gibson flatly denied the charge, and Hatty threatened to sue for slander. Retractions were printed, but soon rumors circulated that Hatty had, in fact, employed Italian craftsmen to execute her designs for her. While Charlotte acknowledged privately that Hatty "deserves much of this—at the same time it will not do to have such things said,"[105] she encouraged Hatty to react resolutely, to respond to this charge directly and in print—as she herself had reacted to unfavorable press early in her own career—and set to rest any implications that women artists were not up to their task. Hatty followed Charlotte's advice and responded by publishing an article in the *Atlantic Monthly*, edited by Charlotte's good friend James T. Fields, explaining the process by which sculptors, male and female, conceived of a work and what part skilled craftsmen played in any piece's execution.

The criticism Hatty received had stung Emma Stebbins and other women artists in their Roman circle. It was, in Emma's mind, "as much an attack on her as a woman worker as it was on Hattie herself."[106] Publicly, Charlotte continued to applaud Hatty's accomplishments, but by the time this scandal broke Charlotte was directing more of her energy toward active support for her partner than for her friend. Charlotte was concerned lest Emma Stebbins's reputation suffer by association as a result of these charges.

And she was particularly disturbed that Emma's response to the accusations was to undertake so much of the strenuous physical labor involved in the direct carving of her marble sculptures herself that her health was affected. Just as Charlotte had, years earlier, acted as intermediary and literary agent for Eliza Cook, exploiting her own popularity on her partner's behalf, Charlotte's efforts to protect Emma Stebbins and secure commissions for her were also untiring. And by this time Charlotte's own reputation had grown so formidable that she usually got her way. On numerous occasions Charlotte still performed as an emissary for many other women artists and literary friends, but once Emma Stebbins was established in Cushman's life her advocacy on behalf of the woman she routinely referred to as her "better half" took precedence over all the others.

One of Emma Stebbins's first major commissions was to produce a commemorative sculpture of the late educator Horace Mann. Hatty Hosmer had also vied for the commission, but Charlotte used her influence with Mann's widow, Mary Peabody Mann, sister of Charlotte's dear friend Elizabeth Peabody, to secure it for Stebbins. The husband of Charlotte's friend Julia Ward Howe was taking up a collection to fund the statue, but only half of the necessary four thousand dollars had been raised. Charlotte knew how much her partner wanted this commission and how expensive it was to produce and cast a bronze sculpture, let alone to ship it from Italy to the United States. And so she interceded and offered help at every stage. Cushman wrote from Rome to tell mutual friends in Boston that Howe had let it be known that "if any responsible, conscientious artist would undertake to furnish them a Bronze Statue [of Mann] . . . they could have the order and he said he found such a responsible conscientious artist in Miss Stebbins." But drawing upon her connections to secure the arrangement wasn't effort enough for Charlotte. "It now becomes necessary to have what would be the cost of *casting* such a work," Cushman wrote. Knowing how powerful a draw her own celebrity was, Charlotte Cushman suggested that Fields "get some mighty clever fellow to write a eulogy" about Mann, which she would deliver "and so raise a fund which shall pay Emma for her work. In this way—*women* will raise the statue."[107]

Emma Stebbins's most renowned sculpture was *Angel of the Waters,* begun in Rome in the early 1860s and commissioned for Bethesda Terrace in New York's Central Park. Charlotte was so excited about her partner's achievement that she was sure that, when set up in New York, "it will be without exception the most magnificent thing in our country."[108] But, despite largely favorable reactions, not everyone agreed. When the fountain was finally displayed, one anonymous journalist in Boston sniped that "New York is poking fun at Miss Stebbins' fountain in Central Park." Perhaps because Emma's brother Henry Stebbins was the New York commissioner of parks, as well as president of the New York Stock Exchange, some critics charged that nepotism rather than talent was the reason Emma had been awarded the commission. Other criticism of the large, powerful, female body in Stebbins's work had a decidedly misogynist tone. "The belief is continually growing," wrote a derisive Boston critic, "that the angel who sat for the model of the buxom deity on top of the concern must have been brought up on pork and hominy."[109] Charlotte was livid. James Fields had influence with the Boston paper, and Charlotte sent the article to his wife, Annie, with a note: "I wish you would have something said in the *Transcript* which shall stultify the effect of the enclosed vileness." Believing the article to be the work of a "miserable jealous artist" with "a dirty mind,"[110] Charlotte offered to send along all of the positive reviews Stebbins's fountain had received in the New York press. But once again she was determined to manage her partner's reputation without Stebbins's knowledge. Charlotte's role as romantic partner and public defender included vigilantly guarding Emma from anything likely to disturb her. "I would not have Emma see this for the world," she wrote.[111]

For the last two decades of her life Charlotte positioned herself as Emma Stebbins's advocate and protector as well as her partner. Although Charlotte often gave precedence to Emma's career over her own, in their relationship Charlotte was still the more acclaimed partner, the star. During their almost twenty years together Charlotte would repeatedly find herself lured out of retirement, despite Emma Stebbins's disdain for the theater. Charlotte was grateful, then, to her "dearest friend" Elizabeth Peabody, to whom she now acknowledged, "My only two very intimate friends of the last 18 years [Matilda Hays and Emma Stebbins] have looked disprisingly upon my art—and this has always hurt me altho' I have not said much. Your honest, tender appreciation of it and me has done me more good than you can think."[112]

For all of Charlotte Cushman's advocacy for and devotion to Emma Stebbins, their life together from the beginning was a series of negotiations. Charlotte decided to return to the stage in 1857, just months after she and Emma Stebbins met, and they planned to travel to the United States together. Louis Harlan, a Philadelphia investor who had been intrusted with tens of thousands of dollars of Charlotte's money, had mismanaged it. She felt she needed to earn more money and arrange to have a more reliable person oversee it for her. Hatty's patron, Wayman Crow, might be just the man to perform this service. Besides, for all the pleasure that Charlotte felt in acting as host, sponsor, head-of-the-household, symbolic center of the women's community, advocate for women artists, and artist-at-leisure, she missed the attention of her fans and the sense of satisfaction she got out of

Angel of the Waters, by Emma Stebbins. Bethesda Fountain,
Central Park, New York. Emma Stebbins's sculpture was
begun in Rome in the 1860s and unveiled in Central Park in
May 1873. Some critics disapproved of the large, powerful
body that Stebbins had given her "Angel"—a body not unlike
Charlotte Cushman's. *(Photograph copyright P. Calkins.)*

performing on the stage. As Kate Field mused shortly after she met Charlotte Cushman during that same year, "it must be so glorious to inspire thousands of people instantaneously." But Field recognized that this glory was ephemeral, since "the singer or actor, if successful, reaps golden harvests" but is only "feted for the time being . . . How fleeting, how sad, is such fame!"[113] At times Charlotte felt similarly. She had been gone five years. If she stayed away too long would she be forgotten? She planned a series of return performances for this trip, during which she would rediscover the pleasure she felt in her active pursuit of her career. And she would meet the "little lover" who would change all their lives.

The Sapphic Family

Temper the fire of your spirit my darling, and I shall be better
in mind and body for these influences are far too subtle for us
in one narrow vision to understand.
                —Charlotte Cushman to Emma Crow, 1860

It was the autumn of 1857 when Charlotte Cushman returned to the United
States to perform. Over the five years she had been away news of her success
in England had crossed the Atlantic, and she had no trouble securing
profitable, starring engagements, despite a now tense economy. Emma
Stebbins, with whom Charlotte had been living since the summer, accompanied Charlotte and Sallie Mercer on this trip, although Charlotte was not
quite sure how she would integrate Emma Stebbins into either her professional tours or the network of friends she had established with Matilda
Hays on her previous trip. "I am situated a little awkwardly I fear," Charlotte explained to her Baltimore friends, Algernon and Emily Chase, "I have
invited my friend Miss Stebbins . . . to go to Phila and Baltimore with me
and I should scarcely feel myself justified in bringing a stranger to you. But
we shall see!" The Chases, who had known and liked Charlotte's former
partner, were told only that "Miss Hays has not come to America this
time—she is busy editing a Journal in London in company with a friend."
Charlotte was pleased to report that her return performances in New York
were so successful that they were being extended, so she was unsure when
she would get away, but "at all events you shall have timely warning of my
coming southward, and not be unexpectedly *pounced upon!*"[1]

After an extraordinarily successful month-long run in New York,
where among her well-known roles Charlotte played Cardinal Wolsey in
Henry the VIII for the first time, she left Emma Stebbins in New York with
her own family and set out with Sallie Mercer for a series of engagements
that would take them west to Chicago and then south to St. Louis. There
Charlotte planned to meet Hatty's patron, Wayman Crow, to seek his

financial advice. Sixty years later Wayman Crow's daughter Emma still vividly remembered her first impressions of the woman who would become the emotional center of her life: "It was in the year 1858 that Charlotte Cushman came to the city of St. Louis to play an engagement of two weeks. She brought letters of introduction to my father . . . from Harriet Hosmer and from Mrs. Fanny Kemble," Emma recalled. "The play which took place that evening was *Romeo and Juliet*. Never having seen it until then, Miss Cushman as Romeo seemed the incarnation of the ideal lover and realized all the dreams that flitted through a girl's fancy." In her brief, unpublished memoir Emma Crow did not present as strange or unique the fact that a young woman's ideal lover would be another *woman*.[2] What did the eighteen-year-old Emma Crow see that led her to read Charlotte as the realization of *her* ideal lover? Charlotte was forty-two years old and heavier and more powerful than ever. As we saw in chapter 5, even in the costume of the prototypical romantic male lover Charlotte's buxom body was visibly female. And this female Romeo was clearly moved by Mary Devlin, the delicate and inexperienced actress who played Juliet. Seeing the erotic tension between the two women on stage, Emma Crow "felt a thrill when in the balcony scene at the moment of impassioned parting, Romeo returned again and again for a last embrace and finally pressed one of [Juliet's] ringlets to his lips." Watching the two women embrace, Crow attested that Charlotte's display of passion as the ardent lover of young Juliet won Charlotte "more hearts than Juliet's," especially Emma Crow's.[3] For the next two weeks Emma Crow spent as much time as she could with Charlotte, relishing long rides in the afternoons and visits to Charlotte's dressing room before the evening performances, although "the price of this much coveted privilege was the complete effacement of my presence."[4] Emma Crow wanted Charlotte's company *and* her attention.

Like the many female fans who had seen in Charlotte a palpable alternative to heterosexual passion, from this first performance Emma embraced Charlotte Cushman as the object of her desire. By the time Charlotte left town to resume her Southern tour the feeling was reciprocated. Charlotte found herself drawn to "the dear 'little lover' I have inspired in my 'old age' who made my time pass quickly and agreeably in St. Louis after she dawned upon my path and who proved the devotion she professed in so many ways."[5] In the first of the hundreds of letters that were to pass between Charlotte and Emma Crow from 1858 until the end of Charlotte's life, eighteen years later, Charlotte encouraged the demonstrations of devotion the younger woman was so eager to "prove." Sounding much as she had in letters to Sarah Anderton a decade earlier, Charlotte told Emma Crow that "it is sweet to be loved by a young fresh heart and the enthusiasm of youth is too precious not to be gathered up as I gather yours dear." But

Charlotte was concerned that Emma might come to "see the little idol which you have raised on my altar tumble to pieces at your feet." Female fans had idolized her for decades, and Charlotte feared that this young woman might outgrow her worshipful infatuation and "wonder you ever could have declared so fervent a love for *me*."[6]

Emma Crow's response to this letter, and to all those that followed, is unknown, since none of her letters to Charlotte have survived. But from the multitudes of Charlotte's letters to her, which Emma saved despite Charlotte's occasional exhortations over the years to burn them, we can hear Charlotte's replies to her "little lover's" passionate expressions and plaintive requests for the same from Charlotte, whom she called her "ladie lover." Two days later Charlotte wrote again, assuring Emma, "I will write to you whenever I possibly can—but you must never doubt my love for you if circumstances prevent my writing as often as you wish to hear. I *love* you! I *love* you! . . . I kiss your soft loving eyes and hands."[7]

Charlotte flirted, teased, and cajoled her little lover. In one letter, playfully chastising Emma for not writing sooner, Charlotte asked, "Did my note frighten you that you were making a monster which you could not easily subdue? . . . Why then am I so long without a word? . . . You are naughty and don't deserve the comfort which you say you find in my picture . . . and I am half inclined to take it away from you when I come back again—or else not come back at all."[8] What passions had been aroused in each other that Charlotte could imagine seeming "monstrous"? Women's enthusiasms and their passionate expression might be seen as monstrous—unnatural, excessive—by some, but clearly Emma Crow was not frightened, nor did she want to "subdue" her growing fervor.

While Charlotte was on tour throughout the South, Emma had asked her to come back through St. Louis on her return northward. Not entirely sure how Emma understood the feelings they expressed to each other, Charlotte wondered, "What will your dear little young head make out of my anxiety to hear from you?" Flattering Emma, Charlotte announced that she planned "to travel twenty-six hours without stopping" to St. Louis for one day only "solely and entirely to see you!"[9] Writing as she sped back toward St. Louis, Charlotte encouraged her young lover and described in Emma Crow a desire she recognized in herself: "All that is young and fresh and enthusiastic has especial charm for me," Charlotte wrote. "I see my own young aspirations and feelings reflected and wondering how *I* ever should excite such feelings which others have excited in me—a mixture of such sensations give me pleasure, and I am getting to an age where pleasures are rare."[10]

But, as much as Charlotte relished the prospect of spending more time with her devoted young "love," she had also come to recognize the need "to talk to you as I must seriously about myself, and of my many obligations in affection to show you where I am and what you have to expect with one who has so many claims upon her." Their letters had been getting increasingly passionate, and Charlotte recognized the need to clarify her feelings for Emma Crow. For all that was wonderful about this new, exciting relationship, Charlotte had to be careful. Emma Crow had to be made to understand the nature of the prior commitment Charlotte had made to Emma Stebbins. And, perhaps remembering Benjamin Brewster's censure years ago, Charlotte did not want to risk condemnation by Emma Stebbins or the Crow family. Besides, the young woman who professed such devotion might outgrow her feelings, particularly if they were based more on Emma Crow's perception of Charlotte the celebrated actress "playing the part" of a romantic lover, rather than Charlotte the woman as an actual or potential lover. "Don't love me too much and think me too good or you will see your god tumble and you will walk over the fragments," Charlotte warned in response to one of Emma Crow's expressions of "enthusiasm" for her.[11]

Charlotte needed to be absolutely sure of the meaning of Emma's fervent feelings, for, as we have seen, women's protestations of love for each other could indicate a multitude of different and paradoxical feelings, from companionable friendship to passionate desire.[12] From Nashville, as she neared St. Louis, Charlotte wrote, "You say in your note . . .—'Do you . . . really love me? How *funny!*' Is it funny dear, or only strange—or does your '*funny*' mean '*strange*' you dear little patronizing monkey? Explain your meaning. 'Funny' to me implies something *ludicrous!* and that is an element I don't like in love!" Charlotte was aware that the desire she and Emma sensed exceeded what much of middle-class Victorian society thought women should feel for each other. Charlotte was used to being regarded as strange or unusual, but the prospect of her love being characterized as ridiculous or laughable was painful to her, particularly since she acknowledged what today would be considered the lesbian nature of her passions: "I do not think we can help our *feelings* or impulses," Charlotte explained, "so you were not wrong for wishing to come to *see me.*"[13]

But Emma Crow proposed to do more than see Charlotte when she returned to St. Louis; Emma wanted to come to the hotel and sleep with her. Charlotte was wary. "For coming to the Hotel to sleep with me, darling—I think if I were your Papa or Mama—I should be sorry to refuse you—but I should be sorry to have you do such a thing. I need not assure you of the true pleasure it would be to me. Your own heart tells you that . . . if you doubt that *I want you.*" Charlotte, however, had another plan: "If I were on a visit to your house I would open my arms gladly to such a visitor and you should talk to me and keep me awake all night if you would."

Perhaps Emma could arrange an invitation. Charlotte suggested, "If I do sleep with you I will cut off one of your curls as you lay sleeping by my side. I will kiss you for the pretty thought of getting me a little picture of you."[14] Charlotte knew that whatever physical expressions of desire the two woman might share as they lay in bed together kissing could very well challenge the bounds of acceptable "romantic friendship." But as a visitor to the Crow home Charlotte could more easily "open her arms" to Emma and spend the night with her without arousing suspicion. It is impossible to determine exactly what happened between the two during Charlotte's visit, but from the letters that followed the emotional bond between them was clearly strengthened. For almost two decades Charlotte would attempt to negotiate the tensions between her desire to experience the passionate feelings she had for Emma Crow and her need to keep those feelings within bounds that would be accepted by the society at large, so as not to threaten her professional reputation or upset their families—or Emma Stebbins.

Ironically, as in Charlotte's earlier relationships, the general acceptance of romantic friendships afforded Charlotte and Emma Crow great latitude to express their affection. From Rome Hatty Hosmer reported to Wayman Crow that she "had a letter from Miss Cushman . . . I am so pleased that you have seen so much of her. . . . She is a noble woman and as much of a mother to me as you are a Father. . . . I perceive that she and Emma are what we on this side of the ocean call 'lovers'—but I am not jealous and only admire Emma for her taste."[15] Apparently, at first Hatty thought the notion of Charlotte and Emma Crow being considered "lovers" was innocent and conventional enough to be mentioned casually to Emma's father. Hatty herself admired Charlotte and described her in romantic terms as well as maternal terms. But within a few months the intensity between Charlotte and Emma Crow must have seemed increasingly excessive and erotic, for Hatty offered to "keep a sharper lookout at Miss Cushman and not allow her to go on in this serious manner with Emma—it is really dreadful and I am really jealous."[16] What made some expressions of love between women too "serious" or "dreadful" than others? Emma Donoghue has identified a range of possible interpretations of the passions between women in an earlier period: "The same pair of women could be idealised as romantic friends by one observer and suspected of unnatural acts by another, or even in some cases idealised and suspected by the same person."[17]

Hatty was evidently responding to some concern Wayman Crow felt as he witnessed his daughter's emotions so affected by her frequent correspondence with her beloved Charlotte, who was now back in Rome and encouraging Emma Crow to visit. While Hatty assured her patron of her

Charlotte Cushman (seated) and Emma Crow (kneeling).
When they first met, Emma Crow was eighteen years old and
completely infatuated with the forty-two-year-old Cushman.
Within weeks Cushman, whom Crow called her "ladie lover,"
and Emma Crow, Cushman's "little lover," were writing passionate letters to each other. *(Charlotte Cushman Photo Album.*
Prints and Photographs Division. Library of Congress.)

support and made it clear that she too was concerned, she subtly reminded
him that she also had chosen a woman-centered life. "You may tell her if
you like, that unless she restrains her emotions she will never get a husband.
Tell her I speak from experience."[18] In the past Hatty had repeatedly
expressed both to Emma's sister Cornelia and to Wayman Crow himself
her *own* ambivalences about marriage and her belief that women artists
could not maintain a professional life if they were married. "Ambitious
spirits" like her own needed more than a home life and a husband.[19]

Heterosexual marriage was not an attractive option to independent women like Hatty Hosmer, Charlotte Cushman, and Emma Stebbins, who actively chose to pursue their artistic careers and found emotional sustenance in their all-female households. Charlotte was frequently dismissive about the prospect of marriage—to Emma Crow she first characterized it as "that awful question and more awful responsibility." But in the same letter Charlotte followed these sentiments with a surprisingly blunt acknowledgment of her relationship with Emma Stebbins: "Do you not know that I am already married and wear the badge upon the third finger of my left hand?"[20] Although Charlotte signified herself "already" married and equated a marriage between women with the commitment people generally assumed of the legal arrangement between opposite-sex partners, she maintained a distinction between her marriage and many heterosexual marriages. Charlotte, like her former partner Matilda Hays, saw the loveless marriages around them as despicable forms of prostitution or sexual slavery. Several months later Charlotte wrote to Emma Crow that she thought "marriage without love is in truth too miserable a contract for any woman with intelligence or heart to enter into. It is a sin which brings its own punishment." But Charlotte was not only warning against a loveless marriage: "I confess to feeling a secret pain at the thought of anyone coming so near to you as to admit your harboring a thought that you could love them well enough to marry for some years yet."[21]

Perhaps the younger woman was attempting to tease out her own feelings about relationships with men and using Charlotte as a sounding board. Or perhaps—knowing the commitment Charlotte had with Emma Stebbins—Emma Crow was trying to make her lover jealous. Charlotte was annoyed: "As it is, I repeat—your letter gave me unnecessary pain. Did you mean that it should dear?" And, rather than fulfill what Charlotte assumed were Emma Crow's expectations that she write back immediately and beg Crow not to marry, Charlotte warned: "If so darling, you have mistaken me. I could not write to you and have not since felt like essaying a letter to you and even now find it a difficult matter."[22] Although she experienced herself as married to Stebbins, she would not compete with anyone else for Crow's affections. For all the desire she felt for her little lover, Charlotte Cushman, newly reunited with her "wife," Emma Stebbins, began to attempt to negotiate the shifting priorities that each of these women would represent for her and to articulate the terms of their relationships.

Increasingly aware of how her relationship with Emma Crow might appear to others, a new concern crept into Charlotte's letters. Now when she asked Emma to "tell me of your love for me," she suggested, as though to encourage Emma's expression, "if you wish . . . your letters shall be destroyed."[23] Although Charlotte felt reasonably certain that Emma Crow's letters to her—her "heart records"—were safe, it started to occur to her that the depth of emotion she expressed for the younger woman might place them both at risk. What *was* Charlotte afraid of as she implored: "Darling mine, I wish you would *burn* my letters, I have asked you to do so—you do not know into whose hands an accident might make them fall. Suppose anything should chance to you suddenly and your papers were *to be looked through*"? Charlotte was concerned enough to threaten "if you do not promise me to burn them, I shall have to be careful how I write and you will not like that."[24]

Although years later Charlotte's letters, and her relationship with Emma Crow, *were* read by some friends and family members of both women as dangerously passionate—evidence of an erotic connection between them—Emma Crow fortunately did not destroy Charlotte's letters, despite her requests to do so. Instead, the hundreds of letters, most on tiny tissue paper–thin sheets with fading ink, were lovingly cherished and saved. After Emma's death they were donated to the Library of Congress. Those unpublished letters—"the[ir] contents . . . almost lost to the present and all future time"[25]—form the primary base of *this* narrative. I think Emma Crow intended that someday their story would be told. In her unpublished memoir she wrote that Charlotte's letters "were almost too intimate to publish, even in these days when nothing is too private or too sacred to be withheld from the public, but if I were to print them *as I had hoped might be done later,* I should try to choose portions of them which would show what a range of subjects she dealt with and how far-reaching were her interests."[26] Inevitably, I have made other editorial choices, deciding instead to focus on the changing tenor and quality of the relationship between the two women as Charlotte "performed" it in these letters and to speculate on the silences, the absences—those things not said or not saved in these representations of ongoing affection and desire between women. Secure that the secrecy she requested would protect them, Charlotte assured Emma, "I *do* love you very earnestly and sincerely perhaps too much" and repeatedly entreated Emma to "write me all[,] everything you will and your letters shall be destroyed as soon as I have mastered contents. . . . Write to me freely, w/out fear. My letters are quite safe from observation."[27]

In July 1858, when Charlotte Cushman left the United States, she returned to Europe and the life she had constructed with her "dear, dear friend," as she depicted Emma Stebbins. In her next letter to Emma Crow, Charlotte apologized for her delay in writing since her arrival in England: "Forgive the writer for making a lady wait!" Charlotte asked—playfully invoking the gender stereotypes her relationship with Emma Crow confounded—"but then you are not a lady—if you are my lover and hence I am by all Woman's laws justified by precedent in making you wait!"[28] In this eroticized relationship between two women, who was the "lady" and who the "lover"? For most Victorians these were constructed as mutually exclusive heterosexual categories, but in Charlotte's teasing note even these roles were fluid. At times Emma Crow was the "lady," and Charlotte's almost chivalrous affect toward her both epitomized and mocked the codes of heterosexual flirtation. But, as Charlotte noted in jest, since she herself was a woman, to most people her lover could not possibly be a "lady." And so Charlotte's capricious behavior toward the "lover" who desired her was an integral part of her own enactment as the "lady."

In the letters between the two women, they did more than express their mutual longing; they started to plan for a future time when they could be together again. Charlotte suggested that Emma Crow and her sister Mary come to Rome on an extended holiday and stay with Charlotte, Emma Stebbins, and Hatty Hosmer. Hatty was already practically a surrogate sister to Emma Crow. Surely the Crows wouldn't object to a visit, since Hatty had moved into Charlotte's Via Gregoriana home. There, Charlotte told Emma Crow, she might "pass the winter w/ Hattie and me," not even mentioning the third member of their household—Emma Stebbins.[29] But to Wayman Crow, who was now investing money for Charlotte in the United States, she suggested that he "entrust [Emma and her sister Mary] to Miss Stebbins and myself—two careful spinsters of an age to be trusted, we would take very good care of them."[30] Hatty wrote to assure Wayman Crow that Charlotte "suggest[ed] that I look after their morals and she their creature comforts."[31] For all of Charlotte's teasing, the underlying erotic energy between Charlotte and Emma Crow was curiously both reinforced and safely deflected by Charlotte's thinly veiled acknowledgments that the Crow family might not think her trustworthy to uphold their young daughters' morals. Charlotte's broaching the subject and offering these arrangements forced those around her into the awkward position of having to articulate exactly *which* aspects of women's closeness made them uncomfortable or threatened their codes of morality.

As she continued to lay the groundwork for a reunion visit, Charlotte could not help but be aware of Emma Stebbins's discomfort with the prospect of further closeness between her partner and the younger woman who adored her. Emma Stebbins may not have expressed her displeasure directly; after all, that would mean acknowledging the erotic connection between Charlotte and Emma Crow. But Emma Stebbins indicated her feelings in less direct ways. In March 1859, after not hearing from Emma Crow for an unusually long time, Charlotte conjectured, "I am very afraid that . . . you have not received all the notes which I have sent for you. I dare say Miss Stebbins has put the letters in her pocket intending to forward them and has most likely forgotten them."[32] It is impossible to know whether Charlotte was intending to excuse her partner, indict her, or excuse herself for not writing, but in any case it was becoming clear that it would not be easy to reconcile the passion she shared with Emma Crow with the emotional commitment she had made to Emma Stebbins. And Charlotte—who, as we have seen, frequently maintained relationships with more than one woman at a time—would attempt to protect the prior relationship she had forged with Stebbins even while she nurtured the connection with Crow that threatened to upset it.

Throughout the spring of 1859 Charlotte started to draw Emma Crow into connections with her family of origin as well as with her family of choice. Besides writing about Hatty's continued artistic success and adventures, Charlotte told Emma Crow about the adventures of her nephew and adopted son, Ned, then visiting in Rome. The young man Charlotte had helped to raise since infancy was the same age as her "little lover." Charlotte wrote, "Ned has run away with your picture—it seems a strange coincidence for he knows nothing of you save as he hears Hattie and I speak of you all."[33] But Charlotte, curiously, both invited and discouraged Emma Crow's and Ned's interest in each other. "Ned is such an absolute sailor *boy*, that my little love will never take a fancy to him," Charlotte avowed. "She will find that he has not sufficient weight of character or rather force of character for a life companion. . . . [B]esides she loves me and will wish to be with me and that makes all the difference. But then—if her illusion w/ regard to her 'ladie' should wear off and when she joins her abroad she should find that she's not exactly the goddess she has pictured her in her poetical imagination—what then? What is to become of me and my boy?"[34] In Rome, without the trappings of the theatrical world to heighten Charlotte's appeal, the image Emma Crow had of Charlotte might be destroyed. In fact, the passionate young Emma Crow might come to prefer Ned to the powerful older woman she claimed to love. Charlotte's overt competition with her nephew would soon be resolved in a most unusual way. But, before Charlotte could further anticipate Emma Crow's response to Charlotte *or* her nephew, both Ned and Charlotte were suddenly summoned to Liverpool, where Susan Cushman Muspratt lay dying.

It was May 1859. In the ten years that Susan Cushman and Sheridan Muspratt had been married Charlotte had only seen them sporadically. While there had always been tension between the two sisters, whose personalities and life choices were so markedly different, Charlotte felt a strong sense of familial loyalty and responsibility. Charlotte confided to Sallie Mercer after Susan's sudden death, "when the Dr. [Muspratt] told me she

Edwin Charles ("Ned") Cushman. Charlotte Cushman adopted her nephew, whom she had supported since his infancy. (*Charlotte Cushman Photo Album. Prints and Photographs Division. Library of Congress.*)

was 'sinking fast' I could not believe it, but so it proved. [S]he breathed her last without a struggle, poor dear. I am very sad dear Sallie and hardly know which way to turn or what to do, yet I am obliged to keep up everybody here. Poor dear Ned is almost crazy. Ah Sallie," Charlotte disclosed to the maid and companion who had witnessed the complex relationships in the Cushman family for more than fifteen years, "you know in spite of all things I loved my sister dearly and am very sad."[35]

The suddenness and finality of her younger sister's death unsettled Charlotte. Once back in Rome she needed something to look forward to. She repeated her invitation that Emma Crow come to visit. To Charlotte's surprise, Wayman Crow agreed, and by October Emma and Mary Crow and their chaperone, Miss Whitwell, were in Rome. Charlotte was still concerned that Emma Crow might see only "plain prosaic Miss Cushman, a housekeeper." Of all the roles Charlotte enacted in Rome, however, "prosaic housekeeper" was not among them, but undoubtedly Emma Crow would see Charlotte as the head of her Via Gregoriana household—and as partner to Emma Stebbins. "What shall I do about Miss Stebbins who already has a disposition to be tenacious about my affection for my dear little love. I shall have to leave it to you to love *me* and not scare [?] my beloved friend," Charlotte warned.[36] Nevertheless, when Emma Crow arrived, her feelings for Charlotte were not diminished in the least, and once again she eagerly sought to demonstrate the nature and the intensity of her desire. Although Emma Crow's side of the correspondence is missing, we can hear in Charlotte's responses to her Emma Crow's plaintive requests for more shared time and more unrestrained outpourings of affection from Charlotte. Charlotte, on the other hand, was still cautious. "I fear we should not only bring upon ourselves injurious remark—but such discomfort as would make us both *very* miserable," she cautioned. "*I* must be prudent for both and for those around us we must be considerate. I love you dearly!! As you would have me!" Charlotte assured her, "and yet I would rather sacrifice my own peace any day than give pain to any who are dependent upon me for happiness. . . . Therefore I am careful when we are in the presence of others and when we are alone I am careful for you and for myself."[37] Although Emma Crow was not pleased at Charlotte's "prudence," Charlotte implored her: "You should not condemn this prudence in me but rather be glad of an influence which should seem to balance our separate or united positions. Be patient darling, and all will be well."[38]

It seems that the delicately featured, conventionally feminine Emma Crow was often the initiator in this relationship. In public, and occasionally even in private, out of loyalty to Emma Stebbins, Charlotte may have attempted to resist the physical intimacy Emma Crow sought, but Charlotte characterized her prudence as a sacrifice. Yet Charlotte's responses were always complex: while denying herself and Emma Crow their expressions of affection in order to protect others, Charlotte was also particularly eager to avoid whatever "injurious remarks" women who demonstrated their erotic desire for each other might bring upon themselves. And Charlotte—the older, more visibly "mannish" lover of another woman—had ample reason to be wary. As a renowned public figure and a professional woman, Charlotte had boldly claimed such traditionally male roles as head of the household, powerful businessperson, successful and independent artist, and supporter—as well as lover—of other women. Charlotte had been subject to public and familial censure for her gender transgressions before, and so she was vigilant about attempting to control what others saw in her relationship with Emma Crow. Since Ned would be in Rome for the winter, perhaps he, as Charlotte informed Emma Crow, would "escort you to *some* of your sightseeings. I hope he may be of some use to you."[39] Perhaps Ned could deflect some of the erotic tension in the household.

As it turned out, Ned proved to be even more significant to the two women, who struggled to find a way to construct a life together. Ned had already indicated his attraction for Emma Crow. Once Ned and Emma met in Rome, Charlotte encouraged his interest in Emma and hers in him. If Ned Cushman and Emma Crow were to marry, Charlotte would have a "legitimate" reason to have her "little lover" with her as much as she liked. Even Emma Stebbins could not complain if, in addition to being the most passionate of friends, Emma Crow became Charlotte's niece. Somehow the subject was broached. Despite all that Charlotte believed about marriage—and had conveyed to Emma Crow on the subject—Emma Crow agreed to marry Ned. By the end of the winter, when Charlotte saw her off at the train station in Rome, as she set out to see more of Europe, all was settled.

The arrangement forged with Ned had not diminished Emma Crow's passion for Charlotte in the slightest. In fact, once again Charlotte counseled Emma Crow to "temper the fire of your spirit my darling, and I shall be better in mind and body for these influences are far too subtle for us in one narrow vision to understand." Believing "our effect upon each other more terrible than we can see or calculate!" Charlotte asked: "Will you suffer your love for me to subdue its nature sufficiently w/out losing its sweet vitality[?] . . . [D]elicious as this love is which I know for you and which I find in you, . . . [it] makes me fearful for myself and my darling."[40] The intense, "terrible," incalculable feelings the two women shared could be much more easily contained in relationships that conventionally called for effusive emotional expression between women. Emma Crow would be Charlotte's niece, Charlotte's daughter, and—in a vicarious way—even Charlotte's wife, for Charlotte characterized Ned and Emma's upcoming marriage as *her* "ultimate entire union" with her lover. Charlotte continued, "With tears in my throat, I anticipated my pleasure."[41]

It is not clear how Emma Crow felt about this proposed change in her status with her beloved Charlotte. Emma may have been uncomfortable when Charlotte started signing her love notes "Auntie" or "Auntie Ladie." Yet Emma seemed to genuinely care for Ned and this new arrangement might afford her more time and closeness than ever with Charlotte. In April, responding to a letter Emma Crow wrote to Ned, Charlotte—teasing her—asked: "Dear do you know you write much nicer letters to Ned than you used to write to me, but perhaps *that* was because you were not *engaged* to me. Are you engaged to me *now?*"[42] In a manner of speaking she was. Both women recognized what Ned may not have. As much as Emma would grow to care deeply for Ned in his own right, initially he was, in part, a means to facilitate her life with Charlotte. Ned was certainly her fiancé, but the center of Emma Crow's life was, and would continue to be, Charlotte Cushman.

With the context of their new relationship to shield them from injurious remarks, Charlotte's letters were more fervent than ever. "I must send you one line to tell you that . . . I long for you—want you—as perhaps you do not dream—that no human being exercises so peculiar a power as you do over me and that I am not *whole* without you."[43] And Charlotte proposed to express her longing in person. She suggested that Emma Crow meet her in Paris before Charlotte went back to the United States to perform again. "I must be in the same hotel with you somewhere before I go to America," Charlotte entreated.[44]

As much as she cautioned Emma Crow to guard against too visible a display of their attachment to each other, believing that "it is necessary that we should keep all expression of it to ourselves—and not demonstrate too clearly our great devotion to each other: we only excite observation and envy and jealousy and this is best avoided,"[45] still the physical aspect of their love was vital to Charlotte as well, as long as they were discreet. Toward the end of May 1860 Charlotte met Emma Crow in Paris. In a brief note she arranged the logistics: "Not that I do not want *you* the moment we arrive— but . . . [l]et Ned get his sight of you first—Then you can go to your room and watch for me."[46]

Whatever intimacies the two women shared in their hotel in Paris, apparently their time together was more intense than ever. Two months later, as she summoned up the bodily memories of this passionate time, Charlotte mused, "I wonder whether I ought to school myself to live without such love? But ah how hard it would be now that I have tasted the sweets of such communion as is given to few to know. Ah, my darling, do you remember our last night in Paris—ah what delirium is in the memory. Every nerve in me thrills as I look back and feel you in my arms held to my heart so closely so entirely mine in every sense as I was yours."[47]

Charlotte's description of her bodily response to Emma Crow in her arms—to the sweet communion she "tasted"—was cast in unusually sensual language, even given the tendency for sentimental letters between women. Charlotte believed few others "knew" of the pleasure and passionate "delirium" possible in the "communion" between two female lovers, and she was particularly concerned that others might read this desire in her relationship with Emma Crow. Charlotte kept scrupulous records of the letters she wrote and received, and, when she missed one of Emma Crow's letters, she implored her to write to the post office for it, claiming: "I don't like such dear letters addressed to me to be sent to the dead letter office, if an unscrupulous person should find it, my reputation might be lost forever."[48] Whatever degree of physical affection she shared with Emma Stebbins, Charlotte realized that her partner would be devastated "if she thought or dreamed *how* I love you [Emma Crow] it would go near to kill her."[49]

Emma Stebbins's jealousy was a continual source of concern to Charlotte. "I am tied down by circumstances, constrained in my action[,] denied my . . . frank expression of love for you for fear of wounding and hurting others—even Ned," Charlotte wrote regretfully, mentioning almost as an afterthought the fiancé and nephew she cared for and the man with whom Emma Crow would spend the rest of her life. "Will the time ever come when I may show all my earnest love for you as it exists and have no restraint upon me? Alas I fear!"[50] Although Charlotte attempted to mollify Emma Crow, she never diminished the significant part Emma Stebbins would continue to play in her life. Referring to Stebbins as "Aunt Emma," Charlotte acknowledged that, despite Emma Stebbins's "little pang of jealousy as she saw me holding your hand . . . I very soon settled Aunt Emma—who is as sweet as a summer's morning—she knows how dearly I love her and allows me to smooth her ruffled [feathers.]"[51]

Ironically, most of what we can deduce about Emma Stebbins and Charlotte's relationship is recorded in Charlotte's letters to Emma Crow. In them Charlotte constructed a rich, multilayered world of female relationships. Sometimes deploying the tone of a quasiparental figure, she advised Emma Crow about domestic concerns and wrote of her own relationship with "Aunt Em." At other times Charlotte presented herself as an eager lover desperate to be reunited with her beloved. Since correspondence from only one side of this tumultuous homoerotic triangle remains, it is impossible to determine exactly how Cushman presented the relationship to Stebbins. What is clear is that, even while Charlotte attempted to cajole, tease, or woo Emma Crow, she made it evident that, though realizing the pact to have her younger lover with her permanently, Emma Crow would have to accept Charlotte on *her* terms— with Emma Stebbins as her partner.

As she frequently did in her role as head of her various households, Charlotte saw to most of the material details. At first Wayman Crow objected to the marriage between his daughter and Charlotte's adopted son, citing Ned's inexperience in business and his consequent inability to support himself and a wife. Charlotte worked hard to remove this concern as an obstacle to Wayman Crow's approval. Warning Emma Crow that Ned "has not the most remote idea of routine and business" and fearing that "he would find that any business which forced him to deny himself anything was a bore," she developed a plan of action. If Abraham Lincoln won the upcoming election, her friend Senator William Seward would be secretary of state. Seward would then be in a position to appoint Ned

United States consul in Rome. If Ned accepted this largely honorary position, Charlotte confided to Emma Crow, "we could be *together* as much as
I thought would be happiest for us."[52] But that possibility was still a few
years away.

For the present Charlotte wrote to James T. Fields, her publisher friend
in Boston. While Fields was helping her secure sculpture commissions for
Emma Stebbins, perhaps he could make arrangements for Ned as well.
Charlotte thanked Fields for his "kind interest in and efforts for her boy"
and asked for his help finding Ned a "good genteel place" to board and
work, requesting that he provide Ned with books and money on her
account.[53] Just as she had supported Susan and Ned before Susan's second
marriage, supplemented her brother Charlie's employment in London, and
provided for her mother, Charlotte now took an active hand in making
arrangements and decisions for Ned and Emma Crow. To Emma Crow she
confided: "I have told your father my wishes w/regard to Ned in business. I
have let him see what my property is, and how it will be disposed when I am
under the sod, for I have taken his advice w/regard to the making of my
Will and so he knows what Ned's expectations may be!"[54] Charlotte's little
lover would be well cared for.

Occasionally, Charlotte had second thoughts about the upcoming
marriage, at one point asking Emma whether she "would be allowed to
come and live with me" if Emma did not marry Ned.[55] Whether out of her
own discomfort at the prospect of "sharing" her young lover with her
nephew or concern that Emma was taking this step primarily to be with
her, Charlotte confessed, "darling, I am so troubled about you and Ned. I
do not in my soul think him equal to you in any respect."[56] But her misgivings were sporadic. In most of her letters Charlotte continued to make
arrangements for "that dear moment when I can in truth call you my
own."[57] As they ultimately agreed, in a graphic admission of their intentions, since Charlotte could not, as she said, "have you to myself, other
obligations were strong upon me before I knew and loved you . . . you must
belong to me in the nearest way that could be devised—I could not let you
go out of my life[,] out of my own world to belong to anyone else."[58]

Now Charlotte set out to explain to her brother and mother how
Emma Crow would fit into the Cushman family. To her brother she
described Ned as a "lucky fellow" and wrote that Emma Crow "sends her
'love to Uncle Charley,'" noting that Ned "could not have made a choice
more to my liking in every way."[59] With irony that may have been lost on
her brother, Charlotte exclaimed that Emma Crow "is a darling and I love
her as much as if she were *my own*."[60] Soon Emma Crow's relationship to
Charlotte would be solidified. By marrying Emma Crow to her nephew and
adopted son, Cushman could subsume her passion for and maintain the

lifelong connection she desired with Emma Crow within a constellation of relationships that included "dearest niece" and "darling daughter" as well as "little lover." To other members of Charlotte's family Emma Stebbins was now more conventionally recast as "Aunt Emma—as Ned and Emma call her to distinguish her."[61] Families—of any kind—could be shaped, nurtured, constituted by language. By attempting to frame the terms in which family members experienced one another, Charlotte took an active hand in creating familial sentiment through the networks of confidence and gossip that formed her letters. "I try to put everyone on good feeling towards each other," she conceded.[62]

Having returned to the United States as Ned and Emma Crow were planning their future wedding, Charlotte decided once again to perform. In early October 1860 Charlotte happily reported to Emma Crow that "everybody says your darling 'ladie' is acting very well, better than ever."[63] Busy with rehearsals during the day and performances in the evening, Charlotte was determined to add to her savings and make up for money she had lost due to the mismanagement of her investments left in Philadelphia. Now, with Wayman Crow supervising her finances, she felt "for the 1st time . . . to be in the hands of an honest friend . . . I am working hard to put as much money into his hands to invest for me as I possibly can so that I may have enough to live comfortably and happily in a style which my many years of hard work entitle me to."[64] As she described it, a prosperous retirement was still her goal.

For eight weeks New York audiences flocked to see Charlotte Cushman perform. Despite the fact that at forty-four years old she had become, in Mary Eliza Cushman's words, "as fat as a great porpoise,"[65] she played Romeo again and Cardinal Wolsey. All in all Charlotte's two-month engagement in New York was "of much good" to her "socially, morally and physically"—and financially, for she "earned $8,600 in eight weeks!" Charlotte reported jubilantly to Emma Crow, "You see your darling is worth something to the public yet—old as she is."[66]

During her New York engagement Charlotte and Sallie Mercer had stayed with Emma Stebbins and her family. As always, Sallie took care of Charlotte's clothes and "theatrical matters," serving as dresser and occasionally even as prompter for Charlotte. "Sallie always has the direction of my houses and I know nothing but to go into them," Charlotte explained to Emma Crow. But in the Stebbins household, where Sallie had neither the responsibility nor the authority to supervise other servants and direct the house, there was "a sort of uncomfortable atmosphere."[67]

Charlotte relished being back at work, and the professional activity seemed to energize her. In Rome Emma Stebbins's work and the art of other women had taken prominence; now, on tour, Charlotte encountered again the pleasures and the frustrations of being engaged in her own work. Just before Christmas, Charlotte had gone to Philadelphia with Sallie to perform, having left Emma Stebbins with her family in New York. Charlotte had arrived the previous day at one o'clock, "tired, weary—footsore, heart tired," rehearsed, and then performed to "a very fine house" on Christmas Eve 1860. In a rare admission of her feelings for Emma Stebbins, Charlotte confided to Annie Fields, "I feel so lonely without my other and much better half—Sallie is out to dinner and so I am alone for the rest of the day . . . but on this day of all others one wants *somebody*, do they not?"[68] Hard at work, Charlotte related that she "had to re-study Portia and Katharine" the previous week and Nancy Sykes—a part she had "steadfastly objected to doing" but obliged because it was so popular with American audiences.[69] Charlotte was also playing Hamlet, a "most awfully exhausting part" but, as she described to Emma Crow, "such a magnificent character and I can assure you that though I was very nervous lest all the words should not be right, I acted the part as much better than anything else I have done here, that I am amazed at myself."[70] Despite all the strenuous effort, Charlotte was enjoying herself and reveling in her success. Although her life of *dolce far niento*—sweet idleness—in Rome was delightful, performing and playing the role of the starring artist lauded by enthusiastic fans was even sweeter.

Emma Crow and Ned Cushman's wedding would have to be worked around Charlotte's performance schedule, for, as she wrote, "If my darling wants to be with me during my last engagement in Boston—she must be married the early part of the 1st week in April and come straight to Boston w/ me and her honeymoon shall be spent with me."[71] But, just as Emma Crow planned her marriage to Ned to suit Charlotte's career, Charlotte arranged *her* professional engagements to suit Emma Stebbins. "Your Aunt Emma has work to do," Charlotte noted, explaining why she had to return to Europe in June: "She has given up a year to me and I must not make any further demands upon her time or patience."[72]

Ned Cushman and Emma Crow were married in St. Louis on 3 April 1861.[73] Charlotte was present for the wedding and then hurried back to finish the last few months of her tour. When Charlotte was in Boston with Ned and Emma a few weeks later, she helped them set up their home and introduced them to her Boston friends, then she resumed her tour through New England. In one of her first letters to Emma Crow Cushman, Charlotte referred to the younger woman who adored her as her "daughter"—and Emma was not pleased. She had not taken this step to resign her role as Charlotte's "little lover," and the feelings she cherished for Charlotte were far from those she identified between mothers and daughters. Charlotte tried to explain:

"Lovers I may have *little* and big, but nobody else in the world can be my daughter but my 'little lover.'" As Charlotte saw it, the loverlike feelings she had for Emma were not eclipsed by their new relationship, merely supplemented. But, she noted, "If being my daughter enforces you to give me a letter which is a sort of bill of fare," rather than the emotional expressions Emma usually sent, Charlotte would rather that Emma "consider herself what she will, so that she writes to me frankly, tenderly, lovingly as usual."[74]

The complicated role of daughter *and* lover that Charlotte cast Emma Crow Cushman in allowed her to offer Charlotte what no other female partner could—a link to the future, to immortality, by bearing children who would carry on "her" name. Now Charlotte had another reason to encourage Emma to edit her letters, warning her that, "if read by other eyes," their letters "might assume gigantic importance appalling to you[,] to me, to Ned[,] to your Father and Mother and everybody."[75] On paper the "appalling" interpretations Charlotte feared—the lesbian nature of their relationship—could be read by others. The desire conveyed in their letters could assume "gigantic," and dangerous, "importance." Soon, however, another thought occurred to her, and she suggested Emma save them for posterity. But if Emma were to do so, Charlotte would have to represent herself differently:

> Sometimes I think that in my correspondence w/ my dear new daughter I will avoid all love words or epithets save those which might meet *any* eye, only putting a blank__ there which she can fill up w/ anything in the world she pleases—and then keep her Auntie's letters [from which] one of these days [she would] make a journal of her aunty from the time she initially belonged to that aunty and show them to her daughters as a record of affection which they might be made to care for.[76]

Typically, however, Charlotte expressed her ambivalence about sacrificing her expressions of passion: "Will you forgo the love words for the sake of making your children love me and know me when I am passed away[?]" The letters that Charlotte wrote regularly to Emma Crow Cushman, letters that she had been writing almost religiously for three years—and would continue to write for the rest of her life—were the most complete account of her day-to-day life, her "outgoings and incomings," as she called them, that she ever kept. In addition to expressing her sentiments for Emma Crow Cushman, Charlotte had used these letters to explore her feelings on a range of subjects, from her performance career to the political issues of the day to her retirement in Rome with Emma Stebbins. This opportunity for reflection was valuable to Charlotte and cherished by Emma Crow Cushman, but, as Charlotte astutely recognized, it might have value for others as well.

Thinking back to the time she first arrived in England, when she corresponded regularly with whichever woman was her partner at the time, Charlotte recounted, "My 1st six months letters were destroyed, written to Miss Sully. . . . My next were written to my friend Eliza Cook—the poetess—and they have been destroyed."[77] It is not clear how Charlotte *knew* that her letters to Rosalie Sully and Eliza Cook were destroyed. Perhaps she had asked her partners to do so, or at the end of these relationships she may have requested her letters back and destroyed them herself. "Since then I have scarcely been separated from my friend and companion whomever that might be at the time, so my letters have not been worth much," only dealing with "immediate incidents," Charlotte explained, referring to her letters to Matilda Hays and Emma Stebbins.[78] So it seems that, in her letters to Emma Crow, Charlotte was actively constructing the self or image of herself by which she wanted to be remembered; the letters between them would ultimately constitute the fullest account remaining of Charlotte's self-portrayal of her emotional life. Whatever agreement Charlotte and Emma Crow reached, Emma seemed to recognize that the earlier passionate letters and those after her marriage, which included a mix of romantic love, familial concern, and parental advice, were worth making available to posterity.

Charlotte and Emma Crow Cushman would be separated, and soon, much to the younger woman's dissatisfaction, as Charlotte prepared to return to Rome and her comfortable life with Emma Stebbins. "I love you better than anything in the world, and my heart is broken at the idea of leaving you," Charlotte assured her shortly before she returned to Europe in July, "but it is better for you, better for Ned, better in every way that you should be left to yourselves for a season."[79] It certainly was better for *Charlotte,* who may have found it uncomfortable to "recognize that it has been for me and solely for me" that Emma had "assumed those cares" of her marriage to Ned and that Charlotte had allowed "such a sacrifice" on her account.[80] Emma would have to learn to make a life with Ned and build a relationship with him that would bring her satisfaction. Charlotte imagined herself in Ned's place and commiserated with her new niece: "Oh dear, if I were only a man, that I could teach him how to care for a woman."[81] There was no question in her mind that Charlotte knew better how to "care for" another woman than did Ned. But Charlotte had another woman to care for as well. In a particularly candid recognition of her feelings for Emma Stebbins, Charlotte admitted to Emma Crow Cushman, "Darling if I could have been with you this winter it would not have been well for *me,* for *you,* for *Ned*[,] for Aunt *Emma,* for heaven, nor for earth! I love you . . . dearly . . . too dearly for the peace perhaps of any of us! . . . but . . . I will not have anything *in the future* to reproach myself for, however much I *may* have in the past!"[82] Charlotte was returning to Rome.

Although Charlotte's family had grudgingly accepted her lifestyle with a woman partner and, lately, the household of female friends she had established in Rome, there were always tensions between Charlotte's allegiance to the family she created with friends and lovers and her obligations to her family of origin. Members of the Cushman family had resented the material support Charlotte gave her partners, and many of their letters imply discomfort with her living so publicly in a female household. "It has made my blood boil with indignation how my mother (and Ned) have felt and spoken with regard to Miss Stebbins," Charlotte fumed. With pride and pique Charlotte asserted that since she had "earned everything for herself and not chosen to marry and give everything away from her family . . . she had a perfect right to do what she pleased."[83] Now, interestingly, through her marriage to Ned Cushman, Emma Crow would be considered part of Charlotte's socially recognized family unit. While Emma Crow Cushman had reasons of her own to resent Charlotte's attentions to Emma Stebbins, ironically her resentment fell in line with that expressed by Charlotte's mother, brother, and nephew. At the same time, then, Emma Stebbins's jealousy of Emma Crow as Charlotte's object of desire was now somewhat silenced because it would have pitted her against Charlotte's "family." The two Emmas—the two women in Charlotte's life—were each jealous of the prominence that the other enjoyed with Charlotte.

Comparing herself to Ned, and Emma Stebbins to Emma Crow Cushman, Charlotte maintained, "I love my friends as he loves his—I would do as much for those to whom I give my most intimate friendship as he would do for you. It is necessary for me to have a home. Better for him that a woman and a friend should share that home than that a husband should come in to take all away from my family."[84] Therefore, Charlotte implied, her "children" had no legitimate grounds for complaint. But Emma Crow Cushman was *not* merely one of Charlotte's children; in fact, with Emma's marriage to Ned, "my darling is now my own—she belongs to me as fully as two beings born, educated, living and thinking apart for days and months and years—can become one."[85] But that may not have been enough for Emma Crow. As Charlotte resumed her Roman life of leisure, providing emotional as well as material support to Emma Stebbins, Hatty Hosmer, and the other women of their Roman circle, she was repeatedly compelled to reassure Emma Crow Cushman, "I love you as intensely as I have ever done. I know no love which admits of such passionate *expression.* I *have* never known it."[86] In the family they had constructed Emma Crow Cushman's primary bond was with Charlotte; her marriage to Ned offered (heterosexual) intimacies that, curiously, strengthened the women's close-ness. For Emma was about to bring something else into Charlotte's life: she was pregnant.

Soon Charlotte's letters were infused with maternal advice along with notes of passion. Some of her suggestions were unconventional: she believed Emma should raise a child of either sex as Hatty had been raised—without physical restrictions but rather like "a strong animal with keen per-ceptions." Other sentiments echoed more traditional thinking, such as Charlotte's assertion that "no artist work is so high, so noble[,] so grand[,] so enduring[,] so important for all time as the making of a perfect charac-ter in a child."[87] This was a curious sentiment to express at the very same time Charlotte was actively securing commissions for her *artist*-partner in Rome. Perhaps Charlotte wanted to reassure Emma Crow Cushman of her primacy in Charlotte's life by implying that works created by artists like Emma Stebbins were not as important as the family Emma Crow Cushman was creating for Charlotte. But, as with all private correspondence, it is impossible to know whether Charlotte actually believed what she professed in her letters, or merely chose to present this side of herself to her corre-spondent.

What she did convey in her letters, however, is the impression that she and her "little lover" were having this baby together—as an expression of *their* love for each other. Although Ned was an integral part of the family unit, Charlotte and Emma Crow were shaping a female-centered family. When Emma indicated her preference for a girl child, Charlotte cautioned her, lest she be disappointed and "not love the little man child . . . Remem-ber *my name* can only live through a male child." Later Emma could have "a little Carlotta."[88] By adopting Ned, Charlotte had set up a matrilineal family. It was *her* name, her legacy, that Emma Crow Cushman would carry on through her own children. Curiously, Charlotte never mentioned the possibility of *female* children who might do as she had—remain unmar-ried, keep their own name, and adopt children of their own.

Yet there was no question for either woman that the ideal object of desire in their fantasies of domestic bliss was another woman. "You are right darling, in what you say about a strong woman's coming nearer one's ideal for a lover than any man comes," Charlotte agreed, conceding that such women were rare "and yet do you know, I have met very few women in the world whom I could have accepted for a lover or a husband any more than I could have accepted any man."[89] But she had met *some.* "There have been 2 or 3 and that is a great thing to be able to say. . . . You must reflect how exceptional the nature must be which can admit that," Charlotte granted.[90] Emma Crow Cushman and Charlotte Cushman were such women to each other. But Emma's overtly erotic expressions continued to be both enticing and threatening to Charlotte, who was concerned that "so few people understand our feeling." Guarding against the disapproval of others, she discouraged Emma's plan to come to Europe to be with her as soon as the baby was born. And Charlotte would not leave Emma Stebbins to join her in the United States, since, she explained, "I cannot be the means of giving pain to those who are more dependent on my presence than even you are."[91]

In Rome Emma Stebbins was hard at work on her commemorative statute of Horace Mann, Charlotte's new friend Peggy Foley was "plugging away cutting cameos," Hatty Hosmer was busy working on a commissioned monument of Missouri senator Thomas Hart Benton, so, as Charlotte explained, "it would not be fulfilling dutifully my responsibilities if I should rush off *to you*."[92] Only truly dire circumstances would make it possible for "Aunt Emma to let me go and not die every day while I was gone."[93] Charlotte repeatedly invoked Emma Stebbins's emotional dependency as an explanation for her own actions, and, by casting Stebbins's need for her in life or death terms, Charlotte reinforced her own powerful role as caregiver and supporter to her partner.

Even so, over the course of the next several weeks Charlotte and Emma Crow Cushman tried to devise some contingency that would help them arrange to be together by the summer. But their problem was unexpectedly and sadly resolved when Emma had a miscarriage in the spring of 1862. To help her get over her loss Wayman Crow sent his daughter to England— and to Charlotte. Charlotte would have to wait longer than she had hoped for the "little pilgrim" who would be born into the Cushman family, but in the meantime she and Emma Crow Cushman would be together.

In July, when Charlotte told James and Annie Fields, who had been particularly helpful to Ned and Emma in Boston, how happy she was to see her "'child' again after her sad disappointment," Charlotte presented her concern as maternal. To her friends Emma Crow Cushman was her child, while Emma Stebbins was "*our* Emma," her partner and her "better half." When Emma Crow Cushman returned to the United States, she and Ned had planned to leave Boston and move to St. Louis. Charlotte confided to the Fields that she was "conflicted . . . [at] the thought of the 'children' leaving Boston for a St. Louis home."[94] But the United States was now in the throes of the Civil War, and, although Charlotte's sympathies were staunchly with the Union and with the Republican administration her friend William Seward so ably served as secretary of state, she understood Emma's desire to be near her family.

After Ned and Emma's wedding, a year earlier, Charlotte had stopped in Washington, where she had visited and "been treated with great courtesy and marked respect by Mr. Lincoln and [her] dear old friend Mr. Seward."[95] As the news of the Civil War reached her, filling her with "terror and dismay," Charlotte felt from early reports that "the South comes rightfully by her success . . . for the devil always helps his own, at first."[96] In letters to Wayman Crow as well as to Emma, Charlotte expressed her concern and her political sympathies and her worries about the soundness of her investments in the United States. "From my girlhood up, the battle of life, the political battles of the world have filled me with the intensest interest," Charlotte explained, predicting that, when the war ended "cotton shall continue to be raised by blacks, but by *free* blacks, dominated by a wise and beneficent government which will see them well paid for their labour. . . . Believe me dear," Charlotte asserted, "the hour has come."[97] With the war at home worsening, Charlotte bemoaned her "ignoble ease" in Rome. Believing that her "own earnest convictions . . . might be able to move others who are lethargic or selfish at home," Charlotte decided to return to America.[98] Leaving Emma Stebbins in Italy, Charlotte and Sallie sailed in June 1863 for the United States, where Charlotte acted in a series of benefits for the American Sanitary Commission.

Emma Stebbins was not happy about Charlotte's decision. "The thought of being separated from me gives her great sorrow and makes her thin and haggard and nervous so that I am anxious about her," Charlotte admitted.[99] Yet the trip would afford Charlotte and Emma Crow Cushman much intimate time together. Charlotte suggested staying "at the Hotel where I brought you when you were first married and were so dreadfully distressed at my leaving you and where we would rendezvous promising to love each other forever and forever and best most best!"[100] Almost an incantation, the pet words of affection—loving each other "best most best"—summoned, like a talisman, the connection between them, and implied that Charlotte loved Emma Crow Cushman more than anyone else. It had been "far better," Charlotte reasoned, that she had stayed away from Emma and Ned when they were first married. After all, Emma Crow's "respect and admiration" for her "would not have failed to show itself: and there would have been much consequent misery and jealousy. . . . Now all is as it should be," Charlotte determined in a letter to Emma before she arrived. "You love him [Ned] more—he loves you more confidently and I love you just as fondly."[101]

Charlotte had planned a brief stay and few performances. She had only brought costumes for Meg and Lady Macbeth. After visits with various friends in New England and with William Seward in Washington, she was to perform one night each in five major cities as benefits for the Sanitary Commission. And she planned to enjoy herself, for much of the time Emma Crow Cushman would be at her side. When in late June 1863 Charlotte and Emma were in Washington with William Seward, the human dimensions of the war were brought home to her. As Emma Crow Cushman remembered, Sallie, who usually accompanied her "mistress" every-where, had stayed behind in Philadelphia to visit her own family while Charlotte and Emma were with Seward. "One day Mr. Seward came in from the State Department and smilingly handed us the following tele-gram." From Philadelphia Sallie Mercer, a free woman of color, had the temerity to telegram Seward, her employer's friend: "The rebels are expected here. What shall Sallie do?" As Emma recalled, "great as was the tension of that time, it amused Mr. Seward. . . . Even the President [Lin-coln] found momentary relief in his sense of humour and I recall his expression when his face lighted up with a humorous smile and then relapsed into the saddest I have ever seen."[102] For years Charlotte's trusted servant and companion had functioned as her courier and confidently saw to travel arrangements throughout Europe and the United States. Seward and Lincoln were grimly amused and then sorrowful as they contemplated the impact of the war on this woman they knew as Charlotte's "right hand."

Charlotte was doing her part for the war effort with her Sanitary Fund performances, but she expected to reinforce her popularity as well, so she was resolute about which roles she would play. Edwin Booth, who was managing some of the tour, tried to talk Charlotte out of performing Lady Macbeth: "To cast *Macbeth* we must send to N.Y. for people and their expenses and salaries will of course have to be deducted from the receipts, *all* of which should be given to the soldiers."[103] Charlotte remained firm about choice of roles, although she offered to help publicize the perfor-mances. When Charlotte wrote to accept Annie Fields's dinner invitation in Boston several weeks later, Charlotte suggested that James Fields "give a little help to the Benefit for the Sanitary Commission . . . by calling the attention of people generally through his paper . . . to the fact that I have returned to the stage . . . in aid of this charity and that they will not see me again professionally."[104] In Philadelphia, New York, Boston, Washington, and Baltimore audiences clamored to see Charlotte Cushman as much as to support the cause.

Charlotte was pleased to be performing again, for, as much as she enjoyed her life in Italy, she still craved the attention she garnered on the stage. The Sanitary Commission had enriched its coffers by more than eight thousand dollars for Charlotte's five nights of work. As she headed back to Rome, again to retirement, she may have felt a bittersweet tug when female fans like Sallie Bridges eulogized her career.

But now the stage again beholds
Its sov'reign abdicate her sway!
The muse must weep, the world deplore;
Her brow is weary of its bay!

Yet still within a happy home
Dear friends shall speak her worshipp'd name
And love shall give her woman-heart
More true content than shouts of fame.[105]

Perhaps. But Charlotte's "woman-heart" may have preferred occupation outside of her "happy home" as well. And by 1864 the complex arrangements she had forged with her "dear friends" and lovers were being reconfigured. In Rome Hatty was moving into her own apartment near the Via Gregoriana. Hatty's increasing social and professional prominence, coupled with Charlotte's efforts to secure commissions for Emma Stebbins over Hatty, had created inevitable uneasiness in the household. Emma Stebbins was busy "working splendidly," as Charlotte bragged to Bessie Rayner Parkes, but Charlotte described her "children"—Ned and Emma Crow Cushman—as "the joys and rewards of my life."[106]

Now, in addition to supporting the efforts of the women artists in her Roman community, Charlotte turned her energy toward arranging a way for Emma and Ned to come and live with her. The household that she was heading could be home for them as well, particularly if Seward came through and appointed Ned as the American consul in Rome. In the meantime Emma Crow was pregnant again. Together she and Charlotte decided that she should have her baby in England, where Charlotte, Emma Stebbins, and Sallie Mercer regularly passed the summer months to escape the heat. After spending some time in Harrogate, Charlotte rented a house for all of them near Manchester, until "the event" was over. Pregnant women in Cushman's era frequently referred to and experienced their pregnancies as a "confinement." But, rather than being restricted to her home and husband or even her continent, Emma Crow Cushman crossed the Atlantic Ocean so that she could be with the woman she loved—her beloved Charlotte—when she gave birth. The cool English summer in which Emma could derive "much benefit from the fine pure clear air" was the explanation Charlotte offered those who asked,[107] for there was some concern that Emma might miscarry again; but Charlotte, as well as Emma Crow Cushman, wanted the baby to "be near me [Charlotte] in his early days and learn to love" her.[108] Emma and Ned's first son, Wayman Crow Cushman, was born in October. Along with Ned, Charlotte—who now referred to herself as "Big Mamma"—was with Emma Crow at the baby's birth, as she would be for his three brothers. Charlotte wrote Emma's sister Cornelia, as soon as the baby was born, "I was called into the room and baby deposited in my arms. . . . I was too thankful . . . that she [Emma] was through her hour of labour and had ceased moaning to care to know whether baby was boy or girl."[109]

Years later, when Emma Stebbins described the extended family that Charlotte nurtured, she attributed her partner's attachment to "her nephew's children" to Charlotte's "passionate love for children" in general and the "maternal and protecting element" in Charlotte's personality. No doubt this accounts in part for her interest—and certainly echoes how Charlotte in her role as Big Mamma portrayed her concern. But in her published memoir Stebbins eradicated all mention of Charlotte's passionate love for the children's *mother,* noting only that Charlotte "would travel any distance to be present at their birth, even on one occasion crossing the ocean for that purpose. It was her great joy to be the first to receive them in her arms, and she had a feeling this ceremony made them more her own."[110] To Emma Crow Cushman, Charlotte wrote as though the children *were* her own: "The one wish of my life has been for some child to love me dearly and tenderly." Now that "God has blessed me with such a darling," Charlotte explained, "I love you for yourself—then as baby's Mamma, then for baby and then for myself"—but Charlotte crossed out *myself*—and added, as an afterthought, "Ned dear."[111]

With the birth of Wayman, followed by Allerton, Edwin, and Victor in the next eight years,[112] Charlotte's relationship to Emma Crow Cushman grew more complex, and the roles they played in each others' lives grew incrementally more complicated, conflating the erotic and the familial, and finding in each the possibility of the other. "Dearest and Sweetest daughter[,] niece, friend and lover," Charlotte wrote early in 1865, "only think how many things combined in any one of these words—for surely *any* one in *our* case comprehends the whole! . . . I could never have hoped to combine in one person so many happy relations as come to me through you my darling—who never fails me."[113] The multiple roles that Emma Crow Cushman played in Charlotte's life had their corollary in the parts Charlotte embodied for and with her. With Emma, Charlotte was aunt, mother, adored older woman friend and lover, as well as "Big Mamma" to the growing family they nurtured together. All that was left was for them to live together as well.

Since Emma Stebbins was determined to remain in Rome and work at her sculpture, Charlotte would stay with her also; Ned and Emma Cushman would have to move to Italy. Now that Hatty had moved into her own "cosy snug little place,"[114] the fourth floor of 38 Via Gregoriana would make a lovely home for Ned, Emma, and their baby. Charlotte had prevailed with William Seward. When Lincoln was reelected and Charlotte's adversary, United States consul William J. Stillman, resigned his post in Rome and was reassigned to Crete, Ned Cushman was appointed to take his place.[115]

As Ned and Emma Cushman's arrival grew nearer, Emma Stebbins was anxious about the anticipated changes once they moved into the home she

Emma Crow Cushman, after her marriage to Ned Cushman.
(*Charlotte Cushman Photo Album. Prints and Photographs
Division. Library of Congress.*)

shared with Charlotte. Before they all set up a household together Charlotte
had to clarify, once again, the terms of the "association" with her romantic
friend, "which has been productive of so much happiness to me."[116] To
Emma Crow Cushman, who was now included in the category of official
family—an option that was forever foreclosed to Charlotte's partner—
Charlotte declared that Emma Stebbins was "*a part of me* as much as a life
of eight years of the most intimate association can make her." Charlotte
implored her "dear children" to "love Aunt Em for all her sweetness and
goodness and love to me." The thought that "my children are coming into

my life—not liking her, determined to thrust her out" would be disastrous. In an acknowledgment of the complicated degrees of affection and commitment between women who choose to make a life together, Charlotte admitted that "I have allowed myself to be untrue to much which I promised her. . . . [W]hen first I knew her I took the obligation of her life and future upon me and did not know of . . . other loves and affections which were in store for me. . . . I have tried to reconcile too many things . . . and not preserved my life intact for her when I took the responsibility of her life upon myself."[117] To Emma Crow Cushman, Charlotte revealed that Emma Stebbins "has always been a little afraid of you—I have not been considerate or thoughtful enough of and for her . . . now . . . I feel how wrong I have been."[118]

As a further demonstration of her loyalty, in the spring of 1865 Charlotte planned to travel to the United States with Emma Stebbins just as Ned and Emma Cushman were expected to arrive in Rome. Stebbins's statue of Horace Mann was due to be unveiled in Boston. "At the time I worked to get the order for Aunt Em—I promised to give something towards it— Nothing could do so much towards this as my going home to act for it," Charlotte explained.[119] Once they returned Charlotte would be hardpressed to reconcile the simultaneous and competing presence of the two women in her life.

For the next few years they all tried to make the arrangement work, but it was always tense. "Be patient with me," Charlotte implored Emma Crow Cushman, "I am steering a bark through troubled waters but shall come out all right bringing with me what I have so dearly prized for 8½ years that I cannot give it up without a struggle and consequent suffering. You know your Auntie's is an adhesive nature, that what she once loves she never wholly gives up."[120] *Adhesive* was a contemporary phrenological term which Walt Whitman, among others, used to indicate the emotional intensity and the spiritual connection they experienced in their attraction to their samesex intimate partners. But, whereas Charlotte Cushman acknowledged this aspect of her "nature" uncritically, Whitman wrote in his diary of his struggle to "depress" his "adhesive nature," feeling that it was "in excess—making life a torment / All this feverish, disproportionate adhesiveness."[121] Charlotte had "adhered to" Emma Stebbins as well as to Emma Crow Cushman. Now Charlotte expected Emma Crow Cushman to sanction her attempt to reinforce Charlotte's alliance with Emma Stebbins, her recognized partner, even at the sacrifice of some of their own intimacy. "I have in the past year narrowed much my business relations and now I shall narrow my social ones and it will be better for all in the future," Charlotte announced.[122]

But Charlotte's social relations grew more demanding and exciting than ever. With Ned and Emma Cushman living with her in Rome, Charlotte, always needing to be in control, expected to have a hand in Ned's conduct as consul. After all, everyone recognized that it was on her behalf that Seward had appointed Ned to the post. As long as Seward was in office, Charlotte was to take on an increasingly influential role with the expatriate community. And her extended family duties were growing also. In June 1867 Emma gave birth to Allerton Seward Cushman, named in part for his statesman godfather. Charlotte was thrilled to be at the center of it all.

Occasionally, the conflicts in the Roman household were overt, as Charlotte's friend Elizabeth Peabody noticed when she visited Via Gregoriana during the winter of 1867. The frustrations of living with Emma and Ned had taken a toll on Charlotte and Emma Stebbins's relationship. Charlotte, Emma Stebbins, and, as always, Sallie Mercer, planned another trip back to the United States. Perhaps Charlotte hoped that time away with Emma Stebbins would rekindle the closeness between them, but the tensions were palpable. While Sallie Mercer was off on a vacation, Charlotte wrote to Emma Crow Cushman from Emma Stebbins's sister's estate in Hyde Park, New York. "I miss Sallie more than I can tell you—but I have given her a fortnight's holiday. . . . She is the only human being after you who thoroughly loves me." Charlotte was not feeling well and complained that "I cannot get on in this loveless way when I am ailing."[123] Other women friends also knew of the "lovelessness" Charlotte now felt herself to suffer with Emma Stebbins, but she presented their intimacy differently to them than she did to Emma Crow Cushman. To Elizabeth Peabody, Charlotte confided: "Emma Stebbins and I are getting on very much better . . . but no one *outside* can judge. If Miss S had never been any more demonstrative— I should have been a fool to look for it—or disappointed not to find it. I have not grieved over the *lack*—but the *loss!* Not over the absence of expression—but the change from *great*—to none! However, it cannot be helped . . . I shall tell you more when we meet."[124]

What did it mean for Emma Stebbins to be "demonstrative"? And what exactly had changed between them? From this juncture in time and through the few remaining letters that survive about Emma Stebbins, it is impossible to know what "great expressions" of affection the two women shared and whether or how the women expressed their affection physically. Unlike the unmistakable passion in Charlotte's responses to Emma Crow Cushman and her abiding fear that their intimacy might be read as exceeding the bounds others deemed acceptable, Charlotte's letters about Emma Stebbins repeatedly speak of her "true" and "noble" nature and imply Stebbins's unfailing respectability. Certainly, Stebbins was more outwardly reserved than was Emma Crow Cushman. The letter to Elizabeth Peabody, however, suggests that a certain intensity, if not physicality, had one time been part of Charlotte's relationship with Emma Stebbins.

But what is missing, edited, destroyed? Most of what we know of the shifting allegiances and jealousies between all three primary members of this "sapphic" household comes from those letters Emma Crow Cushman saved. And letters are, after all, constructions—narratives shaped by the writer's rhetorical purpose—rather than a pure "factual" account of one's feelings. What image of herself and the two women in her life was Charlotte striving to present, assuage, protect, as tensions between the two Emmas threatened to reach a breaking point in the autumn of 1868? Perhaps Charlotte, with her concern for social status despite her unconventionality, chose to characterize her relationship with Stebbins as a companionable romantic friendship. Emma Crow Cushman was pregnant with her third child and hoping once again for a girl she could name after her beloved Charlotte. As Charlotte rushed back to Rome to be with Emma for the birth of her third son, Edwin Charles Cushman Jr., at the end of November, disharmony between the two women in Charlotte's life was as strong as ever. Although, paradoxically, to most outside observers Emma Crow Cushman appeared to be a conventional, heterosexual married woman, she was still passionately engaged with Charlotte and jealous whenever Charlotte's relationship with Emma Stebbins appeared to take primacy.

"You are entirely wrong with regard to an influence which you suppose to be at work with me against you," Charlotte asserted to Emma Crow Cushman in a letter from England, en route to Rome. "It is possible, and perhaps natural that there should have been some jealousy on the part of 'the influence' [Emma Stebbins] with regard to you . . . for I know what that passion is and how easily it may be excited when one loves much and is very dependent. I have felt it with regard to you and to her. . . . I am unhappy enough . . . without you telling me . . . of your 'wasted life.' You did what you did with your eyes open—as open as any girls [*sic*] eyes ever are—you loved me—you wanted to help me and *you have helped me*," Charlotte claimed.[125] Had Emma married Ned to please or to be close to Charlotte? Perhaps now, in the discomfort of living together with Charlotte and her partner, Emma regretted that choice. The starkness of Emma Crow Cushman's admission of her "wasted life" may have annoyed Charlotte or triggered a feeling of guilt. But, however the women understood and attempted to reconcile passions that led each to take the respective steps she had to construct a home and family together, they were about to face an even more severe obstacle than the jealousy that threatened to tear their home asunder; in England, in the spring of 1869, Charlotte Cushman was diagnosed with breast cancer.

In July Charlotte went back to Malvern to try the water cure. The spa regimen had helped her over other ailments before. Sallie Mercer, Emma Stebbins, and Emma Crow Cushman, "with her lovely babies," would be there as well, unified in their hope for Charlotte's cure. But the hydropathy treatment was unsuccessful, and by August Charlotte, with Sallie Mercer and Emma Stebbins accompanying her, went on to Edinburgh for "heroic treatment"—an operation by surgeon Sir James Simpson. Emma Crow Cushman and the children waited nervously in Malvern for word. Afterward Charlotte scrawled a note to assure Ned that she would "pull through this dark valley." Longer letters to Emma Crow Cushman and "the family" Charlotte dictated, and Emma Stebbins dutifully wrote, but it would take some months of recuperation before they would all be reunited for the winter in Rome. Emma Crow Cushman went on ahead with the children. Charlotte and Emma Stebbins followed as soon as they could. Sadly, Emma Stebbins remembered, "in the course of the winter it became evident that the evil was not entirely eradicated."[126] Despite additional medical care, Charlotte's symptoms returned. With Emma Stebbins, Charlotte decided to move back to the United States.

Much of the pleasure had gone out of Charlotte's Roman life. In addition to the fear and pain of living with breast cancer, coupled with whatever tension still existed between the two Emmas, Charlotte's seventeen-year-long friendship with Hatty Hosmer had disintegrated. The two women had grown increasingly estranged from the time Hatty had moved out of the Via Gregoriana home to establish her own household, but the final rupture in their friendship came over something surprisingly incidental. Charlotte felt that Ned had been slighted by Hatty. Protesting that Americans were never awarded the highest foxhunting honors, no matter how well they rode, Hatty and Ned had both resigned from the hunts held in the *campagna*. When Italian Prince Bandini invited Hatty, and not Ned, to return to the hunt and Hatty accepted, Charlotte was insulted and accused her of "show[ing] off." Because of Charlotte's illness, Hatty determined that it was "not the moment to gather up old grievances," and so the frustrations that had been building over the years were never addressed. Nonetheless, when all the members of Charlotte's household left Rome "without so much as a goodbye," Hatty took it as "a cut direct." If members of Charlotte's family wanted Hatty back in the inner circle, she told Emma Crow Cushman's sister Cornelia, "they must come and fetch me."[127]

But Charlotte had other things to worry about. Several years earlier she had given up her London home, since she was there so infrequently. In October she would leave Europe. Ned and Emma were leaving the Via Gregoriana also, to return to St. Louis. Because of Seward's resignation in 1869, Ned was out of work. Although Charlotte originally told Emma Crow

Cushman that from now on home for her would be wherever "her children are," it was with Emma Stebbins and Sallie Mercer that Charlotte would live permanently. Charlotte expected they would all be together again for summers on the East Coast. "I shall be with you in the West whenever I am physically able to be there," Charlotte told Emma Crow Cushman, "but I am a wanderer, or rather a bird of passage, henceforth seeking where and how I can best preserve my health."[128] On 22 October 1870 Charlotte Cushman, Emma Stebbins, and Sallie Mercer left Liverpool on the *Scotia* and sailed across the Atlantic for the last time.

From the Stebbins family home in Hyde Park Charlotte implored Emma Crow Cushman not to "let the children lose me from their minds."[129] Charlotte was planning a visit to St. Louis in the spring, but in the meantime she was looking for a house in Newport where they might all be together again. Word of Charlotte's return to the United States brought floods of requests for her to perform again. Sorely tempted by offers "to read or lecture or act," Charlotte was offered more money "for a night than I ever made two before."[130] At first she resisted, finding it sadly ironic that "now when I can no longer act with safety I am offered . . . six or seven hundred dollars a night!"[131] But the offer Charlotte accepted was from Edwin Booth, who wrote "begging me to entertain the thought of acting with him next Fall. He says I need only act Queen Katharine which will not fatigue me much and he will revive it with the greatest magnificence and will give me better terms than anyone else will."[132] Emma Stebbins preferred that Charlotte conserve her strength, but the excitement of being back at work was exhilarating to Charlotte. While Stebbins spent most of the month of July with her sister at Hyde Park, "Emma Cushman and her bairn" summered in Newport with Charlotte as she rested and anticipated her September opening.[133]

Whenever all three women were together, the difference between the two Emmas had a decided effect on Charlotte. Emma Stebbins was frequently filled with anxiety and dread and depended upon Charlotte to take care of her. Now that Charlotte was ill, she herself wanted "to be taken up bodily and made to do whatever is right and good and *pleasant*." Emma Crow Cushman had taken Charlotte with her for a jaunt in Swampscott, which had done her much good, Charlotte claimed. But Emma Stebbins was "difficult to move—and perhaps that is why I am less energetic."[134] As always, the two women in Charlotte's life demanded that she play different roles, and Charlotte responded reciprocally, as supporter to Emma Stebbins and passionate companion to Emma Crow Cushman.

But, less than a month after Charlotte bemoaned her lack of energy, fans at New York's Booth's Theatre heralded her return to the stage. Although, according to Emma Stebbins, "Miss Cushman's nearest friends were anxious and troubled when she came to this resolution to continue working,"[135] Charlotte followed her New York engagement with an equally successful run in Boston, and she performed as Lady Macbeth and Meg Merrilies as well as Queen Katharine. Charlotte was pragmatic about her success. As always, she realized that her immense popularity was constructed as much from the mystique created by laudatory theater reviews as from the fact of her initial unavailability and ambivalence about returning to the stage. "My being careless whether they want me or not is a great thing[,] for of course they want me all the more"[136]—so much so that she would earn fifty thousand dollars for the season. New York critics, praising Charlotte, claimed she now had more "grace" as a performer, but Charlotte thought otherwise: "I dare say I have grown intellectually, and my suffering has been sent to me in vain if I have not improved in spirit during all the time I have been away from my profession; but as a mere actress, I was as good, if not better, eleven years ago than I am now. But," Charlotte recognized, "what is printed lives for us, and what is conceived and acted lives only in the *memory* of the beholder; thus I am glad that such things should be *printed* of me."[137]

Once again reviewers intimated that Charlotte was performing in her closing engagements—and that the fifty-five-year-old actress would soon retire—but Charlotte contradicted these intimations of finality with the rigorous tour of performances and readings she undertook in the spring of 1872. Charlotte Cushman was not yet ready to be a mere memory to her fans. As always, Sallie traveled with her, seeing to details of travel arrangements and costumes. Emma Stebbins spent more of her time at Hyde Park, explaining to Annie Fields that "it did not seem possible to me, to make the long cold journies she [Charlotte] was obliged to make."[138] In actuality, Charlotte's winter performances had been scheduled to take her to St. Louis in February, when Emma Crow Cushman was due to give birth to her fourth child, Victor. Charlotte was there to hold the newborn baby and then return him to the nurse's arms before she rushed off to dress for her evening performance.[139] Charlotte's tour was a lifeline as well as an excuse to see Emma. When friends were incredulous that she was still acting, Charlotte claimed that the only time she wasn't in pain was when she was onstage—or asleep.

To her old friend Mary Lloyd, Charlotte explained that "work was absolutely necessary for me, *society* was not sufficient."[140] Charlotte was wracked with anxiety about her medical condition unless she was doing something "which would so take me out of myself—that I should forget my own troubles . . . so I went to work in my old profession—which I did wrong ever to leave, for anything else . . . even for my pleasant (sometimes) life in Rome." Wasting what she considered her God-given talent had "brought its own punishment—a healthy prosecution of my profession and I should have been saved all the pain mental and bodily which I have ever known."[141] That Roman life, with Emma Stebbins and Hatty Hosmer and the circle of women Charlotte supported, had been focused on the artistic productions of others. In the time left to her Charlotte intended to continue to work for the "pleasure and profit" she realized for herself.

Charlotte wanted to play a more active part in the lives of her children—Ned, Emma, and their sons—once again. In the summer of 1872, when her Newport home was completed, they would all live together again in "Villa Cushman." But when the summers ended and the children departed, Charlotte found herself unexpectedly depressed. Acting was becoming an increasingly strenuous effort, and so she began to complement her acting performances with stage readings. Charlotte's first reading had been scheduled for 18 December 1871, in Providence, Rhode Island. Soon booking agents solicited her for readings all over the country.[142]

As she pushed on with her performances, at times illness and loneliness overtook her, and she had to cancel or reschedule appearances. Because readings were less rigorous than full performances, increasingly Charlotte read, rather than acted, the Shakespearean texts with which she was identified. For a time she did both, and she continued playing Meg Merrilies, on occasion losing her voice as she strained to render Meg's hollow and eerie tones. Despite Charlotte's strong will to keep on working, her health steadily declined.

In 1874 she embarked on a series of final "farewell" performances. For years Charlotte had marketed her ambivalence—publicizing every tour as her "farewell" and making a fortune as fans flocked to her "one last time." After years of threatening to retire permanently and then being drawn back to the work she loved, Charlotte now had no choice. Although she still intended to give professional readings, acting was proving too arduous for her. In New York, after her last performance as Lady Macbeth, spectacular festivities were planned. On 31 October, the management of Booth's Theatre had published a four-page announcement detailing the great ceremony to be given after Charlotte's performance the following week. At eleven o'clock, on 7 November 1874, after the play ended, poet William Cullen Bryant recited an ode in her honor, naming her Shakespeare's "grand interpreter" and "queen" of her profession. Fans who had been crowding the streets since dusk heard Charlotte respond with an address she had planned and agonized over. Saying farewell now had an ominous ring to it.

Charlotte thanked the assembled well-wishers who complimented her "honorable life." How did Charlotte's experience of herself—a lover of women—lead her to be applauded for living an honorable life? The now

Charlotte Cushman. Portrait engraving by Alonzo Chappel.
Charlotte Cushman on the reading platform, ca. 1872.
(Author's collection.)

fifty-eight-year-old actress, without the hint of any emotional or sexual entanglements with men in her past to dishonor or distract her, told the throng of fans that "art is an absolute mistress; she will not be coquetted with or slighted; she requires the most entire self-devotion, and she repays with grand triumphs."[143] Charlotte had cast her mistress—her passion, her art—in female terms. And it was as a *woman* lover to such a mistress that Charlotte Cushman was being lauded.

After the gala event a torchlight procession accompanied Charlotte to the Fifth Avenue Hotel, where tens of thousands of fans had gathered to see the fireworks display provided for the occasion and catch a final glimpse of their "Queen." To Emma Crow Cushman, Charlotte poured out her ambivalent feelings about retiring. On the one hand, she referred to the ceremony as "that fearful event after the play on Saturday," but she mentioned, nonetheless, that she "wish[ed] the children [Emma's sons] could have seen it; it was a thing they should have seen, to remember in connection with their 'big mama.'"[144]

After the New York event Charlotte went on to have lucrative farewell festivities in Philadelphia and Boston, giving readings and continuing to act all the while in cities from Buffalo to Cincinnati to Chicago, despite having announced her retirement. Charlotte Cushman concluded her last season of acting in Boston on 15 May, and gave readings until 2 June 1875. After all the well-publicized festivities in Charlotte's honor, Hatty Hosmer confided to Cornelia Crow, "I hear that Miss Cushman is so poorly and it is only her heroism that has kept her alive so long."[145] Charlotte's on- and offstage characterizations as hero were to be among her most enduring.

Despite her heroic efforts, by the winter it was clear that Charlotte's condition had worsened. She was too sick to join Ned and Emma and their sons in Newport for Christmas. Instead, she and Sallie and Emma Stebbins spent the winter at Parker House, in Boston, where Charlotte was undergoing medical treatment. Every day, immediately after breakfast, Charlotte wrote "with her own hand to her family at Newport."[146] Emma Stebbins, her partner, was at her side; Emma Crow Cushman, Charlotte's "family," was in Newport waiting for news. Despite the severity of her illness, Charlotte remained determined. On 13 February, although she was too ill to sit up, Charlotte sent off a penciled note (because of the breast cancer she could no longer exert the effort needed to write with a pen) to theatrical manager John McCullough, asking "if next November and December were engaged at your theatre in California. I hope to be able to get well and go there."[147] Charlotte never did recover. As Charlotte had throughout her eighteen years with Emma Stebbins, "she it was who sustained others; she held them up in her strong arms and comforted them, instead of leaning heavily upon them. In her sick-room," to Emma Stebbins's eyes, Charlotte "was still as much a queen as when, in the role of Katharine, she drew the faithful picture of a noble and saintly death bed."[148]

On the morning of 18 February 1876 Charlotte Cushman died. She had, "mercifully" according to Stebbins, lapsed into unconsciousness the day before; those around her "were not called upon to see one moment of weakness in the heroic picture of her last days."[149] For Emma Stebbins, as for many of Charlotte's fans, her resolute, powerful embodiment of female strength and almost chivalrous support for other women were Charlotte's most legible and definitive characteristics: these would constitute the primary elements of the picture that Charlotte, the icon, left behind. But whereas, in her relationship with Emma Stebbins, Charlotte was consistently called upon to play the "hero," to Emma Crow Cushman, Charlotte's most enduring role was that of lover, her Romeo.

In Emma Crow Cushman's brief memoir, which opens this chapter, she mentioned a vivid recollection of her first image of Charlotte onstage as Romeo. More than forty years after Charlotte's death Emma Crow Cushman was still trying to piece together her palpable, embodied response to the woman she had loved so passionately: "It is difficult to describe wherein her charm lay—she had no physical beauty as beauty is commonly rated, but when one came into her presence it was as if one came to a warm fire when one had been cold, and suddenly felt thawed out."[150]

Ultimately, the radiating warmth that Emma Crow Cushman remembered feeling in response to the woman she loved was as ephemeral as the powerful performances Charlotte's spectators had witnessed onstage for forty years. Charlotte had been concerned about how she would be remembered, and Emma "once heard Miss Cushman say, 'While painters, sculptors or poets leave some visible proof of their work behind them, an actor leaves nothing but a memory, and even that is not left when those who knew him [sic] personally have gone.'"[151] Once the lived experiences of Charlotte and the women closest to her passed away like quicksilver with the memories of those who shared them, what artifacts would remain? And how would Charlotte Cushman's various and contradictory narratives of her experience as an autonomous, ambitious woman who loved other women be told and reconstructed—and erased—in the years to follow?

The Backlash and Beyond

Miss Cushman possessed in a remarkable degree the power of
attaching women to her. They loved her with utter devotion,
and she repaid them with the wealth of her great warm heart.
—Obituary, "Charlotte Cushman,"
Boston Advertiser, 19 February 1876

On 18 February 1876, when Charlotte Cushman died, the entire nation
mourned her passing. Among the hundreds at her funeral were scores of
dignitaries: highly esteemed writers, performers, even public figures such as
the governor and lieutenant-governor of Massachusetts and the mayor of
Boston. Charlotte's family and friends had already gathered in King's
Chapel when, at twenty minutes past eleven o'clock, the doors opened to
the public. The church was filled instantly, and hundreds of women "tried
in vain" to get inside. Following a brief service a procession of forty-six car-
riages slowly traveled through Boston and Cambridge to Mount Auburn
cemetery, where Charlotte was laid to rest.[1] After four decades of a spectacularly successful public life Charlotte was, arguably, one of the most
famous women in the English-speaking world. "No other woman of our
day—in America at least, was as well known to so many people," claimed
Scribner's Magazine, "for it is probable that . . . in her forty years of professional life, she had been seen by millions."[2] In magazines and newspapers
and from pulpits nationwide, acquaintances, journalists, and clergymen
offered tributes to Cushman. The New York *Tribune* predicted that "the
historian of our time will review many significant lives, and will lay the lau-
rel upon many a storied tomb; but he will honor no genius more stately or
singular. . . . The future will speak of Charlotte Cushman with pride and
gladness."[3] In Boston alone the Reverends Foote, Bartol, Cooke, and Murray all published sermons that included "Lessons" to be learned from "the
life of Charlotte Cushman."[4] What qualities did her contemporaries see in
the life of this woman they commended, and what was overlooked or illeg-
ible to them?

Through Cushman's example, Reverend Foote claimed, parishioners
might learn that "an honest, true and noble life is not incompatible with an

actor's profession."[5] Throughout her lifetime Charlotte had been heralded as a model of chaste respectability, a quality rarely associated with a woman on the stage. Because she had no close attachments to men, she brought the appearance of "purity" and respectability to the theater. In return, a stage career had granted her a degree of independence that was almost unprecedented for women of her time. Curiously, given this unusual circumstance, to Reverend Bartol, Charlotte was the epitome of middle-class, female propriety. Although an actress, she had been in his eyes a "true woman": "conservative in her stand, no radical, free religionist or woman-suffragist, a lover of the old ways and solemn forms of worship."[6] A woman who attempted to exert her "moral" influence to "purify" the licentious world of the stage must have appeared to be upholding traditional values he admired. While it is accurate to say that Charlotte was not a "woman-suffragist," she had hoped her model of self-sufficiency would help emancipate women just the same. Charlotte, always eager for respectability, had been willing to deploy the conventions of middle-class femininity whenever it suited her.

Reverend W. H. H. Murray of Boston wrote appreciatively that in Charlotte Cushman "the strength of the masculine and the tenderness of the feminine nature were blended. She seemed to stand complete in nature, with the finest qualities of either sex. Her strength was that of a man, her tenderness that of a woman."[7] For a woman so "complete," associations with men were unnecessary; to Murray it was advantageous that she had possessed qualities of both sexes. And for the journalist from the *Boston Advertiser* Charlotte Cushman's greatest strength was her "character," which earned her "the perfect service of the purest friendship, and beyond that, numbers of noble women waiting to give and receive unfailing sympathy and affection."[8] Why do we know so little about her today? Why has she not been remembered with "pride and gladness"? I contend that for each of Charlotte's eulogizers the very qualities they applauded—her androgyny, her lifelong affectionate "friendships" with other sympathetic women, the absence of any relationships with men that might tarnish her noble reputation—would come to be represented and understood differently in the years that followed as norms of gender and sexuality changed over time. Several months after her death John D. Stockton wrote: "The very fame of the actor finally suffers from the limitations of his art; and though the greatness of Charlotte Cushman is unquestioned now, it will be doubted hereafter."[9] Stockton attributed the waning of an actor's popularity to the ephemeral nature of theatrical performance. That is, once the performer and those who had witnessed her performances were gone, nothing of the live experience shared between actor and audience would remain. But Cushman's greatness began to be doubted even while many people who had known and admired her were still living. Within a few decades after her death the very aspects of her life that had brought her such acclaim had fallen into disfavor.

As we have seen, while Charlotte was alive she constructed and reconfigured the various narratives of her life story against the backdrop of changing and contradictory beliefs about women, about performers, about Americans, about women who loved other women. To some extent her greatness lay in her ambiguity: she served different roles for different audiences, each of whom might find some aspect of her to admire and with which to identify. Charlotte had become a popular cultural artifact—an icon who both embodied and disturbed her culture's dominant ideologies about gender and sexuality. In death, as in life, "Charlotte-the icon" would be seized upon as a symbol who either reflected, expanded, or overturned her era's expectations of womanly behavior. Like most symbols, what "Charlotte Cushman" came to represent was arbitrary and unstable, shifting as attitudes about women, about performance, and about desire changed. It was, I suggest, the specific characteristics she embodied as an autonomous, assertive, "masculine" woman who loved other women that contributed to her unprecedented success. As the available meanings of women's love for each other and their performance of gender changed, so did Charlotte's posthumous reputation.

Charlotte had lived in an era when the separation of domestic and public spheres created a female homosocial world that allowed for intimate relationships between women as part of everyday middle-class life.[10] In addition, a commonly expressed medical belief held that respectable women were innately incapable of feeling sexual passion, so the closeness they shared must necessarily be innocent. For the most part during the mid-nineteenth century *sex* was defined as a heterosexual act of procreation in which women indulged merely to gratify their husbands, not out of any desire of their own. Such an esteemed medical authority as Britain's William Acton claimed that it was a "vile aspersion" to say that women were capable of sexual feeling.[11] According to Augustus Kinsley Gardner, Acton's American counterpart, "sensuality . . . [was] unusual in the sex."[12] Therefore, during Charlotte's lifetime writers like William Alger, in 1868, had *encouraged* unmarried female readers to form intense friendships with each other that would occupy their time and emotions.[13]

We have seen in the varied responses to Charlotte during her life, however, that such romantic friendships were not always casually accepted; nor were all women thought to be passionless. Some women—working-class women, actresses, women who attempted to pass as men, "exotic" women of non-European background—were regarded as dangerously sexual. In addition, some women—even respectable women—were aware of their

Charlotte and Susan Cushman as Romeo and Juliet. Stafford-
shire figurine. This figurine, modeled on Margaret Gillies's
1846 drawing, demonstrates how Charlotte's Romeo was
accepted and commodified as standard theater memorabilia
in the mid-nineteenth century. *(From the Art Collection of the
Folger Shakespeare Library.)*

own desire, a fact Charlotte's letters make abundantly clear. Thus Charlotte, recognizing her own desire *and* striving for middle-class respectability, had been wary about others reading her letters or seeing the passionate
attachment she shared with some of the women in her life. Competing
interpretations of *purity, chastity,* and *sex* opened a space for erotic and sexual love between women that outwardly appeared to affirm many of the
values of Victorian society—a space that, I would suggest, Charlotte negotiated quite well.

Certainly, there were many people, such as well-known actor Lawrence Barrett, who extolled Charlotte's closeness to her dear "friend," Emma Stebbins, seeing the intimate, affectionate bond of their romantic friendship as *evidence of* Charlotte's high moral character. After her death, Barrett published a brief memoir of Charlotte in which he made special mention of the fact that "she was supported for years by the companionship of a friend who survived her, and whose devotion is a testimony to the winning and attractive character of her lost friend."[14] Barrett was eager to elevate the social status and moral reputation of a theatrical career, so he portrayed Charlotte as a purifying, ennobling force who "left the stage better than she found it" and resisting its temptations, "preserved her fame pure and unstained."[15] For him, Charlotte's particular representation of her chastity—or, I might suggest, her disinterest in or disdain for heterosexual sex—counteracted the commonly held association between actresses and "fallen women," or prostitutes. Charlotte, then, emerged in such early posthumous accounts as she had during her lifetime: as evidence that a woman could achieve eminence in the profession while leading a virtuous life. In one commemorative article an anonymous eulogizer asserted that Charlotte "furnished a worthy example for all vocations":

> but to the theatre she has been especially useful. . . . Miss Cushman's strong, wholesome and somewhat austere character was felt, more or less in every playhouse in America. Her individuality steadily elevated her calling and constantly reminded young people who sought dramatic honors that these were to be reached not only without sacrifice of self-respect, but by its distinct and continual assertion.[16]

Without "compromising her values," nineteenth-century code for engaging in illicit relationships with men that might rob her of her "virtue," Charlotte Cushman had become, according to George C. D. Odell, "the greatest tragedienne of her time."[17] And her widespread popularity had done much to improve the respectability of actresses generally. Her supposedly pure and wholesome example helped make it more acceptable for other middle-class women who were drawn to a stage career as a means to improve their economic status, to express their artistic inclinations, and to assert their autonomy. During her lifetime Charlotte had received scores of requests from women who wished to go onto the stage and emulate her example. One young woman wrote, "I partake of the noble ambition of minds like your own that have made for your profession friends who were enemies and judges without mercy."[18] Another aspiring performer had solicited Charlotte's advice "not because of your artistic abilities, but because of your virtue."[19]

After Charlotte's death Emma Stebbins had a stake in perpetuating the

THE LATE CHARLOTTE CUSHMAN AND HER PRINCIPAL CHARACTERS.

Cover of the *Daily Graphic* (New York), 4 March 1876. Two weeks after Charlotte Cushman's death this illustration featured Emma Stebbins's bust of Cushman and flattering depictions of her major female characters, omitting Romeo and her other breeches roles. *(Harvard Theatre Collection. Houghton Library.)*

impression that the partner with whom she had shared her life had been a loving, virtuous, moral paragon. Just weeks after Charlotte died a despondent and grieving Emma Stebbins wrote to Charlotte's friend Sidney Lanier about collaborating with him on a "memoir which must be written by those who loved her, lest unworthy and careless hands undertake it."[20] It seemed inevitable that Charlotte Cushman's "life story" would be told and re-presented. Believing that on some spiritual plane Charlotte "exists and loves me still,"[21] Emma Stebbins resolved "to produce a worthy memorial of this great life . . . in its material aspects as well as in its high moral and spiritual significance." Like the women in Charlotte's literary circle decades earlier who had created fictionalized depictions of actresses, Stebbins set out to present an idealized refinement of "nature." That presentation was shaped by what Eve Sedgwick has called the "wider mappings of secrecy and disclosure" that dictated the available terms for understanding lesbian desire.[22] Emma Stebbins was determined to control Charlotte's posthumous representation: "no one but her nearest and dearest as I was and *am* thank God!" could sift through and authorize the letters, diaries, and private papers that would constitute the published story of her life. "It will be necessary for all to pass through my hands first," Emma Stebbins determined.[23] She claimed that Charlotte had initially wanted her to write the memoir, but she had felt daunted by the task. Although "the darling always believed I could do anything I willed to do," Stebbins put it dejectedly, acknowledging her dependency on her deceased companion, "I was never anything but through her—she bore me up in her strong will & made me whatever I was."[24]

In the last weeks of Charlotte's life Emma Stebbins had been so upset about her partner's condition that she couldn't stand to speak with Charlotte about her imminent death. When Charlotte called Ned and Emma Crow Cushman to her to whisper about settlements and funeral arrangements, Emma Stebbins fled from the room. The one thing Stebbins *had* discussed with Charlotte was the production of a memoir of Charlotte's life. Years before, Emma Stebbins had sculpted a bust of her famous partner, but words were not her chosen medium. Now that Charlotte was gone, it was up to Stebbins to determine how she would be remembered.

But there was less material available than Emma Stebbins had hoped. She *did* have in her possession the diary filled with Charlotte's fears about her reception in England and her longing for Rosalie Sully. But Stebbins commented to Sidney Lanier that "much of it [the diary] [was] written in pencil—so fine and pale that I can scarcely decypher [*sic*] it even with a magnifying glass."[25] Although the tiny pencil notations *are* difficult to read, they are readable, so the diary's illegibility is not sufficient to explain Stebbins's reluctance to use it. She simply did not want to include any material of such a "personal" nature. Virtually all correspondence from Charlotte's early life in England had been destroyed.

As Stebbins explained to Lanier, she herself had "destroyed quantities" of Charlotte's letters to her before she realized their prospective value for this project. Besides, they were of a "personal character, which require[d] careful gleaning" before they could be used in a public document. She wanted to provide facts, to detail the events that had shaped the remarkable life of her partner. But there were few facts to go on. As we have seen, Charlotte had built her personal narratives of her early life on shifting accounts. In her creation of her public persona, uncomfortable details—such as her parents' separation, the actual date of her father's death, the circumstances of Susan's marriage to Ned Merriman, and the shadowy details of Merriman's death—all these were either omitted or reshaped as Charlotte had seen fit. Even the occasion of Charlotte's first breeches performances had been given contradictory dates and explanations. Facts, then, were sketchy and unclear. Out of the mix of facts and intentional gaps through which Charlotte had fashioned her public self, Emma Stebbins would have to craft the "official account."

What criteria, then, did Emma use for her sifting the "too personal" from the suitably public persona she would craft for her readers? And what other information could she rely on? For almost two decades Charlotte had written religiously to her *other* lover, Emma Crow Cushman. To this "voluminous correspondence with her Aunt"—as Stebbins characterized the relationship—"I trusted for much help." But once Emma Crow Cushman could bring herself to look over the cherished correspondence, she decided that her letters from Charlotte—the letters that form most of *this* narrative—were so "purely personal and private" that she "could not think of putting them into any other hands."[26] Particularly Emma Stebbins's hands. Or so Emma Stebbins reported to Lanier. Although she felt the memoir was her "sacred duty," Stebbins suggested they delay the project "unless the materials come forward much more freely" from "Mrs. Cushman" [Emma Crow].[27] Sidney Lanier abandoned the project, but Stebbins, determined to complete her memoir, gained access to at least a portion of Charlotte's letters to Emma Crow.

Two years after Charlotte Cushman's death, her fans read an account of Charlotte's life and stage career constructed as consciously and carefully as Charlotte's own self-presentation had been, fully in keeping with what Lawrence Barrett praised as "the quiet and uneventful character of her [Charlotte's] domestic history."[28] There was, of course, nothing quiet and "uneventful" about Charlotte's domestic history. Nevertheless, as with virtually all published memoirs of this period, passionate, homoerotic relationships between women were reconfigured or edited out of Stebbins's volume. Emma Crow Cushman is only briefly identified as Charlotte's "dearly beloved niece."[29] Although whole paragraphs of Charlotte's letters to her and to Sarah Anderton are incorporated into Emma Stebbins's text, the letters were edited so that the eroticism evident in the original letters is omitted. Hatty Hosmer, with whom Charlotte and Emma Stebbins lived for years, is only mentioned once. Eliza Cook is reduced to "a devoted friend" who "celebrated her friendship in many fervid lines."[30] And Rosalie Sully and Matilda Hays are omitted entirely. Instead, the image of Charlotte Cushman that her surviving partner forged from "the current of their two lives [which] ran, with rare exceptions, side by side," emphasized Charlotte's "pure" life and the dramatic profession that she had "honored" with her "noble" character.[31]

Now that I have read the original letters and compared them with Stebbins's highly censored narrative, I wonder how consciously the women who loved Charlotte negotiated the rules that governed proper gender behavior and participated in what Jennifer Terry calls "the policing of lesbian desire."[32] Did Emma Stebbins recognize excessive erotic overtones in the few letters to Emma Crow that she eventually included and, so, edit them? Or did Emma Crow provide Stebbins with her own censored versions of the few letters? And, if so, *who* was she trying to protect? Emma Stebbins? Charlotte? Herself? In any case, by 1878 clearly *someone* determined that the passionate expressions of attachment to women had no place in the official narrative of Charlotte's life, despite the fact that romantic friendships between women were presumed to be platonic.

Or were they? Shortly after Charlotte died the romantic friendships so lauded in some contexts were increasingly open to redefinition and contestation, depending upon whether love between women was seen as either supporting or threatening the status quo.[33] But this process had been going on at least through Charlotte Cushman's adult life. My study of Cushman certainly lends further support to Martha Vicinus's claim that some scholars "may have exaggerated the acceptability of romantic friendships."[34] The same prescriptive literature that heralded the purity of women and encouraged women's friendships had warned against excessively passionate emotional bonds. Even if only in codes and whispers, suspicions of women's passion had coexisted for decades alongside idealized accounts of virtuous female friendships. In 1858—a year after Emma Stebbins and Charlotte Cushman met—one of the most popular volumes of prescriptive literature, Dinah Craik's *Woman's Thoughts about Women,* had described female "sentimental" friendships in contradictory terms: "Though often most noble, unselfish, and true, [they are] in some forms ludicrous, in others dangerous. For two women, past earliest girlhood, to be completely absorbed in one another, and make public demonstration of the fact, by caresses or quarrels, is so repugnant to common sense, that where it ceases to be silly it becomes actually wrong."[35] Craik did not articulate explicitly *what* was "dangerous" and "wrong" about such close affectional bonds.[36]

And yet, as an observer of numerous female couples, Craik felt that close friendships between women could be laudable: "to see two women, whom Providence has denied nearer ties, by a wise substitution making the best of fate, loving, sustaining, and comforting one another, with a tenderness often closer than that of sisters, because it has all the novelty of election which belongs to the conjugal tie itself—this, I say is an honourable and lovely sight."[37] For the last twenty years of her life Charlotte Cushman and Emma Stebbins had elected to live together in such an apparently affectionate and tender relationship, presenting themselves as respectable spinsters and romantic friends, rather than as women who had actively desired each other. But missing from Stebbins's published account of their life together, as from Craik's depiction of women's romantic friendships, was a clear and consistent sense of exactly how the absorbing, demonstrative, and "dangerous" passionate relationships between women differed from the "honourable and lovely" connections that were encouraged. What was missing was a way politely to allude to women's erotic desire.

Throughout her life Charlotte had guarded against being characterized as deviant or unnatural. Aware that, as Charlotte warned Emma Crow, "if any unscrupulous person or persons" should find Emma Crow's "dear letters" to her, "[her] reputation might be lost forever,"[38] in her letters to Emma Crow, Charlotte had attempted to negotiate what Jennifer Terry has called "the contradictory relationships between . . . the demands of the desiring body and the probabilities of risk."[39] As a result, in part, of Charlotte's careful accommodations to, and appropriations of, the conventional discourse about women's purity, Charlotte's contemporaries found her close attachments to women praiseworthy. "Miss Cushman possessed in a remarkable degree the power of attaching women to her. They loved her with utter devotion, and she repaid them with the wealth of her great warm heart," the *Boston Advertiser* eulogized. "Young girls gave her genuine hero worship, which she received with a gracious kindness that neither encouraged the worship nor wounded the worshipper; mature women loved and trusted her wholly."[40]

How were these supposedly virtuous female friendships differentiated from the same-sex erotic possibilities that might threaten Charlotte's reputation? Lesbian sexuality was a muted discourse, an unarticulated possibility. Women's potential desire for each other had been a current running through their relationships, although it was rarely named or discussed. And yet, Peter Gay has noted that "it would be a gross misreading of the bourgeois experience to think that the nineteenth century bourgeois did not know or did not practice, or did not enjoy what they did not discuss."[41] While largely eliminated from public discourse, women's erotic preferences for each other—and the possibility that they acted on them—were coded and hinted at in women's diaries and private correspondence long before they had been featured in medical texts and court transcripts.[42]

Yet even in public texts there had been suggestions of such preferences,

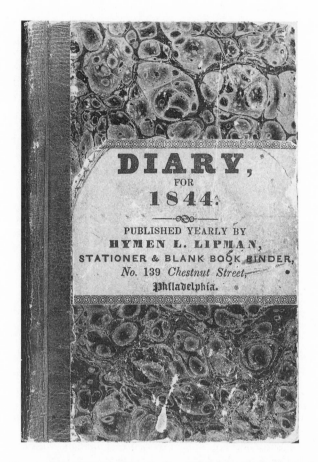

Cover of Charlotte Cushman's diary. The diary Cushman took
to England serves as an artifact of her attempts to "trace [her
private] thoughts" about the women in her life and to record
details of her public performances. *(Dramatic Museum Collection. Rare Book and Manuscript Library. Columbia University.)*

often inscribed in the racialized scientific discourse of the time onto women
who were assumed to be anatomically "unnatural" and otherwise different:
exotic East Asian or African hermaphrodites, decadent French aristocratic
tribades, or indolent courtesans in Eastern harems might be considered capable of engaging in sexual acts with each other. But surely the revered and
reserved American actress who was believed to have had Pilgrim forebears,
who had been friends with presidents and British nobility, whom *Scribner's
Magazine* had lauded as having stood higher in her profession than her "sister" artists Charlotte Brontë, George Eliot, Elizabeth Barrett Browning, and
George Sand[43] stood in their own, could not be considered unnatural—or
could she?

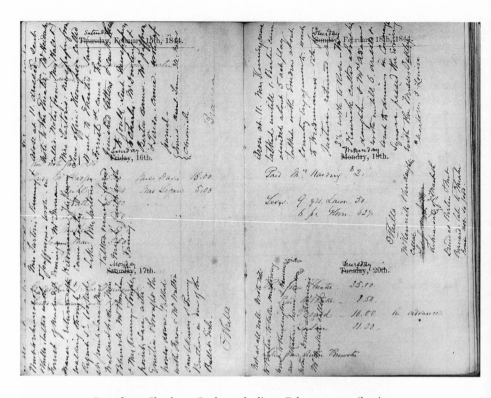

Page from Charlotte Cushman's diary, February 1844 (horizontal) and 1845 (vertical). Cushman's use of pencil and ink in overlapping lines to preserve paper also had the effect of disguising some accounts of her experiences. *(Dramatic Museum Collection. Rare Book and Manuscript Library. Columbia University.)*

Reading Gender and Sexuality

Throughout her life Charlotte Cushman had often been described as "masculine" or "manly." When I started this book, I pored over available images of Charlotte, trying to detect the "majesty," the power, the passion, that so many had read in her presence. I saw a large woman, solid, square-jawed, not conventionally attractive, but direct in her gaze: a masculine woman, a precursor to a "mannish" lesbian. Illustrations and photographs of Charlotte Cushman, like Manet's *Olympia,* stare back—almost challenging the spectator to take her seriously. Here was a woman to be reckoned with.

In a 1913 issue of *Theatre Magazine* Marguerite Merington attempted to explain Charlotte's proclivity for playing male roles onstage by suggesting that "Miss Cushman's active nature rebelled against the encumbrance, physical and psychic, of petticoats in the exercise of art."[44] Reading a dawning recognition of sexuality onto Charlotte's dress, body, and demeanor, Merington compared her to the esteemed French artist (and another lesbian) Rosa Bonheur: "Indeed, placing the portraits of these two women side by side one notes many points of resemblance in the square outline that marked each face, the strong yet mobile features, the clear, direct gaze, and a certain manliness in the general effect, that nevertheless does not gainsay a lovable femininity."[45] What did Merington recognize in Charlotte? What do I see as well? Bonheur and Cushman *did* resemble each other. But more significant than any visible physical features they may have had in common was the fact of their assertiveness, their direct-ness, their lack of coyness or deference to men. These characteristics became legible to general viewers and spectators in the years after Char-lotte's death in a way that had earlier only been read by other women who shared her erotic desires—or desired *her*. These were "mannish" women who demanded and exercised the same privileges as men. Strong, smart, and businesslike, these autonomous, active women had centered their emotional lives around their female friends or partners. Other than describing her in the gender-inflected terms of *manliness* or *masculinity*, most critics writing about Charlotte in the years immediately following her death did not have another agreed-upon name or a category to depict what they saw—or imagined.

Toward the end of Charlotte Cushman's life and increasingly after her death, the very appearance of mannishness in a woman came to signify less an admirable quality of mind or character than a deficiency of feminine attractiveness of the body; it now threatened to mark a woman as "unnat-ural," "odd," or "epicene." Odd women, unmarried spinsters competing with men for employment—described by Elaine Showalter as "women left over"—were increasingly depicted in medical discourses and in popular culture as threatening the established social order.[46] Autonomous, power-ful women who supported themselves and preferred the company of other women were characterized by Charlotte's contemporary and former friend, Eliza Lynn Linton, as "the Epicene sex" and "women of doubtful gender," part male and part female. During the 1860s and 1870s, in her virulently antifeminist column in the *Saturday Review,* Linton lambasted the modern "Girl of the Period" and leveled fiercest indignation at those "hard, unblushing, unloving women whose ideal of happiness lies in swagger and notoriety." Clearly differentiated, mutually exclusive categories of "manly men" and "feminine women" were the ideal "outgrowths of a natural law," according to Linton, who also felt "disgust . . . for men who paint and pad and wear stays."[47] Although Linton herself was a "mannish," established professional woman, in her influential articles she railed against any effacing of the distinctions between the sexes:

> If the interlacing margins of certain things are lovely, as colours which blend together are more harmonious than those which are crudely distinct, it is not so with the interlacing margin of sex. Let men be men, and women women, unmistakably definite; but to have an ambiguous sex which is neither one nor the other, possessing the coarser passions and instincts of men without their strength or better judgment, and the position and privileges of women without their tenderness, their sense of duty, or their modesty, is a state of things that we should like to see abolished by public opinion.[48]

Linton was not alone in her condemnation. Women like Charlotte had always been on the margins of a Victorian culture that assumed mutually exclusive categories of man and woman. Posthumous descriptions of Charlotte Cushman came to focus on what Gamaliel Bradford called "a virile element in her, which she strove neither to diminish nor conceal."[49] Although W. T. Price's 1894 biography of Cushman commended her "virile genius," he was aware that in other memoirs—Stebbins's among them—Charlotte's masculinity and her choice to portray male characters had been intentionally downplayed. Price, however, believed that "there is not only no apology needed for Charlotte Cushman's Romeo as her female biographers seem to imagine, but it was one of her most remarkable achievements."[50] Other journalists, critics, and early theater historians described Charlotte's masculine physical features as either a "lack" of feminine beauty that she had struggled to overcome or as the intrinsic motivation for the male parts she played onstage. "Charlotte Cushman did more than merely succeed as an actor; she conquered circumstances. She turned the natural awkwardness of a tall bony frame into picturesque majesty," claimed a critic in 1893.[51] The implication was that Charlotte's body might have determined her fate—but that she had skillfully either transcended or exploited her physical limitations. But, like other "border cases" of her culture's predominant definitions of femininity and masculinity, Charlotte's androgynous style, manner, and appearance had what Mary Poovey calls "the potential to expose the artificiality of the binary logic that governed the Victorian symbolic economy . . . the opposition between men and women."[52] For, despite protests like Linton's, it was becoming increasingly clear that, as much as the Victorians heralded the presumed distinctness between the abilities, activities, and behavior of men and women, these categories were not hard and fast: the presence of visibly "manly" women and "feminine" men threatened to upset the boundaries.

At this time, the medical discourse of sexology was positing the existence of an "intermediate sex," a category for men and women who felt sexual desire for members of their own sex. It was not until the close of the nineteenth century and the early years of the twentieth century that the theories of sexologists Havelock Ellis and Richard von Krafft-Ebing[53] and of Sigmund Freud became generally available to English-speaking readers, although German psychiatrist Karl Friedrich Otto Westphal[54] had been studying homosexual desire since 1869. In fact, Ellis's collaborator, John Addington Symonds, hypothesized what Eliza Linton had most feared: that homosexuals were a separate sex altogether. Furthermore, in the 1890s Havelock Ellis helped popularize the notion that females were, indeed, capable of sexual feelings, just as men were. Therefore, it was possible to concede that women might have sexual feelings for each other.

Suddenly, close expressions of affection between middle-class same-sex "friends" that had been generally acceptable in an earlier era came to be considered abnormal; the behavior itself had not changed, only its interpretation. In fact, Ellis depicted same-sex erotic desire as innate in some women but abnormal, or "inverted."[55] The "invert," or lesbian, was so described not because of specific acts she might commit but because of who she *was;* her emotions, her responses to others, her sense of herself, were inverted, the reverse of social norms. Rather than choosing domestic lives with men, inverted women sought active, professional lives of their own, often in the company of other women. Sexuality came to be considered a critical aspect of one's innate identity, rather than a series of behaviors an individual might choose or refuse to perform. And a woman like Charlotte Cushman could no longer be considered a paragon of chaste virtue merely because she had abstained from relationships with men.

Although the word *lesbianism* was not widely used, sexual desire between women was one of the "sexual perversions" described in Krafft-Ebing's *Psychopathia Sexualis.* Using the word *uranism* to indicate homosexuality, Krafft-Ebing described lesbians along a scale from "invisible" to highly masculinized. While some women who loved other women appeared conventionally feminine, and therefore were not easily detected, he maintained that "uranism may nearly always be suspected in females wearing their hair short, or who dress in the fashion of men . . . also in opera singers and *actresses who appear in male attire on the stage by preference.*"[56] Charlotte Cushman, the most highly acclaimed breeches performer of her day, was clearly suspect.

Those who remembered Charlotte onstage, like critic William Winter, writing in 1906, now represented her and accounted for her celebrity in light of this new awareness: "You might resent her dominance and shrink from it, calling it 'masculine'; you could not doubt her massive reality, nor escape the spell of her imperial power. She was a tall woman, of large person and commanding aspect, and in her demeanor, when she was thoroughly aroused, there was an innate grandeur of authority that no sensitive soul could resist," Winter claimed.[57] Winter had known Charlotte when her powerful, decisive manner was considered noble, regal, honorable, as respectable as the female monarch on the British throne. But in the ensuing years Havelock Ellis had warned readers that "there are all sorts of instinctive gestures and habits" a woman might display "which may suggest . . . that such a person 'ought to have been a man.'" With a description that could have been taken from one of Charlotte's early theater reviews, Ellis warned, "The brusque, energetic movements, the attitude of the arms, the direct speech, the inflections of the voice, the masculine straightforwardness and sense of honour, and especially the attitude towards men, free from any suggestion either of shyness or audacity, will often suggest psychic abnormality to a keen observer."[58]

As newly available "knowledge" about sexuality shaped what people saw, recollections of Charlotte and of other powerful, independent women who had refused to be deferential to men were cast in the light of these pathologizing discourses. Other sexologists and compilers of information about homosexuals—also referred to by the terms *similisexuals, intersexes, urnings,* as well as *uranians* and *uraniads*—identified Charlotte more directly, naming her not just as a woman who had masculine qualities but as a woman who was identifiably lesbian. In 1909 the topic of same-sex desire was still largely forbidden in the American and English commercial press, subject to censorship and obscenity laws, so American writer Edward Prime Stevenson resorted to printing privately 125 copies of his mammoth study *The Intersexes,* one of the first in-depth discussions in English outside of medical journals of members of the "intermediate sexes." Publishing under the pseudonym Xavier Mayne, Stevenson claimed that "nature has always maintained . . . a series of graduated and necessary intersexes" whose "natural" desire is for members of their own sex, although "the average eye and mind have never learned even how to look for them."[59] He bemoaned the fact that "to too many medical men, similisexualism seems 'wholly a pathologic affair,' a disease, a 'morbid' abnormalism. They do not accept or admit similisexualism as the eternal manifestation of any distinct—or indistinct Intersexes."[60] Much of Stevenson's book, which tried to refute the tendency to "pathologize" homosexuality, consists of case studies and examples of homosexual men and lesbians. One of them was Charlotte. "A strongly uraniadistic actress (psychically) was the noted American tragedian, Charlotte Cushman," Stevenson asserted. "She was acceptable in male roles; at her best only in the severer and almost unfeminine characters, her bodily personality being rather virile than female."[61]

Whether invoked as evidence of her sexual "identity"—a new concept linked to the idea that a person might innately *be* lesbian, rather than just engage in lesbian acts—or implied in hints and whispers, Charlotte's masculine appearance and demeanor were seized upon as a causal explanation for the male parts she had played so successfully. George C. D. Odell wrote in the *Annals of the New York Stage* that "Miss Cushman's homely features and lack of feminine charm drove her to masculine characters; her success in them helped to perpetuate throughout the best years of the century the very bad custom of female Romeos, Hamlets, etc."[62] Henry James remembered having seen Charlotte perform when he was a child. "Miss Cushman [was] . . . markedly destitute of beauty or the feminine attractive," James recalled, claiming her appearance was the reason she was "thereby reduced to the interpretation of a small number of parts."[63]

Instead of signifying Charlotte's power or unique talents, as it had at the time she was performing, her "mannishness" or "masculinity" was now regarded as a handicap that had decidedly limited her potential. Writing at the same time—thirty years after Charlotte's death—Gamaliel Bradford announced definitively that "there was no feminine charm, no grace, no witching tenderness" in Charlotte. "Instead, there was a deep, resonant, immensely varied, but always slightly masculine voice, strongly marked features and a commanding presence, which impressed and imposed, but hardly fascinated."[64] But Bradford, like Odell and James, considered Charlotte Cushman from the perspective of a male spectator, and, as we have seen, Charlotte had no particular desire to "charm" or "fascinate" *men*. Although it was unimaginable to most of the critics writing immediately after her death, Charlotte had been most fascinating to her lesbian spectators.

The appeal of a masculine woman as the object of another woman's desire continued to confound critics, like theater impresario David Belasco. When Belasco heard that Charlotte's contemporary, actress Anna Cora Mowatt, had preferred playing Juliet to another female Romeo, Fanny Vining, Belasco remarked incredulously, "I cannot believe that any woman was ever really satisfied with an imitation man, any more than any man was ever really satisfied with an imitation woman." Discounting all possibilities of homoerotic desire—and the spark it had ignited in female spectators—Belasco announced, "All epicene anomalies are, to say the very least, superfluous upon the stage."[65] It was easier to attempt to dismiss or diminish that which one could not understand.

For many early twentieth-century critics, erotic relationships between women seemed not to exist. In a commemorative article published on 23 July 1916, exactly one hundred years after she was born, Charlotte Cushman was described as "a woman of striking personality and stormy nature" whose "professional struggles and emotional conflict were rewarded by fame and wealth" but who *"knew little love or happiness."*[66] Thus, despite the intense love and support from other women that Charlotte's eulogizers had recognized and openly acknowledged forty years earlier, in these later accounts her relationships with other women were either rendered unhealthy or erased. Charlotte was now pitied as a chaste spinster: not only was erotic desire missing from the official account of her life, but even the emotional sustenance she shared with other women was eliminated.

Although much misunderstood, Charlotte continued to fascinate people. By 1940, when Lyman Beecher Stowe planned to write a biography of Charlotte Cushman, the competing discourses that rendered lesbians either invisible or pathological continued to shape reactions to her. As the theories of the sexologists and, especially, Freud came to be accepted as common knowledge, they provided a weapon against both same-sex love and androgynous behavior. To research his never-completed biography Stowe contacted a range of people who might provide information. Walter Eaton, then dean of the Yale School of Drama, answered Stowe's inquiry for information about Charlotte. "I used to hear my mother talk about her with awe," Eaton wrote, "but she lived such a blameless life that you'll be denied the normal fancy trimmings of the theatrical biography. One horror she committed—Romeo to her sister's Juliet. I did see Bernhart play Hamlet, and that was enough."[67] Eaton, apparently, dismissed the practice of women playing breeches roles as a "horror," and he assumed the absence of male love interests in Charlotte's life rendered her chaste, blameless, boring. Without relationships with men to provide the "trimmings," Charlotte's life might not be of sufficient interest to the presumably heterosexual readers who yearned for a romantic plot in the life stories they read.

But Stowe, influenced by Freudian notions of lesbianism, was able to see what was invisible to Eaton. Ned and Emma Crow Cushman's son, Victor, and Victor's wife, Louise Foraker Cushman, had just donated Charlotte's letters to Emma Crow to the Library of Congress. Although the library's guide to the Charlotte Cushman Papers describes the collection as primarily "family correspondence" from Charlotte to her brother Charles and her adopted nephew, Ned,[68] Stowe could see that something was amiss. In his notes after reading some of the letters—most of which have no salutation—he wrote that "when I came upon this I thought I had discovered a love letter and so it is, but a love letter from one woman to another. . . . I suppose the prurient modern mind would give a sinister interpretation to the relationship."[69] Although Stowe recognized the possibility of a lesbian reading of Charlotte's passionate expressions, he made several crucial errors, misreading the letters as addressed to an even younger (nonexistent) grandniece, "Emily" Crow. As I have discovered, Charlotte's ardent expressions to her "little lover," Emma Crow Cushman—whose initials, like Ned's, were *also* E. C. C.—were indeed love letters, not affectionate family correspondence or the overeffusive expressions of a great aunt to a beloved grandniece. Stowe never completed the project, but biographies of other women in Charlotte's circle, other women who loved women, suffered under the glare of a Freudian interpretation of lesbian sexuality.

As we have seen in chapter 6, novelist Geraldine Jewsbury and her intimate friend Jane Carlyle were each closely associated with Charlotte Cushman over a period of many years. Jewsbury and Carlyle's letters to each other and to Cushman were full of loving references and expressions of jealousy. By 1935, however, Jewsbury's biographer Susanne Howe argued: "Some of these letters are too revealing. They make uncomfortable reading. They were not meant for the eyes of the casual twentieth-century reader with his Freudian vocabulary."[70] The "casual twentieth-century reader" was likely to see suppressed sexual motives in the expressions of sentiment that, during the Victorian era, had largely fallen within the realm of acceptable female friendship. When the letters were written, sentimental and romantic language was used in a broad range of female relationships, thereby permitting some letters of passionate love between women to "pass" as "normal." Because of the pronounced emphasis on heterosexual behavior as "normal" and the belief that effusive expressions of affection should be reserved for opposite-sex partners, the letters in question would now be read as signifying the writer's "deviancy."

Freud's theories were even more troubling than those of the early sexologists. In popular readings of Freud, homosexuals were individuals who had not reached their full sexual maturity and were, therefore, unhealthy. Thus, Howe was careful to point out to her readers that although Geraldine Jewsbury "fell deeply in love" with Jane Carlyle, their friendship was never "morbid" (i.e., lesbian).[71] Countless other female relationships were edited out of biographies and histories in an attempt to "protect" the subjects from this kind of Freudian interpretation. Women who identified primarily with other women and women who attempted to become independent and change their subordinate status in any way risked being labeled aberrant.[72] According to Freud, women who resisted stereotypical notions of femininity were believed to suffer from "masculine striving," in which "the wish for masculinity persists in the unconscious" and exercises "a disturbing influence."[73] Freud's notion of penis envy and other theories were repeatedly invoked to discourage autonomous and androgynous behavior in women.[74] Furthermore, unlike those sexologists who saw homosexuality as a hereditary condition that could not be "cured," Freud claimed that homosexuality was the result of a disruption of "normal" sexual development. Women like Charlotte Cushman were no longer considered appropriate role models for future generations; they were now regarded, retrospectively, as symbols of abnormality and arrested development. No wonder the most highly acclaimed actress of her time was largely edited out of theater history texts or relegated to mention as a mere oddity or "vagary" of performance history.

One hundred years after Charlotte's death, in his book on the history of Shakespearean performance, Bernard Grebanier described what he called "the inexplicable obsession which has driven some women to assume men's roles" as an "inversion"[75]—language that clearly echoed the sexologists. And, to further reinforce the association, Grebanier claimed that Charlotte Cushman "never in her life managed to act with grace of movement," although "she projected dignity with her commanding presence."[76] After mentioning her relationships with her partners Rosalie Sully and Eliza Cook, Grebanier concluded that Charlotte had "at least strong tendencies in her makeup toward lesbianism."[77]

As recently as 1973, Robert Speaight described what he called Charlotte's "celibate life and total lack of sex appeal," sarcastically asserting that, if Charlotte Cushman "had not died in her virginity, we should be tempted to describe her as the last and not the least of the Pilgrim mothers."[78] Apparently like the Victorians, who believed that sex only "counted" if men were involved, Speaight imagined Charlotte to have been celibate and virginal, since she appeared neither to appeal to nor to be interested in men. Of course, these twentieth-century accounts miss the very qualities that made her such an object of desire for many of her female spectators. "One inclines to the opinion that the only thing wrong with Charlotte Cushman as an actress was that she ought to have been a man,"[79] Speaight remarked. Who is the "one" presumptive in Speaight's narrative? Clearly, the women in Charlotte's intimate life, and those who admired her on the stage, located their erotic response in her as a *woman*.

Other twentieth-century critics also read Charlotte's "masculine" body and voice as emblematic of an androgynous "temperament" that became a determining factor in her performance style. In Garff Wilson's history of American acting he noted the "powerful influence" of Charlotte's appearance on the parts she played. "She was a tall woman, with square shoulders and a sturdy frame. . . . She was generally described as commanding, rather than handsome, and as masculine in appearance, rather than dainty or feminine." But, unlike most mid-twentieth-century critics and historians, Wilson saw these attributes as beneficial to her, believing that, "if Miss Cushman's endowments hindered her assumption of certain roles, they were nonetheless her principal assets, for they enabled her to act great roles greatly and to project a stage magnetism few players have ever equaled."[80] Describing Charlotte's performance as Romeo late in her career, Wilson commented that "her success in the part continued to be great in spite of the minority opinion which deprecated the unnatural spectacle of a woman, in male costume, making passionate love to another woman." Without considering the "naturalness" of women's lovemaking, Wilson seemed surprised that "a photograph of Miss Cushman as Romeo shows a large lady wearing a skirt-like costume of knee-length, a fancy sword, white hose, black slippers, and a cap set rakishly on a rather thick head of hair. The figure is broad of hip and full of bosom and, to the modern eye, looks precisely like what it is: a large woman of middle age masquerading as a man."[81] But, as I have asserted earlier, it may have been Charlotte's very legibility as a *woman* making love to another woman and not her skill at "imitating" a man that accounted for the erotics of her Romeo. As we have seen in chapter 5, Charlotte's male personifications pointed out to her audiences how provisional any performance of gender could be and how it was possible to uncouple gender and biological sex, masculinity and male bodies.

Even Charlotte's *handwriting* has come under the scrutinizing eye of critics and historians determined to police gender behavior. In *Titans of the American Stage* Dale Shaw described the letters Charlotte wrote to Edwin Booth negotiating the terms of her return to the stage after being diagnosed with breast cancer. "In letter after letter she dickered coyly, referring to the advice of doctors on rare illnesses and closing with requests for fantastically high fees. Written in a dainty hand, on scented violet stationery, the notes seemed to come from a petite girl. Actually Cushman was statuesque, an Amazon."[82]

For many of Charlotte Cushman's twentieth-century male critics and historians the message was clear. A woman who was too large, too powerful, too androgynous, was subject to ridicule. Shaw called her "gargantuan." The monstrous woman, the excessive woman, the lesbian, was an object of fear or loathing or disbelief. So much more so if, incredibly, she had once been considered the greatest actress in the English-speaking world. In light of her "peculiarities" Charlotte's popularity as an actress was unfathomable to many critics. But Charlotte's magnetism was felt most powerfully by female spectators, and women have continued to be fascinated.

In 1929 Jennie Lorenz, a theater historian, wrote an unpublished master's thesis about Charlotte Cushman. Lorenz was born in 1886—too late to have seen Charlotte perform but still close enough in time to correspond with and interview people who had known her. For the rest of her life Lorenz continued to be intrigued with Charlotte, and until her death in 1962 she continued to examine Charlotte's correspondence and follow up leads for a proposed biography. While researching this book a few years ago, after months of poring over Charlotte's papers, one of the research librarians at the Library of Congress asked if I wished to see the Jennie Lorenz Papers as well. Lorenz had died without having completed her biography, but she had bequeathed all her painstaking notes about Cushman from letters and clippings in repositories and collections around the country—and the trunk she collected them in—to the library. A gift to the future. To me. I had also written about Charlotte, ten years earlier, and was now drawn again to find secrets coded in the volumes of Charlotte's letters. Lorenz's notes, sitting in the library for decades, had only been cataloged in 1991. Clearly, Jennie Lorenz had also seen something in Charlotte that continued to captivate her, something more than the conventional narrative about the life of an extraordinary actress that she had written for her thesis. In Lorenz's papers were letters from Helen Thomson, yet another woman who had planned, unsuccessfully, to publish a biography of Charlotte Cushman. For several years, from 1956 to 1960, Thomson and Lorenz had compared notes and exchanged leads, speculating about Charlotte's relationships with women and the identity of her purported early male love interest. In keeping with a Freudian interpretation of Charlotte's life, Thomson thought that the women Charlotte Cushman loved had filled a void, making up for the coldness Mary Eliza Cushman felt toward her daughter; she likened Charlotte's "marriage" to Matilda Hays to the intense emotional attachments of adolescent girls for one another. What Lorenz saw in the same-sex love relationships of the woman who had fascinated her for thirty years is unclear. In 1960 Thomson wrote Lorenz that, after nine years of work on her study of "our mutual friend, Charlotte C," four publishers had turned down her manuscript on the grounds that Charlotte had not been an "important enough" figure in theater history to warrant publishing her biography. Thomson was surprised, expecting that publishers would be as intrigued with Cushman as she and Lorenz were.

Ten years later, in 1970, Joseph Leach published the first and, until now, the only modern biography of Charlotte Cushman. Based on many of the manuscript sources I have examined here, Leach produced a solid chronological narrative of Charlotte Cushman's life. However comprehensively Leach chronicled the "facts" of Charlotte's family life and professional career, his book only hints at her erotic relationships with the women who played the most significant parts in her emotional life. In 1970—at the dawning of the contemporary gay rights movement—Leach's ambiguous characterization of Cushman's relationships with her lovers was commented on in a review in the lesbian periodical, the *Ladder*. Critic Lennox Strong found Leach's book commendable—"the final word on her"—but qualified her praise: "Final, that is, until some woman does it better, and . . . it might be good if someday somebody does." Where Leach was "hopelessly confused," according to Strong, was in understanding the nuances of erotic relationships between Charlotte and her lovers in the various women-centered households she established in Rome.[83] Although Leach does mention the affectional bonds Charlotte established with several of her female companions, Leach—like Dinah Craik a century earlier—drew the line at any discussion of homoerotic passion, jealousy, and desire. Relying largely upon Leach for her discussion of Cushman, Lillian Faderman, in her study of love and friendship between women, claimed that the openness with which Charlotte Cushman discussed her love for her female friends in her letters and diary was evidence that "Charlotte did not feel intrepid in her amorous pursuits" and that she did not consider her relationships "unorthodox."[84] Yet, as we have seen, far from assuming that others would routinely accept the passionate aspects of her relationships, Charlotte was vigilant about policing the boundaries that determined what *aspects* of those relationships could safely be represented to others. As I have shown, Charlotte Cushman and the relationships she formed with other women cannot be read as a straightforward example of the acceptability of romantic friendship in her era.

Much of Charlotte's extraordinary success as a performer was due to the pleasures and identifications of other women who loved women, women who saw in Charlotte something both recognizable and worthy of their society's respect. Even for members of her virtual community of spectators, Charlotte the actress, the artifact, was an unstable icon who could be seen to represent and signify at least two seemingly contradictory ways of conceptualizing women's same-sex desire. As a woman who clearly preferred the company of members of her own sex and lived openly in a series of long-term relationships with other women that may have resembled romantic friendships, she could embody what Eve Sedgwick has called the trope of "gender separatism," privileging women and their presumed moral superiority and locating women's desire for each other in their identification as, and with, other women and their consequent distinctness from men. Charlotte's audiences, admirers, and critics might respond to her, reject her, or desire her as the embodiment of the erotics of "sameness" in same-sex desire, appreciating as Emma Crow did, that "a strong woman come[s] nearer one's ideal for a lover than any man comes."[85]

Yet, as a transgressive, cross-dressing woman who displayed many so-called masculine attributes, she could also be seen to signify the contradictory trope that came to be known as "inversion."[86] This way of understanding women's same-sex desire—as an animating force between two *different* kinds of women, one more masculine or inverted and the other appearing more feminine—has structured the reactions of those who responded to Charlotte across the boundaries of gender, highlighting her masculine or "butch" qualities and being drawn to or rejecting her for her autonomy, her assertiveness, her so-called "mannishness." Consequently, Charlotte's "masculinity" was read not only into her performances and demeanor, but also in contrast to her female partners. Lilla Wheeler, who as a girl spent time with Charlotte and Emma Stebbins together, remembered that Charlotte's "great friend, Miss Stebbins, was as gentle and feminine as Miss C was the reverse. Miss C dominated any company in which she found herself."[87] For spectators familiar with these codes of lesbian desire Charlotte could stand for *both* the erotic potential experienced in female couples who were drawn to each other's differences as well as those erotic pairings of women drawn to each other's similarities and identifications *as* women, combining, as Martha Vicinus has observed, "the outward appearance of the cross-dressed woman and the inner, emotional life of a romantic friendship."[88]

Whatever position a late-twentieth-century viewer or reader takes toward Charlotte, I am aware that responses to her can never be completely free of the pathologizing discourses that have constructed and still characterize powerful women who love other women as deviant.[89] As we have seen in Charlotte's own correspondence, there were times when, in order to stave off the potential of being seen as "epicene," she strategically appropriated conventional expectations about women to account for her ambition, her cross-dressing, her choice to love other women. At other times she resisted predominant Victorian meanings for any of these acts. Charlotte Cushman, remarkable woman that she was, led neither a "blameless life" nor a "sinister" one. Rather, she was a powerful, intelligent, resolute woman who was able to use the social norms to her advantage. She was a woman who loved other women, a lesbian. As the available meanings of that love changed, so did responses to her. The attempts to erase her or render her merely unusual, "odd,"[90] or inconsequential have not been accidental; each largely reflects the attitudes toward gender and sexuality at the time the accounts were written, rather than attempts to locate the significance of such attitudes in her time.

But, despite the editing, the trivializing, and the diminishing of her reputation in the years since she died, Charlotte Cushman, the artifact, was there all along, in the letters she left, in the reactions and reviews of those who saw her. She was there for the critics, for Jennie Lorenz, for Emma Stebbins, and for Emma Crow. I imagine her somewhere, and she is winking, knowing I have looked for her in the possibilities and foreclosures of her era and in the constructions of ours. She will continue to change, as more letters, hints, gossip, and diaries surface and as more women who love women talk about their desire and look to an artifact, an icon, a star, for personifications of that passion.

Notes

The following abbreviations have been used for frequently cited sources:

BRPP   Bessie Rayner Parkes Papers, Girton College, Cambridge University
CC   Charlotte Cushman
CCP   Charlotte Cushman Papers, Manuscript Division,
                     Library of Congress
DMA   Dramatic Museum Archives, Rare Book and Manuscript Library,
                     Columbia University
Fields Collection Fields Collection, Huntington Library, San Marino, CA
G-O Papers   Gay-Otis Family Papers, Rare Book and Manuscript Library,
                     Columbia University
HGH   Harriet Goodhue Hosmer Collection, Schlesinger Library,
                     Radcliffe College
HH   Harriet Hosmer
HTC   Harvard Theatre Collection, Houghton Library,
                     Harvard University
LBS Collection   Lyman Beecher Stowe Collection, Schlesinger Library,
                     Radcliffe College
Lorenz Papers   Papers of Jennie Lorenz, Manuscript Division, Library of Congress
NLS   National Library of Scotland, Edinburgh

Preface

1. Charles H. Shattuck, *Shakespeare on the American Stage* (Washington, DC: Folger Shakespeare Library, 1976), 96.

2. Henry James, *William Wetmore Story and His Friends: From Letters, Diaries and Recollections,* 2 vols. (London: Thames and Hudson, 1903), 1:260.

3. Geraldine Jewsbury to Emma Stebbins, 6 February 1877, Charlotte Cushman Papers (hereafter CCP), 11:3462–63, Manuscript Division, Library of Congress, Washington, DC.

4. Henry Alden to Charlotte Cushman, 3 November 1874, CCP, vol. 9.

5. See Judith Butler, *Gender Trouble: Feminism and the Subversion of Identity* (New York: Routledge, 1990); and *Bodies That Matter: On the Discursive Limits of "Sex"* (New York: Routledge, 1993).

6. See Erving Goffman, *Presentation of Self in Everyday Life* (New York: Anchor Books, Doubleday, 1959); Andrew Parker and Eve Kosofsky Sedgwick, eds., *Performativity and Performance* (New York: Routledge, 1995); Victor Turner, *The Anthropology of Performance* (New York: Performing Arts Journal Publications, 1987).

7. See Terry Castle, *The Apparitional Lesbian: Female Sexuality and Modern Cul-*

ture (New York: Columbia University Press, 1993); George Chauncey Jr., "From Sexual Inversion to Homosexuality: Medicine and the Changing Conceptualization of Female Deviance," *Salmagundi* 58–59 (fall 1982–winter 1983): 114–45; Martha Vicinus, "'They Wonder to Which Sex I Belong': The Historical Roots of the Modern Lesbian Identity," *Feminist Studies* 18 (fall 1992): 467–97; Vicinus, "Lesbian History: All Theory and No Facts or All Facts and No Theory?" *Radical History Review* 60 (1994): 57–75.

8. See Sue-Ellen Case, ed., *Performing Feminisms: Feminist Critical Theory and Theatre* (Baltimore: Johns Hopkins University Press, 1990); Teresa de Lauretis, "Sexual Indifference and Lesbian Representation," in Case, *Performing Feminisms;* Kate Davy, "Constructing the Spectator: Reception, Context, and Address in Lesbian Performance," *Performing Arts Journal* 10, no. 2 (1986): 74–87; Jill Dolan, *The Feminist Spectator as Critic* (Ann Arbor: University of Michigan Press, 1991).

9. Charlotte Cushman to Miss Booth, 27 July 1874, Harvard Theatre Collection, Houghton Library, Harvard University, Cambridge, MA.

Chapter 1

1. Martha Vicinus has noted that "virtually every historian of sexuality has argued that the present day sexual identity *of both* homosexuals and heterosexuals is socially constructed and historically specific. Yet same-sex erotic attraction appears to be transhistorical and transcultural." Because, as Vicinus claims, all societies "have denied, controlled, or muted the public expression of active female sexuality, . . . we must first decode female sexual desire, and then within it, find same-sex desire" (" 'They Wonder to Which Sex I Belong': The Historical Roots of the Modern Lesbian Identity," *Feminist Studies* 18, no. 3 [fall 1992]: 469).

2. Charlotte Cushman, diary (hereafter cited as CC diary), 28 October 1844, Dramatic Museum Collection, Rare Book and Manuscript Library, Columbia University, New York.

3. CC diary, 30 October 1844.

4. CC diary, 30 October 1844.

5. CC diary, 30 October 1844.

6. Carolyn Heilbrun, *Writing a Woman's Life* (New York: Norton, 1988), 48.

7. CC diary, 30 October 1844.

8. CC diary, 30 October 1844.

9. CC diary, 30 October 1844.

10. William Toynbee, ed., *The Diaries of William Charles Macready, 1833–1851*, 2 vols. (1912; rpt., New York: Blom, 1969), 2:270. Although Macready voiced decidedly pro-American sentiments in other contexts, expressions like this revealed his class biases; see chap. 3.

11. Anne Brewster, "Miss Cushman," *Blackwood's Edinburgh Magazine* 124 (August 1878): 173.

12. CC diary, 4 November 1844.

13. CC diary, 8 November 1844.

14. CC diary, 5 November 1844.

15. CC diary, 1 November 1844.

16. CC diary, 3 November 1844.

17. Lillian Faderman, *Surpassing the Love of Men* (New York: Morrow, 1981), 16. Faderman's work is among those histories of lesbians that followed Carroll Smith-

Rosenberg's groundbreaking article "The Female World of Love and Ritual," *Signs* 1 (1975):1–29. These early works stress the social acceptability of female friendships in the nineteenth century and emphasize the romantic and emotional, rather than the possible erotic or sexual, nature of these friendships.

18. As gender theorist Judith Butler asserts, "naming is at once the setting of a boundary, and also the inculcation of a norm" (*Bodies That Matter* [New York: Routledge, 1993], 8). Two of the major theorists on the construction of "homosexual" as an identity category in the late nineteenth century are Jeffrey Weeks, *Sex, Politics and Society: The Regulation of Sexuality since 1800* (London: Longman, 1981); and Michel Foucault, *The History of Sexuality*, trans. Robert Hurley (1978; New York: Vintage, 1990). See chap. 9 for a further discussion of the impact of the sexologists.

19. Lisa Merrill, "Charlotte Cushman: American Actress on the Vanguard of New Roles for Women" (Ph.D. diss., New York University, 1984). My earlier research on Cushman has been cited in Lesley Ferris, *Acting Women: Images of Women in Theatre* (London: Macmillan, 1990); and Faye E. Dudden, *Women in the American Theatre: Actresses and Audiences, 1790–1876* (New Haven: Yale University Press, 1994).

20. Vicinus, "'They Wonder to Which Sex I Belong'"; Emma Donoghue, *Passions between Women: British Lesbian Culture, 1668–1801* (London: Scarlet, 1993); Terry Castle, *The Appartitional Lesbian: Female Homosexuality and Modern Culture* (New York: Columbia University Press, 1993); see also George Chauncey Jr., "From Sexual Inversion to Homosexuality: Medicine and the Changing Conceptualization of Female Deviance" *Salmagundi* (fall 1982–winter 1983): 58–59, 114–45; Lisa Moore, "'Something More Tender Still than Friendship': Romantic Friendship in Early-Nineteenth-Century England," *Feminist Studies* 18, no. 3 (fall 1992):499–520.

21. Rosalie Sully to CC, 21 May 1845, CCP, 14:3970.

22. CC diary, 6 November 1844.

23. CC diary, 1 June 1844. Charlotte noted that she "wrote to Rose, sent *Ring*." Cushman, always careful to keep track of her finances, noted "[Ring] $4.00 Rose's Birthday" on 3 June.

24. CC diary, 5 July 1844.

25. CC diary, 6 July 1844.

26. As feminist biographer Susan Ware notes, "we do not demand proof of sexual activity as a badge of heterosexuality" ("Unlocking the Porter-Dewson Partnership: A Challenge for the Feminist Biographer," in *The Challenge of Feminist Biography: Writing the Lives of Modern American Women*, ed. Sara Alpern, Joyce Antler, Elizabeth Israels Perry, and Ingrid Winther Scobie [Urbana: University of Illinois Press, 1992], 59).

27. CC diary, 6 November 1844.

28. Rosalie Sully to CC, May 1845, CCP, 14:3970.

29. CC diary, 15 November 1844.

30. CC diary, 14 November 1844.

31. CC diary, 3 November 1844.

32. Monroe Fabian, *Mr. Sully, Portrait Painter: The Works of Thomas Sully (1783–1872)* (Washington, DC: Smithsonian Institution Press, 1983), 62. Rosalie Sully died on 8 July 1847, in Philadelphia. Even in this century art historians, discussing the work of her famous father, note that the miniatures Rosalie painted, which "are sometimes incorrectly attributed to her father, are also evidence that a promising career ended when she died at age twenty-nine." Two of the miniatures posthumously identified as painted by Rosalie Sully are of Charlotte Cushman. Shortly after the death of his daughter Rosalie and her brother Thomas, Thomas Sully wrote to his sister that

he hoped "to earn enough" from his painting "to keep the female part of my family enough w/care and a little industry on their part to 'keep the wolf from their door.'" His earnings had been affected since "he could not leave home . . . [as] the family were too depressed over our recent loss" (qtd. in Edward Biddle and Mantle Fielding, *The Life and Works of Thomas Sully* [New York: Kennedy Graphics, 1970], 71).

33. CC diary, 15 November 1844.

34. CC diary, 16 November 1844.

35. Jennifer Terry also notes that "instead of positing a fixed deviant subject position, the new archivist finds a provisional position corresponding to a discursively fashioned, outlawed, or pathologized sexual identity—the location from which a resistant historiography can be generated ("Theorizing Deviant Historiography," in *Feminists Revision History*, ed. Ann-Louise Shapiro [New Brunswick, NJ: Rutgers University Press, 1994], 289). This is certainly my goal with Cushman.

Chapter 2

1. "Notes Taken from Charlotte Cushman's Own Lips," 1875, Charlotte Cushman Papers (hereafter CCP), 15:3991–4000, Manuscript Division, Library of Congress, Washington, DC.

2. Emma Stebbins, *Charlotte Cushman: Her Letters and Memories of Her Life* (1879; rpt., New York: Blom, 1972), 12.

3. Stephen Greenblatt also notes the importance played by "narrative selection" in self-fashioning, particularly the choice to recount turning points or incidents of "mobility" in one's life narrative (*Renaissance Self-Fashioning: From More to Shakespeare* [Chicago: University of Chicago Press, 1980], 2–3). See also Stephen Orgel, *The Illusion of Power: Political Theatre in the English Renaissance* (1975; rpt., Berkeley: University of California, 1991), 60.

4. Felicity A. Nussbaum, "Eighteenth-Century Women," in *The Private Self: Theory and Practice of Women's Autobiographical Writings*, ed. Shari Benstock (Chapel Hill: University of North Carolina Press, 1988), 154. Stephen Greenblatt also explores the relationship between a "cultural system of meanings" and their embodiment; following Greenblatt, I explore some of the symbolic structures perceivable in Cushman's self-expression and those in the larger social world in which she lived (Greenblatt, *Renaissance Self-Fashioning*, 3–6).

5. Stebbins does not mention Charlotte's grandmother's separation from her husband, but she does speculate about Erasmus Babbit's low fees and his preference for music over a legal career. Joseph Leach provides the dates of the births and marriages, but neither speculates about the discrepancies in "official" accounts or their potential impact on Charlotte's early life. Mary Howitt claims that Mary Saunders Babbit had never gotten over her attachment to an earlier suitor. See Emma Stebbins, *Charlotte Cushman*, 12; Joseph Leach, *Bright Particular Star: The Life and Times of Charlotte Cushman* (New Haven: Yale University Press, 1970), 2–3; Mary Howitt, "The Miss Cushmans," *People's Journal* 2 (18 July 1846): 30–33, 47–49.

6. Howitt, "The Miss Cushmans."

7. Manning Leonard to Emma Stebbins, 29 November 1876, CCP, 12:3521. Leonard is referring to H. W. Cushman, *A Historical and Biographical Genealogy of the Cushmans: The Descendants of Robert Cushman, the Puritan, of the Year 1617 to 1855* (Boston: Little, Brown, 1855), 170. Although I follow the official accounts of Charlotte's

birth, which cite her birthdate as 23 July 1816, an obituary in the *New York Clipper* claimed she was born on 23 July 1815, the same year her parents were married. Given Charlotte's lifelong desire for respectability, the possibility that she was born in 1815 might suggest further motivation for her depiction and configuration of her genealogy and family background in the narratives she authorized ("Charlotte Cushman: The Versatilities of a Great Career," 13 May 1876).

8. Leonard to Stebbins, 29 November 1876, CCP, 12:3521.

9. "Notes," CCP, 15:3991–4000.

10. "Notes," CCP, 15:3991–4000.

11. "Notes," CCP, 15:3991–4000. Although Charlotte's accounts mention only these siblings, H. W. Cushman mentions another brother, Fitz Henry, who was born in 1820 and died in infancy in 1821 (*Historical and Biographical Genealogy*, 511).

12. Leach, *Bright Particular Star*, 10.

13. Carroll Smith-Rosenberg, "Beauty, the Beast, and the Militant Woman," in *A Heritage of Her Own*, ed. Nancy F. Cott and Elizabeth H. Pleck (New York: Simon, 1979), 198.

14. "Notes," CCP, 15:3991–4000.

15. "Notes," CCP, 15:3991–4000. Also cited in Stebbins, *Charlotte Cushman*, 17.

16. See, for example, Samuel Miller, *Theatrical Exhibitions: Their Influence on the Character of Individuals and the Community* (New York: n.p., 1812), 25; David Grimsted, *Melodrama Unveiled* (Chicago: University of Chicago Press, 1968), 27; Jonas Barish, *The Antitheatrical Prejudice* (Berkeley: University of California Press), 1981.

17. Although Emma Stebbins reprints the letter of Charlotte's childhood friend, "H.W.," she does not comment on the use of the term *boys* in Charlotte's description of her childhood. See Stebbins, *Charlotte Cushman*, 17.

18. "Introduction," *Women in American Theatre*, ed. Helen Krich Chinoy and Linda Walsh Jenkins (New York: Crown, 1981), 3.

19. James Henry Wiggin, "A House and a Name," *Bostonian* 1 (October 1894): 87–97. Although Joseph Leach spells Charles Wiggin's nickname "Charley," Wiggin spells his relative's name "Charlie," which I follow here.

20. Elkanah Cushman's disappearance can be deduced from several sources. Charlotte is (intentionally?) vague in her account, merely mentioning her need to drop out of school and contribute to the family's support. Charlotte's letters to and from the Judds refer to him living in Boston with the children from his first marriage. See also Leach, *Bright Particular Star*, 13; and Cushman, *Historical and Biographical Genealogy*, 302.

21. Heilbrun, *Writing a Woman's Life*, 48.

22. "Notes," CCP, 15:3991–4000. Also cited in Stebbins, *Charlotte Cushman*, 19.

23. Barbara Welter, "The Cult of True Womanhood," in *The American Family in Social-Historical Perspective*, ed. Michael Gordon (New York: St. Martin's, 1978), 313–33. Welter found that *True Womanhood* was the phrase used by authors who addressed themselves to the subject of women in the mid-nineteenth century as frequently as writers on religion mentioned God.

24. Welter, "True Womanhood," 313.

25. Nancy F. Cott, intro., *Heritage of Her Own*, 19.

26. Mrs. J. H. Hanaford, "Interview with Charlotte Cushman," *Boston Journal*, 24 August 1858.

27. Carolyn Steedman, "Why Clio Doesn't Care," in *Feminists Revision History*, ed. Ann-Louise Shapiro (New Brunswick, NJ: Rutgers University Press, 1994), 77.

28. Louise Hall Tharp, *The Peabody Sisters of Salem* (Boston: Little, Brown, 1988), 50.

29. Susan Rutherford, "The Voice of Freedom: Images of the Prima Donna," in *The New Woman and Her Sisters: Feminism and Theatre, 1850–1914*, ed. Vivien Gardner and Susan Rutherford (Ann Arbor: University of Michigan Press, 1992), 97.

30. George T. Ferris, "Charlotte Cushman," *Appleton's Journal*, 21 March 1874, 354.

31. "Notes," CCP, 15:3991–4000.

32. Mary Ann Wood to CC, 19 January 1833, CCP, vol. 14.

33. Walter M. Leman, *Memories of an Old Actor* (San Francisco: Roman, 1886), 111–12.

34. Ferris, "Charlotte Cushman," 355.

35. Wiggin, "House and a Name," 87. Another young man, Charles Spalding, also appears to have been interested in Charlotte at this time, although she did not reciprocate his romantic interest. After Spalding's death in 1835, Charlotte and Mary Eliza Cushman returned Spalding's miniature to his mother (H. Spalding to Mary Eliza Cushman, 31 May 1835, CCP, vol. 13).

36. "Notes," CCP, 15:3991–4000.

37. *Sunday Dispatch*; qtd. in Leach, *Bright Particular Star*, 31.

38. Edward G. Fletcher, "Charlotte Cushman's Theatrical Debut," *Texas University Studies in English* 20 (1940): 166.

39. *Boston Daily Atlas*, 11 April 1835.

40. *Spirit of the Times* (New York), 18 April 1835.

41. John Paddon, letter, *Boston Transcript*, 18 April 1835.

42. *Pearl* (Boston), 18 April 1835.

43. Stebbins, *Charlotte Cushman*, 22.

44. *New Orleans Bee*, 4 December 1835.

45. H. P. Phelps, *Players of a Century* (1880; rpt., New York: Blom, 1972), 199–200.

46. *New Orleans Bee*, 12 April 1836.

47. Bruce A. McConachie, *Melodramatic Formations: American Theatre and Society, 1820–1870* (Iowa City: University of Iowa, 1992), 120. McConachie has identified the emergence of several melodramatic forms in the American theater between 1820 and 1870 and the range of class interests they served. He contends that in the earlier part of the century elite audiences gravitated toward paternalistic fairytale melodramas that legitimated patrician values. From the 1830s to the mid-1850s (the time period in which Charlotte first performed) the heroic melodrama and its subgenre, the apocalyptic melodrama, came into vogue in the United States and emphasized working-class notions of heroic honor and combative action. Beginning around 1845, moral reform melodramas directed toward the interests of business-class "respectable" families emerged.

48. E. F. [E. Burke Fisher], *New Yorker*, 27 August 1836, 367.

49. Philip Hone, former mayor of New York City, had remarked ten years earlier, when the Bowery Theatre first opened, that it was "incumbent upon those whose standing in society enables them to control the opinions and direct the judgment of others, to encourage, by their countenance and support, a well-regulated theatre" (*New-York Mirror*, 24 January 1826, 32).

50. E. Burke Fisher to CC, 13 September 1836, CCP, 11:3312.

51. E. Burke Fisher to CC, 13 September 1836, CCP, 11:3312.

52. E. Burke Fisher to CC, 13 September 1836, CCP, 11:3312.

53. *Evening Star* [New York], 13 September 1836.

54. James H. Dormon Jr., *Theatre in the Ante-Bellum South, 1815–1861* (Chapel Hill: University of North Carolina Press, 1967), vii. Live theater in the nineteenth century played the role that film, television, concerts, and sporting events do today, providing entertainment, amusement, relaxation, and access to what has been called the cultural imaginary.

55. Garff Wilson, *A History of American Acting* (Bloomington: Indiana University Press, 1966), 105. See McConachie, *Melodramatic Formations,* for a discussion of the relationship between the development of transportation networks, the growing star system, and the breakup of permanent acting companies.

56. Grimsted, *Melodrama Unveiled,* 26. See also Barish, *Antitheatrical Prejudice.* Tracy C. Davis discusses the interplay between society and theater in the neighborhoods that surrounded English playhouses of this period (*Actresses as Working Women: Their Social Identity in Victorian Culture* [London: Routledge, 1991]).

57. Dormon, *Theatre in the Ante-Bellum South,* 236.

58. Grimsted, *Melodrama Unveiled,* 55.

59. *New Orleans Bee,* 8 December 1835; qtd. in Grimsted, *Melodrama Unveiled,* 236. In December 1835 Cushman performed at the St. Charles Theatre.

60. Davis, *Actresses as Working Women,* 69.

61. Tom Gunning, "The Horror of Opacity: The Melodrama of Sensation in the Plays of André de Lorde," in *Melodrama: Stage, Picture, Screen,* ed. Jacky Bratton, Jim Cook, and Christine Gledhill (London: British Film Institute, 1994), 51. This is not to imply that melodramas offered spectators only one hegemonic position from which to understand their world. In fact, the very excesses upon which melodrama depends opened the way for a range of possible identifications. Gunning describes melodrama as a "dialectical interaction between moral significance and an excess aimed precisely at non-cognitive affects, thrills, sensations, and strong affective attractions" (51). I explore this point further in chap. 4. See also Rosemarie K. Bank, "The Second Fall of the Idol: Women in Melodrama," in *Women in American Theatre,* ed. Helen Krich Chinoy and Linda Walsh Jenkins (New York: Crown, 1981), 238–43.

62. Mark Twain, *Contributions to the Galaxy,* ed. Bruce McElberry Jr. (Gainesville, FL: n.p., 1961), 128–29.

63. Dormon, *Theatre in the Ante-Bellum South,* 258.

64. Nellie Smither, "'The Sovereign in the Ascendant': Charlotte Cushman's First New York Engagement," *Bulletin of the New York Public Library,* 1970:419–24.

65. Walter M. Leman, an actor who worked with Clara Fisher at the Tremont in 1828, was one of the many who noticed that Fisher "played male characters with spirit" and that her "archness of manner . . . capture[d] the young men . . . who thronged to see her" (*Memories of an Old Actor,* 73). See also Yvonne Shafer, "Women in Male Roles: Charlotte Cushman and Others," in Chinoy and Jenkins, *Women in American Theatre,* 74–81.

66. In fact, the Bowery theater had burned down before and would suffer the same fate a third time in years to come. Theatrical fires were so frequent that Leman, who had experienced several, claimed that "the liability to conflagration in any building devoted to theatrical uses is so great, that it has been said that the average life of a theatre cannot exceed fifteen years" (*Memories of an Old Actor,* 126).

67. E. Burke Fisher to Francis C. Wemyss, 27 September 1836, Harvard Theatre Collection, Houghton Library (hereafter HTC), Harvard University, Cambridge, MA.

68. Fisher to Wemyss, 27 September 1836, HTC.

69. E. Burke Fisher to CC, 7 October 1836, CCP, vol. 11.

70. As Helen Krich Chinoy and Linda Walsh Jenkins note, "To the usual limits on female career aspirations—marriage, family, appropriate submissive behavior and acceptable feminine appearance—theatre has imposed further restrictions by being socially and morally suspect in puritanical middle class America" (intro., *Women in American Theatre*, 3).

71. Christopher Kent, "Image and Reality: The Actress and Society," in *A Widening Sphere: Changing Roles of Victorian Women*, ed. Martha Vicinus (Bloomington: Indiana University Press, 1980), 94.

72. Fisher to CC, 7 October 1836, CCP, vol. 11.

73. Francis Wemyss, *Twenty-Six Years of the Life of an Actor and Manager* (New York: Burgess, 1846), 336; my emphasis.

74. Benjamin McArthur, *Actors and American Culture, 1880–1920* (Philadelphia: Temple University Press, 1984), 143. While McArthur does not mention Charlotte's intentional deployment of the popular press, he does discuss how "a flourishing mass media was . . . crucial for the expanding social role of actors," particularly in the years immediately after her death. I contend that she anticipated and contributed to this trend. Wemyss apparently concurs.

75. Charlotte S. Cushman, "The Actress: Extracts from My Journal," *Godey's Lady's Book* (February 1837): 70–73. In choosing the unconventional name Leoline, Charlotte, who was interested in mesmerism and spiritualism, may have drawn on her own horoscope sign, Leo, to further link herself with the character. Furthermore, just as Charlotte made her dramatic debut as Lady Macbeth, Leoline debuted in a Shakespearean role, as Cordelia in *King Lear*.

76. Cushman, "Actress," 71.

77. Cushman, "Actress," 70.

78. Cushman, "Actress," 70.

79. Cushman, "Actress," 71. In Cushman's stories about her actual family, as we have seen, she alluded to her own father's business losses as an explanation for her initial choice to perform onstage but did not explicitly refer to his abandonment of the family. In fact, she may have actively created the impression that he, like Leoline's father, died before his daughter performed onstage; numerous journalists and memoirists writing of Charlotte Cushman described, either through her own intentional misrepresentation or their mistake, her father's death as the circumstance that led her to a career onstage.

80. Cushman, "Actress," 72.

81. Cushman, "Actress," 73.

82. E. Burke Fisher to CC, 8 October 1836, CCP, vol. 2.

83. Fisher to CC, 8 October 1836, CCP, vol. 2.

84. CC to E. Burke Fisher, 8 October 1836, HTC.

85. Emma Donoghue notes that in the eighteenth and nineteenth centuries "this 'early jilting' motif was such a conventional and acceptable reason for being an old maid that it could function as a cover for a woman's basic disdain for heterosexuality" (*Passions between Women: British Lesbian Culture, 1668–1801* [London: Scarlet, 1993], 124). I believe that the stories about Cushman's presumed early suitors were deployed in this fashion.

86. Captain Frederick Marryat to CC, 14 August [1837], CCP, 13:3565.

87. As Aileen Kraditor has asserted in her discussions of nineteenth-century feminism, "the common denominator, the fundamental desire of feminists, can perhaps be

designated by the term 'autonomy.'" Kraditor claims that, regardless of whether or not women desired to have rights and privileges that were equal to men or accepted the notion that women and men occupied different "spheres of life, the essential change demanded has always been that women's 'sphere' must be defined by women" (*Up from the Pedestal* [Chicago: Quadrangle, 1968], 7–8).

88. Henry Dickinson Stone, *Theatrical Reminiscences* (New York: Blom, 1873), 118.

89. J. S. Bratton, "Irrational Dress," in Gardner and Rutherford, *New Woman and Her Sisters*, 83.

90. McConachie, *Melodramatic Formations*, 75–77.

91. "Literary Notices," *Ladies Companion* 6 (1837): 201–2.

92. Stone, *Theatrical Reminiscences*, 53.

93. Phelps, *Players of a Century*, 201.

94. Phelps, *Players of a Century*, 203.

95. Lesley Ferris has discussed how frequently female performers were associated with the parts they played. See Ferris, *Acting Women: Images of Women in Theatre* (London: Macmillan, 1990), 149.

96. Richard Moody dates the first performance of Joseph Stevens Jones's play *The Liberty Tree, or Boston Boys in '76* as 17 June 1832, Warren Theatre, Boston. See Richard Moody, *America Takes the Stage: Romanticism in American Drama and Theater, 1750–1900* (Bloomington: Indiana University Press, 1955), 289.

97. Charlotte Cushman's holograph copy of this poem, CCP, vol. 15.

98. "Literary Notices," 201.

99. *Advertiser,* 1 April 1837; qtd. in Phelps, *Players of a Century,* 204.

100. "Charlotte Cushman: Her Debut as Meg Merrilies," Robinson Locke Scrapbook, 139, New York City Library for the Performing Arts, Lincoln Center, New York.

101. *Doat:* "to be crazed or simple-minded from age" (*Oxford English Dictionary*).

102. Qtd. in Stebbins, *Charlotte Cushman,* 149.

103. See Howitt, "Miss Cushmans." When questions were raised about Susan's marital status, Charlotte claimed she had to send for official papers to squelch rumors alleging that Susan had not been legally married. H. W. Cushman states that Susan married Merriman on 14 March 1836 (*Historical and Biographical Genealogy,* 511), but Charlotte attested to the 4 November date (George Combe to CC, 9 February 1846, NLS, MS 7390:295). Sometime after Merriman abandoned Susan, he apparently disappeared. Howitt reported that Susan had been granted a divorce decree in the early or mid-1840s on the grounds of Merriman's desertion and that he died months later, "somewhere in the Far West." In 1851 Charlotte received a letter from a friend of Merriman's in St. Louis claiming Merriman had died on 17 November 1848—considerably after Charlotte had indicated (E. Keener to CC, 1851, CCP, vol. 12).

104. Lawrence Barrett, *Charlotte Cushman* (New York: Dunlap Society, 1889), 39. Barrett dates Cushman's performance as Nahmeokee as 26 December 1837 and her performance as John Rolfe as 8 February 1838. Richard Moody dates the first performance of Robert Dale Owen's *Pocahontas* (published in 1837) as 8 February 1838, so apparently Cushman was the original Rolfe in Owen's version (*America Takes the Stage,* 101).

105. Moody, *America Takes the Stage,* 101–2.

106. Walt Whitman, *Brooklyn Eagle,* 14 August 1846, recalling earlier performances.

107. Yvonne Shafer has alleged that one of the motivations for portraying male characters was "the urge to take the lead and compete with men in a very direct way . . .

Actresses playing . . . leading male roles undoubtedly found pleasure in playing the central part" while men played supporting roles ("Women in Male Roles," 74–81).

108. Phelps, *Players of a Century*, 203.

109. *Spirit of the Times*, 30 June 1838, 153.

110. See chap. 4 for the competition between Cushman and Forrest.

111. Anne Brewster, "Miss Cushman," *Blackwood's Edinburgh Magazine* 124 (August 1878):173.

112. Whitman, *Brooklyn Eagle*, 14 August 1846. The realism of Cushman's portrayal startled her audiences and has gone largely unacknowledged by theater historians, who date the origin of realistic acting techniques to the late nineteenth century. Cushman's narrative about this performance offered pragmatic rather than aesthetic motivations for her choices and so may have been overlooked—or edited out—of the historical record.

113. Qtd. in Clara Erskine Clement (Waters), *Charlotte Cushman* (Boston: Osgood, 1882), 16–17.

114. Qtd. in Clement (Waters), *Charlotte Cushman*, 25.

115. Brewster, "Miss Cushman," 174.

116. Brewster, "Miss Cushman," 175.

117. Ferris, "Charlotte Cushman," 356.

118. Epes Sargent originally published his play under the title *The Bride of Genoa* (1836). Set in fourteenth-century Genoa, the play was concerned with the struggles of the patrician and plebeian characters. It was first produced under the title *The Genoese* on 13 February 1837, at the Tremont Theatre, Boston. See Moody, *America Takes the Stage*, 198.

119. Clement (Waters), *Charlotte Cushman*, 21. See also Howitt, "The Miss Cushmans."

120. Charlotte Cushman to [Mrs.] Creswick, 7 February 1841, Lyman Beecher Stowe Collection, Folder 429, Schlesinger Library, Radcliffe College, Cambridge, MA.

121. Leach, *Bright Particular Star*, 100.

122. Qtd. in C. D. Odell, *Annals of the New York Stage* (New York: Columbia University Press, 1931), 4:468.

123. Winthrop Babbit to CC, 13 June 1841, CCP, vol. 9.

124. Walt Whitman, "Specimen Days," *Leaves of Grass and Selected Prose*, ed. John Kouwenhoven (New York: Modern Library, 1950), 572.

125. J. S. Bratton, "Irrational Dress," 83–84.

126. Qtd. in W. T. Price, *A Life of Charlotte Cushman* (New York: Brentano's, 1894), 47.

127. CC to Park Benjamin, 14 October 1841, HTC.

Chapter 3

1. "Address by Charlotte Cushman on Taking Management of Walnut Street Theatre, October 1842," Charlotte Cushman Papers (hereafter CCP), vol. 1, Manuscript Division, Library of Congress, Washington, DC.

2. CC, "Address."

3. CC, "Address." With this conscious strategy to encourage middle-class families' attendance at the theater she was managing, Cushman was on the vanguard of a trend that many theater historians identify primarily as a mid- or late-nineteenth-cen-

tury phenomenon. See Bruce A. McConachie, *Melodramatic Formations: American The-atre and Society, 1820–1870* (Iowa City: University of Iowa Press, 1992).

4. William T. Hamilton, *A Sermon on Theatrical Entertainments* (Mobile, AL: n.p., 1841); qtd. in David Grimsted, *Melodrama Unveiled*, 25.

5. For Stephen Greenblatt transitions "out of a narrowly circumscribed social sphere" bring people into close contact with a range of disparate persons and their cir-cumstances, thus situating them to construct and experience themselves differently. See Stephen Greenblatt, *Renaissance Self-Fashioning: From More to Shakespeare* (Chicago: University of Chicago Press, 1980). At this point Cushman was at a transition in her pro-fessional life and was also experiencing the impact of her passion for other women.

6. CC to "Chip" [William Chippendale], 8 August 1842, Harvard Theatre Col-lection (hereafter HTC), Houghton Library, Harvard University, Cambridge, MA.

7. See CC, "Address."

8. Anna Cora Mowatt, *Autobiography of an Actress, or Eight Years on the Stage* (Boston: Ticknor, Reed and Fields, 1854), 152.

9. Mowatt, *Autobiography*, 154.

10. Mowatt, *Autobiography*, 214, 215, 429.

11. See Barbara Welter, "The Cult of True Womanhood," in *The American Fam-ily in Social-Historical Perspective*, ed. Michael Gordon (New York: St. Martin's, 1978), 313–33. Apparently they were successful; as contemporary critic William Winter alleged, "no sympathic mind can contemplate [these lives] without emotion or without improvement" ("Eminent Women of the Drama," *Eminent Women of the Age* [Hart-ford: Betts, 1868], 440). See Tracy C. Davis, *Actresses as Working Women: Their Social Identity in Victorian Culture* (London: Routledge, 1991), 71, on the importance of women's acceptance of actresses.

12. Literary critic Mary Poovey has identified two primary cultural narratives about gender that were predominant in Cushman's era: a "domestic" narrative of nur-turing self-sacrifice and a complementary "military" narrative of heroic individual assertion and will. See Poovey, *Uneven Developments: The Ideological Work of Gender in Mid-Victorian England* (Chicago: University of Chicago, 1988). Poovey explores the embodiment of both of these qualities in narratives about Florence Nightingale; I con-tend that these traits also converged in Charlotte Cushman, whose accounts of her early years contained aspects of both kinds of stories.

13. Martha Vicinus has asserted that the nineteenth-century stage "was one of the few spheres in which women could be involved in the creation of a persona, rather than wait passively to be acted upon" (intro., *A Widening Sphere: Changing Roles of Victorian Women* [Bloomington: Indiana University Press, 1980], xviii–xix).

14. George Vandenhoff, *Leaves from an Actor's Note-book* (New York: Appleton, 1860), 186.

15. Vandenhoff, *Leaves from an Actor's Note-book*, 194.

16. Historian Carroll Smith-Rosenberg contends that as a result of the "rigid gender-role differentiation within the family and within society as a whole . . . a sup-portive female world, a woman's network developed" in mid-nineteenth-century America in which "women routinely formed emotional ties with other women" ("The Female World of Love and Ritual," in Gordon, *American Family*, 339). While Smith-Rosenberg suggests that these relationships were generally accepted, my examination of Cushman's letters reveals both her awareness of the degree to which those women's intimate relationships that appeared to threaten the status quo pro-

voked rejection in some of her contemporaries and Cushman's vigilance to protect herself and her partners.

17. Anne Hampton Brewster, "Miss Cushman," *Blackwood's Edinburgh Magazine* 124 (August 1878): 174.

18. Anne Hampton Brewster, diary II, 18 February 1849, recalling an earlier time. Anne Hampton Brewster Papers (hereafter cited as Brewster Papers), Library Company of Philadelphia, Philadelphia.

19. Brewster, "Miss Cushman."

20. Brewster diary I, 2 June 1847.

21. Nancy F. Cott, "Passionlessness: An Interpretation of Victorian Sexual Ideology, 1790–1850," in *A Heritage of Her Own*, ed. Nancy F. Cott and Elizabeth H. Pleck (New York: Simon, 1979), 73.

22. Brewster diary II, 18 February 1849.

23. Brewster diary I, 2 June 1847; my emphasis.

24. Brewster diary I, 2 June 1847.

25. Brewster diary II, 18 February 1849.

26. Vandenhoff, *Leaves from an Actor's Note-book,* 194.

27. Walter M. Leman, *Memories of an Old Actor* (San Francisco: Roman, 1886), 24, 179–80.

28. Brewster, "Miss Cushman," 171.

29. Brewster, "Miss Cushman," 171–72.

30. Qtd. in William Toynbee, ed., *The Diaries of William Charles Macready* (1912; rpt. New York: Blom, 1969), 2:230.

31. Vandenhoff, *Leaves from an Actor's Note-book,* 221.

32. Vandenhoff, *Leaves from an Actor's Note-book,* 222.

33. Toynbee, *Diaries of William Charles Macready,* 2:235, 239–40.

34. Actress and playwright Anna Cora Mowatt, describing her choice to debut as a public reader in Boston rather than New York, noted that "Boston had been pronounced the most intellectual city of the Union—the American Athens" (*Autobiography,* 141). Macready, among others, referred to Boston in these laudatory terms as well.

35. George T. Ferris, *Appleton's Journal,* 21 March 1874, 356.

36. Toynbee, *Diaries of William Charles Macready,* 2:241.

37. *Spirit of the Times,* 9 December 1843, 492.

38. Toynbee, *Diaries of William Charles Macready,* 2:242.

39. Toynbee, *Diaries of William Charles Macready,* 2:241.

40. Toynbee, *Diaries of William Charles Macready,* 2:243.

41. CC to "Chip" [William Chippendale], 27 December 1843, HTC.

42. Toynbee, *Diaries of William Charles Macready,* 2:243.

43. William Charles Macready to CC, 24 December 1843, CCP, 12:3542.

44. Thomas Colley Grattan to CC [1843], CCP, 11:3351.

45. Thomas Colley Grattan to CC [1843], CCP, 11:3351.

46. Toynbee, *Diaries of William Charles Macready,* 2:305.

47. William Charles Macready to CC, 13 March 1844, CCP, vol. 16.

48. Charlotte Cushman, diary (hereafter CC diary), 11 January 1844, Dramatic Museum Archives, Rare Book and Manuscript Library, Columbia University.

49. CC diary, 12 January 1844.

50. Qtd. in Margaret Armstrong, *Fanny Kemble: A Passionate Victorian* (New York: Macmillan, 1938), 165.

51. Mowatt also claimed that, despite her colleagues' protests and affectations,

"Without some decided attachment for the profession, I cannot conceive how the fatigues, the vexations, the disappointments incident even upon the most successful theatrical career, could be supported" (*Autobiography*, 425–26). It took someone with Mowatt's impeccable social pedigree to challenge public opinion so directly.

52. CC diary, 11 January 1844.

53. Fanny Kemble Butler to CC [27 November 1843], CCP, vol. 9.

54. Butler to CC [n.d.], CCP, vol. 9.

55. Butler to CC [n.d.], CCP, vol. 9. CC noted in her diary on 24 January 1844 that she received a "train" and a note from F. B.

56. CC diary, 5 January 1844.

57. CC diary, 7 January 1844.

58. CC diary, 6 January 1844.

59. CC diary [n.d., 1844].

60. Butler to CC [n.d.], CCP, vol. 9.

61. Butler to CC [n.d.], CCP, vol. 9.

62. Butler to CC [n.d.], CCP, vol. 9.

63. Butler to CC [n.d.], CCP, vol. 9.

64. Butler to CC [n.d.], CCP, vol. 9.

65. Almost two decades later Charlotte Cushman remarked of Fanny Kemble Butler, "What a strange woman she is, and how little to be depended upon" (CC to Emma Crow Cushman, 14 February 1862, CCP, vol. 2). Although Cushman acknowledged, finally, that some of the discomfort between them may have been the result of a misunderstanding, she noted that she had been "indignant with her [Fanny Kemble Butler] for years" (CC to Emma Crow Cushman, 23 January 1862, CCP, vol. 2).

66. Cushman had this concern about meeting more publicly visible women throughout her life. For example, she mentioned her "reverence" and her insecurity when first meeting George Sand and Elizabeth Barrett Browning (CC to Emma Crow Cushman, 3 January 1862, CCP, vol. 2).

67. Born in England in 1783, Thomas Sully was from an acting family who emigrated to the United States. After years of living in the South, Thomas married the widow of his elder brother and moved to New York in 1806, at the encouragement of actor and impresario Thomas Abthorpe Cooper, who wanted Sully to set up his studio at New York's Park Theatre, of which Cooper was then lessee. Within two years the Sullys relocated to Philadelphia, where they were to become an established part of Philadelphia cultural life. See Edward Biddle and Mantle Fielding, *The Life and Works of Thomas Sully* (New York: Kennedy Graphics, 1970).

68. Butler to CC [n.d.], CCP, vol. 9.

69. CC diary, 19 August and 14 September 1844.

70. On 8 May 1844 Macready recorded that he "wrote to Miss C. Cushman, as I had promised Simpson, wishing her to play here during my engagement" (Toynbee, *Diaries of William Charles Macready*, 2:271). On Macready's attitude about Americans, see Toynbee, *Diaries of William Charles Macready*, 2:233; and Joseph Leach, *Bright Particular Star: The Life and Times of Charlotte Cushman* (New Haven: Yale University Press, 1970), 129–30.

71. See Alan S. Downer, *The Eminent Tragedian: William Charles Macready* (Cambridge, MA: Harvard University Press, 1966), 267.

72. In October 1843, when Edwin Forrest was competing with Macready, and American critics frequently compared the two actors' relative merits, Macready commented in his diary that if Forrest had "cultivate[d]" his powers "as in England, his taste could be formed," but, instead, Forrest's "countrymen['s] . . . extravagant applause"

had led Forrest to overestimate his talents. "He is now only an actor for the less intelligent Americans." Macready, much irritated by the reactions of the American press, wrote of Forrest on 28 October, "Let him be an American actor—and a great American actor—but keep on this side of the Atlantic, and no one will gainsay his comparative excellence." In lambasting the "state of semi-civilization here," Macready was revealing the elitism that Cushman and others detected in him (Toynbee, *Diaries of William Charles Macready*, 2:229–31). The rivalry between Forrest and Macready was to erupt in the Astor Place Riot in 1849, the worst riot in terms of injuries and deaths in New York history.

73. Thomas Colley Grattan to CC, 24 December 1842, CCP, 11:3349.

74. Ferris, "Charlotte Cushman," 357.

75. Emma Stebbins, *Charlotte Cushman: Her Letters and Memories of Her Life* (1879; rpt., New York: Blom, 1972), 31.

76. Vandenhoff, *Leaves from an Actor's Note-book*, 197.

77. CC diary, 3 November 1844.

78. CC diary, 3 November 1844.

79. Clara Erskine Clement (Waters), *Charlotte Cushman* (Boston: Osgood, 1882), 33.

80. Stebbins, *Charlotte Cushman*, 37.

81. Stebbins, *Charlotte Cushman*, 37.

82. Joseph Leach, in 1970, claimed that Sallie Mercer "delightedly agreed" to accompany Cushman to England but that Mercer's mother complained "lest she never see her daughter again" (*Bright Particular Star*, 127). Neither his nor Stebbins's sketchy explanations calls into question the assumption that the young African American woman's fate would be determined by her white mistress, rather than by her own family.

83. Thomas Colley Grattan to CC, [1843], CCP, 11:3351.

Chapter 4

1. CC to Mary Eliza Cushman, 18 November 1844, Charlotte Cushman Papers (hereafter CCP), Manuscript Division, Library of Congress, Washington, DC.

2. CC to Mary Eliza Cushman, 2 December 1844, CCP, vol. 1.

3. Benjamin McArthur, *Actors and American Culture, 1880–1920* (Philadelphia: Temple University Press, 1984), 186.

4. George T. Ferris, "Charlotte Cushman," *Appleton's Journal*, 21 March 1874, 357.

5. Joseph Leach, a biographer of Cushman's, assumes this as well (*Bright Particular Star: The Life and Times of Charlotte Cushman* [New Haven: Yale University Press, 1970], 140).

6. George Vandenhoff, *Leaves from an Actor's Note-book* (New York: Appleton, 1860), 198–99. Vandenhoff had first performed with Charlotte Cushman in the Walnut Street Theatre company she had managed in Philadelphia. She had been of service to him then, since he had recently arrived from England, and she provided him with letters of introduction to theatrical contacts in Boston who might help with his career. It is extremely likely that Vandenhoff returned the favor by writing to Maddox and other managers some of the letters that introduced her to English contacts.

7. Peter Brooks, *The Melodramatic Imagination: Balzac, Henry James, Melo-*

drama, and the Mode of Excess (1976; rpt., New Haven: Yale University Press, 1995), 36–37.

8. Dutton Cook, "Charlotte Cushman," *Great Men and Famous Women* (New York: Selman Hess), pt. 66, pp. 355–60, 359.

9. These anecdotes also feature the calculating or capricious behaviors of Maddox. Many reports by contemporary actors of their dealings with Maddox foreground his "Jewishness" and seize upon anti-Semitic explanations for his contrivances in negotiating with actors. Charles Cushman's account of Charlotte's dealings with Maddox is no exception. Like Vandenhoff, who said of Maddox, "the little Hebrew was obdurate as Shylock" (Vandenhoff, *Leaves from an Actor's Note-book,* 198), Charles remembered Maddox as "a shrewd old rascal of the Israelitish persuasion" who initially contracted to pay Charlotte 7 pounds per night for her performances and refused to raise her salary even after her spectacular success (Charles Cushman to Emma [Stebbins], n.d. [1876], CCP, 8:2499–2508). In this first engagement Charlotte accepted his terms, although in later years she enacted her resentment of Maddox in a manner that would become characteristic for her. As her friend George William Bell remembered, Charlotte would imitate Maddox, who spoke with a decided Yiddish accent, "until tears ran down our faces from excess of laughter" (Bell to Charles Cushman, 20 May 1876, CCP, vol. 9).

10. Lawrence Barrett, *Charlotte Cushman* (New York: Dunlap Society, 1889), 20.

11. Qtd. in Clara Erskine Clement (Waters), *Charlotte Cushman* (Boston: Osgood, 1882*)*, 37.

12. Brooks, *Melodramatic Imagination,* 20.

13. Qtd. in Emma Stebbins, *Charlotte Cushman: Her Letters and Memories of Her Life* (1878; rpt., New York: Blom, 1972), 73.

14. Cook, "Charlotte Cushman," 359.

15. Qtd. in Clement (Waters), *Charlotte Cushman,* 38–39.

16. "The Princess Theatre," *English Gentleman* [February 1845], Charlotte Cushman Scrapbook, CCP, vol. 20.

17. "Princess Theatre."

18. [John Forster], *Examiner;* qtd. in James Willis Yeater, "Charlotte Cushman: American Actress" (Ph.D. diss., University of Illinois, 1959), 55.

19. In this gendered, dichotomous marking of mind versus body, we can see what Eve Kosofsky Sedgwick has described as "a structuring force for nodes of thought, for axes of cultural discrimination, whose thematic subject isn't explicitly gendered at all" and yet serves as implicit cultural "allegories of the relations of men and women" (*Epistemology of the Closet* [Berkeley: University of California Press, 1990], 34).

20. Qtd. in Clement (Waters), *Charlotte Cushman,* 37.

21. CC to Mary Eliza Cushman, 2 March 1845, CCP, vol. 1.

22. CC to Mary Eliza Cushman, 2 March 1845, CCP, vol. 1.

23. In chap. 6 I discuss Jewsbury's fictional depiction of Cushman/Bianca in the context of their relationship.

24. Sedgwick, *Epistemology of the Closet,* 2.

25. "Public Amusements: Haymarket," *Dispatch* (London), [January 1855?], CCP, vol. 19.

26. "Public Amusements: Haymarket."

27. "Public Amusements: Haymarket."

28. Westland Marston, *Our Recent Actors: Being Recollections Critical, and in Many Cases Personal, of Late Distinguished Performers of Both Sexes* (London: Low, Marston, Searle, and Rivington, 1890), 232–33.

29. See John Coleman, *Fifty Years of an Actor's Life,* 2 vols. (New York: Pott, 1904), 1:295. Coleman was recounting his memory of Cushman's first performance of Bianca in Edinburgh several months after her London opening.

30. "Haymarket Theatre," *Morning Post* (London), 28 January [1854], CCP, vol. 19; my emphasis.

31. "The Princess Theatre," *Times* (London), 18 February 1845, CC Scrapbook, CCP, vol. 20.

32. [John Forster], "Princess's," *Weekly Examiner* [February 1845], CC Scrapbook, CCP, vol. 20.

33. [Forster], "Princess's."

34. "Princess Theatre," *English Gentleman.*

35. "Princess Theatre," *Times* (London).

36. CC to Mary Eliza Cushman, 28 March 1845, CCP, vol. 1.

37. CC to Susan Cushman, 1 April 1845, CCP, vol. 1.

38. CC to Mary Eliza Cushman, 2 March 1845, CCP, vol. 1.

39. Anna Jameson, *Visits and Sketches at Home and Abroad,* 3 vols. (London: Saunders and Otley, 1835), 3:33–38.

40. Clement (Waters), *Charlotte Cushman,* 173.

41. William Winter, "Players: Past and Present: Great Actress and Great Woman, Charlotte Cushman," *Saturday Evening Post,* 29 September 1906, 10.

42. Winter, "Players," 10.

43. *Times* (London), 22 February 1845.

44. Barrett, *Charlotte Cushman,* 14.

45. Unidentified newspaper clipping, CC Scrapbook, CCP, vol. 20.

46. *Times* (London), 22 February 1845.

47. On Forrest and the class interests he represented for spectators, see Bruce A. McConachie, *Melodramatic Formations: American Theatre and Society, 1820–1870* (Iowa City: University of Iowa Press, 1992).

48. Vandenhoff, *Leaves from an Actor's Note-book,* 196.

49. Qtd. in Richard Lockridge, *Darling of Misfortune: Edwin Booth, 1833–1893* (New York: Century, 1932), 96.

50. Winter, "Players," 10.

51. Qtd. in Coleman, *Fifty Years in an Actor's Life,* 336.

52. William Winter, *Shakespeare on the Stage* (New York: Moffat, Yard, 1911), 480.

53. Mrs. J. H. Hanaford, "Interview with Charlotte Cushman," *Boston Journal,* 24 August 1858, CCP, vol. 19.

54. Emily Faithfull, *Three Visits to America* (Edinburgh: Douglas, 1884), 116.

55. See McArthur, *Actors and American Culture.*

56. George L. Mosse, *Nationalism and Sexuality: Middle-Class Morality and Sexual Norms in Modern Europe* (Madison: University of Wisconsin Press, 1985), 13.

57. Unidentified newspaper clipping [February 1845], CC Scrapbook, CCP, vol. 20.

58. James Murdoch, *The Stage, or, Recollections of Actors and Acting from an Experience of Fifty Years* (1880; rpt., New York: Blom, 1969), 238.

59. Unidentified newspaper clipping, CC Scrapbook, CCP, vol. 20.

60. Murdoch, *Stage,* 239.

61. "Charlotte Cushman," *Chicago Times,* 17 March 1872.

62. Clement (Waters), *Charlotte Cushman,* 174.

63. Henry Augustin Clapp, *Boston Advertiser,* May 1875.

64. [James Oakes], "Letter from 'Acorn': Theatricals in Boston," *Spirit of the Times,* 12 June 1858. Given Oakes's intimate friendship with and loyalty to Edwin Forrest, these particular allegations may have been a form of revenge against Cushman for upstaging Forrest in England.

65. "Letter from 'Acorn.'"

66. "Letter from 'Acorn.'"

67. Winter, "Players," 10.

68. Unidentified clipping [February 1845], CC Scrapbook, CCP, vol. 20.

69. John Ranken Towse, *Sixty Years of the Theatre* (1916); qtd. in Arthur Hornblow, *A History of the Theatre in America from Its Beginnings to the Present Time,* 2 vols. (New York: Lippincott, 1919), 2:129.

70. David Grimstead notes that Shakespeare's "poetic power, his breadth of understanding, his inclusiveness, indeed his lack of concern for classical standards endeared him to Romantic critics" throughout the nineteenth century (*Melodrama Unveiled* [Chicago: University of Chicago Press, 1968], 112).

71. Towse, *Sixty Years of the Theatre,* qtd. in Hornblow, *History of the Theatre,* 2:129.

72. Wisner Payne Kinne, *George Pierce Baker and the American Theatre* (Cambridge, MA: Harvard University Press, 1954), 5.

73. CC to Mary Eliza Cushman, 1 May 1845, CCP, vol. 1.

74. Charles Cushman to Emma [Stebbins], [1876], CCP, 8:2499–2508.

75. Charles Cushman to [Stebbins], [1876], CCP, 8:2499–2508.

76. Marston, *Our Recent Actors,* 239–40.

77. CCP, 11:3467.

78. Qtd. in Clement (Waters), *Charlotte Cushman,* 63–65.

79. Qtd. in Clement (Waters), *Charlotte Cushman,* 62.

80. Qtd. in Clement (Waters), *Charlotte Cushman,* 64.

81. Catherine Mary Reignolds Winslow, *Yesterdays with Actors* (Boston: Cupples and Hurd, 1887), 19–20.

82. William Winter, *Other Days* (New York: Moffat, Yard, 1908); qtd. in Hornblow, *History of the Theatre,* 2:128.

83. Promptbook for Daniel Terry, *Guy Mannering; or the Gypsy Prophecy* (New York: French, 1816). This and all subsequent references to the play itself, unless noted, are to Charlotte Cushman's annotated copy of the promptbook, now known as the James E. Kirkwood Promptbook, Players Club, New York.

84. Qtd. in Stebbins, *Charlotte Cushman,* 149.

85. Mary Anderson de Navarro, *A Few More Memories* (London: Hutchinson, 1936), 268.

86. Leach, *Bright Particular Star,* 160.

87. George Rowell, *Queen Victoria Goes to the Theatre* (London: Elek, 1978), 74. Victoria is commenting on a production of *Guy Mannering* at the Haymarket Theatre, 17 February 1854.

88. "Sallie Mercer, Obituary," n.d., CCP.

89. Stebbins, *Charlotte Cushman,* 151.

90. Stebbins, *Charlotte Cushman,* 150–52.

91. Stebbins, *Charlotte Cushman,* 150.

92. George William Bell to Charles Cushman, 20 May 1876, CCP, vol. 9.

93. Stebbins, *Charlotte Cushman,* 152.

94. CC to Emma Crow Cushman, 26 October 1871, CCP, vol. 5.

95. Joseph Francis Daly, *The Life of Augustin Daly* (New York: Macmillan, 1917), 134.

96. Garff Wilson, *A History of American Acting* (Bloomington: Indiana University Press, 1966), 50–51.

97. de Navarro, *A Few More Memories*, 269.

98. Barrett, *Charlotte Cushman*, 20.

99. "Miss Cushman's Last Appearance in America," *Prompter*, [1850], Harvard Theatre Collection (hereafter HTC), Houghton Library, Harvard University, Cambridge, MA.

100. *Herald* (New York), [1870s], HTC.

101. Unidentified clipping, "Booth's Theatre: King Henry VII" [1871?], HTC; Barbara Welter, "The Culture of True Womanhood," in *The American Family in Social-Historical Perspective*, ed. Michael Gordon (New York: St. Martin's, 1978), 323.

102. Rosalie Sully died on 8 July 1847 in Philadelphia. Correspondence from Geraldine Jewsbury and Henry Chorley in CCP attests to Cushman's physical and emotional state at the time. In a letter to her agent-friend John Povey, Cushman described the "miserable illness" that "shattered" her but did not specify the cause (CC to John Povey, 17 October 1847, Players Club, New York).

103. Henry Chorley to CC, 28 October 1847, CCP, vol. 10.

104. Unidentified newspaper clipping [1870s], CCP, vol. 19.

105. *Daily Advertiser* (Boston), n.d., CCP, vol. 19.

106. Clement (Waters), *Charlotte Cushman*, 170.

107. George William Bell to Charles Cushman, 20 May 1876, CCP, vol. 9.

108. Winter, "Players: Past and Present," 10.

109. *World* (New York), n.d., CCP, vol. 19; my emphasis.

110. Unidentified newspaper clipping, CCP, vol. 19.

111. Sarah Stickney Ellis, *The Daughters of England* (London: n.p., 1845), 73.

112. *Boston Post*, n.d., CCP, vol. 19.

113. "Acorn" [James Oakes], *Spirit of the Times*, n.d., CCP, vol. 19.

114. Clement (Waters), *Charlotte Cushman*, 171.

115. *World* (New York), n.d., CCP, vol. 19.

116. *Daily Advertiser* (Boston) , n.d., CCP, vol. 19.

117. Unidentified newspaper clipping, HTC.

118. Marston, *Our Recent Actors*, 239.

119. Marston, *Our Recent Actors*, 239.

120. Barrett, *Charlotte Cushman*, 21.

121. Barrett, *Charlotte Cushman*, 14.

122. Qtd. in Robert Browning, *Dearest Isa: Robert Browning's Letters to Isa Blagden*, ed. Edward C. McAleer (Austin: University of Texas Press, 1951), 27.

Chapter 5

1. Westland Marston, *Our Recent Actors: Being Recollections Critical and in Many Cases Personal of Late Distinguished Performers of Both Sexes* (London: Low, Marston, Searle, and Rivington, 1890), 238.

2. Garff Wilson, *A History of American Acting* (Bloomington: Indiana University Press, 1966), 143.

3. During her short stint at the Bowery Theatre, immediately after leaving the

Maeders, Cushman acted with Ann Waring Sefton, who included Romeo in her repertoire. And, while Cushman was serving her tenure as "utility actress" at the Park, the leading actress, Mrs. Hamblin Shaw, was popular in male roles as well. In addition to Romeo, Mrs. Shaw played Hamlet opposite Cushman's Gertrude. W. T. Price, an early Cushman biographer, believed that Shaw's success as a breeches actress had much influence on Cushman (*A Life of Charlotte Cushman* [New York: Brentano's, 1894], 124; see also Montrose J. Moses, *Famous Actor Families in America* [1906; rpt., New York: Greenwood, 1968], 215).

4. Numerous theater historians have explored the multiple meanings and erotic valences available to spectators witnessing cross-dressed performers in a variety of different time periods. See, for example, Lesley Ferris, ed., *Crossing the Stage: Controversies on Cross-Dressing* (London: Routledge, 1993); Laurence Senelick, ed., *Gender in Performance* (Hanover, NH: University Press of New England, 1992); Sue-Ellen Case, ed., *Performing Feminisms: Feminist Critical Theory and Theatre* (Baltimore: Johns Hopkins University Press, 1990); and J. S. Bratton, "Irrational Dress," in *The New Woman and Her Sisters: Feminism and Theatre, 1850–1914*, ed. Vivien Gardner and Susan Rutherford (Ann Arbor: University of Michigan Press, 1992). On the potential homoeroticism of male actors playing female characters, see Stephen Orgel, *Impersonations: The Performance of Gender in Shakespeare's England* (Cambridge: Cambridge University Press, 1996).

5. Qtd. in George C. D. Odell, *Annals of the New York Stage*, 4 vols. (New York: Columbia University Press, 1931), 4:147.

6. H. P. Phelps, *Players of a Century* (1880; rpt., New York: Blom, 1972), 205.

7. Our Lady Correspondent, "Theatricals in Boston," *Spirit of the Times*, 12 June 1858.

8. CC to Mary Eliza Cushman, 1 May 1845, Charlotte Cushman Papers (hereafter CCP), vol. 1, Manuscript Division, Library of Congress, Washington, DC.

9. CC to George Combe, 21 November 1845, National Library of Scotland (hereafter NLS), MS 7275, Edinburgh.

10. CC to Mary Howitt, [July 1845], Folger Shakespeare Library, YC 968 (16), Washington, DC.

11. CC to Mary Eliza Cushman, 17 April 1845, CCP, vol. 1.

12. CC to George Combe, 21 November 1845, NLS, MS 7275.

13. Martha Vicinus has discussed the need to "recogniz[e] the power of not naming—of the unsaid," that is, the need to read silences and absences—and I would include denials—as a conceptual tool for lesbian history. See Martha Vicinus, "Lesbian History: All Theory and No Facts or All Facts and No Theory?" *Radical History Review* 60 (1994): 57–75, 1994.

14. George Combe to CC, 11 December 1845, NLS , MS 7390.

15. George Combe to CC, 11 December 1845, NLS, MS 7390.

16. CC to Mrs. [James] Darbishire, [October 1845], Harvard Theatre Collection (hereafter HTC), Houghton Library, Harvard University, Cambridge, MA. Mrs. Darbishire had hosted a large party for Cushman in Manchester after her performances there in September 1845. This entry into Darbishire's esteemed Unitarian social circle helped Charlotte's popularity enormously.

17. Mary Jean Corbett, *Representing Femininity: Middle-Class Subjectivity in Victorian and Edwardian Women's Autobiographies* (New York: Oxford University Press, 1992), 108.

18. *Spirit of the Times* (New York), 1846.

19. Elizabeth M. Puknat, "Romeo Was a Lady: Charlotte Cushman's London Triumph," *Theatre Annual* 9 (1951): 65; and Emma Stebbins, *Charlotte Cushman: Her Letters and Her Memories of Her Life* (1880; rpt., New York: Blom, 1972), 58–59.

20. CC to Benjamin Webster, n.d. [1846], HTC.

21. Charles Cushman to Emma Stebbins, CCP, 10:3144.

22. *Times* (London), 3 January 1846, CC Scrapbook, CCP, vol. 20.

23. *Atlas* (London), 3 January 1846, CC Scrapbook, CCP, vol. 20.

24. *Atlas* (London), 3 January 1846.

25. Marjorie Garber has claimed that the cross-dressed figure serves as "an aesthetic and psychological agent of destabilization, desire and fantasy." See Marjorie Garber, *Vested Interests: Cross-Dressing and Cultural Anxiety* (New York: HarperCollins, 1993), 70–71. While most breeches actresses directed their performances to the erotic responses of male spectators, I contend that Cushman served as an agent of desire and destabilization for many female members of her audience.

26. *Britannia* (London), 3 January 1846, CC Scrapbook, CCP, vol. 20.

27. "J. M. W." [Jessie Meriton White], "First Impressions of Miss Cushman's Romeo," *People's Journal* 2 (18 July 1846): 118.

28. After a visit to the Haymarket Theatre on 22 February 1855, no less a spectator than Queen Victoria would assert that when "Miss Cushman took the part of Romeo . . . no one would ever have imagined her a woman, her figure and voice being so masculine." The British monarch found Charlotte's acting "not pleasing, though clever, and [felt] she entered well into the character, bringing out so forcibly its impetuosity" (George Rowell, *Queen Victoria Goes to the Theatre* [London: Elek, 1978], 74).

29. Stephen Orgel, *Impersonations*, 70, 165 n. 24. Although Orgel is writing of the Elizabethans, his comments on the need to understand specific cultural constructions of gender hold for other historical periods as well.

30. [Henry Chorley], *Athenaeum*, 3 January 1846, 19.

31. However well Charlotte evidently played Romeo, her youth was not the causative factor, as she was still playing the role in 1860, when she was forty-four. See Stebbins, *Charlotte Cushman*, 59–60.

32. N. M. Ludlow, *Dramatic Life as I Found It: A Record of Personal Experience, Etc.* (St. Louis, MO: Jones, 1880), 316.

33. Dutton Cook, *Hours with the Players*, 2 vols. (London: Chatto and Windus, 1881), 2:197.

34. Robert Browning to Elizabeth Barrett, 31 January 1846, *Letters of Robert Browning and Elizabeth Barrett*, 1, 443.

35. *Theatrical Journal* 7 (1846): 380; qtd. in Puknat, "Romeo Was a Lady," 65–66.

36. Qtd. in Cuthbert Bede, "Miss Cushman: A Reminiscence," *Belgravia* 29 (May 1876): 338.

37. John Sheridan Knowles, *Spirit of the Times* (New York), 4 July 1846.

38. Stebbins, *Charlotte Cushman*, 63.

39. Knowles, *Spirit of the Times*, 4 July 1846.

40. *English Gentleman* [1846], CC Scrapbook, CCP, vol. 20.

41. Knowles, *Spirit of the Times*, 4 July 1846. See also George C. D. Odell, *Shakespeare from Betterton to Irving*, 2 vols. (New York: Scribner's, 1920), 2:272.

42. CC to [Benjamin Webster], 3 January [1846], Folger Shakespeare Library, YC 968.

43. *Era* (London), 3 January 1846, CC Scrapbook, CCP, vol. 20.

44. Walter Herries Pollock, "A Forgotten Romeo," *Saturday Review*, n.d., CC

Scrapbook, Robinson Locke Scrapbook Collection, New York Public Library for the Performing Arts, Lincoln Center.

45. This illustration is, unfortunately, undated. Although it is impossible to know whether the discrepancies between the drawings are a result of the artist's rendering or of different performances, both actresses appear to be wearing simpler costumes.

46. John Coleman, *Fifty Years of an Actor's Life*, 2 vols. (New York: Pott, 1904), 361–63.

47. Emma Crow Cushman, "Charlotte Cushman: A Memory" (unpublished memoir, 1918), CCP, 15:4019–36.

48. Judith Butler, *Gender Trouble* (New York: Routledge, 1990) 140, 137. See also Judith Butler, *Bodies That Matter* (New York: Routledge, 1993). According to Butler, the social performances that constitute gender are stylized repetitive acts that are performed under duress, but the genesis of these "punitively regulated cultural fictions" is generally concealed, thereby contributing to the impression of their "necessity and naturalness." See Judith Butler, "Performative Acts and Gender Constitution," in *Performing Feminisms: Feminist Critical Theory and Theatre*, ed. Sue-Ellen Case (Baltimore: Johns Hopkins University Press, 1990), 273. I contend that those critics who responded negatively to Cushman may well have been threatened—albeit unconsciously—by her exposure of conventional gender behavior as merely an "act," a set of attributes that were "performed" rather than innate.

49. *Britannia* (London), 3 January 1846, CC Scrapbook, CCP, vol. 20; my emphasis.

50. *Britannia* (London), 3 January 1846. Invoking Sappho called up a range of associations in the mid-nineteenth century. For many readers the intense love between women that Sappho's poetry celebrated was romantic, rather than sexual, hence this critic's contention that two women lovers would not "suggest . . . a thought of vice," while passionate opposite-sex lovers would offend contemporary audiences. The majority of English and German classicists of the time publicly claimed that Sappho's relationships with women had been "innocent" or that her professed love for the male youth Phaon surpassed her love for women; in this version, that her love for Phaon was unrequited led to her suicide. See Peter Gay, *The Tender Passion: The Bourgeois Experience, Victoria to Freud* (Oxford: Oxford University Press, 1986), 238. Yet, as Emma Donoghue has clearly established, the terms *Sapphist* and *Sapphic* had appeared in various seventeenth- and eighteenth-century sources to refer to explicitly sexual passion between women, often with overtones of decadence, long before the *Oxford English Dictionary* records the terms' usage. See Emma Donoghue, *Passions between Women: British Lesbian Culture 1668–1801* (London: Scarlet, 1993), 3–4, 253–63. Furthermore, an article about Sappho in an 1867 issue of the London-based *Queen* asserts that "the principal theme of her [Sappho's] songs was a passionate love for her lady friends" and claims that the Sappho who committed suicide because of Phaon's neglect was a different woman of the same name. See "Gallery of Celebrated Women: Sappho," *Queen*, 17 August 1867, 129. That the nature and intensity of Sappho's love and her objects of desire were debated in the nineteenth century allows for a historical reading of the *Britannia* review that suggests that while the general public may not have recognized an allusion to Sappho as a reference to sexual love between women, for spectators familiar with the classical story such a recognition *was* possible.

51. *Britannia* (London), 3 January 1846.

52. Coleman, *Fifty Years of an Actor's Life*, 363.

53. *Era* (London), 3 January 1846, CC Scrapbook, CCP, vol. 20.

54. Mary Howitt, "The Miss Cushmans," *People's Journal* 2 (18 July 1846): 30. Howitt's article served as the public narrative of Cushman's respectability, which George Combe had belabored Cushman to provide. In chap. 6, I explore how instrumental Howitt's friendship was for Cushman.

55. George T. Ferris, "Charlotte Cushman," *Appleton's Journal,* 21 March 1874, 357.

56. As Mary Poovey notes, "signification is not a singular process; signifying practices always produce meanings in excess of what seems to be the text's explicit design" (*Uneven Developments: The Ideological Work of Gender in Mid-Victorian England* [Chicago: University of Chicago Press, 1988], 16). On the process of decoding and the various positions spectators can occupy in decoding a performance or text, see Stuart Hall, "Encoding/Decoding," in *Culture, Media, Language,* ed. Stuart Hall, Dorothy Hobson, Andrew Lowe, and Paul Wills (London: Unwin, 1980), 128–38.

57. George Vandenhoff, *Leaves from an Actor's Note-book* (New York: Appleton, 1860), 217.

58. Vandenhoff, *Leaves from an Actor's Notebook,* 217–18.

59. Qtd. in Leach, *Bright Particular Star,* 241; Clara Eskine Clement (Waters), *Charlotte Cushman* (Boston: Osgood, 1882), 68.

60. "Amusements," *New York Times,* 16 November 1860.

61. "Amusements."

62. Martha Le Baron to CC, Friday, 17 May [n.d.], CCP, vol. 16.

63. CC to Charles Cushman, 21 May 1861, CCP, vol. 16.

64. Martha Le Baron to CC, n.d., CCP, vol. 16.

65. Jill Dolan has explored ways in which lesbian spectators read and resist dominant cultural meanings about gender in the representations they witness. While Dolan investigates contemporary performance and spectatorial practices and communities, her insights on spectators' interpretations of representations have bearing on responses Cushman received as Romeo, a point I explore further in subsequent chapters. See Jill Dolan, *The Feminist Spectator as Critic* (Ann Arbor: University of Michigan Press, 1991); and *Presence and Desire: Essays on Gender, Sexuality, Performance* (Ann Arbor: University of Michigan Press, 1993).

66. CC to [Emma Crow], 27 April 1858, CCP, vol. 1. I discuss Emma Crow's relationship with Charlotte Cushman in more detail in chap. 8.

67. CC to [Emma Crow], 15 November 1860, CCP, vol. 1.

68. Kate Field to Emma Crow, 20 May 1860, CCP, vol. 11.

69. "J. M. W." [Jessie Meriton White], "First Impressions of Miss Cushman's Romeo," *People's Journal,* 118.

70. Alan S. Downer, *The Eminent Tragedian William Charles Macready* (Cambridge, MA: Harvard University Press, 1966), 141.

71. Unidentified clipping, "Haymarket Theatre" [1846], CCP, vol. 19.

72. CC to Benjamin Webster, 21 March [1846], HTC.

73. Stebbins, *Charlotte Cushman,* 217.

74. For the stage history of female Hamlets, see Jill Edmonds, "Princess Hamlet," in Gardner and Rutherford, *New Woman and Her Sisters,* 59–75.

75. Edwin Booth to Richard F. Cary, 4 December 1860, Edwina Booth Grossmann, *Edwin Booth: Recollections by His Daughter* (1894; rpt., Freeport, NY: Books for Libraries, 1970), 133–34.

76. CC to Mary Devlin Booth [1861], Players Club, New York. This often

repeated story is cited in, among other sources, Lawrence Barrett, *Charlotte Cushman* (New York: Dunlap Society, 1889), 21.

77. CC to Emma Crow, Philadelphia, 29 January 1861, CCP, vol. 1.

78. "Amusements," unidentified clipping, 16 February [1861], CCP, vol. 19.

79. Qtd. in [Lester] Bangs, *New York Clipper,* 7 September 1876, CC Clipping File, HTC.

80. "Amusements."

81. Harriet Hosmer to Cornelia Crow [n.d.], Harriet Goodhue Hosmer Collection, folder 111, Schlesinger Library, Radcliffe College, Cambridge, MA.

82. Laurence Hutton, *Curiosities of the American Stage* (New York: Harper and Bros., 1891), 302.

83. Barrett, *Charlotte Cushman,* 21.

84. Qtd. in *Philadelphia Bulletin,* 24 May 1898, CC Clipping File, HTC.

85. CC to "Fred" [William Fredericks], 25 September [1851], HTC.

86. Unidentified clipping, "Dramatic: Miss Cushman as 'Cardinal Wolsey,'" CCP, vol. 19.

87. "Dramatic: Miss Cushman as 'Cardinal Wolsey.'"

88. "Dramatic: Miss Cushman as 'Cardinal Wolsey.'"

89. Barrett, *Charlotte Cushman,* 20–21.

90. Unidentified clipping, "Charlotte Cushman as Wolsey," CCP, vol. 19.

91. "Dramatic: Miss Cushman as 'Cardinal Wolsey.'"

92. Unidentified clipping, "Before the Curtain: Dramatic: The Walnut—'Cardinal Wolsey'" CCP, vol. 19.

93. "Before the Curtain: Dramatic: The Walnut—'Cardinal Wolsey.'"

94. "Before the Curtain: Dramatic: The Walnut—'Cardinal Wolsey.'"

95. Sidonie Smith, *Subjectivity, Identity, and the Body: Women's Autobiographical Practices in the Twentieth Century* (Bloomington: Indiana University Press, 1993), 130.

96. Qtd. in Smith, *Subjectivity,* 23.

97. Marjorie Garber, *Vested Interests,* 161. While Garber is not discussing Cushman, the danger and the anxiety that, as Garber notes, exist along with the erotics of "boundary crossing" were certainly operative for Cushman and those spectators who could decode her.

98. Tracy C. Davis, *Actresses as Working Women: Their Social Identity in Victorian Culture* (London: Routledge, 1991), 107. Although Davis neither examines Cushman's performances, nor the particular points of reference or readings that might be shared by lesbian spectators, her notions that "sexuality exerts a strong influence on interpretation" and that some "encodings were intended to be perceived by only a limited portion of the audience attuned to the covert meanings and prone to enjoy sexuality" are undoubtably as applicable to female spectators who experienced desire for other women as for heterosexual spectators.

99. Sallie Bridges to CC, October 1863, CCP, vol. 9.

Chapter 6

1. Norma Clarke, *Ambitious Heights: Writing, Friendship, Love, the Jewsbury Sisters, Felicia Hemans and Jane Carlyle* (London: Routledge, 1990), 21.

2. Nathaniel Hawthorne complained to George Ticknor in 1855 that "America is now wholly given over to a d[amne]d mob of scribbling women, and I should have no

chance of success while the public taste is occupied with their trash" (qtd. in James Mellow, *Nathaniel Hawthorne in His Times* [New York: Houghton Mifflin, 1980], 457). Hawthorne used this phrase on other occasions as well.

3. Qtd. in Patricia Thomson, *George Sand and the Victorians: Her Influence and Reputation in Nineteenth-Century England* (New York: Columbia University Press, 1977), 24.

4. Carl Ray Woodring, *Victorian Samplers: William and Mary Howitt* (Lawrence: University of Kansas Press, 1952), 104.

5. Mary Howitt to CC [n.d. 1845], Charlotte Cushman Papers (hereafter CCP), 11:3393, Manuscript Division, Library of Congress, Washington, DC.

6. CC to Mary Howitt, 17 September [1845], CCP, 16:15,019.

7. CC to Mary Eliza Cushman, 28 March 1845, CCP, vol. 1.

8. Although the term *feminist* was not in use until the 1890s, the advocacy for recognition of women as a class that experiences oppression and for increased social, political, and economic opportunities for women that it marks aptly describes many women of the Victorian period. Anna Jameson (1794–1860) had been enamored of Fanny Kemble for years. In Jameson's later life the emotional center of her life was Ottilie von Goethe. Her marriage to Robert Jameson in 1825 was, by all accounts, disastrous. The Jamesons only lived together for a few years before an acrimonious formal separation, and Anna was forced to support herself through her writing. Anna and Charlotte remained friends until Anna's death in 1860. See Clara Thomas, *Love and Work Enough: The Life of Anna Jameson* (Toronto: University of Toronto Press, 1967).

9. CC to Anna Jameson [1845], Harvard Theatre Collection (hereafter HTC), Houghton Library, Harvard University, Cambridge, MA.

10. Mary Howitt, "The Miss Cushmans," *People's Journal* 2 (18 July 1846): 30.

11. CC to Mary Eliza Cushman, 28 March 1845, CCP, vol. 1.

12. Charles Cushman to Emma Stebbins [n.d.; after 1876], CCP, 10:3144.

13. *News* [New York], CC Scrapbook, CCP, vol. 19.

14. Eliza Cook, "To Charlotte Cushman, on Seeing Her Play 'Bianca' in Milman's Tragedy of 'Fazio,'" *Poems by Eliza Cook*, 5th ed., 3 vols. (London: Simkin, Marshall, 1848), 3:78–79.

15. Eliza Cook, pen and ink drawing, CCP, 10:2970.

16. Cook, "Stanzas, Addressed to Charlotte Cushman," *Poems by Eliza Cook*, 3:12–17.

17. Charles Cushman to Emma [Stebbins], [n.d.; after 1876], CCP, 8:2499–2508.

18. Charlotte chastised her mother that "the spirit in which" Mary Eliza mentioned Rosalie Sully and Lizzie Gardette (another American woman who had been attached to Charlotte) "is most painful to me" (CC to Mary Eliza Cushman, 2 March 1845, CCP, vol. 1). Mary Eliza Cushman's disapproval of Charlotte's subsequent relationships with other women is evidenced in numerous other letters between them.

19. Eliza Cook, *Lays of a Wild Harp: A Collection of Metrical Pieces* (London: n.p., 1835); Eliza Cook, *Melaia and Other Poems* (London: n.p., 1838).

20. *Notable Women of Our Own Times* (London: Ward, Lock, n.d. [1882]), 138–49.

21. *Notable Women*, 143, 144.

22. Qtd. in *Notable Women*, 149.

23. "Limnings of Literary People," *New York Daily Times*, 30 September 1851. The charge that Cook appeared "half Bloomerish" was an allusion to the growing women's rights movement, many of whose leaders championed dress reform and advocated

women's adoption of a short dress and pantaloons. This outfit, which was called a "Bloomer" costume, was identified with Amelia Bloomer, editor of the American women's periodical the *Lily*, who championed the Bloomer outfit in the pages of her paper. I have no indication that Cook ever wore a Bloomer outfit; however, her masculine appearance and clothing were commented on by others as well.

24. Charles Cushman to Emma [Stebbins], [n.d.; after 1876], CCP, 8:2499–2508.

25. CC to Harry Langley, 3 July 1845, Chicago Historical Society; transcription in the Papers of Jennie Lorenz (hereafter Lorenz Papers), Manuscript Division, Library of Congress.

26. *News* [New York], [n.d.], CC Scrapbook, CCP, vol. 19.

27. CC to Mrs. Sarah J. Hale, 22 September 18[50], typescript in Lyman Beecher Stowe Collection, folder 429, Schlesinger Library, Radcliffe College, Cambridge, MA. Hale's book was published as *Women's Record* (New York: Harper and Brothers, 1855).

28. Mary Howitt, *An Autobiography*, ed. Margaret Howitt, 2 vols. (Boston: Houghton Mifflin, 1889), 2:37. Howitt's mother's remarks were, in all likelihood, directed at Cushman and Anna Cora Mowatt, both of whom the Howitts befriended. This objection, that actors are duplicitous and will become that which they pretend to be, is one of the tenets of the antitheatrical prejudice. See Jonas Barish, *The Antitheatrical Prejudice* (Berkeley: University of California Press, 1981). Howitt attempted to forestall such assumptions by claiming that Cushman's acting was not imitative; it was natural "action." See also chap. 5.

29. Howitt, *Autobiography*, 2:37.

30. CC to Susan Cushman, 1 April 1845, CCP, vol. 1; CC diary, 10 May 1845, Dramatic Museum Archives, Rare Book and Manuscript Library, Columbia University, New York.

31. Cook, "Stanzas," *Poems by Eliza Cook*, 14.

32. Charlotte Cushman's unpublished letters to Sarah Anderton frequently have no salutation or use endearments like "my pet" or "Dearest," and I have only been able to identify them by their content. Shortly after advising the eighteen-year-old in Sheffield to consider a stage career, Charlotte wrote about securing costumes for her and informed her correspondent that they were being made in the name of "Sarah Anderton," implying that Sarah had chosen not to use her birth name on the stage. Anderton and Cushman maintained a lifelong friendship. After acting for ten years, Anderton retired to marry Geraldine Jewsbury's friend Stavros Dilberoglue, to whom Charlotte had introduced her. Throughout her career and until her marriage Sarah was known to her friends as Sarah Anderton. After tracing her marriage certificate, however, I have established her birth name to have been Sarah Coxon.

33. CC to "Dearest" [Sarah Anderton], 9 December 1845, CCP, vol. 1.

34. CC to [Sarah Anderton], 21 November [1845], CCP, 7:2299.

35. CC to [Sarah Anderton], 30 November [1845], CCP, vol 7.

36. CC to "Dearest" [Sarah Anderton], 9 December 1845, CCP, vol. 1.

37. CC to "Dearest" [Sarah Anderton], 9 December 1845, CCP, vol. 1.

38. CC to "My Sweet Friend" [Sarah Anderton], 9 November [1845], CCP, 7:2287–91.

39. CC to "Dearest" [Sarah Anderton], 9 December 1845, CCP, vol. 1.

40. CC to [Sarah Anderton], 30 November [1845], CCP, vol. 7. Once again Charlotte Cushman seized upon the discourse of "true womanhood" to advocate for her progressive and nontraditional partner, Eliza Cook, as the "truest" of women.

41. CC to "My dear little pet" [Sarah Anderton], [December 1845], CCP, 7:2247.

42. Jane Carlyle to Jeannie Welsh, 19 January 1846, in *Jane Welsh Carlyle: Letters to Her Family*, ed. Leonard Huxley (London: John Murrary, 1924), 261. Elizabeth ("Betsy") Newton Paulet, of Seaforth, Liverpool, became close friends with both Geraldine Jewsbury and Jane Carlyle; all three women corresponded and provided suggestions about Geraldine Jewsbury's first novel, *Zoe*.

43. Geraldine Jewsbury to CC, postmarked 4 April 1846, CCP, 11:3458. Writing in 1935, Susanne Howe claimed that Geraldine Jewsbury's "friendships with women were never 'morbid,'" a term the sexologists then used to refer to lesbianism. (*Geraldine Jewsbury: Her Life and Her Errors* [London: Allen and Unwin, 1935]). However physical Geraldine Jewsbury and Jane Carlyle's relationship may or may not have been, it was so emotionally intense that Jane implored Geraldine to destroy all Jane's letters to her, a promise Geraldine carried out on her deathbed. Annie Ireland, a witness to this act of self-censoring of the material evidence of Geraldine and Jane's intimacy, described it as an act of loyalty. Ireland noted that Geraldine and Jane "could weep together, quarrel like lovers, [and] make peace like lovers . . . [W]hat a woman is to a woman, only a woman knows" (*Selections from the Letters of Geraldine Endsor Jewsbury to Jane Welsh Carlyle*, ed. Annie Ireland [London: Longmans, 1892], xiv).

44. Geraldine Jewsbury to CC, postmarked 4 April 1846, CCP, 11:3458.

45. Geraldine Jewsbury to CC [n.d.], CCP, 11:3449; Eliza Cook to [?], 26 November 1846, Pierpont Morgan Library, New York.

46. Geraldine Jewsbury to CC [n.d.], CCP, 11:3455.

47. Norma Clarke describes Charlotte Cushman's influence on Jewsbury as "an artistically enabling one," claiming that it "form[ed] the basis of Geraldine's portrait of Bianca—one of Cushman's most famous roles—in the *Half Sisters*" (*Ambitious Heights*, 178). In the *Half Sisters* Bianca also discusses playing the roles of Mrs. Haller, Queen Katharine, and "if [she] were a man" Hamlet, all roles Cushman played.

48. Geraldine Endsor Jewsbury, *The Half Sisters: A Tale*, 2 vols. (London: Chapman and Hall, 1848), 1:49.

49. Jewsbury, *Half Sisters*, 1:44.

50. Jewsbury, *Half Sisters*, 1:245–46.

51. Jewsbury, *Half Sisters*, 1:206.

52. Jewsbury, *Half Sisters*, 2:7.

53. Jewsbury, *Half Sisters*, 2:22.

54. Jewsbury, *Half Sisters*, 2:23.

55. Jewsbury, *Half Sisters*, 2:24.

56. Jewsbury, *Half Sisters*, 2:28, 29, 83.

57. For example, writing to her friend Eliza Fox about an upcoming visit she and Charlotte Cushman were planning, Eliza Cook reminded Fox: "When you have me with my American Ally please let it be when her sister is uninvited. I will explain when I see you" (Cook to Fox, 7 December 1847, Gay-Otis Family Papers [hereafter G-O Papers], Rare Book and Manuscript Library, Columbia University, New York).

58. Geraldine Jewsbury to CC [n.d.], CCP, vol. 11.

59. Rosalie Sully to CC, 11 May 1845, CCP, 14:3970.

60. Geraldine Jewsbury to CC [n.d.], CCP, 11:3455.

61. Cook, "Stanzas," *Poems by Eliza Cook*, 14–15.

62. [Charles Cushman] to Emma [Stebbins], [n.d.], CCP, 8:2499–2508.

63. [Charles Cushman] to Emma [Stebbins], [n.d.], CCP, 8:2499–2508.

64. Charles Cushman to Emma Stebbins [n.d.; after 1876], CCP, 10:3144. A self-professed "Literary Lady," or " L.L.," as George Eliot derisively referred to her, Lynn wrote articles and short stories for popular journals, like *Ainsworth's,* and in 1846 published her first book, *Azeth, the Egyptian,* a historical novel she had been researching assiduously at the British Museum. In the 1850s she became the first woman hired as a staff writer for a mainstream periodical (*The George Eliot Letters,* ed. Gordon Haight, 8 vols. [New Haven: Yale University Press, 1954], 2:11).

65. Nancy Fix Anderson, *Woman against Women in Victorian England: A Life of Eliza Lynn Linton* (Bloomington: Indiana University Press, 1987), 39.

66. CC, diary, 9 February, 10 March, 2, 4 April [1845], Dramatic Museum Archives (hereafter DMA), Rare Book and Manuscript Library, Columbia University.

67. Eliza Lynn Linton, *My Literary Life* (London: Hodder and Stoughton, 1899), 17. Eliza Lynn Linton, writing a half-century later, misspells several of the names of members of this circle as *Matilda Hayes, Edward Larkin,* and *Mrs. Brazier.* "Mrs. Brazier" is almost certainly Matilda Hays's close friend, Mrs. Braysher, mentioned in Cushman's correspondence. Mrs. Braysher was also a friend of Helen Faucit and William Charles Macready, who also knew Matilda Hays at this period. Matilda Betham-Edwards identifies Ellen Braysher as the "lifelong friend" of writer and Egyptologist Amelia Edwards; the two women are buried together (*Friendly Faces* [1919; rpt., Freeport, NY: Books for Libraries Press, 1969], 69).

68. Charles Cushman to Emma Stebbins [n.d.; after 1876], CCP, 8:2499–2508.

69. Linton, *My Literary Life,* 31.

70. Qtd. in Anderson, *Woman against Women,* 42.

71. *Mercury* [Liverpool], 18 January 1847.

72. *Letters of Geraldine Endsor Jewsbury to Jane Welsh Carlyle,* 347.

73. Jane Carlyle to CC, 31 January [1862], CCP, vol. 16. After years of tension between them Cushman and Jane Carlyle met at the home of mutual friend, Sarah Anderton Dilberoglue. They became close immediately, as their extremely passionate letters attest. Carlyle opens this letter: "My Dear! I want to put my arms round your neck, and give you—oh! Such a good kiss!"

74. CC to Eliza Meteyard, 21 September [1848], CCP, 16:12,391.

75. Joseph Leach claims that Cushman and Hays first met in 1848, when Hays came to Cushman for acting lessons (*Bright Particular Star: The Life and Times of Charlotte Cushman* [New Haven: Yale University Press, 1970], 207). Given how many close friends they had in common before this time (see n. 65), I am certain they were acquainted earlier. I have in my possession a copy of Eliza Cook's *Poems* inscribed by Eliza to Matilda Hays.

76. Matilda Hays, *Helen Stanley* (London: Churton, 1846).

77. Hays, *Helen Stanley,* 41.

78. Edmund Roberts Larken (1810–95) was later to be instrumental in helping to fund another progressive literary venture that grew out of this circle, George Henry Lewes's and Thornton Hunt's journal, the *Leader.*

79. Theodosia, Dowager Lady Monson (1803–91) was an ardent feminist, like Matilda Hays. Born Theodosia Blacker, she married Frederick John, fifth Baron Monson of Burton (1809–41), on 21 June 1832 but lived with him for less than a week. Lady Monson was also a close friend of Anna Jameson, who similarly identified herself as an advocate for women, and separated from her husband after a brief married life (*The George Eliot Letters,* ed. Gordon Haight, 8 vols. [New Haven: Yale University Press, 1954], 2:82–83).

80. Mary Poovey has observed, "Because literary texts mobilize fantasies without legislating action, they provide a site at which shared anxieties and tensions can surface as well as be symbolically addressed." See Mary Poovey, *Uneven Developments: The Ideological Work of Gender in Mid-Victorian England* (Chicago: University of Chicago Press, 1988), 124. In her chapter "David Copperfield and the Professional Writer" Poovey discusses how the nineteenth-century subject was constructed by the cultural discourse of contemporary literature.

81. According to Patricia Thomson, Thomas Carlyle used the phrase "to convey all he attributed to the novelist—tolerance of immorality, romantic effusiveness, lack of common sense, high flown sentiments, concentration on love" (*George Sand and the Victorians: Her Influence and Reputation in Nineteenth Century England* [New York: Columbia University Press, 1977], 28–29).

82. *Quarterly Review* 81 (September 1849): 533; qtd. in Thomson, *George Sand*, 24.

83. See *Correspondence de Sand*, T. VII, 3575bis D, a Giuseppe Mazzini, 16 January 1847, 603–5.

84. Eliza Ashurst to Eliza Neall Gay, 31 July 1848, G-O Papers.

85. *English Gentlemen*, n.p., n.d., CC Scrapbook, CCP, vol. 20.

86. Matilda Mary Hays, "Memorial of Matilda M. Hays," Application as Candidate for a Civil List Pension from the Govermental Literary Fund, February 1865, Parliamentary Papers, 944/66, Public Records Office, London.

87. Mary Howitt to Sarah Hale, 1 October 1847, Huntington Library, HM 7199, San Marino, CA.

88. CC to Eliza Meteyard, 19 July 1848, Stead Collection, New York Public Library.

89. Hays, "Memorial."

90. Hays, "Memorial." Like Cushman, Matilda Hays had an elderly father who not only could no longer provide for her, but was increasingly dependent upon his daughter's support. When John Hays died in 1862, he was ninety-seven years old.

91. CC to Emma Crow Cushman, 15 January 1864, CCP, vol. 2.

92. Hays, "Memorial"; *Theatrical Times* 3 (October 1848): 411–12; and 4 (January 1849), 23.

93. Matilda Hays eventually was part of the group of women who formed the *English Woman's Journal* in 1857; they often referred to one another by male nicknames; see Jane Rendall, "'A Moral Engine'? Feminism, Liberalism and the *English Woman's Journal*," in *Equal or Different: Women's Politics, 1800–1914*, ed. Jane Rendall (London: Blackwell, 1987). I am indebted to Jane Rendall for her discovery of all the male nicknames used by members of this group and for her generosity in sharing her research notes. Denise Quirk's recent work on this group has informed my thinking about Hays ("The 'Working Woman' of Langham Place: At the Crossroads of Desire, Work, and Domesticity" and "The 'Empire of Public Opinion': The Women's and Feminist Press in Imperial Britain," MSS, 1997).

94. Qtd. in Robert Browning, *Dearest Isa: Robert Browning's Letters to Isabella Blagden*, ed. Edward C. McAleer (Austin: University of Texas Press, 1951), 27.

95. Cook, "Dedication: To Charlotte Cushman," *Poems by Eliza Cook*, 1:iv.

96. CC to "My Dear Child" [Sarah Anderton], [19 December 1848], CCP, 7:2314.

97. CC to "My Wee One" [Sarah Anderton], 26 January [1849], CCP, 7:2219. This performance was reviewed in *Theatrical Times* 4 (January 1849).

98. Hays, "Memorial."

99. "Miss Cushman" [1849], transcription from the scrapbook of Mrs. Persewan, Lorenz Papers.

100. Eliza Ashurst Barouneau-Narcy to Elizabeth Neall Gay, 30 August 1849, G-O Papers.

101. Barouneau-Narcy to Gay, 24 August 1850, G-O Papers.

102. *Promiscuous* was a term frequently used in the Victorian era to refer to encounters in which men and women were in each other's company under circumstances not deemed socially appropriate. Although *promiscuous* did not refer to a specifically sexual encounter, the term invokes the *presumptive possibility* of sex in any heterosexual grouping. Obviously, all theatrical audiences are potentially "promiscuous" in these terms.

103. CC to William Henry Chippendale, 20 September 1849, HTC.

104. George G. Foster, *New York by Gas-Light and Other Urban Sketches,* ed. and intro. Stuart M. Blumin (1850; rpt., Berkeley: University of California Press, 1990), 150–53.

105. Anne Hampton Brewster, diary II, 18 November 1849, Anne Hampton Brewster Papers (hereafter Brewster Papers), Library Company of Philadelphia, Philadelphia.

106. CC to "Fred" [William Fredericks], 8 November 1850, MS letter in extra-illustrated copy of Clara Erskine Clement (Waters), *Charlotte Cushman* (Boston: Osgood, 1882), HTC.

107. Brewster, diary II, 6 November 1849, Brewster Papers.

108. Brewster, diary II, 31 October 1849, Brewster Papers.

109. Brewster, diary II, 18 February 1849, Brewster Papers.

110. Brewster, diary II, 6 November 1849, Brewster Papers.

111. Brewster, diary II, 27 November 1849, Brewster Papers.

112. Eliza Cook, "Our Rambles by the Dove: Addressed to C.C. in America," *Eliza Cook's Journal* 2, no. 39 (January 1850): 208.

113. Hays, "Memorial."

114. Matilda Hays, trans., *Fadette: A Domestic Story from the French,* by George Sand (New York: Putnam, 1851).

115. "Miss Charlotte Cushman's Last Appearance in America," *Prompter* [1850], HTC.

116. Elizabeth Ashurst to Elizabeth Neall Gay, 24 August 1850, G-O Papers. Joseph Leach incorrectly attributes Charlotte's abrupt departure to the sudden illness of her niece Ida (*Bright Particular Star,* 231). Although Ida did die at a young age, clearly Charlotte interrupted her American tour to be with Eliza Cook, who was closer "family" to her than her niece.

117. Charles Cushman to Emma [Stebbins], [after 1876], CCP, 8:2499–2508. Eliza Cook died in 1889. According to her obituary, "in her will she expressed her earnest wish that no information should be given to anyone for the purpose of compiling memoirs of her life" (*Women's Penny Paper* 2:122, 4 January 1890). I read Cook's hypervigilance to withhold all details of her personal life as evidence of the silences and absences that constitute much of lesbian history.

118. Unidentified clipping, 1 August 1851, transcription from Detroit Public Library, Lorenz Papers.

119. Nina Auerbach, *Communities of Women: An Idea of Fiction* (Cambridge, MA: Harvard University Press, 1978), 8–9.

120. Bessie Rayner Parkes Belloc, *A Passing World* (London: Ward and Downey,

1897), 40. I have seen no substantive evidence to support claims made by Leach that Charlotte's degree of emotional attachment to Clarke called into question her choice of women as life partners. The sources Leach cites appear to be from a period when women's decisions to lead female-centered lives were usually explained as reactions to failed heterosexual romances (*Bright Particular Star,* 234–36).

121. Harriet Hosmer to Cornelia Crow [n.d.] Harriet Goodhue Hosmer Collection (hereafter HGH), folder 111, Schlesinger Library, Radcliffe College. Occasionally, Hatty spelled her nickname "Hattie," as Charlotte did. For the sake of consistency I refer to her as "Hatty" throughout.

122. HH to Cornelia Crow [n.d.], HGH, folder 111.

123. Grace Greenwood was the pen name of Sara Jane Clarke (Lippincott). A prolific writer, she used her pen name in private correspondence as well, and close friends like Cushman referred to her as Grace.

124. CC to Mr. Schwab, n.d., DMA. Charlotte used this term to describe her group of friends in Rome to numerous correspondents.

125. HH to Cornelia Crow [n.d.], HGH, folder 111.

126. Ned [Charles Edwin] Cushman to CC, 14 January 1852, CCP, 10:3149.

127. CC to Grace Greenwood, 9 July 1852, DMA.

128. CC to [Sarah Anderton], 20 February [1846?], CCP, 7:2223.

Chapter 7

1. Harriet Hosmer to Cornelia Crow, 7 December [1852], Harriet Goodhue Hosmer Collection (hereafter HGH), Schlesinger Library, Radcliffe College, Cambridge, MA. Also traveling with them was a Mrs. Bayne; Miss Smith may have been Anne (Nannie) Leigh Smith, the sister of Barbara Leigh Smith, who was to found the *English Woman's Journal* with Bessie Rayner Parkes and Matilda Hays in 1857.

2. Henry James, *William Wetmore Story and His Friends: From Letters, Diaries and Recollections,* 2 vols. (London: Thames and Hudson, 1903), 1:254.

3. Emma Stebbins, *Charlotte Cushman: Her Letters and Memories of Her Life* (1879; rpt., New York: Blom, 1972), 176. "Mrs. Grundy" was an icon for the watchful eye of bourgeois social respectability.

4. HH to Cornelia Crow, 7 December [1852], HGH.

5. Dolly Sherwood, *Harriet Hosmer: American Sculptor, 1830–1908* (Columbia: University of Missouri Press, 1991), 66.

6. Gertrude Reece Hudson, *Browning to His American Friends* (New York: Barnes and Noble, 1965), 271.

7. HH to Cornelia Crow [1852], HGH, reel 4, folder 111.

8. Grace Greenwood, "Harriet Hosmer and Charlotte Cushman," *Chicagoan* [n.d., but after 1858], Charlotte Cushman Papers (hereafter CCP), vol. 19, Manuscript Division, Library of Congress, Washington, DC. This article is a response to the article about Harriet Hosmer that Matilda Hays had written for the *English Woman's Journal* (July 1858) after her breakup with Cushman. Hays's article, while "very full," according to Greenwood, had "one strange omission": Matilda Hays had eliminated all mention of the role played by Charlotte Cushman in Hosmer's career.

9. Hudson, *Browning to His American Friends,* 272. Story's friend James Russell Lowell had been acquainted with Hiram Hosmer in Massachusetts and had requested Story's help in finding a suitable master sculptor for Hatty to study with.

10. Grace Greenwood, *Haps and Mishaps of a Tour in Europe* (London: Bentley, 1854).

11. Greenwood, "Harriet Hosmer and Charlotte Cushman."

12. Hudson, *Browning to His American Friends*, 271.

13. Stebbins, *Charlotte Cushman*, 105.

14. CC to Grace Greenwood, 13 June 1854, Dramatic Museum Archives (hereafter DMA), Rare Book and Manuscript Library, Columbia University.

15. Leonee Ormond and Richard Ormond, *Lord Leighton* (New Haven: Yale University Press, 1975), 22. Leighton's sexuality, and Hosmer's, is discussed in Emmanuel Cooper, *The Sexual Perspective: Homosexuality and Art in the Last Hundred Years in the West* (London: Routledge, 1986).

16. HH to Cornelia Crow, 22 April [1853], HGH, reel 4, folder 112.

17. HH to Cornelia Crow, 30 October 18[53], HGH, reel 4, folder 112.

18. CC to Grace Greenwood, 13 June 1854, DMA.

19. Ned [Charles Edwin] Cushman to Susan Cushman Muspratt, 30 September [1853], CCP, 10:3218.

20. EBB to Henrietta, 23 December 1853, *Elizabeth Barrett Browning: Letters to Her Sister 1846–1859*, ed. Leonard Huxley (London: Murray, 1929), 196.

21. EBB to Henry Fothergill Chorley, 10 August [1853], Huntington Library, HM 7798, San Marino, CA. For a discussion of the nineteenth-century distinction between *manly* and *masculine*, see Gail Bederman, *Manliness and Civilization* (Chicago: University of Chicago, Press), 1995.

22. EBB to Henrietta, 23 December 1853, *EBB: Letters to Her Sister*, 196.

23. Bessie Rayner Parkes to Elizabeth Parkes, 21 April 1857, Bessie Rayner Parkes Papers (hereafter BRPP), II/17, Girton College, Cambridge University.

24. Bessie Rayner Parkes to Elizabeth Parkes, 21 April 1857, BRPP, II/7.

25. Bessie Rayner Parkes to Elizabeth Parkes, 21 April 1857, BRPP, II/7.

26. CC to Grace Greenwood, 13 June 1854, DMA.

27. Isa Blagden to Elizabeth Kinney, 9 September [1855?], Edmund C. Stedman Papers, Rare Book and Manuscript Library, Columbia University.

28. Laura Stedman and George M. Gould, eds., *Life and Letters of Edmund Clarence Stedman* (New York: Moffat, Yard, 1910). Edmund Stedman was a poet and literary critic and the son of Elizabeth Kinney. In this biography he is quoted as faulting his mother for her "hero-worship" of Charlotte Cushman: "You speak of *courage* to shew [*sic*] 'Our Charlotte' your drama. Now have more self-respect and less 'hero-worship'" (1:131).

29. CC to Grace Greenwood, 13 June 1854, DMA.

30. CC to Grace Greenwood, 13 June 1854, DMA. Charlotte also explained to Grace that during Charlotte's successful season, when Matilda was in Rome, Charlotte visited and stayed with Matilda's old friend, Mrs. Ellen Braysher, who initially had been disapproving of Matilda's relationship with Charlotte. Matilda was indignant to discover now that Charlotte "had almost seemed to take her place" in Mrs. Braysher's affections. "This has of course caused a breach between Mrs. B & Miss H." The jealousy among Charlotte Cushman, Matilda Hays, and Ellen Braysher, like that among Charlotte, Matilda, and Hatty Hosmer, is evidence of the complex and often competing understandings of attraction, attachment, and primacy of emotional commitment between and among women in these circles.

31. CC to Grace Greenwood, 13 June 1854, DMA.

32. CC to Grace Greenwood, 13 June 1854, DMA.

33. Bessie Rayner Parkes to Barbara Leigh Smith, 1 September 1855, BRPP, V/76. "Currer Bell" was Charlotte Brontë's pseudonym.

34. Bessie Rayner Parkes to Barbara Leigh Smith, 10 August 1855, BRPP, V/70.

35. Matilda M. Hays to Cornelia Crow, n.d. [1856/57?], HGH.

36. Bessie Rayner Parkes to Elizabeth Parkes, 21 April 1857, BRPP, II/7.

37. Anne Hampton Brewster, diary, 5 June 1876, Box 3, Anne Hampton Brewster Papers (hereafter Brewster Papers), Library Company of Philadelphia, Philadelphia.

38. Ned [Charles Edwin] Cushman to Susan Cushman Muspratt, 6 April [1857?], CCP, 10:3145.

39. Bessie Rayner Parkes Belloc, *A Passing World* (London: Ward and Downey, 1897), 40. The mutual friend was Mary Merryweather, known for her work in hospitals among the poor.

40. Brewster, diary, 5 June 1876, Box 3, Brewster Papers. Brewster wrote this lengthy entry in her diary in Albano, Italy, after a visit with Hatty Hosmer several months after Charlotte Cushman's death: ". . . we talked of poor Charlotte Cushman and laughed over some of her curious droll ways and droller social life as it was about twenty years ago. She had with her always a female companion with whom she quarrelled when she did not reign as tyrant. There was a certain Matilda Hayes [*sic*] who held this difficult post with her for a few years." Hatty related the instances that Anne recorded. In her diary Anne Brewster remarked upon the fact that Hatty appeared to hold Matilda Hays solely responsible for the incident. Anne felt instead: "Of course Miss H was in the wrong and behaved like a beast, but surely part of the blame rested on C.C. for allowing such a scene to occur. It could not have taken place if C.C. had acted with proper dignity during their previous intercourse."

41. John F. Kasson, *Rudeness and Civility: Manners in Nineteenth-Century Urban America* (New York: Hill and Wang, 1990), 161.

42. Eliza Leslie, *Miss Leslie's Behavior Book* (1853; rpt., New York: Arno, 1972), 47–48. This book and the use of etiquette manuals to control women's "emotional excesses" is discussed in Kasson, *Rudeness and Civility*.

43. Leslie, *Miss Leslie's*, 47–48.

44. Brewster, diary, 5 June 1876, Box 3, Brewster Papers. I am not aware of how actively Matilda tried to pursue her case through the courts, if at all, before Charlotte agreed to this settlement. Regardless of whether any suit was filed, Hatty Hosmer's knowledge of the monetary settlement of "a thousand or two dollars" (not as small a sum in the mid-nineteenth century, as Anne Brewster claims) attests to the significance women in their circle placed on the *right* as well as the *need* for women to be self-supporting.

45. Jane Rendall has discussed the importance of the *English Woman's Journal* to the beginning of the organized feminist movement in Britain. See Rendall, *The Origins of Modern Feminism: Women in Britain, France and the United States, 1780–1860* (New York: Schocken, 1984), 184–87, 314–20; "'A Moral Engine'? Feminism, Liberalism and the *English Woman's Journal*," in *Equal or Different: Women's Politics, 1800–1914*, ed. Jane Rendall (London: Blackwell, 1987).

46. Matilda Mary Hays, "Memorial of Matilda M. Hays," Application as Candidate for a Civil List Pension from the Governmental Literary Fund, February, 1865, Parliamentary Papers, 944/66, Public Records Office, London. With the help of Bessie Rayner Parkes, Mary Howitt, and Alfred Tennyson, Matilda Hays was awarded a Civil List Pension of 100 pounds in 1866.

47. Matilda Hays, *Adrienne Hope: The Story of a Life*, 2 vols. (London: Newby, 1866), 1:217.

48. Hays, *Adrienne Hope*, 1:231.

49. Elizabeth Blackwell to "the Reform Club" [Barbara Leigh Smith and Bessie Rayner Parkes], 3 June 1856. After Matilda Hays's breakup with Cushman she formed an intense attachment to poet Adelaide Procter, also of the *English Woman's Journal* circle. Procter died in 1864 and is mentioned in *Adrienne Hope*. Little is known of the last thirty years of Hays's life, after she left the *EWJ*, other than that she spent many years as a companion to Lady Theodosia Monson and lived much of the time in a rooming house she owned in Malvern. Hays died on 3 July 1897.

50. Stebbins, *Charlotte Cushman*, 100.

51. Stebbins, *Charlotte Cushman*, 101.

52. Stebbins, *Charlotte Cushman*, 112.

53. Stebbins, *Charlotte Cushman*, 114.

54. Stebbins, *Charlotte Cushman*, 114.

55. Unidentified newspaper clipping, "Sallie Mercer" obituary, 1894, CCP, vol. 20. In all probability Emma Crow Cushman wrote the obituary that is cited here. There are few extant letters to or by Sallie Mercer. Those friends or correspondents who mention her, such as Geraldine Jewsbury and Emma Crow, speak of Mercer's extraordinary loyalty to Charlotte and unfailing competence. For the remainder of her life, Cushman obviously trusted and depended upon Mercer. In her will Cushman stated that Mercer would receive a lifetime inheritance of five hundred dollars a year and would have a home with the Cushman family, with whom Mercer lived until her own death. See Joseph Leach, *Bright Particular Star: The Life and Times of Charlotte Cushman* (New Haven: Yale University Press, 1970), 363. In 1884, eight years after Cushman's death, Mercer wrote to a friend of Cushman's that "only those who have lived under the shelter of her [Cushman's] angel's wings can know" what it was like "while there was her smile to reward every little effort far beyond its worth" (Mercer to Dennis Alward, 26 December 1884, Harvard Theatre Collection, Houghton Library, Harvard University, Cambridge, MA). While a fuller exploration of the dynamics and implications of Cushman and Mercer's relationship as mistress/star and maid/companion/dresser would be fascinating, the primary information is scanty. Rather than speculate about the contours and dimensions of such a complex and charged area, in the interests of length and the book's primary focus, I have chosen to limit my discussion of Mercer to her participation in the narrative of Cushman's life when she appears in the sources.

56. HH to Cornelia Crow, 12 November 1858; qtd. in Sherwood, *Harriet Hosmer*, 173.

57. HH to [Wayman Crow], 4 July 1862 [fragment], HGH.

58. HH to Wayman Crow, 9 December 1857, HGH.

59. See, for example, HH to Wayman Crow, 11 June [1853], HGH.

60. HH to Wayman Crow, 4 June [1863], HGH.

61. CC to Emma Crow, 26 November 1858, CCP, vol. 1.

62. CC to Emma Crow Cushman, 11 May 1865, CCP, vol. 3.

63. CC to Emma Crow Cushman, 11 May 1865, CCP, vol. 3.

64. Brewster, diary, 5 June 1876, Box 3, Brewster Papers.

65. *The Art of Conversing* (Boston: French, 1846), 27; qtd. in Kasson, *Rudeness and Civility*, 176.

66. Stebbins, *Charlotte Cushman*, 108.

67. See Sue-Ellen Case, *Feminism and Theatre* (New York: Methuen, 1988),

46–47. Case also discusses the set and costume designers' roles in these personal theaters as arbiters of taste who decorate the home and set the dress code. In Cushman's salon these were roles Emma Stebbins undertook. As Cushman's salon became an almost exclusively female-centered space, women guests reacted most enthusiastically to her personal performances, as I discuss later in this chapter.

68. [Dinah Mulock Craik], *A Woman's Thoughts about Women* (London: Hurst and Blackett, 1858), 174.

69. [Craik], *Woman's Thoughts about Women,* 58–60.

70. William James Stillman, *The Autobiography of a Journalist,* 2 vols. (Boston: Houghton Mifflin, 1901), 1:359.

71. Stillman, *Autobiography,* 1:363.

72. Stillman, *Autobiography,* 1:361–62.

73. Stebbins, *Charlotte Cushman,* 102.

74. Stebbins, *Charlotte Cushman,* 102.

75. Francis Power Cobbe, *Life of Frances Power Cobbe, as Told by Herself,* posthumous ed. (London: Swan Sorrenschein, 1904), 392.

76. Cobbe, *Life,* 391–92.

77. Emilie Ashurst to CC, 10 December 1859, CCP, 9:2628.

78. CC to Bessie Rayner Parkes, February 1864, BRPP, IX/132.

79. CC to Bessie Rayner Parkes, February 1864, BRPP, IX/132.

80. Bessie Rayner Parkes to Barbara Leigh Smith Bodichon, 20 March 1864, BRPP, V/130.

81. Kate Field to CC, 15 March 1860, CCP, 11:3295.

82. Kate Field to Emma Crow, 20 May 1860, CCP, vol. 11.

83. Kate Field to CC, 15 March 1860, CCP, 11:3295.

84. Kate Field to CC, 15 March 1860, CCP, 11:3295.

85. Cobbe, *Life,* 392.

86. Cobbe, *Life,* 392.

87. Isa Blagden, *Agnes Tremone,* xxii; qtd. in *Dearest Isa: Robert Browning's Letters to Isabella Blagden,* ed. Robert McAleer (Austin: University of Texas Press, 1951), 37.

88. Rosalie Osborne Binstadt to CC, n.d. [1868], CCP, vol. 9. Binstadt's summoning up of the steadfast relationship enjoyed by the earlier couple to refute "malicious" allegations of women's faithlessness—to each other—is yet another example of the complex climate of awareness and naivete that shaped women, like Charlotte, who pledged to spend their lives with a female partner. See Elizabeth Mavor, *The Ladies of Llangollen* (Harmondsworth, UK: Penguin, 1973).

89. Uncatalogued, accession number 1976:116, Prints and Photographs Division, Library of Congress.

90. CC to Emma Crow Cushman, 17 September 1861, CCP, vol. 1.

91. CC to Emma Crow Cushman, 17 September 1861, CCP, vol. 1.

92. Stillman, *Autobiography,* 1:359.

93. Stillman, *Autobiography,* 1:359.

94. William Wetmore Story to Charles Eliot Norton [1863 or 1864]; qtd. in James, *William Wetmore Story,* 2:127.

95. Greenwood, "Harriet Hosmer and Charlotte Cushman."

96. CC to Emma Crow Cushman, 21 August 1865, CCP, vol. 3.

97. Sherwood, *Harriet Hosmer,* 119.

98. James, *William Wetmore Story,* 1:257.

99. James, *William Wetmore Story,* 1:257.

100. Sara Foose Parrott, "Networking in Italy: Charlotte Cushman and 'The White Marmorean Flock,'" *Women's Studies* 14, no. 4 (1988): 305–38. Parrott makes this point as well and explores the lives of these sculptors in Cushman's circle in some detail.

101. Margaret Ferrand Thorp, "The White Marmorean Flock," *New England Quarterly* (June 1959): 147–69, 164.

102. CC to "Sir" [president YMCA, Boston], May 1867, CCP, vol. 3.

103. H. L. Robbins to CC, n.d., CCP, 12:3654.

104. CC to "Sir" [president YMCA, Boston], May 1867, CCP, vol. 3.

105. CC to Emma Crow Cushman, April 1862, CCP, vol. 2.

106. CC to Emma Crow Cushman, February 1864, CCP, vol. 2.

107. CC to James T. Fields, 26 June 1861, Fields Collection, Huntington Library, FI 686.

108. CC to Annie Fields, 26 February 1868, Fields Collection, FI 692.

109. Unidentified newspaper clipping, in CC to Annie Fields, 29 June 1873, Fields Collection, FI 706.

110. CC to Annie Fields, 29 June 1873, Fields Collection, FI 706.

111. CC to Annie Fields, 29 June 1873, Fields Collection, FI 706.

112. CC to "My dearest friend" [Elizabeth Peabody], 12 May [1868], HTC.

113. Lilian Whiting, *Kate Field: A Record* (Boston: Little, Brown, 1899), 77–78.

Chapter 8

1. CC to Chase, 8 October 1857, New York Public Library.

2. Emma Crow Cushman, "Charlotte Cushman: A Memory" (unpublished memoir), Charlotte Cushman Papers (hereafter CCP), 15:4019–36, Manuscript Division, Library of Congress, Washington, DC. Handwritten note at the top reads "written in 1918 when Mrs. Cushman was 78 years old."

3. ECC, "Charlotte Cushman: A Memory."

4. ECC, "Charlotte Cushman: A Memory."

5. CC to Emma Crow, 3 February 1858, CCP, vol. 1.

6. CC to Emma Crow, 3 February 1858, CCP, vol. 1.

7. CC to Emma Crow, 5 February 1858, CCP, vol. 1.

8. CC to Emma Crow, 22 February 1858, CCP, vol. 1.

9. CC to Emma Crow, 21 March 1858, CCP, vol. 1.

10. CC to Emma Crow, 21 March 1858, CCP, vol. 1.

11. CC to Emma Crow, 22 February 1858, CCP, vol. 1.

12. See chap. 1, esp. n. 18. On the various meanings suggested by the term *Sapphic* in the nineteenth century, see chap. 5, n. 50.

13. CC to Emma Crow, 31 March 1858, CCP, vol. 1.

14. CC to Emma Crow, 31 March 1858, CCP, vol. 1.

15. HH to Wayman Crow, 17 July 1858, Harriet Goodhue Hosmer Collection (hereafter HGH), reel 3, Schlesinger Library, Radcliffe College, Cambridge, MA. To Cornelia, Hatty described Emma as Charlotte's "inamorata," the Italian word for *lover*.

16. HH to Wayman Crow, 22 December 1858, HGH, reel 3.

17. Emma Donoghue, *Passions between Women: British Lesbian Culture, 1668–1801* (London: Scarlet, 1993), 148, 143.

18. HH to Wayman Crow, 22 December 1858, HGH, reel 3.

19. HH to Wayman Crow, 7 August 1855, HGH.

20. CC to Emma Crow, 27 April 1858, CCP, vol. 1.

21. CC to [Emma Crow], 22 January 1859, CCP, vol. 1.

22. CC to [Emma Crow], 22 January 1859, CCP, vol. 1.

23. CC to [Emma Crow], 11 May 1858, CCP, 16:1858.

24. CC to [Emma Crow], 20 June 1858, CCP, vol. 1.

25. ECC, "Charlotte Cushman: A Memory."

26. ECC, "Charlotte Cushman: A Memory"; my emphasis.

27. CC to [Emma Crow], 30 June 1858, CCP, vol. 1.

28. CC to [Emma Crow], 12 August 1858, CCP, vol. 1.

29. CC to [Emma Crow], 22 January 1859, CCP, vol. 1.

30. CC to Wayman Crow, 17 August 1859, CCP, vol. 1. As Emma Donoghue has noted, spinsterhood was a palpable threat to the institution of marriage (*Passions between Women*, 121–24).

31. HH to Wayman Crow, 14 October [1859], HGH, reel 3.

32. CC to [Emma Crow], 18 March 1859, CCP, vol. 1.

33. CC to [Emma Crow], 18 March 1859, CCP, vol. 1.

34. CC to [Emma Crow] [n.d.], CCP, vol. 1.

35. CC to Sallie Mercer [May 1859], CCP, vol. 7. The cause of Susan's death is not recorded in any of Charlotte's papers nor in any earlier Cushman biographies.

36. CC to [Emma Crow], 18 October 1859, CCP, vol. 1.

37. CC to [Emma Crow] [1859], fragment, CCP, vol. 1.

38. CC to [Emma Crow] [1859], fragment, CCP, vol. 1.

39. CC to [Emma Crow] [1859], fragment, CCP, vol. 1.

40. CC to [Emma Crow], 9 March 1860, CCP, vol. 1.

41. CC to [Emma Crow], 9 March 1860, CCP, vol. 1.

42. CC to [Emma Crow], 17 April 1860, CCP, vol. 1.

43. CC to [Emma Crow], 5 April 1860, CCP, vol. 1.

44. CC to [Emma Crow], 5 April 1860, CCP, vol. 1.

45. CC to [Emma Crow], 3 May 1860, CCP, vol. 1.

46. CC to [Emma Crow], 23 May 1860, CCP, vol. 1.

47. CC to [Emma Crow], 27 July 1860, CCP, vol. 1.

48. CC to [Emma Crow], 12 September 1860, CCP, vol. 1.

49. CC to [Emma Crow], 27 July 1860, CCP, vol. 1.

50. CC to [Emma Crow], 15 July 1860, CCP, vol. 1.

51. CC to [Emma Crow], 20 June 1860, CCP, vol. 1.

52. CC to [Emma Crow], 20 June 1860, CCP, vol. 1.

53. CC to James T. Fields, 25 September [1860], Fields Collection, FI 713.

54. CC to [Emma Crow], 27 July 1860, CCP, vol. 1.

55. CC to [Emma Crow], 24 June 1860, CCP, vol. 1.

56. CC to [Emma Crow], 15 July 1860, CCP, vol. 1.

57. CC to [Emma Crow], 5 October 1860, CCP, vol. 1.

58. CC to [Emma Crow], 23 January 1862, CCP, vol. 1.

59. CC to Charles Cushman, 29 October 1860, CCP, vol. 16. As with the alternate spellings of Hatty/Hattie Hosmer, Charlotte variously spelled her brother's name *Charley* and *Charlie*.

60. CC to [Charles Cushman], n.d. [1860], CCP, vol. 1; my emphasis.

61. CC to Charles Cushman, 29 October 1860, CCP, vol. 16.

62. CC to [Emma Crow], 26 October 1860, CCP, vol. 1.

63. CC to [Emma Crow], 5 October 1860, CCP, vol. 1.

64. CC to [Emma Crow], 26 October 1860, CCP, vol. 1.

65. Mary Eliza Cushman to Charles Cushman, 4 October 1860, CCP, vol. 16.

66. CC to [Emma Crow], 15 November 1860, CCP, vol. 1.

67. CC to [Emma Crow], 5 October 1860, CCP, vol. 1.

68. CC to Annie Fields, 25 December [1860], Fields Collection, FI 685.

69. CC to [Emma Crow], 16 January 1861, CCP, vol. 1.

70. CC to [Emma Crow], 29 January 1861, CCP, vol. 1.

71. CC to [Emma Crow], 16 January 1861, CCP, vol. 1.

72. CC to [Emma Crow], 29 January 1861, CCP, vol. 1.

73. Dolly Sherwood, *Harriet Hosmer: American Sculptor, 1830–1908* (Columbia: University of Missouri Press, 1991), 198.

74. CC to [Emma Crow Cushman], June 1861, CCP, vol. 1.

75. CC to [Emma Crow], 26 February 1861, CCP, vol. 1.

76. CC to [Emma Crow Cushman], 29 June 1861, CCP, vol. 1.

77. CC to [Emma Crow Cushman], 29 June 1861, CCP, vol. 1.

78. CC to [Emma Crow Cushman], 29 June 1861, CCP, vol. 1.

79. CC to [Emma Crow Cushman], July 1861, CCP, vol. 1.

80. CC to [Emma Crow Cushman], 28 October 1861, CCP, vol. 1.

81. CC to [Emma Crow Cushman], 28 October 1861, CCP, vol. 1.

82. CC to [Emma Crow Cushman], 7 November 1861, CCP, vol. 1.

83. CC to [Emma Crow Cushman], 16 August 1861, CCP, vol. 1.

84. CC to [Emma Crow Cushman], 16 August 1861, CCP, vol. 1.

85. CC to [Emma Crow Cushman], 30 August 1861, CCP, vol. 1.

86. CC to [Emma Crow Cushman], 23 January 1862, CCP, vol. 2.

87. CC to [Emma Crow Cushman], 23 January 1862, CCP, vol. 2.

88. CC to [Emma Crow Cushman], 13 March 1862, CCP, vol. 2.

89. CC to [Emma Crow Cushman], 13 March 1862, CCP, vol. 2.

90. CC to [Emma Crow Cushman], 13 March 1862, CCP, vol. 2.

91. CC to [Emma Crow Cushman], 26 March 1862, CCP, vol. 2.

92. See chap. 7 for a discussion of Charlotte's role in the Roman community of expatriate sculptors. See also HH to Wayman Crow, 15 March 1862, HGH, reel 3; CC to James T. Fields, 15 March 1862, Fields Collection, FI 687; and CC to [Emma Crow Cushman], April 1862, CCP, vol. 2.

93. CC to [Emma Crow Cushman], May 1862, CCP, vol. 2.

94. CC to James and Annie Fields, 25 July 1862, Fields Collection, FI 688.

95. CC to [Emma Crow Cushman], 2 July 1861, CCP, vol. 1.

96. CC to [Emma Crow Cushman], July 1861, CCP, vol. 1.

97. CC to [Emma Crow Cushman], 8 December 1861, CCP, vol. 1.

98. CC to [Emma Crow Cushman], 8 December 1861, CCP, vol. 1.

99. CC to [Emma Crow Cushman], 3 April 1863, CCP.

100. CC to [Emma Crow Cushman], 3 April 1863, CCP.

101. CC to [Emma Crow Cushman], 3 April 1863, CCP.

102. ECC, "Charlotte Cushman: A Memory"; Sallie Mercer, telegram, 29 June 1863, CCP.

103. Edwin Booth to CC, 3 September 1863, CCP, vol. 9.

104. CC to Annie Fields [September 1863], Fields Collection, FI 714.

105. Sally Bridges to CC, October 1863, CCP, vol. 9.

106. CC to Bessie Rayner Parkes, 11 February 1864, Bessie Rayner Parkes Papers, IX/132, Girton College, Cambridge.

107. CC to James T. Fields, 27 August 1864, Fields Collection, FI 690.

108. CC to [Emma Crow Cushman], 20 January 1865, CCP, vol. 3:735.

109. CC to Cornelia Crow Carr, 15 October 1864, HGH, reel 7, folder 152.

110. Emma Stebbins, *Charlotte Cushman: Her Letters and Memories of Her Life* (1879; rpt., New York: Blom, 1972), 170–71.

111. CC to [Emma Crow Cushman], 20 January 1865, CCP, 3:735. In this manuscript letter Charlotte's cross-outs and additions are clearly visible.

112. A fifth son, Guy, was born in 1876 after Charlotte's death.

113. CC to [Emma Crow Cushman], 26 January 1865, CCP, 3:736–38.

114. HH to Cornelia Crow Carr, 3 July [1865], HGH, folder 116.

115. William J. Stillman, *The Autobiography of a Journalist*, 2 vols. (Boston: Houghton Mifflin, 1901), 1:361–62. Years later an embittered Stillman still felt that Charlotte had been "not at all scrupulous in the attainment of her purposes, and was, in effect, that most dangerous member of society, a strong-willed and large-brained woman without a vestige of principle." It seems likely that much of Stillman's dislike for Charlotte was a result of his suspicions of Charlotte's machinations on Ned's behalf.

116. CC to [Emma Crow Cushman], 11 May 1865, CCP, vol. 3.

117. CC to [Emma Crow Cushman], 11 May 1865, CCP, vol. 3.

118. CC to [Emma Crow Cushman], 11 May 1865, CCP, vol. 3.

119. CC to [Emma Crow Cushman], 15 April 1865, CCP, vol. 3.

120. CC to [Emma Crow Cushman], 21 August 1865, CCP, vol. 3.

121. John D'Emilio and Estelle B. Freedman, *Intimate Matters: A History of Sexuality in America* (New York: Harper and Row, 1988), 127–29.

122. CC to [Emma Crow Cushman], 21 August 1865, CCP, vol. 3.

123. CC to Emma Crow Cushman, 26 July 1868, CCP, vol. 3.

124. CC to [Elizabeth Peabody], 8 September 1868, transcription from Massachusetts Historical Society in Papers of Jennie Lorenz, Manuscript Division, Library of Congress.

125. CC to Emma Crow Cushman, 28 June 1869, CCP, vol. 4.

126. Stebbins, *Charlotte Cushman*, 230.

127. HH to Cornelia Crow Carr, 16 August [1870], HGH, reel 7, folder 139.

128. CC to Emma Crow Cushman, 9 October 1870, CCP, vol. 4.

129. CC to Emma Crow Cushman, 25 November 1870, CCP, vol. 4.

130. CC to James and Annie Fields, 5 January 1871, Fields Collection, FI 698.

131. CC to Emma Crow Cushman, 16 January 1871, CCP, vol. 5.

132. CC to Emma Crow Cushman, 12 February 1871, CCP, vol. 5.

133. CC to Annie Fields, 31 July 1871, Fields Collection, FI 702.

134. CC to Annie Fields, 29 August 1871, Fields Collection, FI 703. In later years Annie Fields might better understand how one woman can "move" another, for after James Fields's death Annie would spend the rest of her life as partner to Sarah Orne Jewett.

135. Stebbins, *Charlotte Cushman*, 212.

136. CC to Emma Crow Cushman, 29 October 1871, CCP, vol. 5.

137. CC; qtd. in Stebbins, *Charlotte Cushman*, 238.

138. Emma Stebbins to Annie Fields, 8 February 1872, Fields Collection, FI 1699.

139. CC to Charles Cushman, 14 February 1872, CCP, vol. 5.

140. CC to Mary Lloyd, 23 September 1874, Huntington Library, CB 378.

141. CC to Mary Lloyd, 23 September 1874, Huntington Library, CB 378.

142. Cushman's career as a platform reader raises other questions about spectatorship and performance that are beyond the scope of this book. Some of these questions have been addressed by John Gentile, *Cast of One: One-Person Shows from the Chautauqua Platform to the Broadway Stage* (Urbana: University of Illinois Press, 1989); and David W. Thompson, "Early Actress-Readers: Mowatt, Kemble, and Cushman," in *Performance of Literature in Historical Perspective*, ed. David W. Thompson (Lanham, MD: University Press of America, 1983), 629–50. Yet, as Elizabeth Bell has persuasively argued, nineteenth-century women platform readers negotiated gender prohibitions in a particular space "between the sexually charged stage and the rhetorically charged political platform" of women's activism. To appreciate fully Cushman's successful receptions as a platform reader, one would have to locate her—and the act of public readings—within the larger context. See Elizabeth Bell, "Performance Studies as Women's Work: Historical Sights/Sites/Citations from the Margin," *Text and Performance Quarterly* 13 (1993): 350–74.

143. Stebbins, *Charlotte Cushman*, 263–64.

144. CC; qtd. in Stebbins, *Charlotte Cushman*, 264–65.

145. HH to Cornelia Crow Carr, 1 July [1875], HGH, reel 5, folder 120.

146. Stebbins, *Charlotte Cushman*, 278.

147. CC to John McCullough, 13 February 1876, Harvard Theatre Collection, Houghton Library, Harvard University, Cambridge, MA.

148. Stebbins, *Charlotte Cushman*, 212.

149. Stebbins, *Charlotte Cushman*, 285.

150. ECC, "Charlotte Cushman: A Memory."

151. ECC, "Charlotte Cushman: A Memory." Ned and Emma Cushman lived together for the remainder of their lives. Emma Crow Cushman, the last member of Charlotte's immediate circle, died on 15 September 1920. Ned Cushman had died six years earlier, in Rome. Until World War I Emma spent her winters in Rome and summers in Bar Harbor, Maine. She continued to cherish her memories of Charlotte throughout her life. Emma spent her final two decades with a companion and friend, Miss Ludwig (unidentified clipping, "Services for Mrs. Cushman Thursday," obituary, 15 September 1920, CCP, vol. 19).

Chapter 9

1. Unidentified clipping, "Charlotte Cushman: The Funeral Services in King's Chapel," Harriet Goodhue Hosmer Collection, Schlesinger Library, Radcliffe College, Cambridge, MA.

2. *Scribner's Magazine*, Lyman Beecher Stowe Collection (hereafter LBS Collection), 217, Schlesinger Library.

3. "Charlotte Cushman: A Great Life Ended," *Tribune* (New York), 21 February 1876, 2.

4. "Tributes to Charlotte Cushman," *Boston Evening Transcript*, 28 February 1876.

5. "Tributes to Charlotte Cushman."

6. "Tributes to Charlotte Cushman."

7. "A Tribute by Reverend W. H. H. Murray of Boston," 1 March 1876, Charlotte Cushman Papers (hereafter CCP), vol. 15, Manuscript Division, Library of Congress, Washington, DC.

8. *Boston Advertiser,* 19 February 1876.

9. John D. Stockton, *Scribner's Magazine,* 18 June 1876, 265.

10. See chap. 1 n. 17.

11. Qtd. in G. Rattray Taylor, *Sex in History* (New York: Harper and Row, 1970), 210.

12. Augustus Kinsley Gardner, *The Causes and Curative Treatment of Sterility* (New York: DeWitt and Davenport, 1856), 111.

13. William Rounseville Alger, *The Friendships of Women* (Boston: Roberts, 1868), 346–58.

14. Lawrence Barrett, *Charlotte Cushman: A Lecture* (New York: Dunlap Society, 1889), 23.

15. Barrett, *Charlotte Cushman,* 22.

16. Unidentified newspaper clipping, n.p., n.d., Charlotte Cushman Clipping File, Harvard Theatre Collection (hereafter HTC), Houghton Library, Harvard University, Cambridge, MA.

17. George C. D. Odell, *Shakespeare from Betterton to Irving,* 2 vols. (1920; rpt., New York: Dover, 1966), 1:251.

18. Emma S. Stilwell to CC, 21 June 1875, CCP, vol. 13.

19. J. J. Borg to CC, 2 December 1874, CCP, vol. 9.

20. Emma Stebbins to Sidney Lanier, 1 March 1876, transcript, Papers of Jenny Lorenz (hereafter Lorenz Papers), Manuscript Division, Library of Congress. Cushman's novelist friend Helen Hunt had wanted to write Charlotte's memoir, but Stebbins thought she was "not the right one for the task." Hunt had suggested having the book come out in the autumn, but Stebbins claimed she wanted it "done with care and love, not gotten up to meet an excited market" eager for an account of Cushman's life.

21. Stebbins to Lanier, 1 March 1876, transcript, Lorenz Papers.

22. Eve Kosofsky Sedgwick, *Epistemology of the Closet* (Berkeley: University of California Press, 1990), 71.

23. Stebbins to Lanier, 27 March 1876, transcript, Lorenz Papers.

24. Stebbins to Lanier, 1 March 1876, transcript, Lorenz Papers.

25. Stebbins to Lanier, 6 July 1876, transcript, Lorenz Papers.

26. Stebbins to Lanier, 27 July 1876, transcript, Lorenz Papers.

27. Stebbins to Lanier, 6 July 1876, transcript, Lorenz Papers.

28. Barrett, *Charlotte Cushman,* 24. Although this image of Charlotte suited Barrett's intention to depict her as a noble, moralizing force, there is ample evidence of her tumultuous years with Matilda Hays and the frequent tensions between Emma Crow and Emma Stebbins. See chaps. 6, 7, and 8.

29. Emma Stebbins, *Charlotte Cushman: Her Letters and Memories of Her Life* (1878; rpt., New York: Benjamin Blom, 1972), 192.

30. Stebbins, *Charlotte Cushman,* 57.

31. Stebbins, *Charlotte Cushman,* 162.

32. Jennifer Terry, "Theorizing Deviant Historiography," in *Feminists Revision History,* ed. Ann-Louise Shapiro (New Brunswick, NJ: Rutgers University Press, 1994), 297. See also Lisa Moore, "'Something More Tender than Friendship': Romantic Friendship in Early-Nineteenth-Century England," *Feminist Studies* 18, no. 3 (fall 1992): 507.

33. Emma Donoghue, *Passions between Women: British Lesbian Culture, 1668–1801* (London: Scarlet, 1993), 7. See also Martha Vicinus, "'They Wonder to Which Sex I Belong': The Historical Roots of the Modern Lesbian Identity," *Feminist Studies* 18, no. 3 (fall 1992): 467–89. Vicinus is here disputing Lillian Faderman and Caroll Smith-

Rosenberg's earlier claims that women's romantic friendships were generally accepted without fear of social stigma in the Victorian era.

34. Vicinus, "'They Wonder to Which Sex I Belong,'" 483.

35. [Dinah Mulock Craik], *A Woman's Thoughts about Women* (London: Hurst and Blackett, 1858), 174–75.

36. Nor was anything explicitly named when Craik's acquaintance—and Charlotte Cushman's friend—Emily Faithfull was implicated in the 1864 *Codrington v. Codrington* divorce case. In the testimony of this trial, covered religiously in the London *Times,* there were accusations not only that Faithfull was an accomplice to Helen Codrington's adulterous affairs with men but also that the "warm" attachment between the two women interfered with the Codrington marriage. The details of the case are recounted in William E. Fredeman, "Emily Faithfull and the Victoria Press: An Experiment in Sociological Bibliography," *Library,* 5th ser., 29, no. 2 (June 1974): 139–64. The lesbian implications are discussed in Denise Quirk, "The Women of Langham Place: Presses, Publications, and Platforms," MS, 1996; and, more recently, Martha Vicinus, "Lesbian Perversity and Victorian Marriage: The 1864 Codrington Divorce Trial," *Journal of British Studies* 36 (January 1997): 70–98.

37. [Craik], *A Woman's Thoughts about Women,* 174–75.

38. CC to [Emma Crow Cushman], 12 September 1860, CCP, vol. 1. See also CC to [Emma Crow Cushman], 26 March 1862, CCP, vol. 2.

39. Terry, "Theorizing Deviant Historiography," 299.

40. Obituary, "Charlotte Cushman," *Boston Advertiser,* 19 February 1876. Of course, the mere mention of the potential that such worship might "wound" a young woman hints at the danger of such relationships.

41. Peter Gay, *The Bourgeois Experience: Victoria to Freud,* vol. 2: *The Tender Passion* (New York: Oxford University Press, 1986), 4. Martha Vicinus makes the point that what is "not said" and "not seen" is crucial for understanding lesbian history. See Martha Vicinus, "Lesbian History: All Theory and No Facts or All Facts and No Theory?" *Radical History Review* 60 (1994): 57–75.

42. See Lisa Moore, "'Something More Tender than Friendship,'" 499–520. Moore discusses the accounts of sexual affairs between women in the diary of Anne Lister, the court transcripts of two female Scottish teachers charged with having a sexual relationship with each other, and the depiction of the transgressive character Harriot Freke in Maria Edgeworth's 1801 novel, *Belinda,* to explore the ways in which women's same-sex desire was understood in the early nineteenth century.

43. Stockton, "Charlotte Cushman."

44. Marguerite Merington, *Theatre Magazine* [n.d.]; qtd. in Mary Caroline Crawford, *The Romance of the American Theatre* (1913; rpt., New York: Basic, 1940), 343.

45. Merington, *Theatre Magazine;* qtd. in Crawford, *Romance of the American Theatre,* 343. Martha Vicinus has discussed the limitations of visibility as a signifier for lesbians in "Lesbian History."

46. Elaine Showalter, *Sexual Anarchy: Gender and Culture at the Fin de Siècle* (London: Virago, 1992), 19.

47. Eliza Lynn Linton, "The Epicene Sex," *Saturday Review,* 24 August 1872; rptd. in Eliza Lynn Linton, *The Girl of the Period and Other Social Essays,* 2 vols. (London: Bentley, 1883), 2:241.

48. Linton, "Epicene Sex," 2:242.

49. Gamaliel Bradford, *Biography and the Human Heart* (1906; rpt., Boston: Houghton Mifflin, 1932), 114.

50. W. T. Price, *A Life of Charlotte Cushman* (New York: Brentano's, 1894), 120, 140.

51. "Charlotte Cushman," *Inter Ocean* (Chicago), 24 October 1893, clipping file, HTC.

52. Mary Poovey, *Uneven Developments: The Ideological Work of Gender in Mid-Victorian England* (Chicago: University of Chicago Press, 1988), 12.

53. Richard von Krafft-Ebing, *Psychopathia Sexualis* (1882; rpt., translated from the seventh and revised German edition, trans. Charles Gilbert Chaddock, Philadelphia: F. A. Davis, 1893).

54. Karl Friedrich Otto Westphal, "Die contrare Sexualempfindung," *Archiv fur Psychiatrie und Nervenkrankheiten* 2, no. 1 (August 1869): 73–108. In 1871 a review of Westphal's work was published in the London *Journal of Medical Science.*

55. Havelock Ellis, *Studies in the Psychology of Sex: Sexual Inversion* (1897; rpt., Philadelphia: Davis, 1911). Ellis initially collaborated with homosexual literary critic John Addington Symonds on this volume. After Symonds's death his contributions to the volume were minimized. Presumably, both men agreed that homosexuality was congenital and not a series of behaviors an individual chose to engage in, but they disagreed about the "normalcy" of homosexuality. It is significant to note that Ellis's wife, Edith Lee Ellis, was lesbian.

56. Krafft-Ebing, *Psychopathia Sexualis;* qtd. in Showalter, *Sexual Anarchy,* 23; my emphasis.

57. William Winter, "Players: Past and Present: Great Actress and Great Woman, Charlotte Cushman," *Saturday Evening Post,* 29 September 1906, 10.

58. Ellis, *Sexual Inversion,* 250.

59. Xavier Mayne (E. I. Prime Stevenson), *The Intersexes: A Study of Similisexualism as a Problem in Social Life* (1908; rpt., New York: Arno, 1975), 17. I am grateful to Jonathan Ned Katz, through whose groundbreaking volume, *Gay American History* (New York: Crowell, 1976), I first encountered mention of *The Intersexes.* Stevenson mentions in his volume that he had been working on it for more than a decade and had intentionally printed it in Italy, where the typesetters would be unable to read the text.

60. Mayne, *Intersexes,* 553.

61. Mayne, *Intersexes,* 407.

62. George C. D. Odell, *Annals of the New York Stage,* 4 vols. (New York: Columbia University Press, 1927), 4:147.

63. Henry James, *William Wetmore Story and His Friends: From Letters, Diaries, and Recollections,* 2 vols. (London: Thames and Hudson, 1903), 2:260.

64. Bradford, *Biography and the Human Heart,* 113.

65. David Belasco, "Women and the Stage," *Ladies Home Journal* 37 (November 1920): 110.

66. Katharine Wright, "A Century Ago Today Charlotte Cushman, America's Greatest Actress Was Born in Boston," *Sunday Herald* (Boston), 23 July 1916.

67. Walter Eaton to Lyman Beecher Stowe, 25 November 1940, LBS Collection.

68. "Charlotte Cushman Papers," Library of Congress Reader's Guide. The core of the papers in the collection were donated to the library between 1925 and 1927. The current guide to the collection, processed in 1978, reads: "Most of the correspondence is between Charlotte and her older brother, Charles Augustus, her mother, Mary Eliza, and Edwin, the nephew she adopted." It seems unlikely that any earlier note on the collection available to Stowe would have indicated the passionate nature of the bulk of the letters or the fact that they were largely written to Charlotte's nephew's wife, not her nephew.

69. LBS Collection, note cards 306–8.

70. Susanne Howe, *Geraldine Jewsbury: Her Life and Errors* (London: Allen and Unwin, 1935), 47.

71. Howe, *Geraldine Jewsbury*, 45.

72. Faderman, *Surpassing the Love of Men*, 240.

73. Sigmund Freud, "Analysis Terminable and Interminable," *Collected Works*, ed. Joan Rivière (New York: Basic, 1959), 5:355.

74. Freud believed that even the wish "to carry on an intellectual profession—may often be recognized as sublimated modification of . . . the wish to get the longed for penis" ("Femininity," *New Introductory Lectures on Psychoanalysis*, trans. James Strachey [New York: Norton, 1964], 125).

75. Bernard Grebanier, *Then Came Each Actor: Shakespearean Actors, Great and Otherwise* (New York: McKay, 1975), 253.

76. Grebanier, *Then Came Each Actor*, 257.

77. Grebanier, *Then Came Each Actor*, 259.

78. Robert Speaight, *Shakespeare on the Stage* (Boston: Little, Brown, 1973), 79.

79. Speaight, *Shakespeare on the Stage*, 79.

80. Garff Wilson, *A History of American Acting* (Bloomington: Indiana University Press, 1966), 49–50.

81. Wilson, *History of American Acting*, 55.

82. Dale Shaw, *Titans of the American Stage* (Philadelphia: Westminster Press, 1971), 84–85. Ironically, the "coy," "dainty" handwriting of Charlotte's letter, the stationery she wrote on, and the tone she employed were no different than the characteristic style Cushman used in all of her correspondence, including earlier letters to both Edwin Booth and Mary Devlin Booth. Shaw's implication—that Cushman was merely appearing coy to "dicker" an exorbitant salary from Booth—misrepresents her as manipulating gender stereotypes to get what she wanted, to pass herself off as a "dainty" female, ailing from some obscure disease, using duplicitous feminine wiles, when in reality she was far from a helpless, pitiful, weak woman; although suffering from breast cancer, she was still more powerful, and larger, than Booth himself.

83. Lennox Strong, review of *Bright Particular Star* by Joseph Leach, *Ladder* 31 (1970): 29.

84. Faderman, *Surpassing the Love of Men*, 224. Refuting Faderman's claim, Lisa Moore argues that "such accounts . . . draw very partially on the evidence of how these relationships were viewed by contemporaries. [Faderman's and Carroll] Smith-Rosenberg's studies obscure the wariness and even prohibition that sometimes surrounded women's friendships, leaving us with a flattened notion of contesting constructions of female sexuality in late eighteenth century and early nineteenth century England" ("'Something More Tender than Friendship,'" 501).

85. CC to Emma Crow Cushman, 13 March 1862, CCP, vol. 2.

86. Eve Kosofsky Sedgwick, *Epistemology of the Closet* (Berkeley: University of California Press, 1990), 87.

87. Lilla Wheeler to LBS, LBS Collection, folder 433.

88 Vicinus, "'They Wonder to Which Sex I Belong,'" 480. Vicinus has made the point that women like Cushman complicate the notion of mutually exclusive "categories of romantic friendship and butch-femme passion" by appearing to belong to both—or neither. Vicinus suggests that "historians need not seek a coherent lesbian identity in the past or present" ("Lesbian History," 62).

89. Terry, "Theorizing Deviant Historiography," 281–83.

90. Terry Castle persuasively notes that the term *odd* may have been employed as code for *lesbian* in texts as early as 1755. See Castle's powerful book *The Apparitional Lesbian* for a discussion of the erasure or "ghosting" of lesbian subjects in a wide range of nineteenth- and twentieth-century cultural artifacts (*The Apparitional Lesbian: Female Homosexuality and Modern Culture* [New York: Columbia University Press, 1993], 9–10).

Index

breeches performances, 33, 38–39, 110–11; CC's early, 38–40; CC's explanations for, 113–14, 125–26, 135–37; CC's major, 111–35. *See also* cross-dressing

Brewster, Anne: on CC's break with Hays, 183–85; on CC's British celebrity, 163–65; on CC's performances, 46–47; relationship with CC, 52–53, 56–62, 73

Brewster, Benjamin, 56, 58–60

Bridges, Sallie, 137, 229–30

Brooks, Peter, 82, 83, 100

Brougham's Lyceum (New York), 131

Browning, Elizabeth Barrett, 109, 160, 177, 181, 253

Browning, Robert, 118, 140, 177

Bryant, William Cullen, 239

Bulwer-Lytton, Edward, 44

Burton, William E., 48–49, 134

Butler, Judith, 124

Butler, Pierce, 60, 69–71

Cardinal Wolsey (*Henry VIII*): CC as, 133–35, 205, 221; Macready as, 105, 134, 158

Carlyle, Jane, 150–51, 155, 261

Case, Sue-Ellen, 190–91

Castle, Terry, 8

Chappel, Alonzo, portrait of CC, 240

Chase, Algernon and Emily, 205

Child, Lydia Maria, 199

Chippendale, William, 163

Chorley, Henry Fothergill, 105, 116–18, 140

Cinderella, CC in opera of, 27

Civil War, CC's views on, 227–28

Clapp, Henry Augustus, 95

Clarendon, Miss, rivalry with Susan Cushman, 50–51

Clarke, Conrad, 169

Clarke, Norma, 139

Clarke, Sara Jane. *See* Greenwood, Grace

Clement (Waters), Clara Erskine, 106

Cobbe, Frances Power, 193, 195

Coleman, John, 86, 122, 125

Combe, George, 112–14

Corbett, Mary Jean, 114

Cordelia (*King Lear*), CC as, 44

Cott, Nancy, 22, 57–58

Count Belino (*The Devil's Bridge*), CC as, 38, 39, 41

Countess Almavira (*The Marriage of Figaro*), CC as, 24, 26, 27–28

Coxon, Sarah. *See* Anderton (Dilberoglue), Sarah

Craik, Dinah Mulock, 191, 251–52, 265

Cross-dressing, 115, 136. *See also* breeches performance; CC's offstage, 125, 146, 168–70; CC's on stage, 39, 136–37; male costars' reactions to CC's, 122, 125, 126, 131–34.

Crow, Cornelia, 132, 176, 210, 236, 241

Crow, Emma. *See* Cushman, Emma Crow

Crow, Wayman: as CC's financial advisor, 202, 205–6, 221; on Emma Crow's attraction to CC, 209–11, 213; as Hosmer's patron, 176, 189, 198; objections to Emma Crow's marriage, 219

curtain speeches, CC's use of, 39

Cushman, Allerton Seward, 231

Cushman, Augustus, 9, 41

Cushman, Charles, 19, 97–99, 141, 220

Cushman, Charlotte: acts with Booth, 229, 237, 141–50; acts with Forrest, 44–45, 82–83, 87–92; acts with Macready, 31, 53, 56, 61, 63, 65–66, 69, 73–75, 105; adhesive nature of, 233; adopts Edwin "Ned" Cushman, 169–70; as Bianca, 83–87; and breast cancer, 235, 241; breeches roles, 38–40, 111–35; British reactions to, 85, 87–95, 114, 136, 162–63; builds Villa Cushman, 237, 239; as Cardinal Wolsey, 132–35; circumspect about passion for women, 148, 180–81, 208, 212, 223, 252; as cultural icon, 12–13, 42, 82, 108–9, 138–41, 170, 245, 253–54; death of, 242, 249; diary of, 1–14, 68, 69, 70, 73; eulogies of, 243–44, 252, 253, 260; family negotiations, 217, 220–23, 232; farewell performances, 239, 241; funeral of, 243; "genius" of , 44, 86, 119, 181; as Hamlet, 131–33; as head of household, 187–90, 192, 216; as Lady Macbeth, 89–97; London salon, 181; as manager of Walnut Street Theatre, 52–56, 60–61; on marriage, 189–90, 196–97, 210–11, 217; as matriarch, 188–89; as Meg Merrilies, 42–46, 97–104; as "moral influence,"

Cornelia Crow, 132, 176; as sculptor, 174, 176, 181, 191, 197–98, 227; and story of CC's break with Hays, 182–85; Wayman Crow as patron of, 176, 189–90, 202; *Zenobia* scandal, 200

Hosmer, Hiram, 173

Howe, Julia Ward, 201

Howe, Susanne, 261

Howitt, Mary: on CC's relationship with Cook, 145–46; friendship with CC, 112, 138–40, 156; "The Miss Cushmans," 18, 43, 120–22, 125, 139

Hutton, Laurence, 133

Intersexes, The (Mayne), 258

"inversion," 257–59, 262

Ion (Talfourd), CC as, 130

Ireland, Joseph, 80

James, Henry, 198, 259

Jameson, Anna, 89, 138, 140, 172, 177, 182

Jewsbury, Geraldine: attachment to Jane Carlyle, 150–51, 155, 261; attraction to CC, 139, 150–51; *The Half Sisters,* 85, 151–52, 155; hears story of CC's "jilting," 37; jealousy of Cook, 151, 153; meets CC, 139, 156; reactions to CC onstage, 101, 158

Judd, Samuel, 24

Kean, Edmund, CC compared to, 119

Kean, Ellen Tree, 111, 113, 130

Kemble (Butler), Fanny, 4, 133; antitheatrical prejudice of, 76; attempts divorce, 69–71; Combe's appeal to, 112–13; and Crow family, 206; early career in U.S., 24; friendship with CC, 53, 56, 60, 67–72, 89, 140; in Rome, 174, 176; and Sully family, 72–73, 76

Kent, Christopher, 34

Kinney, Elizabeth, 179

Knowles, Sheridan, 65, 119

Krafft-Ebing, Richard von, 257

Ladies Companion, 35, 39, 41, 54

Lady Gay Spanker (*London Assurance*), CC as, 50

Lady of Lyons, The (Bulwer-Lytton), 44

Lady Macbeth, CC as: conception of, 28, 61–62, 64, 89–97, 103–4, 108, 117, 137; debut performances of, 28–29, 32, 38, 89; farewell performances of, 238–39, 241; with Forrest, 89–95; with Macready, 58, 61, 64, 158; for Sanitary Commission, 228–29

Langley, Henry, 144

Lanier, Sidney, 248–50

Larken, Edmund, 154, 157–58

Laurence, Samuel, 154–57

Leach, Joseph, 264–66

Le Baron, Martha, 128–29

Leigh Smith, Barbara, 185

Leighton, Frederick, 175–76

Leman, Walter M., 60

Leonard, Manning, 18–19

lesbian: CC identified as, 113, 196, 258, 260–62, 264–65; expression of desire, 59, 68, 124–26, 128–29, 179, 184–85, 196, 207–9, 217, 223, 259–61; as identity category, 7–8, 160, 255, 257–66; "mannish," 216, 255–56, 262, 265–66; spectatorship, 39, 122, 126, 129, 136–37, 155, 206. *See also* homosexuality; "inversion"; uraniad

Lewes, George Henry, 154, 157

Lewis, Edmonia, 196, 198–200

Lincoln, Abraham, CC meets, 227

Llangollen, ladies of, CC and Stebbins compared to, 196

Lloyd, Mary, 195, 238

London Assurance (Boucicault), 50

Longfellow, Henry Wadsworth, 65

Lorenz, Jennie, 263–64, 266

Lynn, Eliza (Linton), 154–55, 255–57

Macready, William Charles: acts with CC, 31, 53, 56, 61, 63, 65–66, 69, 73–75, 105; antitheatrical prejudice of, 65–66; attitudes toward Americans, 5, 6, 74; compared with CC, 65, 91, 94, 119, 130, 163; competes with Forrest, 81, 87, 91; first performances in U.S., 20; friendship with Hays, 157; reactions to CC, 3, 61, 64–67, 74, 75, 80–81

Maddox, J. M., 81–82, 85, 97

Maeder, James G., 24, 26

Malvern, spa, 153, 176, 236

manliness, British vs. American conceptions of, 87, 88–89, 90, 93–95, 119, 255; Jameson on, 177

Mann, Horace, 23, 135; Stebbins's sculpture of, 201

"mannish" lesbians, 216, 254–56, 262, 265–66

Marriage: between women, 194–97; CC describes relations with Stebbins as, 189–90, 195–97, 211; CC and Hays as a "female marriage," 160; CC as "married" to Sully, 9; warnings against heterosexual, 155, 157, 159; 210–11, 217

Marryat, Frederick, 38

Marshall, E. A., 51

Marston, John Westland, 86, 98, 108, 110

masculinity, and *manliness,* 87, 88–89, 90, 117, 177, 178, 254, 255, 262

Mayne, Xavier. *See* Stevenson, Edward Prime

Mazzini, Guiseppe, 158

McConachie, Bruce, 19, 39

McCullough, John, 241

Melnotte, Claude (*The Lady of Lyons*): CC as, 44–46, 48, 155, 160; Forrest as, 44–46

melodrama, 32, 82, 83, 100

Mercer, Sallie, 6, 80, 82, 112, 169, 214–15, 230; as CC's dresser, 102, 221, 238; comes to work for CC, 77–79; manages CC's household, 175–76, 181, 187; and tensions in CC's household, 234; travels during the Civil War, 228–29

Merington, Marguerite, 254–55

Merrilies, Meg (*Guy Mannering*), CC as: conception of, 102–4, 228, 238, 239; drawing of CC as (Cook), 141–43; in England, 97–104, 108, 117, 180; first performance as, 42–46

Merriman, Nelson, 41, 43, 159, 250

Metamora (Stone), CC's appearance as Nahmeokee in, 44

Meteyard, Eliza, 156, 159

"Miss Cushmans, The" (Howitt), 43

Mitford, Mary, 131, 139

Monson, Lady Theodosia, 157

Montaldo (*The Genoese*), CC as, 48

Mosse, George, 93

Mott, Lucretia, 139

Mount Auburn Cemetery, 243

Mowatt, Anna Cora, 54, 68, 259

Mrs. Haller (*The Stranger*), CC as, 32

Murdoch, James, 95

Murray, W. H. H., delivers eulogy of CC, 234–44

Muspratt, James Sheridan, 159, 167, 169–70

Nahmeokee (*Metamora*), CC as, 44

Naiad Queen, CC's performance in, 49

Nancy Sykes (*Oliver Twist*): attitudes about CC as, 5, 47, 163–64; CC as, 46–47, 222; conception of, 46, 98, 100

nationality, performance of, 81, 85–86, 87–88, 109, 114, 119, 127–28, 136–37

National Theatre (Boston), 127

National Theatre (New York), 41, 111

National Theatre (Philadelphia), 48–49

New Theatre (New York), 134

Nussbaum, Felicity, 16

Oakes, James, 95–96, 107, 168

Oberon, (*Midsummer Night's Dream, A*), CC as, 50

"odd" women, 255, 266

Odell, George C. D., 247, 259

Orgel, Stephen, 16, 116

Owen, Robert Dale, 44

Paddon, John, 23–24, 26–27

Park Theatre (New York), 28, 33, 41, 43, 44, 46, 47–49, 55, 62, 65, 67, 111

Parkes, Bessie Rayner, 168–69, 177, 181, 182, 185, 193–94, 230

"passionlessness," 57–59, 137, 184, 245

Patrick (*The Poor Soldier*), CC as, 33, 41, 44

Peabody, Elizabeth, 201–2, 234

Peabody, Mary, 23, 201

Pearl Street Theatre (Albany), 37, 38, 111

People's Journal, 120, 121, 139

Pleck, Elizabeth A., 22

Pocahontas (Owen), 44

Pollock, Walter Herries, 120

Poovey, Mary, 256

Portia, (*Merchant of Venice*), CC as, 222

press, CC's use of, 26–27, 50–51, 67
Price, Stephen, 46, 48
Price, W. T., 256
Princess Theatre (London), 81, 98, 158

Queen Katharine (*Henry VIII*), CC as, 103, 178, 222, 237; with Booth, 38; Bridges' reactions to, 137; Hosmer's reactions to, 132; with Macready, 158; as "true woman," 104–8

reviews, of CC's performances: by Benjamin, 50; as Bianca, 80, 84, 86; by Fisher, 29–30; as Lady Macbeth, 30, 95, 96; as Meg Merrilies, 104; in *Naiad Queen*, 49; opera 26, 27; as Queen Katharine, 104–8; as Romeo, 111, 115–16, 118–20, 124, 125, 128
Rogers, Randolph, 191–92
Rolfe, John (*Pocahontas*), CC as, 44
romantic friendships: acceptance of, 7, 57–60, 196, 209, 232, 261, 265–66; possible excesses in, 148–51, 160, 184–85, 244–47, 251–52
Rome: artistic community in, 170–72; CC's first visit to, 171–75; CC returns to, 181; CC's salon in, 187, 189–92; community of women sculptors in, 197–202; Ned and Emma Cushman move to, 230; expatriate community in, 172–74, 176
Romeo, CC as: conception of , 103, 110, 114–15; with Susan Cushman, 97, 111–12, 114–16, 120–26, 158–59; female spectators' reaction to , 117, 122, 126–27, 129–30, 242; first performance as, 41; with Hays, 159–60; as "Italian" boy lover, 128; male reactions to, 122, 126–27, 256, 259, 260, 263; reviews in American press of, 111, 120, 128; reviews in British press of, 115–20, 124, 155; "Sapphic," 124; with visual images of , 117, 118, 122, 123, 246

salons, as theaters, 190–93; CC's London, 180–81; CC's Roman, 174–75, 181, 190–92
Sand, George, as icon, 157–58, 181, 196, 253
Sanitary Commission, 228–29

Sappho, nineteenth-century conceptions of, 124, 287
Sartoris, Adelaide Kemble, 174, 176
Sedgwick, Eve Kosofsky, 249, 265
self-fashioning, 16, 116; CC's, 12–14, 15–17, 39, 54, 82
Selim (*Bluebeard*), CC as, 20
Seward, William, 219, 227–29, 231
sexuality: and gender display, 136–37, 254–66; nineteenth-century conceptions of, 245–46; performance of, 212–13
sexually dangerous women, 245, 253
sexologists, 257–58
Shaw, Dale, 263
Showalter, Elaine, 255
Siddons, Sarah, 28, 112, 131; CC compared to, 89, 94
Simpson, Edmund, 28, 41, 48, 49, 55, 73
Simpson, Sir James, 236
Smike (*Nicholas Nickleby*), CC as, 48
Smith, Sidonie, 135
Speaight, Robert, 262
spectacles, on Victorian stage, 49
spectators: British, reactions to Americans, 85–87, 93, 107–8, 127–28; female, 39, 93, 115, 136–37, 155, 178–79, 206–7, 265; importance of middle-class, 52–55, 94, 114; male, response to female performers, 108–9, 111
St. Charles Theatre (New Orleans), 27
Stebbins, Emma: *Angel of the Waters*, 202–3; as CC's "Juliet," 130; CC's loyalty to, 208, 211, 219, 222, 224, 227–28, 233, 250–52; CC as "married" to, 189–90, 196–97; CC's support of, 197, 200–202; family's disapproval of CC, 190; *Horace Mann*, 201, 227; jealousy of Emma Crow, 213–14, 219, 225, 233, 234–35; meets CC, 182–83; memoir of CC, 15, 75, 77, 102, 247, 252; moves in with CC, 186; in posthumous accounts of CC, 247; reactions to CC onstage, 116–17, 131, 192; as "true" woman, 190, 194; at Via Gregoriana, 187–94
Stevenson, Edward Prime (pseud. Xavier Mayne), 258
Stillman, William J., 191, 197, 231

Stockton, John Augustus, 44
Stone, Henry Dickinson, 38
Stone, John Augustus, 244
Story, William Wetmore, 169, 171–75, 191, 197
Stowe, Lyman Beecher, 260
Strong, Lennox, 264–65
strong-mindedness, 108–9, 152–53
Sully, Rosalie Kemble: CC as "married" to, 9; CC's relationship with, 1–4, 6–7, 8–11, 53, 56, 72–74, 76–77; death of, 105, 153; letter to CC, 9, 146–48; as painter, 7, 10; in posthumous accounts of CC, 224, 251, 262, 266
Sully, Thomas, 4, 72, 76
Symonds, John Addington, 257

Terry, Jennifer, 13, 251, 252
theater, as abject zone, 30–32, 54
Thomson, Helen, 264
Trautschold, Wilhelm, portrait of CC, 147
Tremont Theatre (Boston), 20, 24, 26
"true womanhood," 12, 22, 54–55, 57–60; CC and, 104–8; 166, 244, 248; Hale and, 146; Stebbins and, 234

uraniads, and uranians, 258

Vandenhoff, George, 55, 60, 61, 64, 75, 81–82, 91, 126
Via Gregoriana (Rome), CC moves to, 187
Vicinus, Martha, 8, 251, 266

Victoria, Queen: on CC's performances, 101, 105
Villa Cushman (Newport, RI), CC builds, 237, 239
"virtual community," 138–40, 155–56, 168–70, 172, 179

"walking lady," CC as, 41
Walnut Street Theatre (Philadelphia), 3, 51, 52–55, 126, 134; CC as manager of 52–55, 60–61
Washington Theatre (DC), 132
Webster, Benjamin, 114–15, 130
Weld, Isabella Cushman Eaton, 29
Welter, Barbara, 22
Wemyss, Francis, 33–34, 46
Westphal, Karl Friedrich Otto, 257
Wheatley, William, 60
Wheeler, Lilla, 266
White, Jessie Meriton, 116
Whitman, Walt, 44, 46, 233
Wiggin, Charles, 24–26
Wiggin, James Simon, 24
Wilson, Garff, 262–63
Winslow, Kate Reignolds, 100
Winter, William, 89–90, 96, 100, 106, 257–58
Women: as elevating the stage, 53–54, 68; as performers, 21; as self-supporting, 21, 54, 155; as singers vs. actresses, 23; as theatrical managers, 52–55; as writers, 138–40
Wood, Joseph and Mary Ann, 24
Wood, Shakspere, 171, 174